The Culture of Japan as Seen through Its Leisure

SUNY series in
Japan in Transition

Jerry Eades and Takeo Funabiki

Edited by
Sepp Linhart
and
Sabine Frühstück

The Culture of Japan as Seen through Its Leisure

STATE UNIVERSITY OF NEW YORK PRESS

Production by Ruth Fisher
Marketing by Anne M. Valentine
Composition by Doric Lay Publishers

Published by
State University of New York Press, Albany

For information, address the State University of New York Press, State University Plaza, Albany, NY 12246

Library of Congress Cataloging-in-Publication Data

The culture of Japan as seen through its leisure / edited by Sepp
  Linhart and Sabine Frühstück.
      p.   cm. — (SUNY series in Japan in transition)
    Includes bibliographical references and index.
    ISBN 0-7914-3791-4 (alk. paper). — ISBN 0-7914-3792-2 (pbk. :
alk. paper)
    1. Leisure—Social aspects—Japan. 2. Recreation—Social aspects—
Japan. I. Linhart, Sepp. II. Frühstück, Sabine. III. Series.
GV706.5.C86   1998
306.4'812'0952—dc21   97-37508
                                                                   CIP

10 9 8 7 6 5 4 3 2 1

Contents

Preface

This volume comprises most of the papers given at an international conference in Vienna in March 1995, generously sponsored by the Tamaki Foundation, Seattle and Tokyo. The aim of the conference was to bring together people from various disciplines to report about different forms of leisure activities in past and present Japan, thus enriching our knowledge of Japanese culture. Participants of the conference included Japanese, European, Israeli, and American scholars from a number of different disciplines such as anthropology, sociology, cultural history, political science, theatrical science, and others. Some of the participants contributed their first academic paper on leisure, while others are established scholars widely known in the academic community.

This book is not based on a monolithic concept of leisure but—comparing it with music—is rather like a suite or a divertimento with a prelude followed by a number of different dances, some adagio and others presto, some based on a few chords and others rich in variation, but all related to a general theme, namely leisure activities in Japan. By taking this approach we hope to open up in this volume discussion about topics that have been understudied relative to the rest of scholarship on Japan. As a volume in a series on Japanese Studies most authors present the results of empirical research rather than attempts to enhance leisure theory as such. In an area where so much fieldwork remains to be accomplished we think that in this way we are better able to grasp the actual reality of leisure and recreation as well as their social, political, and historical significance within Japanese culture.

The chapters are arranged in five parts according to the leisure activity that has been studied. Part 1 deals with everyday activities as leisure; Part 2 includes papers on sports; Part 3 is concerned with travel and nature; Part 4 deals with theater and music; and Part 5 takes up crucial questions of playing games and gambling. An attempt is made in the introduction to put all the treated leisure acitivities into a historical frame of reference as well as to relate them to the well-known classification scheme of games by Roger Caillois. To our regret, some of the papers presented at the conference could not be included in this volume, either because they were not delivered on time or were not adhering to the overall conference theme as the editors interpreted it. The additional papers read at the conference but not included in this volume are: Rupert Cox's "Playing with tradition: Understanding Japan through *o-keikogo-to*," Henning Gödecke's "Japanese overseas tourism," Shôichi Inoue's "Women on the beach," and Ishikawa Hiroyoshi's "Theories of leisure in Japan from the 1920s to the 1990s."

Throughout the book, Japanese names are presented family name first. For the transcription of Japanese words the Hepburn system is used in a modified way, "n" is not changed to "m" before labials and no apostrophs are used to explicitly mark the beginnings of new syllables. Long vowels are transcribed as â, ê, î, ô, û unless in commonly known words and names such as *Tokyo*. In quotations however the authors keep to the original transcription.

Our thanks go to Gregor Kalinowski for proofreading the contributions of the nonnative speakers, and to Dr. Gabriele Pauer for typing parts of the manuscript and making corrections. We are most grateful to Meriko Tamaki, president of the Tamaki Foundation, to Kozo Yamamura, director of the Tamaki Foundation, and to the members of the board of the Tamaki Foundation, who all showed an extraordinary understanding for the conference as well as for the publishing of its proceedings. We would also like to thank the participants in an, at least for the organizers, exciting conference, and last but not least the authors, who probably had to sacrifice considerable portions of their personal leisure by contributing to this book.

Vienna
Sepp Linhart and Sabine Frühstück

Sepp Linhart

1

Introduction

The Japanese at Play: A Little-Known Dimension of Japan

The Political Meaning of Leisure in Present-Day Japan

Innumerable books have been written in English and other Western languages on Japan, but only a few of these are concerned with Japanese leisure and entertainment. "The Japanese at play" is hardly a commonplace image or stereotype of this Far Eastern nation. Scholars of Japan world-wide have done a lot of research on various facets of Japanese culture such as the tea ceremony or *kabuki* theater, but they usually do not categorize such activities as belonging to the sphere of leisure or entertainment, rather treating them as forms of art. In other words, they do not consider the people involved in those activities—the participants, the spectators, and the performers—but try instead to analyze the activities from an aesthetic, religious, or folkloric perspective.

Why should leisure and entertainment have received so little attention in academic work on Japan? It may be that those of us involved in Japanese studies are too dependent on popular Japanese explanations when approaching our objects of research. When talking about Japan one still frequently hears the opinion that there is no such thing in Japan as "leisure." For many the Japanese unique-

1

ness manifests itself, among other ways, in an insistence that only those phenomena are Japanese and do really take place in Japan for which a genuine Japanese word exists. Hence they will argue that since the Japanese word for leisure is *rejâ*, a loanword derived from English, there is no Japanese concept of leisure, and therefore the concept of leisure is more or less meaningless to the Japanese. Similarly, the Japanese word for leisure, *yoka*, is a Chinese compound, engendered at some time during the Meiji period or even later. Since it means *amaru hima* or "spare time left over," people critical of the concept of leisure as opposed to work frequently employ this "negative" meaning of leisure—as being something left over and with no value of its own—to denounce leisure and anything related to it: vacations, leaving the workplace early (implying when the regular working hours are over) or making private use of one's weekend.[1] It is evident that in such a climate, it has been neither easy nor encouraging to do work on leisure for many years. Sensitive Western researchers, when showing interest in leisure, could sometimes detect an implied criticism that this was not a suitable object of study and that the Westerners wanted to transform the Japanese into a people like themselves: lazy, hedonistic, avoiding hard work, suffering from the English (or French, German, American, or any advanced country's) disease. As the Japanese regarded the concept of leisure critically and suspiciously, for many leisure constituted a problem—*rejâ mondai* or *yoka mondai*. I think that this atmosphere prevalent among many middle-aged and older Japanese is responsible for our insufficient knowledge of the Japanese at play, rather than that all Japanese are so diligent that they make no use of their work-free time for recreational activities.[2]

It has to be added that for several years the leisure behavior of the Japanese has been a constant issue in the ongoing debate on trade imbalances between Japan and most Western nations. Western countries accuse the Japanese of "social dumping" in the realm of working hours and vacations. According to the Westerners they are paying insufficient attention to leisure and too much to work; that is, they are not behaving as the people of a developed, industrialized society, or a postindustrial society should. Rather, the Japanese attitude toward leisure is still one commonly found in an industrializing society. This neglect of leisure results in scant consumption of leisure goods imported from the West, while the concentration on work results in an ever greater industrial output of cheap goods that must be sold in and outside of Japan, exhausting the market for Western products. Extreme psychological pressure on employees to behave according to this pattern leads to a "working-bee" or "ant" society with very little free time and freedom.[3]

Within this political context, Western journalists, following their Japanese colleagues, periodically write sensational reports on tremendous changes in the leisure (and working) values and behavior of the Japanese, using catch phrases spawned by Japanese journalism. This began with the *rejâ bûmu* (leisure boom) around 1960 and *mai-hômu-shugi* (my-home-ism) during the sixties. It found its continuation around 1970 with the Japanese hippies called *futen-zoku*, who were superseded by the *takenoko-zoku*, the "bamboo shoot" people of Harajuku and the *nyû famirî* (new family) of the seventies. The same set of values was again to be found among the *shinjinrui* (new mankind) of the late eighties, which was in turn quickly replaced by the *shin-shin-jinrui*, the "new new mankind"—thus illustrating how short-lived the trends discovered by journalists are. Recently, Karl Taro Greenfeld (1994), also a popular writer, spoke of "speed tribes" when discussing contemporary Japanese youth.

Seen in an historic perspective, it has to be said that the announced sensational changes never held true for the whole society nor for a whole generation. On the other hand, it has to be pointed out that leisure is certainly not unimportant for the whole of Japanese society, as Western critics, and some Japanese intellectuals, tend to claim. In order to demonstrate this I would like to make a historical *tour d'horizon* dealing with the most conspicuous trends and phenomena related to leisure and entertainment in Japan's past.

Leisure in Preindustrial Japan

With respect to the agrarian Japanese society, Japanese ethnologists usually divide time into three categories: *ke*, or normal working time, and special time, which is in turn divided into *hare*, sacred time for the veneration of gods, for example, the time of festivals, and *kegare*, time of pollution, that is, menstruation, childbirth, or death.[4] *Hare* is what comes closest to our understanding of leisure, but as it is time with a strong obligatory character it is fundamentally different from modern leisure. However, recent research has shown that at least from the last quarter of the Edo period onward, uninfluenced by the West, there developed in the villages a yearning for more days of rest and for more entertainment unrelated to religious life. In most cases this desideratum was expressed by the young men's groups (Furukawa 1986).

In the cities, with their luxurious licensed quarters (*yûkaku*), the adjacent theaters, and the dry riverbeds (*kawara*), with abundant places of entertainment that could be visited daily if one had the vigor and the money, the distinction between normal and special time with respect to leisure became meaningless. Furthermore, temples and shrines with their numerous *ennichi* (regular temple festivals with fairs) and *kaichô* (irregular exhibitions of temple or shrine treasures, usually accompanied by a big fair) provided ample opportunities for entertainment. Religion also provided the necessary excuse for traveling, traveling being rather popular during the latter part of the Edo period as Susanne Formanek reports in her contribution to this volume. Since the rigid class structure of the Edo period gave the citizens no possibility for social advancement, much of their energy was channeled into a world of pleasure seeking and entertainment, resulting in the well-known culture of the floating world (*ukiyo*): *kabuki* and *bunraku* (puppet) theater, light and humorous poetry and prose (*gesaku*), *shamisen* music, song and dance of differing styles, and woodblock prints. One of the most popular and, astoundingly, least reported forms of play in the floating world from the beginning of the eighteenth century, namely *ken*, and its decline into a children's game is described and explained in my own contribution to this volume. People who wanted to place emphasis on the moral value of their leisure pursuits did so by designating them a "Way" (*dô*), evident in such expressions as *sadô*, the Way of tea, *kadô*, the Way of flowers, or *kôdô*, the Way of scent.[5] While many forms of entertainment can be identified with social classes—the peasants, the urbanites, the warrior class—there was one form of entertainment in which all Japan participated and indulged and still does: *hanami* or cherry blossom viewing, defined by Emiko Ohnuki-Tierney in her contribution to this volume as "a total social institution."

Development of Modern Patterns of Leisure

In the process of industrialization and Westernization since the second half of the nineteenth century, endogenous leisure activities, most of them still practiced today, albeit by decreasing numbers of people, increasingly coexisted with new activities introduced by the West. Members of the upper class, the people who had most contact with Westerners, often modeled their behavior on what they saw of them. To name only two conspicuous examples, at the beginning of this century they began to spend summer vacations in newly developed resorts like Hakone and Karuizawa and to play golf. One of the most popular forms of entertainment during the Edo period, *kabuki* theater, was reformed almost to the point of extinction. Politicians thought it necessary to "purify" and adapt it to Western standards with the ultimate goal of creating a Japanese national theater, as Annegret Bergmann reports in her chapter.

Great changes also took place in sports, which in the past had only been part of the samurai training in the form of martial arts (*budô*) or performed at village festivals (boat racing, wrestling, stone lifting, etc.). In his chapter, Inoue Shun, using the example of *jûdô*, shows how new traditions in *budô* were created. In its present form this sport goes back no further than the early Meiji period. The most important agents in introducing new concepts and forms of sport were the schools, a proud tradition still seen in various national school sports events, especially the national high school baseball championship at Kôshien stadium every summer.

The greatest changes in leisure behavior occurred, however, with the introduction of mass leisure, first in the twenties[6] and subsequently after World War II. Peter Ackermann's chapter tries to elucidate the leisure activities of people from an old middle-class district of Tokyo, his research based on transcribed recollections from the first two decades of the twentieth century. His most significant observation is that their concepts of leisure, expressed in the words *tanoshimi* (pleasure) and *asobi* (play), are different from the modern concepts of *rejâ* or *yoka*. Katarzyna Cwiertka's and Sabine Frühstück's contributions to this volume, dealing with activities so everyday as to be overlooked in most studies of leisure, namely cooking and sex, are also concerned largely with the first two or three decades of the twentieth century. Although cooking and eating had already become a hobby among the better-off townspeople and rich-er peasants during the Edo period, as Harada (1989, 1995) has con-vincingly shown, it was at that time a hobby predominantly of men when not at home. During the late Meiji and Taishô periods, house-wives of the urban middle class, their ideology influenced by Western thinking, developed a new cooking culture for the family at home, resulting in a new style of family life and leisure. Sex, on the other hand, also came under a strong Western influence when Western medical and sexological knowledge diffused throughout Japan. Sexological journals, booming during the twenties and early thirties, pandered undoubtedly also to the voyeuristic interests of many and thus provided a particular aspect of leisure, but when reading Sabine Frühstück's account one gets the impression that the transformation from traditional sexual behavior to Western-influ-enced sexual behavior took the pleasure out of sex, which, especial-ly during the war, was supposed to serve only limited national goals.

Two chapters in this book are devoted to the Takarazuka the-ater, for some Westerners a curious female musical troupe. However, as Roland Domenig convincingly demonstrates, behind the Takarazuka theater lay Kobayashi Ichizô's ideas of a theater for all Japanese—for rich and poor, for man and woman. This theater swiftly became a vehicle for propagating nationalistic and mili-taristic ideas among the people of Japan, especially after the out-break of the war with China in 1937, as Jennifer Robertson's chap-ter demonstrates.

From 1937 to 1945 leisure had solely to serve two purposes: the recovery from physical fatigue and the strengthening of patriotic spirit. This tradition is still alive in a similar form in many big firms that stress the necessity to spend one's leisure time with col-leagues from work within the leisure and sports facilities provided by the company, either for physical recuperation or work-related education, not to forget how such leisure activities are said to strengthen the team spirit (Linhart 1976:256–65).

The Present Pattern of Leisure

Looking at the present pattern of leisure it has to be noted that, according to various opinion surveys, the Japanese desire for more leisure has been steadily increasing,[7] a desire not compromised by reduced working hours until 1990. On the other hand, in a period of labor shortage, an atmosphere within the firm that permits one to take one's vacations has become an important precondition for many young people when accepting a position. The right to make use of one's vacations is especially pronounced among young females who do not opt for a career within the firm but tend to leave the firm to get married or have a child.

When describing the leisure pattern of the Japanese it is best first to consider differences between sexes and age groups, but of course class differences are also important.[8] Starting with the youngest, it must be noted that most play in the kindergartens is purposeful preparatory education and not carefree enjoyment for its own sake. Kindergarten teachers are under constant pressure from ambitious mothers who demand that their children be taught useful things and not be spoiled with idle play. As regards children below the age of fifteen it has to be mentioned that the severe demands of schools and private evening classes (*juku*) leave little free time for play. Their favorite leisure activities are video games, watching TV, and looking at comic books. The favorite sport among boys is baseball, the Japanese variation of which is so aptly described by William W. Kelly in this volume, whereas girls prefer softball. Conspicuous is the trend among children of this age to spend most of their leisure time alone with the TV or comic book fantasy heroes. The fact that the most popular comic magazine among the dozens of weekly comics for children, *Shônen Janpu* (Young Jump), has a weekly circulation of more than four million shows how well the publishers have established their position and are able to defend it against the new media.

Although it is often heard that Japanese teenagers are generally overburdened with preparatory work for entrance examinations to high schools and universities, it ought to be pointed out that this is only true for maximally one third of this age group.[9] The majority has no great ambitions for higher education and participates fully in the youth culture with its many colorful temptations in the consumer world. As in the West there is a strong tendency among boys and girls to consume music both actively and passively. The expressive creativity of girls often finds outlet in drawing comics or writing diaries and literature. The enormous success in 1987 of

Tawara Machiko's collection of poems in the classical *waka* style with a modern content, *Sarada kinenbi* (Salad Memorial Day), can only be explained upon this background. Group sports like basketball and volleyball for both sexes, as well as soccer for boys, are very popular and are played predominantly by this age group, which can be conceived as expressing a longing for activities with the peer group. To cater to these wishes, high schools and universities offer a wide range of cultural and sports clubs, the popularity of which is also grounded in the fact that they help establish contact with the opposite sex. After the difficult entrance examinations many university students see the years at the university as leisure time. Before entering the strenuous world of work they try to play to the full. Things forbidden up to this age like alcohol, sex, and gambling hold a particular fascination and, together with sports and music, constitute the typical university student's leisure. Sports especially are typical leisure activities of young people. Apart from fishing and golf, favorite pastimes of the older generations, practically all sports are practiced by two or three times as many people in their teens and twenties than by those in the older age brackets.

While university students participate in university sports clubs, the majority that ends education at the age of eighteen often continue with sports in company sports clubs. Young women also tend to acquire traditional Japanese aesthetic skills by learning flower arrangement, tea ceremony, calligraphy, or a Japanese musical instrument, preferably the *koto*, activities also often provided by company clubs. But on the whole these activities, frequently summed up as "bridal training" (*hanayome shûgyô*), have a decreasing popularity and participation rate among young people. Young working women who live with their parents until they marry and therefore need only little money for their daily life, enjoy purchasing relatively luxurious articles both in Japan and abroad. They are also one of the main targets of Japan's tourist industry.

While young and unmarried working women form the group of women for which leisure is most important, young mothers are usually so busy caring for their children and the household that little free time is left them. If they return to work when their youngest child has entered school they have even less free time. On the other hand, housewives whose children are at school usually have considerable free time, which they spend together with female friends from the neighborhood, the PTA, or from their own school days. These women also constitute the bulk of the visitors to the numerous cultural centers (*bunka sentâ*) of which there has been a nationwide boom since the seventies. There women can pursue numerous hobbies, from learning foreign languages and composing poetry to handicrafts. Calling them "nice middies," the Japanese tourist industry has, since the eighties, increasingly courted middle-aged women, who do not travel with their busy husbands but with their female friends.

Japanese working men come nearest to our working-bee image of the Japanese, and the many reports about *karôshi*, death from exhaustive overwork, reinforce this image. But not every salaried man is 100 percent organization man, and even if he should be, he takes various measures to reduce the work stress by leisure activities. Drinking, chatting and singing in bars, playing mah-jong, gambling on the machines in special *pachinko* parlors, gambling at horse races and other racing events, and playing golf are the main leisure activities of adult males. Wolfram Manzenreiter and Nagashima Nobuhiro deal with *pachinko* and other forms of gambling in this book, and both stress the enormous importance of gambling in contemporary society. Another common leisure activity among men is "family service" (*katei sâbisu*), as spending free time with the family is called, for which many men use their free Sundays. The larger firms usually have a variety of leisure and sports facilities and urge their employees to spend their free time together. This is thought to promote the company spirit. Equally, drinking with the office group after work has a strong obligatory character and is therefore sometimes not counted as a leisure activity but rather as a prolongation of work. The leisure behavior of white- and blue-collar workers is rather different, despite the notion that Japan is a big middle-class society without clearly visible class differences. Whereas playing golf (not only in Japan but also in foreign countries such as Singapore, as Eyal Ben-Ari tells us in his vivid description of golfing among expatriates) and mah-jong are activities performed mainly by male office employees, *pachinko* and betting at horse and other races belong to the leisure culture of lower-class men. One possible interpretation is that mah-jong with its complicated estimating and counting is similar to white-collar work, while monotonous *pachinko* resembles blue- or grey-collar work. It is perhaps worth noting that *pachinko* alone makes up about 20 percent of the total Japanese expenditure on leisure, a larger sum than the combined expenditure in Japanese domestic and foreign tourism. Another leisure activity examined in this volume by Eckhart Derschmidt, listening to jazz music, can also be said to be participated in more by males than females and appears to be on the decline.

Since the years of rapid economic growth the elderly have been discarding their traditional role of staying at home in relative inactivity, aside from helping the younger generation with the children and household work. Naturally this is a result of an increasing number of elderly people living in separate households without their children. Old people's clubs and old people's universities, providing both recreation and education, have been booming since the sixties (Linhart 1983). *Karaoke* singing and dancing are popular indoor activities and gateball, a modified Japanese version of croquet, has, since the end of the seventies, become the favorite outdoor game (Iwamoto 1984). More and more Japanese companies try to prepare their older employees for life after retirement by teaching them meaningful hobbies, which they never had time to develop during their company life due to an overdevotion to firm and job.

Other leisure activities, such as watching TV, show little differentiation with regard to age and social class, and among the various TV programs, sports programs, especially during the Olympics or other great international events, seem to be especially attractive. T. J. Pempel's chapter in this volume reminds us that watching international sports events is not always a harmless leisure activity and does not *per se* contribute to an internationalization of society.

Finally we have to consider one more distinction, that made between the urban and the rural "halves" of society. While the ample provisions for leisure in the big cities has been one of the principle motives for generations of Japanese to leave their rural homes, today the countryside has an increasingly important role to fulfill in the leisure context, namely to satisfy the leisure needs of the city dwellers, as Nelson H. H. Graburn explains in his contribution to this volume. As the various rural leisure opportunities offered to the city dwellers provide work for the locals, work available in the leisure industry might provide a motive to remain in the countryside. In her discussion of leisure parks in Japan, Angelika Hamilton-Oehrl is concerned with one of the major facets of this rural leisure industry.

Classification of the Leisure Activities

The well-known study of games by the French philosopher Roger Caillois (1961) partitions games into *agon* (competition), *alea* (chance), *mimicry* (simulation), and *ilinx* (vertigo). When the Japanese cultural historian Yoshida Mitsukuni tried to apply this scheme to the Japanese *asobi* (play), he added a fifth category not on Caillois's list: the cult of the seasons. Although Caillois's scheme is still very helpful as an analytical tool, one must take care not to stretch its applicability, as most leisure activities cannot be classified as belonging to a single one of these five forms of play. Nevertheless, for a brief overview of Japanese leisure activities Caillois's scheme is quite useful.

Agon comprises all kinds of sports, but there is a very important distinction between active and passive participation. Of the "Japanese" sports, only *sumô* wrestling enjoys a huge (TV) audience, while the many sports labeled as "martial arts" (*bujutsu*) are mainly sports for active practitioners. Other sports passively enjoyed and highly popular with the Japanese are baseball and, more recently, soccer, golf, and marathon. If in a big international competition, like a world championship, a Japanese participant is performing well, it makes little difference what kind of sport it is. Apart from sports, *go* and *shôgi* (Japanese chess) are probably among the most widely practiced competitive activities. More traditional ones, like *hyakunin isshu* ("A hundred poems from a hundred poets"), a kind of Japanese memory game requiring a good classical education and formerly an obligatory training for every bride from middle-class standing upward, are now vanishing; albeit societies have been founded to preserve them, as they have, for example, for *tôsenkyô*, a fan-throwing competition. One might cynically say that the creation of such a society means that a form of play is no longer really alive. In this volume the chapters by Eyal Ben-Ari, Inoue Shun, William B. Kelly, T. J. Pempel, and myself concentrate more or less on competitive play.

Games of chance are dealt with in the contributions of Nagashima Nobuhiro and Wolfram Manzenreiter. They deal with the most important forms of gambling, officially licensed gambling and *pachinko*, a game which today is played solely for monetary profit but which is still not officially regarded as gambling. Alongside a rich official gambling culture, illegal gambling involving dice and the card game *hanafuda* seems to be on the decline.

Mimicry, simulational play, is also of enormous importance. This is evident in *karaoke*, singing with the "empty orchestra," now spreading all over the world but as yet without reaching the popularity anywhere that it has in Japan. We must not forget that imitating the master to the nearest possible degree is the ideal of many Japanese art-related leisure activities, and it is surely not far fetched if we interpret the craze for *karaoke* in a similar way. The wish to become a star for a few minutes has, of course, to be seen in relation to everyday societal pressure to conform and behave in a proper, normative way and is thus an important outlet for one's individuality. Another highly important example of *mimicry* is the theme parks discussed in Angelika Hamilton-Oehrl's chapter, and other aspects of mimicry are also dealt with in the contributions by Annegret Bergman, Katarzyna Cwiertka, Eckhart Derschmidt, Roland Domenig, Susanne Formanek, and Jennifer Robertson.

Ilinx, vertigo, is perhaps less apparent in contemporary Japan than it was in earlier periods. It is limited to certain age groups and social outsiders, for example the notorious *bôsô-zoku*, the motorcycle gangs, or the *takenoko-zoku*, the Harajuku people, who perform a kind of carnival every weekend. In this book, the people treating sex as leisure, as discussed by Sabine Frühstück, might best be said to conform to this category of Caillois. In earlier periods, people participating in festivals (*matsuri*), especially those carrying the portable shrine, also exhibited the typical traits ascribed to *ilinx*, but the festivals have since undergone a significant transformation, and most are held only as tourist attractions or as attempts to preserve the past.

Most of the festivals date back at least to the Edo period, but some are recently instituted like the Snow Festival (*yuki matsuri*) of Sapporo. While every community holds one or two small *matsuri* every year, since the 1950s some festivals have become big national events and attract tourists from all over the country, like the "three great festivals of Tôhoku," Nebuta, Kantô, and Tanabata, at the beginning of August. A typical *matsuri* entails a colorful procession, dances, and sportive competitions. Most festivals have religious origins but some older ones, as well as some of the most recent ones, are of a purely secular nature, like the Kobe festival held every summer.

Even though there have been numerous efforts to create modern *matsuri*, the most conspicuous attractions for the modern Japanese citizen are the big sporting events held frequently since the Tokyo Olympics in 1964 and the great expositions, which became common after the successful World Exposition in Osaka in 1970. The latter half of the eighties saw a particularly large number of expositions that, on the whole, boasted a high number of visitors. By entertaining the whole family, they can be compared to the Edo period *kaichô*, special exhibitions in shrines and temples.

The cult of the seasons must take place in natural surroundings, or at least involve viewing nature. The best-known examples are viewing various blossoms and flowers, from the early plum and cherry blossoms, treated in this book by Emiko Ohnuki-Tierney, to the chrysanthemums and red maple leafs, as well as moon viewing in autumn, and, finally, snow viewing in winter. Eating dishes associated with a specific season is another form of enjoyment, often going hand in hand with one of these viewing activities. It goes without saying that there are especially famous places for viewing natural phenomena, both locally and nationally, the logical consequence being a lot of traveling.

Times for Leisure

For many Japanese daily leisure begins rather late. The male office workers have practically no guaranteed maximum of working hours and often stay at the office until late into the night. Only female office workers may frequently leave their working place in accordance with the working-hour regulations, which makes them the object of envy among their male colleagues. Blue-collar workers usually work a fixed amount of overtime, hence their daily free time is also limited. The conditions for weekly leisure have improved greatly since many firms introduced the five-day working week in the 1970s in response to criticism from abroad, but this system is still not universal. For instance, there are many firms who summon their employees to work every other Saturday or ask them to participate "voluntarily" in educational programs on their free Saturdays. But the modifications of the Labour Standard Law in 1987 and 1993, introducing the forty-hour working week as the model to be attained by most firms by 1996, together with the recession starting in 1991, resulted in conspicuously less working time, if we are to believe official working-time statistics. The Japanese average yearly working time is now quickly approaching that of the United States and Great Britain but is still far behind France and Germany.

The special seasonal times of leisure are New Year, when all firms and offices are closed for at least three days; the so-called Golden Week at the end of April and beginning of May, a cluster of national holidays; and the time around the *bon* festival in the middle of August. Many firms have introduced a summer vacation, when they close their doors and force their employees into holiday. Although the legally guaranteed amount of paid vacations was raised to a minimum of ten days in 1987, the Japanese still make comparatively little use of their vacations. The average has been eight or nine days per employee in a year. Female employees tend to make more use of their vacations than male employees. The common pattern is to take a long weekend for a short journey. The Western pattern of taking one or several weeks off and of spending longer vacations with the family is virtually unknown. School vacations are also rather short and, moreover, often used for studying in private schools. In order to counterbalance the unwillingness of Japanese workers to go on holiday the government has tried to create more national holidays in order to preclude foreign criticism of the "working-bee society." In 1995 Japan had fourteen national holidays and was leading the international national holiday table.

What might change the Japanese leisure pattern are the many resorts being constructed. The Resort Law of 1987 gave big capital the possibility to invest large sums in resort areas. More than two hundred resorts from Hokkaidô to Okinawa are said to be under construction. Yet filling all those new resorts with guests, when trips abroad attract more people every year (more than ten million for the first time in 1990 and, after a setback in 1991 and 1992, already more than fifteen million in 1995) will be possible only if the Japanese make more use of their vacations.

An Overview of Leisure Studies on Japan

As stated at the beginning of this introduction, leisure is a rather neglected field in Western Japanese studies. The first full-fledged book on the subject was published by David W. Plath in 1964 in the wake of what the Japanese call the "first leisure boom" around 1960. But after this most promising start, the "economic miracle of Japan" seems to have concentrated most research by sociologists and anthropologists into fields related to Japan's industry and to have hampered further studies on leisure. My own book (1976) on the lifestyles of blue- and white-collar workers, as expressed in their working and leisure behavior, was an attempt to understand the actual meaning of *mai-hômu-shugi* (my-home-ism) among the Japanese employed in big companies at the beginning of the 1970s. In another monograph I dealt with the leisure patterns of the elderly (Linhart 1983).

Other studies on Japan, like Okpyo Moon's (1989) on a skiing resort, Eyal Ben-Ari's (1990) on two suburban neighborhoods, or Michael Ashkenazi's (1993) on the festivals of one town deal partially with leisure without giving it too much prominence. French sociologists like Joffre Dumazedier and Roger Caillois played a pioneering role in developing the sociology of leisure, and their representative works were soon translated, hence their fame in Japan. Given this prominence in leisure studies, it is no wonder then, that the first Western collection of papers on leisure in Japan was edited by Christine Condominas and published in France in 1993. This collection of seventeen papers is based on two French-Japanese colloquia, where the Japanese primarily discussed Japan and the French, with a few exceptions, France. It is evident that in such meetings explanations of one's own society form a major part of the discussion, and therefore many of the papers in that book have a very introductory nature. Similarly, Umesao Tadao, Kumakura Isao, and Brian Powell (1995) edited a volume on amusement in Japan, based on a symposium held at the National Museum of Ethnology in Osaka. The same organizers had previously issued a similar volume on tourism (Umesao, Befu, and Ishimori 1995), one of the better researched fields of leisure studies in Japan. Apart from the books already mentioned, there are a number of articles in academic books and journals, but, as a glance at a recently published annotated bibliography (Manzenreiter 1995), including Japanese as well as Western studies on leisure in Japan, shows, these too are relatively few in number. Often they present nothing more than introductory overviews of Japanese scholars in the form of articles contributed upon invitation to special issues of journals or to symposia, which are later published as books, such as, for instance, that by Koseki Sampei (1989).

The output in the field of mass or popular culture, a related field, is a little more impressive but also far from satisfactory. After the ground-breaking books by Kato Hidetoshi (1959), Donald Richie (1981), Frederick L. Schodt (1983), and Ian Buruma (1984) there followed collections like *The electric geisha* (Ueda 1994) and *Asian popular culture* (Lent 1995), but, like Schodt and Buruma's texts they cater rather to the general reader than to an academic audience. The most recent collection, *Contemporary Japan and popular culture* (Treat 1996), is the most promising one. The *Handbook of Japanese popular culture* (Powers and Katô 1989) is a useful overview of several fields.

The situation in Japan has been quite different. Empirical research on leisure as a means to influence and control the free time of factory workers goes back as far as the 1910s. This did not change until the end of the Pacific War. The aforementioned leisure boom around 1960 provided a great impetus to leisure studies in fields such as sociology. A great number of monographs and series on leisure, amusement (*gôraku*), and recreation (*rekuriêshon*) were published, as were collections of prewar writers (Gonda 1974–1975) and studies (Ishikawa 1989–1990). During the affluent seventies and eighties, *asobi* (play) became more important than ever, and not only for the young. From that time onward books on *asobi*, ranging from very popular to rather academic, streamed into circulation,[10] indicating that this concept holds more interest than the related concepts of *yoka* or *rejâ*, even though, for the scholar, *asobi* is nothing else but a leisure activity. As for empirical research, the Leisure Development Center (Yoka kaihatsu sentâ), a semiofficial institution under the sway of the Ministry of Trade and Industry with the function of promoting the leisure industry, has been doing hundreds of empirical studies since it was founded in 1973. One of its results is the yearly issuance of a Whitebook on Leisure (*Rejâ hakusho*). The periodical surveys by the NHK Research Institute on how people spend their time (*Kokumin seikatsu jikan chôsa*) provide detailed figures that can now be compared over five decades (Nihon Hôsô Bunka Kenkyûsho).[11] Many governmental and other survey agencies also include items on the use and view of leisure in their periodical opinion polls. Seen from an academic point of view, however, it must be said that on the whole very little basic research on the leisure life of the Japanese, with carefully designed surveys of a quantitative or qualitative nature, has been carried out up to now.

Notes

1. Compare also the remarks of Ackermann in his contribution to this volume.

2. To cite just one example: In 1987 Toyama Shigeru, a former manager of the Bank of Japan and various other important economic institutions, when seventy-six years old, published *The Japanese view of diligence and thrift,* as he was of the opinion that the Japanese spirit of diligence and thrift had to prevail (Toyama 1987:216). He devoted a chapter to "The advanced countries' sickness and Japan," and another one to "The problem of leisure in the present age."

3. The most prominent statement accusing the Japanese of being working bees was made by the French ex-prime minister Edith Cresson in July 1991. The same accusations can frequently be found in the writings of the so-called revisionists, a group of Western journalists, the most prominent of which is Karel van Wolferen. They never tire of accusing Japan of unfair trade practices. For a critical academic view of the Japanese leisure society, see McCormack (1991). Cole (1992:53) has pointed out, however, that in official talks the Americans never pressed the Japanese to reduce their working hours.

4. The Japanese anthropologist who did most to clarify these concepts, nowadays standard terminology, is Namihira Emiko (1974 and several later articles and books). For a short discussion of those concepts in English see Linhart (1984).

5. In an earlier article I tried to delineate the main factors as to why there is only limited Japanese research on entertainment in preindustrial society. The places of entertainment, licensed quarters as well as the theaters, were classified during the Edo period as *akusho,* "evil places"; the

people providing entertainment belonged to the outcast class; much entertainment, such as traveling, was disguised as religious activity; and
attempts were made to give other forms of entertainment, which clearly
had no connection with religion, a quasi religious-philosophical significance (Linhart 1990a).

6. Steiner (1943) devotes one chapter to "The changing world of leisure,"
which is an excellent description of the gradual replacement during the
twenties and thirties of traditional Japanese leisure habits by leisure
habits imitating those of the West (Steiner 1943:89–104).

7. Some, but nowhere near all, of the results of the opinion polls are in
Kolatek (1991).

8. A more extensive discussion of the leisure habits of various substra-
ta of Japanese society is contained in Linhart (1990b).

9. Rohlen (1983) has given a very good description of the discrepancies
between the various types of high schools, ranging from those whose grad-
uates have the best chances to enter Tokyo University to those whose grad-
uates can at best be called semiliterate.

10. An impressive list of more than four hundred titles of such books
published until 1993 is contained in number 11 of the journal *Rekuriêshon*
(Anon. 1994).

11. These surveys were held in the years 1941, 1960, 1965, 1970, 1973,
1975, 1980, 1985, 1990, and 1995. The reports on the first three surveys
(1941, 1960, and 1965) were reprinted by Ôsorasha in 1990–91.

———————————— References ————————————

Anon. 1994. "Yoka kanren bunken risuto," *Rekuriêshon* 11, 303–13.
Ashkenazi, Michael. 1993. *Matsuri: Festivals of a Japanese town*. Honolulu:
    University of Hawaii Press.
Ben-Ari, Eyal. 1990. *Changing Japanese suburbia*. London: Kegan Paul.
Buruma, Ian. 1984. *A Japanese mirror: Heroes and villains of Japanese cul-
    ture*. London: Jonathan Cape.
Caillois, Roger. 1961. *Man, play, and games*. Glencoe: Free Press.
    [Translated into Japanese as *Asobi to ningen*. Tokyo: Iwanami shoten,
    1970, by Shimizu Ikutarô and Kiriu Kazuo.]

Cole, Robert E. 1992. "Work and leisure in Japan," *California Management Review* 34/3, 52–63.

Condominas, Christine (ed.). 1993. *Les loisirs au Japon: Actes du colloque "Temps libre, loisirs et tourisme en France et au Japon" de la Maison Franco-Japonaise.* Paris: Edition L'Harmattan.

Furukawa Sadao. 1986. *Mura no asobibi: Kyûjitsu to wakamonogumi no shakai-shi.* Tokyo: Heibonsha (= Heibonsha sensho 99).

Gonda Yasunosuke. 1974–1975. *Gonda Yasunosuke-shû.* 4 vols. Tokyo: Bunwa shobô.

Greenfield, Karl Taro. 1994. *Speed tribes: Children of the Japanese bubble.* London: Boxtree.

Harada Nobuo. 1989. *Edo no ryôri-shi: Ryôri to ryôri bunka.* Tokyo: Chûô kôronsha (= Chûkô shinsho).

———. 1995. "Die Koch- und Eßkultur in der zweiten Hälfte der Edo-Zeit und die Art ihrer Verbreitung," Susanne Formanek and Sepp Linhart (eds.), *Bild und Buch in Japan als gesellschaftliche Kommunikationsmittel einst und jetzt.* Wien: Literas (= Schriftenreihe Japankunde), 93–106.

Ishikawa Hiroyoshi (ed.). 1989–1990. *Yoka, gôraku kenkyû kiso bunken-shû.* 29 + 1 vols. Tokyo: Ôsorasha.

Iwamoto Masayo. 1984. "Gêto bôru kyôgi no hassei to sono fukyû katei," *Minzokugaku kenkyû* 49/2, 174–82.

Kato Hidetoshi (ed.). 1959. *Japanese popular culture: Studies in mass communication and cultural change.* Tokyo: Tuttle.

Kolatek, Claudia. 1991. "Zur Arbeitseinstellung japanischer Beschäftigter. Das japanische Selbstbild und die Entstehung 'typisch' japanischer Arbeitsbeziehungen," Norbert R. Adami and Claudia Kolatek (eds.), *Lebenslust statt Arbeitswut? Moderne Phänomene und geisteshistorische Grundlagen.* München: Iudicium, 13–93.

Koseki Sampei. 1989. "Japan: Homo Ludens Japonicus," Anna Olszewski and Kenneth Roberts (eds.), *Leisure and lifestyle: A comparative analysis of free time.* London: Sage Publications, 115–42.

[Leisure Development Center]. 1978. *Leisure and recreational activities.* Tokyo: Foreign Press Center [1st rev. ed. 1987, 2nd rev. ed. 1990] (= About Japan series 4).

Lent, John A. (ed.). 1995. *Asian popular culture.* Boulder, Colo.: Westview Press.

Linhart, Sepp. 1976. *Arbeit, Freizeit und Familie in Japan: Eine Untersuchung der Lebensweise von Arbeitern und Angestellten in Grossbetrieben.* Wiesbaden: Harrassowitz 1976 (= Schriften des Instituts für Asienkunde in Hamburg 43).

―――. 1983. *Organisationsformen alter Menschen in Japan: Selbstverwirklichung durch Hobbies, Weiterbildung, Arbeit.* Wien: Institut für Japanologie 1983 (= Beiträge zur Japanologie 19).

―――. 1984. "Some observations on the development of 'typical' Japanese attitudes towards working hours and leisure," Gordon Daniels (ed.), *Europe interprets Japan.* Tenterden, Kent: Paul Norbury, 207–14, 269–70.

―――. 1990a. "Verdrängung und Überhöhung als Probleme beim Verständnis von Freizeit und Unterhaltung in Japan am Beispiel der späten Edo-Zeit," Ernst Lokowandt (ed.), *Referate des 1. Japanologentages der OAG in Tokyo, 7./8. April 1988.* München: Iudicium, 29–51.

―――. 1990b. "Arbeite wie ein Präsident, vergnüge dich wie ein König. Einige Bemerkungen zum japanischen Freizeitverhalten," Irene Hardach-Pinke (ed.), *Japan: Eine andere Moderne?* Tübingen: Konkursbuch Verlag Claudia Gehrke, no year indicated, 81–95.

Manzenreiter, Wolfram. 1995. *Leisure in contemporary Japan: An annotated bibliography and list of books and articles.* Wien: Institut für Japanologie (= Beiträge zur Japanologie 33).

McCormack, Gavan. 1991. "The price of affluence: The political economy of Japanese leisure," *New Left Review* 188, 121–34.

Moon Okpyo. 1989. *From paddy field to ski slope: The revitalization of tradition in Japanese village life.* Manchester: Manchester University Press.

Namihira Emiko. 1974. "Nihon minkan shinkô to sono kôzô," *Minzokugaku kenkyû* 38/3–4, 230–56.

Nihon hôsô bunka kenkyûsho (ed.): *Kokumin seikatsu jikan chôsa.* Various years. Tokyo: Nihon hôsô shuppan kyôkai.

Plath, David W. 1964. *The after hours: Modern Japan and the search for enjoyment.* Berkeley: University of California Press.

Powers, Richard G., and Katô Hidetoshi (eds.). 1989. *Handbook of Japanese popular culture.* Westview: Greenwood Press.

Richie, Donald. 1981. *Some aspects of Japanese popular culture.* Tokyo: Shubun International.

Rohlen, Thomas. 1983. *Japan's high schools.* Berkeley, Los Angeles, London: University of California Press.

Schodt, Frederik L. 1983. *Manga! Manga! The world of Japanese comics.* Tokyo: Kodansha International.

Steiner, Jesse F. 1943. *Behind the Japanese mask.* New York: Macmillan.

Toyama Shigeru. 1987. *Nihonjin no kinben, chochikukan.* Tôkyô: Tôyô keizai shinpôsha.

Treat, John Whittier (ed.). 1996. *Contemporary Japan and popular culture.* Richmond, Surrey: Curzon Press (= ConsumAsian Book Series).

Ueda Atsushi (ed.). 1994. *The electric geisha: Exploring Japan's popular culture.* Tokyo, New York, London: Kodansha International.

Umesao Tadao, Harumi Befu, and Ishimori Shuzo (eds.). 1995. *Japanese civilization in the modern world IX: Tourism.* Suita: National Museum of Ethnology (= Senri Ethnological Studies 38).

Umesao Tadao, Kumakura Isao, and Brian Powell (eds.). 1995. *Japanese civilization in the modern world XI: Amusement.* Suita: National Museum of Ethnology (= Senri Ethnological Studies 40).

Yoka kaihatsu sentâ. 1972ff. *Rejâ hakusho.* Tokyo: Yoka Kaihatsu Sentâ. Yearly.

Yoshida Mitsukuni. 1987. *Asobi: The sensibilities at play.* Hiroshima: Mazda Motor Corporation.

PART ONE

Everyday Activities as Leisure

The first few decades of the twentieth century were a time of major changes. On the one hand, new forms of interference of the state that had been developed early in the Meiji period began to have their effect on the everyday life of common people. On the other hand, new challenges such as the emergence of a middle class and accordingly of mass culture had an immense impact on leisure behavior altogether.

Modern concepts for spending free time, such as *yoka* or *rejâ*, seem to rather reflect leisure activities in contemporary Japan. For historical investigations however, older concepts such as *asobi*, associated with play, pleasure, and fun, or *tanoshimi,* associated with delight, happiness, and pleasure prove to be more appropriate and useful, especially when activities are the object of analysis that bear the potential of either being everyday activities or of turning into everyday activities under certain circumstances. The three chapters in Part 1 of this book shed light on a few of these activities and underlying concepts of leisure ranging from entertainment provided by shrines and temples to those provided by the so-called pleasure quarters (see Ackermann's contribution); from cooking taken up as a hobby by middle-class housewives (see Cwiertka's contribution) to discourses on the relationship between sex and leisure that were significantly reshaped during the decades following the turn of the century (see Frühstück).

Peter Ackermann forcefully questions the modern concept of leisure and its application to historiographical work, thus providing insights into how Japanese men in their twenties spent what they vaguely defined as their free time at the beginning of the twentieth century. One particular everyday activity, namely cooking, which became a hobby for many middle-class women during the same period of time is discussed by Katarzyna Cwiertka. Although cooking was chosen as a hobby in relative freedom for its qualities of satisfaction, Cwiertka shows that it was significantly preconditioned by a rhetoric that perceived Western culture and thus also Western culinary culture as superior, and that it was supported by the good wife/wise mother ideology that sought to keep the ideal middle-class woman in the house.

Facets of sex as leisure in contemporary Japan have among others been described by Anne Allison in her study on hostess clubs *Nightwork: Sexuality, pleasure and corporate masculinity in a Tokyo hostess club* (1994); in *Kau otoko, kawanai otoko*, a collection of interviews with men who describe their motifs for visiting a prostitute by Fukushima Mizuho and Nakano Rie (1995); as well as in popular accounts such as Nicholas Bornoff's *Pink samurai* (1991) and Peter Constantine's *Japan's sex trade* (1993). In my own contribution to this volume however, I trace back the relationship between sex and leisure in sexological texts from the Edo period to the early twentieth century. While scholars in and outside of Japan tend to emphasize that the Edo period enjoyed relative freedom in regard to nonreproductive, nonmarital sex as opposed to later periods that came under the strong influence of Western models of morals, I suggest to shift the focus of attention away from matters of degree and instead look at the agents that predominantly defined the relationship between leisure and sex, arguing that major transformations in regard to this relationship concerned these agents.

S. F.

References

Allison, Ann. 1994. *Nightwork: Sexuality, pleasure and corporate masculinity in a Tokyo hostess club.* Chicago: University of Chicago Press.

Bornoff, Nicholas. 1991. *Pink samurai.* London: Grafton Books.

Constantine, Peter. 1993. *Japan's sex trade.* Tokyo: Yenbooks.

Fukushima Mizuho, and Nakano Rie. 1995. *Kau otoko, kawanai otoko.* Tokyo: Gendai shokan.

Peter Ackermann

2

Respite from Everyday Life

Kôtô-ku (Tokyo) in Recollections

Thoughts Concerning the Concept "Leisure"

When discussing a culture we tend to use fairly abstract terms as frames of reference. The classical categories of the academic world have constituted such frames—for instance, religion, literature, art, music, or history. I have often asked myself whether the use of such categories does not hinder the understanding of a culture that has taken shape over centuries of orientation toward frames of reference quite different from our own.

It appears to me that discussions concerning past, present, and desirable forms of society—topics that can in a wide sense be termed political—have also made extensive use of abstract categories formed in the West. Maybe the best known such category applied to Japan is democracy/democratic. Other examples are rationality, equality, efficiency, quality of life, and so on.

It is of course perfectly legitimate for Japanese to pick up such terms, to view their society against a background of Western categories, and, if necessary, restructure their society to conform to these. However, we should not forget how absurd discussions have been that surround, for instance, a term like *rationality*. Japan, measuring itself by means of the Western concept of "rationality"—and also always being measured by this concept—conceived

27

the notion that the West was somehow more rational than Japan. This resulted in silly theories, for example, maintaining that the Japanese language was not rational and therefore could not be learned or understood in a rational way, that is, by anyone not Japanese. Obviously the Japanese language is not irrational, but it has developed within a frame of reference different from the great standard languages of the West, wherein, at some point in history, "rationality" was coupled to the ideal of language as a tool for universal communication.[1]

Now, what about the abstract concept of leisure? In the Oxford dictionary "leisure" is defined as "time at one's own disposal." The Japanese word *yoka* denotes "time at one's own disposal." However, whereas probably few speakers of English would stop to puzzle over the meaning of leisure, I have encountered quite a few Japanese persons who consider *yoka* a very strange word. For some, particularly the first element of *yoka—yo* or *amaru* (to be left over, to be superabundant)—had an extremely negative connotation. Does this imply that the Japanese know no leisure, that they have never learned to free themselves from being enslaved to their work?

The impression that the Japanese have not known leisure is reinforced by the recent adoption into the Japanese language of the foreign term *rejâ* (leisure). Thumbing through a JR (Japan Railways) timetable of 1994 I found this word *rejâ* systematically juxtaposed to the word *bijinesu*. For instance: *Shin toshin Shinjuku. Bijinesu, rejâ no kyoten ni* (Shinjuku, the new City Centre. A base for business and for leisure), or *Bijinesu, rejâ ni San Hoteru Cheenu* (The Sun Hotel Chain, for business and for leisure).

Rejâ is seen here not in a general sense as "leisure," but as something equivalent to work, equivalent in the sense of being a relatively large span of time to be filled with something that can be justified, something that makes "sense." *Rejâ* in other words is not just something that the Japanese did not know before because they "worked like slaves," it is a specific concept related to new forms of organization of time. The *Shin kurashi no jiten* (1983:377) accordingly defines *rejâ*—and also *yoka*—explicitly in relation to *shûkyû futsuka-sei ya kaki renzoku kyûka-sei* (the five-day working week and the institutionalization of consecutive free days in summer). If the discussion of leisure forms part of a discussion of new forms of organization of time, then the absence of something called "leisure" does not necessarily mean that one has absolutely no time to dispose of in a leisurely way.

What forms, then, did "having time" actually assume, and what conceptual categories existed for such "having time"? Such a question may be easy to pose. It cannot, however, be dealt with without some serious considerations as to what kind of material we are basing our argument on, and what specific problems this material presents. Let me therefore insert at this point a few necessary reflections on this topic.

Thoughts Concerning the Use of Japanese Texts Presenting Recollections

To find out what "having time" actually meant for people who did not know leisure, I started to look for published recollections, hoping to find a few indications as to what values were attached to time spans not filled with work, and what terms were used to speak about these.

The search for published recollections proved to be more difficult than I had imagined. First, much of the material consisted of strings of such brief utterances that for me standing outside the cultural context it was hardly possible to grasp their meaning, let alone the background of the experiences recounted.

Second, without exception the texts rendered language as it was actually spoken. Spoken language, however, in contrast to written language, is characterized both by its relationship to an immediate context as well as to the usually quite tiresome process of producing fragments of thought in an often still disorganized form. Thus mere rendering of spoken language in print hardly communicates with people like myself far from the site of the utterance and unable to gather information through direct observation or back-channelling.

A related problem is that all material I found is published giving the exact pronunciation of the speaker. For instance: *horede* (= *sore de*), *so-ntone* (= *sore de ne* / *sô suru to ne*), *nêsanchiniiru* (= *nêsan no uchi ni iru*), *gochisônnannasaittekoto* (= *go-chisô ni narinasai to iu koto*) etc.

This way of rendering the spoken word in a written form that tries to be an exact copy of the phonetic level of speech makes it practically impossible to deal with material originating among people with whose regional dialect one is not acquainted—that is, with the majority of recollections available in print.

To my mind questions related to the language we use and the language we try to interpret are often brushed aside in Japanese Studies in an over-ambitious effort to produce quick information and, perhaps, to conceal the fact that we are battling with formidable difficulties on the communicative level.

The two specific problems I have tried to increase awareness of in the foregoing reflections are, in order to sum up: (a) the fact that the terms we use to define our area of interest have crystallized out of a view of reality that primarily we in the West, or we members of the academic world, possess, and that these terms therefore can easily cast a grid over the object of our interest, which is not the grid that has generated its actual forms; and (b) the fact that the aim of many Japanese publications is explicitly *hitori hitori no katariguchi o dekiru dake ikasu* (as far as possible to bring back to life the words and sounds people have actually used) (KFB 1987:iii). What readership does such material, that is not universally intelligible, appeal to, in what way does this readership approach it, and what is the most adequate way for us to deal with it?

The Concepts of "Asobi" and "Tanoshimi"

During a recent stay in Japan a six-volume publication by the Tôkyô-to Kôtô-ku Sômu-bu Kôhô-ka (Publicity Bureau of the Administration of the Kôtô District in Tokyo) caught my eye. Its title was *Korô ga kataru* (Old residents speak of the past). The volumes, though observing the principle "as far as possible to bring back to life the words and sounds people have actually used," were fortunately not entirely unintelligible to me and were found to contain interviews made in 1984/1985 with 260 persons who lived in Kôtô-ku between the 1890s and 1923.

I was interested in reading these interviews and finding out with what vocabulary reference is made to "having time" and "enjoying respite from everyday life," and how such situations are valued as an organic element of life. The interviews contain no modern expressions like *rejâ* or *yoka*. Even the common word *hima* (time to spare) is rarely used. Though nobody portrays him- or herself as a workaholic, we do see that life was busy and duty very demanding. Against this background, however, it is noteworthy what importance is attached to recollections of *asobi* (play, pleasure, fun) and of *tanoshimi* (delight, happiness, pleasure).

Apart from the distinct field of children's play and children's games, *asobi* and *tanoshimi* are a complementary part of the work of someone else, of someone who provides for the *tanoshimi* and can in a sense be called an entertainer. Moreover, *asobi* and *tanoshimi* lack any reference to a person's own structuring of free time, or to contemplation, rest, or what we like to call "regeneration." Accordingly we find no mention of anything like studying, reading, or of something we might label a "hobby."

How far Kôtô-ku was representative for ways of life widely found in Japan cannot concern us here. At all events, we must keep in mind that Kôtô-ku was a district of Tokyo characterized by *shokunin* (craftsmen) and *shônin* (merchants). The largest proportion of accounts stem from persons who earned their living in the timber business, in fishery, in the shipping business, with *nori* production, with the production of casting nets (*toami*), with cloth dyeing, as operators of filling stations, wholesale merchants for toys, rice dealers, restaurant owners, raftsmen (*kawanami*), carpenters, blacksmiths, and construction workers (*tobi-shoku*).

Occasionally someone in a different type of profession will stand out sharply, for instance *jûshoku* and *gûji* (respectively, chief priest in a temple and chief priest in a shrine), or office worker—I will return to these groups of "outsiders" below. Moreover, the lifestyles of members of farming communities on the far side of Kôtô-ku—closer to the Arakawa than to the Sumidagawa—have characteristics of their own (the children seem to have spent a relatively large amount of time playing in and with nature [KFB 1987:V, 134 ff.], and the people of this area are generally referred to as *jimi* [plain, sober] [KFB 1987:VI, 187]).

Not many interviews make explicit mention of actual working time. Occasionally we encounter the following kinds of remarks: "People in the manufacturing industry have a day off on the first and third Sunday, but many do not take free" (KFB 1987:VI, 164). "Craftsmen have a day off on the 1st and 15th of the month" (KFB 1987:VI, 164). "An apprentice (*hôkô shite iru toki*) is free on the 1st and 15th of the month" (KFB 1987:VI, 185). "An apprentice (*kozô-san*) can almost never take off, perhaps only about four days a year" (KFB 1987:II, 52–53).

Let us now take a closer look at the kinds of *asobi* and *tanoshimi* that are more vividly recalled, and the establishments that lived by providing for these.

Establishments for "Asobi" and "Tanoshimi"

Prominent were theaters of all kinds. When referring to these theaters the general term *shibai* is usually used, but we also find more specific designations, above all *yose* (variety theaters). Sometimes *yose* is further differentiated into *iromono no yose* and *kôdan no yose* (KFB 1987:VI, 165). *Iromono no yose* appear to have been noted for *manzai* (a performing art in which a comic dialogue is carried on by two "comedians"),[2] musical productions, acrobatics, and presentations by magicians. On the other hand, *kôdan no yose*—or simply *kôdan*—were characterized by the presentations of a storyteller. Sitting before a small table, which he beat with a folded fan to mark the rhythm of his words, the *kôdan* storyteller typically recited *gunki* (old war chronicles), *adauchi* (tales of vendettas), *buyû-den* (stories of bravery and heroism), or *kyôkaku-den* (stories of glorified gamblers and gangsters).

The second most frequently mentioned type of establishment is the *eiga-kan* (movie theater). Some interviews show that European and American films were enjoyed (KFB 1987:VI, 165 ff.), but Japanese *jidaigeki* plays portraying the feudal age—with former *kabuki* actors in the key roles (KFB 1987:VI, 163, 186 et al.)—seem to have been cherished most. Moreover, as the films were silent, not only the film itself but also the *benshi* (the speaker) was a central element of attraction (KFB 1987:VI, 163 ff., 186).

A fair number of references are made to *kabuki*-style plays (KFB 1987:VI, 167 ff.) and also to *opera* (presentations of acting and singing) (KFB 1987:VI, 167), to all sorts of performances involving sword fighting, and to *naniwabushi* or *rôkyoku*, emotionally stirring tales narrated to the accompaniment of the three-stringed lute *shamisen* (KFB 1987:VI, 170, 188 et al.).

Some of the establishments frequented by the inhabitants of Kôtô-ku were in their own district, but it appears that whenever possible they went to Asakusa to enjoy the larger variety of theaters there (KFB 1987:VI, 165, 171, 189). As a rule, going to the theater was just one part of an outing, eating and drinking before returning home being of at least equal importance.

Though the majority of the interviewees speak of recitational, musical, and other stage productions from the perspective of passive enjoyment, a few persons also mention amateur theaters and having fun being an amateur actor or narrator oneself (KFB 1987:VI, 178, 182). Concerning amateur productions, there are two interesting references to raftsmen. One took lessons in the extremely high-pitched *kiyomoto* style singing of sentimental[3] texts (KFB 1987:VI, 177). The other raftsman (KFB 1987:VI, 171, 173), known for his good voice, went to learn *shamisen* playing and performed *shinnai nagashi* in the pleasure district of Susaki to earn a few extra pennies (*shinnai nagashi* is a tradition of walking slowly through the streets playing a *shamisen* and singing emotionally stirring accounts).[4]

Even if the interviews show that amateur performances of various kinds did exist, a very clear border was drawn in the world of *asobi* between amateur activity and professionalism. To professionally create the framework for other people's *asobi* was classed *gei o uru* (selling an accomplishment), and a teacher of the arts of *gyôgi* (etiquette, deportment), singing, instrumental play, or dancing was *yakamashii* (severe, rigid, fault finding) when training a professional-to-be (KFB 1987:VI, 197).

Very strict training was a key prerequisite for those persons who were to provide for *asobi* and *tanoshimi* in the "world of blossoms and willows" (*karyûkai*). The *karyûkai* was a specific type of *asobi* insofar as its establishments were a world in themselves, an area into which one consciously had to enter (KFB 1987:VI, 209 et al.). We are not given a complete oversight of the various *karyûkai* in Kôtô-ku, but the most frequently mentioned ones were in the districts of Susaki, Tatsumi, and Kamedo.[5] Moreover, former *geisha* in Kôtô-ku mention having worked in other parts of Tokyo, notably Akasaka and Shinbashi, places that thrived due to patronage of the nearby government buildings (KFB 1987:VI, 192).

The *karyûkai* consisted of a maze of large- and small-scale services of a very tightly interwoven nature. I can only mention the three central types of establishments (KFB 1987:VI, 198), namely the *okiya* (establishments that kept *geisha* and sent them out when they were requested), *machiai* or *machiai-jaya* (tea houses, establishments that rented rooms in which visitors and *geisha* could amuse themselves), and *ryôtei* or *ryôriya* (restaurants).

Let me emphasize at this point that, as *karyûkai* was a place that operated at night, hard work (at daytime) and intensive *asobi* (at night) do not necessarily preclude one another.

We are not given much information on the people who sought their *asobi* in the *karyûkai*. It is certain, though, that there was a wide span between wealthy and poor visitors, and that a wide selection of possibilities existed for both. Types of customers specifically mentioned are iron dealers, shipbuilders, stock brokers, sugar dealers, fish merchants, and, particularly, craftsmen (KFB 1987:VI, 201, 203). One informant says that lengthy visits to the *karyûkai* by a family heir would cause consternation, but in the case of second and third sons one was rather indifferent—*kaseija tsukai da* (when you've earned, you spend!) (KFB 1987:VI, 205).

Against this background of *asobi* a small group of persons stand out, as they appear not to have shown interest in the common forms of *asobi* in Kôtô-ku. Professionally these persons also diverge from the mainstream of the district's inhabitants.

Whereas the *jûshoku* (chief priest) of Entsûji temple mentions his fondness for going to the theater (where he is given a good square to sit in) (KFB 1987:VI, 166), the *gûji* (chief priest) of the Katori shrine finds respite from everyday life in quite a different way (KFB 1987:VI, 181–82). He has vivid recollections of being taken up Mount Mitsumine by his grandfather, and mountain climbing has been an activity of central importance to him ever since. However, the *gûji* is of course not speaking of mountain climbing as a sport or a hobby, but of mountain climbing as *seishin shugyô* (cultivation of the spirit). Accordingly he mentions a visit to a mountain hut built "in the spirit of Shintô" as having been a kind of *misogi* (purification).

We encounter another marked lifestyle in the recollections of an office worker at a department store (KFB 1987:II, 23). After describing the vitality of the trades- and craftsmen he says of himself: "It was also a bit the fault of my parents. ... I spent all day studying, they said I was not allowed to do such disreputable things as carry about the portable shrine at the shrine festival. I was after all not a craftsman. Anyway, in a district of trades- and craftsmen an office worker was rather uncommon."

"Asobi" and "Tanoshimi" Provided by Shrines and Temples

Theaters and specific establishments for *asobi* were not the only institutions that provided respite from everyday life; a very important role in this respect was also played by the local shrines, and, to a certain extent, also by Buddhist temples. Thus, *matsuri* and *ennichi* are among the most emphatically mentioned sources of fun and pleasure. The term *matsuri* probably needs no further explanation here.[6] *Ennichi* is literally a specific day associated with a specific deity—further details will follow.

Besides references to *ennichi* and *matsuri* we find a few recollections concerning participation in a *kô*. *Kô* can here be understood as groups of persons that have organized themselves with the principal aim of undertaking pilgrimages (KFB 1987:IV, 225–27)—the interviewees mention pilgrimages to Mount Ontake in the Kiso region (KFB 1987:II, 95) and to the Fudô deity in Narita (KFB 1987:II, 92). It did, however, come as a bit of a surprise to me that the *nenjû gyôji* (the regular annual observances) such as *o-shôga-tsu* (New Year) or *o-bon* (the Lantern Festival/the Buddhist All Souls' Day) were not mentioned more often as sources of *tanoshi-mi*.[7] I also found no reference to *bon-odori*, the *bon* dances that are such a marked feature of summertime district festivals today.

"Formerly there was not much that could be called recreation, but going to *ennichi* was always enjoyable" (KFB 1987:II, 15). This is a typical utterance concerning *ennichi*. The prominence of *ennichi* had, of course, to do with the fact that there were large numbers of shrines spread all over Kôtô-ku, many of these having their *ennichi* at least once, though usually two or even three times, a month.

In each of these shrines a specific deity was revered, very often Inari, Hachiman, or Fudô, but Shinmei (Amaterasu) (KFB 1987:II, 20, 25, 28), Rakan (the [Five hundred] Arhats) (KFB 1987:II, 144–45), Tenjin (KFB 1987:II, 20, 152), and others are also repeatedly mentioned. However, the fact that the various shrines and temples and their *ennichi* had characteristics that carved themselves deep into one's memory, or that a particular shrine was the shrine of the *ubusuna-gami* (guardian deity of the area), appears to be of far greater importance than the individual deity itself.

The chains of associations that the mention of *ennichi* generate are almost endless. Usually they begin with recollections of a maze of stands arranged inside and outside the shrine precincts. In this world of stands there was plenty of entertainment—tricks and acrobatics, musical performances with flute and drum, and theater (KFB 1987:II, 25)—but particularly vivid are the memories that remain of the many different genres of storytelling, for instance *kami-shibai* (picture-story shows), *nozoki-karakuri* (storytelling together with showing of illustrations to be peeped at through a convex lens) (KFB 1987:II, 16, 83, 144 et al.), and accounts of heaven and hell illustrated with movable dolls swayed on a lotus or attacked by a demon (KFB 1987:II, 83–84).

Undoubtedly the main attraction of *ennichi* was what could be bought there. We have the most animated descriptions of sweets of all kinds, *yaki-imo* (roasted sweet potatoes), toys, balloons, cactuses, and bananas (from Taiwan). The atmosphere is perhaps best captured in the following account of medicine vendors: "They'd use snakes, you know, they'd try to foist medicine or something against the decay of teeth on those who watched, well, you know, in the vein of Matsui Gensui (a vendor of medicine for the teeth who was active in Edo around 1680 and attracted customers with top-spinning show. ...At *ennichi* the things that were sold were often fakes and make-believes. ... You couldn't get anything proper, yet it was fun to just buy" (KFB 1987:II, 13, 24).

Conversely, *matsuri* seem to have been relatively infrequent. In some districts full-scale *matsuri* were held only once every four years (KFB 1987:II, 38, 216–17). We should, moreover, take note of the fact that there were districts without any big *matsuri* at all (KFB 1987:II, 32, 34–35), and several districts that had a few festival carts (*dashi*) but no portable shrines (*mikoshi*) (KFB 1987:II, 35, 135).

In essence, the big *matsuri* are described as outings of the local *mikoshi*, carried by young members of the male population through the district of the *ujiko*—the people of the area for whom the shrine deity is the guardian deity (KFB 1987:II, 4, 99 et al.).

Though the *matsuri* are mentioned in many of the recollections as the greatest *tanoshimi*, they did not necessarily enable participation by all *ujiko*. For one thing the arrangements and activities in conjunction with the *matsuri* were closely interwoven with the social organization of the younger adult male population (KFB 1987:II, 10, 176, 186–87). One informant refers to this fact in the following words: "Nowadays even women, even foreigners carry the portable shrine. This would have been unthinkable formerly."

As many informants point out, *matsuri* were not only male-oriented,[8] they were also an outlet for aggression. Carrying the *mikoshi* through the streets was, we read, not exactly a funeral procession, the *mikoshi* would go forward, backward, crosswise, they would smash into each other, and brawls would ensue (KFB 1987:II, 58, 85).

A particularly impressive element of the *matsuri* were the groups of *kurikara monmon*—the "*yakuza* of former days" (KFB 1987:II, 22, 70, 220)—naked men with huge Kulika dragons[9] tattooed on their backs. There is more than one recollection of groups of young men entering the houses of wealthy and influential persons, extorting sums of money, food and drink, and, in some instances, even smashing up the rooms (KFB 1987:II, 220–21).

Concluding Observations

The six books *Kôtô furusato bunko. Korô ga kataru* by no means give an exhaustive picture of Kôtô-ku at the beginning of this century. However, merely acquainting oneself with personal accounts of the way of life, and with the values attached to this way of life (and especially to situations of "having time"), is in itself time consuming, considering the difficulties presented by Japanese-language interview material.

I am well aware that the books studied are particularly problematic in one respect. Aside from the fact that we have relatively little information on the lives of women, the interviews done in 1984 and 1985 represent memories of people that were youths of thirty and less in the epoch they were interviewed on. Consequently there is a lack of information on the lifestyles of persons from the same epoch who were older.

Let me mention in passing that however young the informants may have been at the time, their experiences are invaluable, as the social fabric of Kôtô-ku has since been destroyed three times: first in the great earthquake of 1923, then by conscription and dispatching the male population to faraway battlefields, and finally in the bombings of World War II.

At the beginning of this century the people of Kôtô-ku did not speak of leisure as an abstract quantity to measure the quality of life, they had their own ways of describing the fact that life did not consist merely of work. The two central terms used when referring explicitly to situations other than work are *asobi* and *tanoshimi*. Where could the basic difference lie between *asobi/tanoshimi* and the present-day concepts of *yoka* and *rejâ*?

As we might remember, the *Shin kurashi no jiten* (1983:377) defines both *rejâ* and *yoka* in relation to the five-day working week and the institutionalization of consecutive free days in the summer. In other words, *rejâ* and *yoka* are closely associated with a long span of time not taken up by work. Thus the problem arises: *ikani yoka o sugosu ka*—how should one spend *yoka* (free time)? How should one structure *yoka*, give it content, make something as sensible as possible out of it? Accordingly, *rejâ* and *yoka* are also spoken of as *katsudô* (activity, action, strenuous exertion), for instance, in the form of a *shumi* (something one is interested in, fond of doing, a hobby), a journey, sports, listening to music, or looking at pictures, and so forth. Japanese persons I asked about *yoka* and *rejâ* spontaneously mentioned tennis, riding, mountain climbing, yachting, and camping.

It is true that some of the *asobi* we encountered in the interviews did demand a degree of planning. However, *asobi* is certainly not a *katsudô*, an activity in the sense of actively doing something sensible. *Asobi* is enjoyment of a more passive kind—others are active, while one's own actions are limited to a minimum. We find no mention of deeper thoughts, or of anything gained in the context of *asobi*, not even in the case of theaters and movies, the contents of which are not reflected on in a single interview.

Asobi and *tanoshimi* do not appear to be opposites of work, rather they are opposites of "content" and "sense." Whereas *yoka* and *rejâ* stand close to respite from work in the form of doing some other sensible thing, or gaining something that cannot be gained through work, *asobi* and *tanoshimi* might be called "respite from content," and consequently from all effort needed for grasping content.

Awareness of the possibility of finding respite from content through *asobi* as we see it in Kôtô-ku at the beginning of the century is probably still there, and it is likely to tinge the meaning of whatever word is used to render the concept of "leisure." To understand aspects of present-day Japan I feel it is important not to project the modern idea of free time onto the past. Instead we should perhaps acknowledge more fully the existence of characteristic forms of respite from everyday life that established themselves in contexts where "free time" was not a subject of lengthy consideration.

──────────────────── /Notes ────────────────────

1. Renaissance, Humanism, and Enlightenment (sixteenth to eighteenth centuries) must be mentioned here. I am not qualified to go into further details on this point, but I wish at least to draw attention to the fact that universality in the Japanese sense is rooted in quite a different philosophical setting and must be understood in conjunction with the specifically Japanese political, social, or religious developments over the past centuries.

2. It is not possible to explain in detail the different genres of entertainment and their characteristics within the limited space of this article. For a deeper understanding of terms like *manzai, naniwabushi, kôdan, yose,* and others either the specific Japanese sources or at least the Kôdansha Encyclopedia of Japan (1983) should be consulted.

3. Such an arbitrary expression may be forgiven here, as it would lead me too far astray to go into detail. A vague idea of the *kiyomoto* style may be conveyed through a glance at the text of the famous *kiyomoto* piece *Yasuna*, found in any larger handbook on *kabuki.*

4. Most closely associated with the *shinnai* style is the account of *Ranchô,* that contains highly emotional scenes surrounding the double suicide of two young lovers. Details on *Ranchô* may also be found in most *kabuki* handbooks.

5. The Susaki *karyûkai* was established in 1888. In the Taishô era it had, according to KFB (1987:VI, 200), around 270 houses with over 2600 women. KFB (1987:VI, 205) speaks of around 330 houses with between 3 and 20 women each in Susaki and 520 houses with 1 to 2 women each in Kamedo.

6. For a detailed account of *matsuri* in its social setting see, for instance, Theodore Bestor, *Neighbourhood Tokyo.* Tokyo and New York: Kodansha International, 1989.

7. One interview mentions old people gathering at the Jizô image for *o-bon* on August 24, chanting *nembutsu* (invocations) and passing a happy day (KFB 1987:II, 185). There is also occasional reference to the construc-

tion of a stage for performances at *o-bon*, and to the pounding of *mochi* (rice cakes) at New Year (KFB 1987:V, 51–53).

8. One informant says that the women's duty was to cater to the needs of the young men (*wakai shû no mendô mitari*) and to serve tea when visitors came (KFB 1987:II, 105).

9. Kurikara (Kulika) is the Sanskrit name of a dragon king who appears as the "black dragon" of esoteric Buddhism.

References

KFB. 1987. *Kôtô furusato bunko. Korô ga kataru.* Tokyo: Tôkyô-to Kôtô-ku sômu-bu kôhô-ka. Vols. 1–6.
Shin kurashi no jiten. 1983. *Shin kurashi no jiten.* [Itô Yoshiichi et al. (eds.)]. Tokyo: Gyôsei.

Katarzyna Cwiertka

————— 3 —————

How Cooking Became a Hobby

Changes in Attitude Toward Cooking in Early Twentieth-Century Japan

Introduction

This chapter examines the change that occurred in Japanese food culture, in particular the change in cooking activities, in the early twentieth century. It views cooking from the perspective of leisure and demonstrates how the first decades of the twentieth century were crucial for the later development of cooking as a hobby.

It ought to be kept in mind that the presented theory is only an outline of the changes, and certain generalizations are inevitable. Moreover, I exclude from my analysis the lower social strata and the elite classes, concentrating on the section of Japanese society that I call the "urban middle class." This focus is determined by two factors. First, members of the elite rarely resorted to cooking, and the hand-to-mouth existence of the poor did not allow for leisure activities. Second, to a certain degree the diet of the early twentieth-century urban middle class may be regarded as representative of the new trends in Japanese food culture, especially with respect to the attitude toward cooking. After World War II, with the gradual dissolution of the extremes of the social ladder, this attitude became a model for the majority of the Japanese.

According to Kaplan's theory, elements of leisure are found in the spheres of work, family, and education. Conversely, elements from those constructs are frequently found in leisure (Kaplan 1975:19). For this reason, I shall first portray the emergence of new responsibilities for women, as well as changes that occurred in the structure of the Japanese family and in women's education. A discussion about leisure will follow. Finally I shall discuss the role that Western civilization played in the process of turning cooking into a leisure activity.

Social Changes

The Meiji restoration (1868) brought changes to Japan's political and bureaucratic structure as well as to its judicial and economic systems. Japan's transition from a preindustrial country, at the end of the Edo period, to an industrial state, at the beginning of the Shôwa period, was also reflected in the country's sociological features.

In 1895 only 12 percent of the forty-two million Japanese lived in cities and towns with more than 10,000 inhabitants. By the mid-1930s over 45 percent of the sixty-nine million Japanese lived in cities with more than 100,000 inhabitants (Reischauer and Craig 1989:206). The traditional Japanese family, where the eldest son and his wife and other unmarried sons and daughters lived with their parents, gradually transformed into a smaller unit. A large number of second and third sons, who, by Japanese law, could not inherit anything, moved to cities and formed nuclear families. The focus came to bear on the husband-wife relationship rather than on a "house." From the late nineteenth century onward, this new type of family was frequently featured in mass media. For example, in the September 1892 edition of the magazine *Katei Zasshi* the conditions for a happy family were illustrated as follows (Ueno 1990:506):

1. man and woman love each other,

2. their relationship is monogamous,

3. the family is nuclear,

4. the man is a salaried worker,

5. the woman is a housewife.

All these conditions were new, and revolutionized the character of the Japanese family.

For the increasing number of wage earners the economic significance of the family as a unit of production began to disappear. In the past, Japanese families had been held together by feudal interdependence and/or economic limitations. In the late nineteenth century these limitations were replaced by the ideology of *ikka danran* (family happiness), which created the basis for the modern family relations in Japan. Diffusion of this ideology into Japanese society was accelerated by the government's involvement in its propagation. *Ikka danran* was given an important role within the governmental policy of building a national state. It was believed that "healthy and happy families form healthy and happy towns and villages, and these create a healthy and happy state" (Yamada Taichirô "An ideal village," 1905, after Ôhama 1989:116).

It ought to be mentioned at this point that the ideology of *ikka danran* was based on the Western ideal of domesticity, as was the *ryôsai kenbo* (good wife, wise mother) ideology that evolved at approximately the same time and that designed the role for women within the new family. Both ideas—of domesticity and of a woman creating a happy atmosphere at home—were introduced into Japan by numerous Protestant mission all-girls schools founded in the early- and mid-Meiji period. The *ryôsai kenbo* ideology, similarly to the *ikka danran* ideology, was incorporated into the social policy of the Japanese government. *Kôtô jogakkô rei* (Order on the women's higher education) issued in 1899 made the *ryôsai kenbo* ideology the only aim of female education in Japan (Oki 1987:208). The *ryôsai kenbo* ideology was combined with the *ikka danran* policy by making the woman responsible for the health and happiness of her family. Slogans like "The woman is the key of the home," "The wise woman builds her house," and "The matters of house are under the control of the wife" depict the placing of women at the center of the *ikka danran* ideology (Ueno 1990:514–15). This focus on family and the responsibility of the woman as wife and mother created the circumstances that led to the changes in home food culture in the early twentieth century.

Changes in Food Culture

A standard menu for a well-off Japanese citizen in the Edo period was rice with *miso*[1] soup for breakfast, rice with boiled vegetables and/or fish for lunch, and rice with pickles for dinner (Watanabe 1964:244). Variations in diet ensued only from the seasonal changes of ingredients. The daily diet of the majority was very simple, and culinary skills of women were limited. For celebrations on special occasions, however, sophisticated dishes were either consumed at restaurants or delivered home. There appears to have been a distinction between home meals and dishes prepared by professional cooks. Accordingly, special dishes were associated with professional cooking and little was expected of the daily meals at home.

Moreover, a distinctive feature of the Edo food culture was a large number of culinary publications (Matsushita 1982:2–5). They can be divided into three general types: cookbooks (*ryôrisho*), compilations of menus (*kondateshû*), and popular cookbooks (*ryôrihon*). The absence of detailed descriptions of cooking techniques and information regarding amounts of ingredients was characteristic for all these publications. *Ryôrisho* were most probably intended for professional cooks already proficient in the details of culinary art. *Kondateshû*, which included only names of dishes, can be classified as advertising material. They were often issued by famous restaurants (Watanabe 1964:225–26). Popular cookbooks (*ryôrihon*) belonged to another group of publications. They placed emphasis on the aesthetic and literary content rather than on the culinary information (Harada 1989:191). Although the large number of reprints discloses that *ryôrihon* were widely read by the general public, it is very unclear whether they had any influence on the diet of the urban population. I would suggest that *ryôrihon* ought to be viewed as essays about food, not intended for kitchen use. They were a kind of popular literature.

Culinary literature preoccupied with Western food culture became popular in Japan in the second half of the nineteenth century. During that period, cookbooks and cooking magazines still had the characteristic features of *ryôrihon* and described Western table etiquette, menus, and dishes in a lapidary and encyclopedic manner. This example is from 1886:

Croquette

Chop finely roasted meat and mix with pepper, finely chopped onions and mashed potatoes. Form the proper shape and deep-fry in fat. (Yoshida 1886:23)

The character of culinary publications did not change before the attitude toward daily meals began to alter with the diffusion of the *ikka danran* ideology. Influenced by Western ideas, the role of a family meal, that of strengthening family ties, was emphasized in several publications.

> Westerners have sophisticated "family dishes," specialities of the house, in their families. Japanese order dishes for special occasions from restaurants, but Westerners enjoy family meals at home. In my opinion, it extremely helps to keep the peace within the family. (Yamamoto 1916:53)

> There is no greater pleasure of the family than when old and young, big and small gather in a happy circle and enjoy a meal together. (Ueno 1990:507)

As a consequence of dining assuming a central position in the *ikka danran* ideology, cooking assumed a central position in the *ryôsai kenbo* ideology. The housewife was encouraged to improve her culinary skills and expand her culinary knowledge in order to prepare tasty, nutritious, and varied meals for her husband and children (see Figure 3.1). It is difficult to assess to what extent the new ideology really affected the life of an average middle-class urban family. Nonetheless, even when considering the fact that the reality of a given situation always differs from the published ideals, a tendency toward variety in the daily diet cannot be denied. Under the influence of the *ikka danran* and the *ryôsai kenbo* ideologies, in the late Meiji period housewives began using cookbooks in order to enhance their culinary skills. As practical, detailed information was required, the character of cookbooks changed. Vague descriptions of ineffable, fancy dishes gradually disappeared and useful, simple recipes began to dominate. Gradually descriptions in cookbooks became more detailed. The two examples given below are, respectively, from 1904 and 1935.

Figure 3.1   New recipes made the daily duty of preparing food more challenging. Here, members of the Young Women's Association (*Joshi seinenkai*) in Kanda (Tokyo) learn how to make ice-cream. (*Asahi gurafu* 5/3, front page, 1925.)

Croquette

First, bake chicken, remove bones and chop meat very finely. Brown flour with butter and thin it with stock and milk to a consistency of sauce. Add chopped meat and boil down. Remove from fire, add yolk, stir well and cool. Later, form using bread crumbs, soak in egg and cover with bread crumbs. Deep-fry in fat. (Hankei 1904:189)

Sanma[2] Croquette

Ingredients: 4 potatoes, 2 pieces of *sanma*, 1 big Chinese lemon, 3 eggs, some flour, milk, bread crumbs, oil, pepper, salt, and seasonings.

Preparation: Peel potatoes, cut them in pieces of about five bu^3 and boil until soft in a large amount of water with a dash of salt, and with lid on. Pour water out and return to fire while shaking the pan. If water has evaporated enough that white powder can be seen on the inside of the pan, take the pan off the fire and mash the potatoes quickly. Next, dry washed and cleaned *sanma* with paper. Using a knife make 3–4 cuts on both sides of the fish and cover the inside with flour. Deep-fry. Separate bones from the fish, chop it finely and pour juice from a Chinese lemon over the fish. Mix with mashed potatoes adding salt, pepper and seasonings. In a different bowl whip egg whites so that they resemble snow, and add quickly to potatoes. Put the dough on a board sprinkled with flour, make croquettes, soak them in a mixture of milk and yolk, then cover with bread crumbs, and deep-fry. When done, take out and put on a paper. Serve still hot with tomato sauce or oyster sauce. (Nihon 1935:157–58)

The use of the words *practical, home*, or *easy* was very common in publication titles on food:

Jitsuyô ryôri kyôhon (*Practical* cooking textbook) 1902

Katei seiyô ryôri (Western *home* cooking) 1905

Keiben shokupan seihô (*Easy* recipes for bread) 1910

Katei nichiyô ryôri (Daily *home* dishes) 1911

Jitsuyô katei shina ryôri (*Practical* Chinese *home* dishes) 1912

Keiben ryôri hô (*Easy* recipes) 1912

Kan'i jitsuyô sakana no ryôri (*Easy* and *practical* fish dishes) 1917

Katei jitsuyô mainichi no oryôri (*Practical* daily *home* dishes) 1925 (Ajinomoto 1992a, b)

New household literature accentuated the necessity of improving home meals. The emphasis on variety in diet became very strong.

Nowadays, the knowledge and interest of people has progressed. The advanced style of work and general rules of life have become more elaborate and complicated. In this situation neither can our body stand simple traditional food, nor can this type of food satisfy our soul. ... Following the development of our interests, we also have come to desire novel tastes with regard to food. (Nihon 1909:1–3)

Western food symbolizing Western political and economic power increasingly gained attention from the Japanese middle class and became a symbol of progress and modernity. Chinese dishes were also adopted, but on a smaller scale. The emergence of so-called *setchû ryôri*, a combination of Western, Japanese, and Chinese elements, was a significant step toward achieving variety in diet. Examples of daily menus for the middle-class family, combining foreign and Japanese culinary elements, appeared frequently in women's magazines from the late Meiji period onward.

Monday
Breakfast: *miso* soup with *nattô*;[4] scrambled egg
Lunch: grilled horse-mackerel with salt; lotus root boiled Korean style
Dinner: fried pork cutlet; boiled Chinese watermelon

Tuesday
Breakfast: *miso* soup with *shijimi*;[5] boiled haricots
Lunch: *sunomono*[6] with mackerel and Japanese ginger; boiled taros
Dinner: deep-fried eggplant; boiled horse-mackerel

Wednesday
Breakfast: *miso* soup with *tôfu*;[7] fried egg
Lunch: boiled mackerel; slightly boiled rape seedlings
Dinner: yam soup; broiled chicken

Thursday
Breakfast: *miso* soup with *unohana*;[8] beef boiled with ginger

Lunch: beef roasted Korean style; *sunomono* with *wakame*[9] and Japanese ginger
Dinner: raw mackerel; *fujimame*[10] flavoured with sesame oil

Friday
Breakfast: egg with *nori*;[11] eggplants boiled with *miso*
Lunch: pork stew
Dinner: broiled salmon; boiled sweet potatoes

Saturday
Breakfast: *yakifu*[12] and Japanese ginger soup; boiled haricots
Lunch: boiled vegetables; boiled *chikuwa*[13]
Dinner: Satsuma-style soup; cucumber flavoured with vinegar and sesame oil

Sunday
Breakfast: radish *miso* soup; Nara-style pickles
Lunch: hamburger steak; deep-fried lobster; apple jelly
Dinner: beef steak; mashed potatoes (Akabori 1915:103)[14]

Despite the growing significance of family meals, the Japanese did not abandon the custom of using the service of professional cooks. On the contrary, in 1906 there were more than three hundred restaurants in Tokyo, forty-two of them serving Western food and two Chinese food (Harada 1989:239).

Nevertheless, with respect to the daily family meal, Japan's food culture underwent radical changes in the early twentieth century, changes that had a great impact on the attitude toward cooking. Some years later the possibility was realized for cooking to attain a hobby status amongst the middle-class housewives.

Cooking as Leisure

From 1868 to 1945 more than three hundred women's magazines were published in Japan (Kindai). Some of them, like *Nihon no jogaku* and *Fujin mondai*, were affiliated with emancipation movements. The majority, however, followed the lines of the *ryôsai kenbo* ideology. The most popular magazines were *Fujin zasshi, Katei zasshi, Ryôri no tomo, Fujin kôron*, and *Shufu no tomo*. Besides advice on makeup, needlework, and raising children, almost every magazine edition presented new recipes and advice on cooking. To a certain degree these magazines included more relevant data for the study of food culture in Japan than cookbooks or textbooks of domestic science curriculums. The growing market of women's magazines resulted in a competitive atmosphere, and, in order to increase sales, the magazines were required to cultivate an ever closer contact with their readers.

Leisure is generally defined as time in which we are freed from the formal duties that a salaried job or other obligatory occupation imposes upon us (Lundberg, Komarovsky, and McInerny 1969:2). However, leisure may also be defined as an "activity chosen in relative freedom for its *qualities of satisfaction. ...* When leisure is defined as a *quality of experience* and as the *meaning of activity*, then it may be almost anything, anywhere, and anytime for someone" (Kelly 1990:2). A similar definition is given by Max Kaplan: "Nothing is definable as leisure per se, and almost anything is definable as leisure" (Kaplan 1975:19). Some sociologists list among the criteria for distinguishing leisure from other activities its being *interesting* (Lundberg, Komarovsky, and McInerny 1969:19).

Accordingly, if cooking was a leisure activity in early twentieth-century Japan, it must have satisfied and interested middle-class housewives. In the titles of the cooking columns of *Shufu no tomo* from 1918 to 1926, words from the four following groups were almost always used:

1. *eiseiteki* (hygienic), *jiyô ippai, jiyô ni tonda* (nutritious)

2. *keizaiteki* (economical)

3. *omoshiroi* (interesting), *mezurashii* (rare, curious), *ki no kiita* (extraordinary), *atarashii* (new)

4. *kantan* (simple), *dare ni mo dekiru* (for everybody), *tegaru ni dekiru* (easy to make), *kanben* (convenient)

The first group reflects a diffusion into Japanese society of Western theories of nutrition and hygiene and the quest for new information concerning healthy cooking. The second group indicates the emphasis on the economic aspects of cooking. Considering that these first two groups do not concern leisure, we will concentrate on the other two groups. Groups 3 and 4 are directly connected with the question of whether cooking was interesting and whether it gave satisfaction to the middle-class Japanese housewives in the early twentieth century. Titles using words from the third group introduced novel and unusual dishes for daily use. Their preparation must have brought changes into the everyday duties of a housewife, and was, therefore, interesting. Slogans from the fourth group encouraged women whose culinary skills were limited to try new recipes. Examples of the titles emphasizing the variety, originality, and novelty in home cooking are listed below.

Warm and tasty *kawarigohan*.[15] Various elegant *kawarigohan easy* to prepare. (Kagami 1922:146)

The pride of our kitchen. Various economical and tasty winter dishes with *unique* home flavours. (Anon. 1 1922:144)

Easy and *attractive* home-made meals for guests. (Kitaôji 1923: 261)

The pride of our kitchen. *Diverse*, tasty side dishes from *various* homes. (Anon. 2 1922:212)

New light *ayu*[16] dishes. Introduction of *various ayu* recipes which will *accent* the summer table. (Matsumura 1924:316)

New, light dishes with fresh-water fish. *Original* recipes that will *accent* your dinner table. (Yamamura 1923:270)

Ten *original*, tasty dishes with *asari*.[17] (Anon. 3 1926:258)

Original recipes with canned or dried fish. Safe consumption guaranteed. (Matsumiya 1925:331)

Attractive vegetarian dishes for summer. (Kamimoto 1925: 331)

Original recipes for Russian sweets. (Nakabayashi 1925:305)

Sociologists stress that how people spend their leisure time depends largely on their training. The choice and technique of avocational and leisure pursuits are not acquired any more spontaneously than are the interests and skills in vocational activities (Lundberg, Komarovsky, and McInerny 1969:248). In Kaplan's theory, the importance of education is emphasized as one of the influences on leisure time due to its impact on lifestyle, taste, curiosity, sense of discrimination, and values (Kaplan 1975:97). Since the early twentieth century, cooking was included in girls' curriculums of primary and high schools. In 1901 Nihon Joshi Daigaku, the first women's university in Japan, was founded, offering a course on domestic science. In 1909 this university started a domestic science correspondence course for those who could not study full time.

Year after year the number of students increased. The feeling of responsibility for the family meal that had catalyzed the interest in cooking gradually gave way to a feeling of pleasure (see Figure 3.2). In early twentieth-century Japan, women had limited opportunities for leisure activities. However, the leisure aspect of cooking could be concealed behind its function. Creating the happy atmosphere within the family was an excuse for housewives to devote more time to cooking.

Isn't it *pleasant* for a wife to cook on Sunday evening an *ayu* caught by her husband. (Matsumura 1924:316)

Summer sweets easy to make. Light, tasty sweets that will *please* everyone. (Nishida 1923:274)

The satisfaction derived from creating a perfect meal—nutritious, interesting, tasty, and cheap—was a source of pleasure for the housewife. On the other hand the importance of such a family meal for family life allowed for this satisfaction. A *Shufu no tomo* series called *Wagaya de jiman no osôzai* (The pride of our kitchen) compiled and published the best recipes sent to the publisher by its readers. If their recipe was published the authors received a prize

Figure 3.2   Convenient canned foods helped to turn cooking into pleasure.
(*Asahi gurafu* 28/20, back cover, 1937.)

of 2 yen. Not only housewives living in Tokyo became involved in
this activity, but names from across the entire country appeared in
the series. This indicates that the rise of interest in cooking was not
limited to Tokyo but diffused gradually throughout all of Japan.

"Pickled sardines" by Kazuko from Okayama (1921/11:186)

"Grilled pickled mackerel" by Masako from Date (1921/11:186)

"Tasty meat dumplings" by Kuniko from Aichi (1921/11:187)

"Pudding" by Fumiko from Ise (1922/5:214)

"Boiled squash" by Kikuko from Hakodate (1922/9: 213)

"Potato and sardine dumplings" by Chiyoko from Hyôgo (1922/12:211)

"Steamed sea bream with radish" by Miyoko from Sasebo (1923/2:204)

"Grilled squid" by Kitsuko from Yamaguchi (1923/2:205)

"*Chawan-mushi*[18] from *jinenjo*"[19] by Sumiko from Niigata (1923/3:219)

"Koshitaka-style *sushi*"[20] by Sakurako from Kagawa (1923/3: 219)

"Prussian carp in *miso* sauce" by Seiko from Kokura (1923/4: 279)

"Elegant soybean curd" by Itoko from Yamagata (1923/5:265)

"Grilled dried cuttlefish" by Teiko from Chiba (1923/5:265)

Conclusion

Based on the study of household literature, we followed the change in attitude toward food, eating, and cooking of the Japanese urban middle class in the early twentieth century. The three stages by way of which cooking becoming a leisure activity were discussed. First, the sociological changes that created the circumstances for the changes in food culture were demonstrated. Second, the changes of attitude toward cooking was examined. Finally, we focused upon the development of cooking as a leisure activity within the greater context of the food culture.

Food has always played an important role in the leisure activities of the upper and middle classes in Japan. Descriptions of court banquets, Tea Ceremony meetings, and Kabuki performances often contained information about the food served on these occasions. However, very little attention was dedicated to the cooking process itself. This attitude might have been caused by the division of roles: the food consumers on the one side and the cooks on the other. Consumers enjoyed eating, but the time-consuming and meticulous duties of the cooks cannot be classified as leisure. From the late Meiji period, this situation started to change as middle-class consumers began to treat cooking as a source of pleasure. It cannot, however, be claimed that from the early twentieth century the majority of Japanese began to perceive cooking as a hobby. For many the economic situation did not allow for a life of leisure. Nevertheless, in the first decades of the twentieth century, the basis for a change of attitude toward cooking was established in the urban middle class. This attitude filtered out into the whole country and society, parallel to Japan's postwar economic growth. In general it may be said that any pleasure concerning food in Japan before the twentieth century was in its consumption. Albeit members of the aristocracy happened to enjoy cooking in premodern Japan as well, it was throughout the twentieth century that preparing food started to be associated with leisure on a wider scale.

The change that occurred in Japanese food culture after 1868 included the introduction of new cooking techniques and new foodstuffs, the modernization of cooking equipment, and the industrialization of food preparation. Aside from these material aspects, the relation between people and food underwent a transition. Food lost its religious meaning and gradually acquired an important role as a source of pleasure for the body and soul (Kumakura 1989:99).

To conclude this discussion concerning cooking in twentieth-century Japan, it must be pointed out that Western civilization contributed greatly to these changes. Western technology influenced Japanese economy, and this in turn influenced the structure of the Japanese family. Western technical innovations, such as matches, the gas stove, and cans, pared down the workload involved in cooking. The Western idea of family and the role of family meals in family relations changed the Japanese attitude toward home cooking. This led to the rise in importance of cooking among housewives' duties. Moreover, the introduction of Western knowledge regarding nutrition and hygiene, followed by the diffusion of the domestic science curriculum into Japanese women's education, influenced the quality of cooking skills and the dietary knowledge among Japanese women. Finally, the adoption of Western dishes and foodstuffs allowed for more variety in the Japanese diet. Western dishes, or combinations of Western and Japanese dishes, made the daily duty of preparing food more attractive. All these changes were essential for the transformation of cooking into a hobby.

─────────────────── *Notes* ───────────────────

1. Paste made of fermented soybeans

2. Pacific saury (*Cololabis saira*)

3. A unit of linear measure (1 *bu* = 0.303 cm)

4. Fermented soybeans

5. Japanese freshwater clam (*Corbicula astarte polaris*)

6. Dressed with vinegar

7. Soybean curd

8. Soybean-curd refuse

9. Seaweed (*Undaria pinnatifida*)

10. Egyptian kidney beans

11. Seaweed (laver)

12. Lightly baked wheat gluten

13. Baked fish paste

14. Every meal in this menu was served with boiled rice

15. = *Gomoku gohan* (rice boiled with fish or meat, and vegetables)

16. Sweetfish (*Plecoglossus altivelis*)

17. Short-necked clam (*Tapes philippinarum*)

18. Steamed savory custard

19. Yam (*Dioscorea japonica*)

20. Vinegared boiled rice with vegetables and/or seafood

──────────────── References ────────────────

Ajinomoto Foundation for Dietary Culture. 1992a. *Bibliography of dietary culture monographs / Meiji period.* Tokyo.

———. 1992b. *Bibliography of dietary culture monographs / Taishô period.* Tokyo.

Akabori Minekichi. 1915. "Jûgatsu no oryôri," *Fujin Zasshi* 4, 103–10.

Anon. 1. 1922. "Wagaya de jiman no osôzai," *Shufu no tomo* 2, 144–45.

Anon. 2. 1922. "Wagaya de jiman no osôzai," *Shufu no tomo* 9, 212–13.

Anon. 3. 1926. "Asari o shu to shita oishikute mezurashii oryôri jûsshu," *Shufu no tomo* 3, 258–60.

Hankei Sanjin. 1904. *Katei jûhô wayô shirôto ryôri.* Tokyo.

Harada Nobuo. 1989. *Edo no ryôrishi. Ryôrihon to ryôri bunka.* Tokyo: Chûô koronsha.

Kagami Kikuko. 1922. "Atatakakute oishii kawari gohan," *Shufu no tomo* 2, 146.

Kamimoto Haruko. 1925. "Yasai o shu to shita natsu no ki no kiita oryôri," *Shufu no tomo* 7, 331–34.

Kaplan, Max. 1975. *Leisure: Theory and policy.* New York: Wiley.

Kelly, John R. 1990. *Leisure.* NJ: Prentice-Hall.

Kindai josei bunkashi kenkyûkai (eds.). 1985. *Kindai fujin zasshi mokuji sôran.* Tokyo: Ozorasha.

Kitaôji Rokyô. 1923. "Tegaru de ki no kiita kateiteki kyakuzen," *Shufu no tomo* 5, 261–62.

Kumakura Isao. 1989. "Shokuji no henka," Ôhama Tetsuya, Kumakura Isao, *Kindai Nihon no seikatsu to shakai.* Tokyo: Nihon hôsô shuppan kyôkai, 91–99.

Lundberg, George A., Mirra Komarovsky, and Mary Alice McInerny. 1969. *Leisure. A suburban study.* New York: Agathon Press.

Matsumiya Shinko. 1925. "Anshin shite taberareru kanzume ya himono no mezurashii oryôri," *Shufu no tomo* 7, 331–34.

Matsumura Aiko. 1924. "Assari shita aji o motsu ayu no shinryôri," *Shufu no tomo* 7, 316–17.

Matsushita Sachiko. 1982. *Edo ryôri dokuhon.* Tokyo: Shibata Shoten.

Nakabayashi Hatsue. 1925. "Mezurashii Roshiya no okashi no seihô," *Shufu no tomo* 5, 305–06.

Nihon hôsô shuppan kyôkai. 1935. *Hôsô ryôri issenshû: Nikurui hen.* Tokyo.

Nihon joshi daigakkô ôfûkai ryôri kenkyûbu. 1909. *Nihon joshi daigaku kôgi, 14: Ryôri.* Tokyo: Nihon joshi daigakkô.

Nishida Miyoko. 1923. "Tegaru ni dekiru natsumuki no okashi," *Shufu no tomo* 8, 274–76.

Ôhama Tetsuya. 1989. "Den'en toshi," Ôhama Tetsuya, Kumakura Isao, *Kindai Nihon no seikatsu to shakai*. Tokyo: Nihon hôsô shuppan kyôkai, 111–23.

Oki Motoko. 1987. "Ryôsai kenboshugi no kyôiku," Wakita Haruko, Hayashi Reiko, and Nagahara Kazuko (eds.). 1987. *Nihon joseishi*. Tokyo: Yoshikawa Kôbunkan, 206–10.

Reischauer, Edwin O., and Albert M. Craig. 1989. *Japan. Tradition and transformation*. Hong Kong: Allen & Unwin.

Ueno Chizuko. 1990. "Kaisetsu (3)," Ogi Shinzô, Kumakura Isao, and Ueno Chizuko. 1990. *Nihon kindai shisô taikei 23: Fûzoku, sei*. Tokyo: Iwanami shoten, 505–50.

Watanabe Minoru. 1964. *Nihon shokuseikatsushi*. Tokyo: Yoshikawa kôbunkan.

Yamamoto Kotoko. 1916. "Shokumotsu no kairyô," *Fujin zasshi* 5, 52–54.

Yamamura Toshiko. 1923. "Assari shita natsu no kawasakana shinryôri," *Shufu no tomo* 8, 270–71.

Yoshida Itarô. 1886. *Seiyô nihon shina reishiki shokuhô daizen*. Tôkyôka and Kaishindô.

Sabine Frühstück

4

Then Science Took Over

Sex, Leisure, and Medicine at the Beginning of the Twentieth Century

Introduction

The relationship between leisure and sex may be defined in several ways. The definition most commonly associated with old Japan paints a picture of the unproblematic uses of sex, of sex as a source of pleasure (from a male standpoint, at least), unconstrained by morals or society, but, by looking at concrete texts, we find a relationship between the two that is not that simple. From early pseudomedical literature such as the *Ishinhô* (The essence of medical prescriptions) of the tenth century to the censorship of erotic wood-block prints or Yoshiwara guide books during the Edo period, from the public dispute on naturalistic literature to the controversies on sexological writing at the beginning of the twentieth century, both advice on sexual behavior and the restrictions on representations of sex are evidence of a relationship between leisure and sex fraught with many more problems and tensions than is generally believed. I will focus on the relationship between male-female sex as leisure and male-female sex as work and its specific problems in the arena of the emerging sexological sciences at the beginning of the twentieth century. Drawing on data from sexological, medical, and general journals as well as from newspapers into which the discussions on sexual activity spread during the second, third and fourth decades of the twentieth century, I will make two principal points restricted to questions concerning heterosexuality.[1]

First, biologists and doctors who called themselves "sexologists" emphasised self-control and the importance of individual responsibility for "correct sexual behavior" based on "scientific knowledge" in their attempt to take over and reshape the discourse on sex and so establish themselves as experts on sexuality. In doing so, they explicitly dismissed leisure-oriented sexual attitudes and commercial sex. They denounced traditional Japanese sex-related ideas such as the popular belief that venereal diseases caught as an effect of sex consumption in the pleasure quarters were "as harmless as catching a cold" (Komatsu 1913), and notions of ancient "bedroom art" such as the belief that "since one gets sick in this way [via sexual intercourse], one can also get cured in this way" (*Ishinhô* cf. Ishihara and Levy 1968:114). And they declaimed against traditional Japanese creators of sex "knowledge"—quacks, artists, literary writers, street society, etc.—as "premodern" or "uncivilized."

Second, to strengthen the status and general acceptance of their new field, to ensure their authority and make legitimate the dissemination of their knowledge, early sexologists had to keep the lay public interested in their journals. As mass culture developed and competition in the print media market escalated, they livened up their serious articles with erotic stories of grotesque overtones, thus reintroducing a leisure element into scientific sexual writing.

Early Pseudomedical "Bedroom Warnings"

The twenty-eighth section of the *Ishinhô*, appropriately called "Within the bedroom," mentions a host of afflictions to which sexual intercourse at improper times leads. The emphasis is on having intercourse after midnight and as dawn approaches. During coitus, one is advised to be leisurely in movement and to adjust one's breathing accordingly. Taoist gymnastics and breathing exercises are also prescribed as ways to strengthen the eyes, ears, and digestive organs and the waist and back muscles; these exercises were thought to have curative value. Apart from conferring these side benefits, the main purpose of Taoist "bedroom techniques" was to assure the "return of the semen" (Ishihara and Levy 1968:114). Far from being the individual's private business, having no partner was still considered somewhat unnatural for both sexes at the beginning of the Edo period (1603–1867). The couple represented the link between heaven and earth. The lack of sexual unification was compared with the experience of a year with spring and summer (*yin*) but lacking autumn and winter (*yang*). Both single men and single women would constantly try to control their hearts and consequently begin to suffer from various diseases (*Enju satsuyô* 1631 cf. Shimizu 1989:199–206). According to old pseudomedical ideas, sexual activity was, aside from the restrictions concerning the location, organized along a system of two time coordinates. One was the individual's age, the other the time of the day, month, or year.

Varying with individual age, people in their twenties were meant to climax once every four days, people in their thirties once every eight days, people in their forties once every sixteen days, and people in their fifties once every twenty days. Once reaching the age of sixty one was meant to cease sexual activity. This was intended to provide a general guideline. Though controling and resisting one's sexual drive was considered unhealthy and capable of causing an abscess, it was thought that performing sex at the wrong time could lead to illness or even death. In the case of young people in the flush of youth who didn't feel sexually aroused more than twice a month, they were not to give in to it more often if they didn't feel like it. While the authors of old pseudomedical books such as the *Yôjôkun* (1714) were aware that there were also some exceptional people in their seventies who enjoyed perfect physical strength and engaged in sexual activities even resulting in offspring, they warned average people against emulating them. Although sexual activity was thought to guarantee a long life, sexual activity at a late point of life could also be a cause of premature death (*Yôjôkun* 1714 cf. Shimizu 1989:199–206).

In relation to the second time coordinate, "bedroom warnings" claimed that sexual intercourse was to be avoided during solar eclipse and full moon, at times of severe rainfall, snowfall, or storm, during extremely hot or cold periods, and at times when there were rainbows and earthquakes.

Furthermore, it seems to have been the general belief that the correct amount of sexual activity was physiologically necessary for good health. In 1688, Ihara Saikaku said: "As I observe with care, the young merchants of fabric stores in Edo are full of blood, yet most of them are pallid in face and will gradually become ill; eventually many of them die. This is because they are so occupied with their business, sparing no time to go to the pleasure quarter. Their bachelor life suffices with tea and shelled clams and cold rice for a quick supper, and for their only treat, drinking the famous good sake from Osaka. They have plenty of money to spend, but they have never seen the Yoshiwara" (*Kôshoku seisuiki* cf. Seigle 1993: 153). Saikaku proceeds to observe that the young clerks of the fabric shops of Kyoto are so devoted to pleasure that they succumb to what the Edo-period Japanese called *jinkyo*, or "hollow kidney (semen)," meaning exhausted libido. It was believed that *jinkyo* was a common (and incurable) cause of premature death. "Therefore," comments Saikaku, "virile men of Edo die from frustration and melancholy, while young men of Kyoto die from excess of sex." Everything in moderation, Saikaku cautions with his characteristic mock seriousness (Seigle 1993:154).

Another seventeenth-century writer observed: "Since olden times, no intelligent man has disliked this matter," and "no matter how superior a man, if he does not buy prostitutes, he is incomplete and tends to be uncouth" (*Yoshiwara shittsui* 1674 cf. Seigle 1993: 153–54). Books on sexual love such as Saikaku's *Nanshoku ôkagami* (The great mirror of male love, 1687), flourished in the seventeenth century in response to a demand from Japan's emergent urban class of merchants and artisans, called "townsmen" (*chônin*). These books reflected the cultural assumption that romantic love was to be found not in the institution of marriage but in the realm of prostitution. Recreational sex with both female and young male prostitutes was a townsman's prerogative if he could afford their fees, and he chose between them without stigma. A cult of sexual connoisseurship grew up around each: *nyôdô*, "the way of loving women," and *wakashudô*, "the way of loving boys" (Schalow 1990: introduction).

As for men of *samurai* status, it has been stated that "men in seventeenth-century and early eighteenth-century Edo were socialized to experience sexual attraction to both males and females" (Leupp 1995b), and, in fact, for an adult male, say a thirty-year-old *samurai* with a small stipend, a relationship with a partner (or partners) who either required no financial support, or who, while receiving such support, also provided nonsexual services, was certainly the most economical means of acquiring sexual satisfaction. The other two options, marriage[2] or a visit to the Yoshiwara[3] involved considerable expense. Although attitudes toward pleasure quarters and prostitution had changed considerably by the end of the nineteenth century, as we will see below, glimpses of people spending time in the pleasure quarters enjoying the sexual services of a prostitute as a leisurely affair keep showing up in popular culture as late as the semiliberal years of the late Taishô era (1912–1926). When "erotic grotesque nonsense" (*ero-guro-nansensu*) became a catch phrase illustrating the loose morals of Taishô-era youth culture, a song became popular, the lines of which referred to this attitude of leisure toward commercial sexual services: "Today is our day off. Shall we buy a *geisha* or a prostitute?" (Takemura 1986:4).

Although the early Yoshiwara was primarily a site of entertainment and socializing, with sex usually described as a discreet and secondary aspect of the business, the Edo period produced an abundance of pornographic *ukiyoe* called *shunga* (spring pictures) or *waraie* (laughing pictures), which survived (together with illustrated books including sparse but graphic texts by top *ukiyoe* artists) despite severe government controls.[4] Government controls were based on regulations concerning the representations of sex. From time to time they underwent changes as part of extensive law reforms, and culminated after the Meiji restoration in a number of regulations under the all-purpose rubric "injurious to public morals." This covered the prohibition of *shunga*[5] (*Shunga no kinshi*) in 1869, the suppression of Edo classics, the banning of the complete works of Saikaku in 1894, and the prohibition in 1906 of the twenty-eighth section of the *Ishinhô*[6] concerning bedroom arts as being injurious to social customs (Ishihara and Levy 1968:9). Naturalistic literature[7] featuring adultery or premarital sex as well as sexological writings published during the first three decades of the twentieth century also came under these regulations.

Science, Sex, and Politics

The all-embracing attempt to modernize and civilize the "physical and spiritual entity of the Japanese people" after the Meiji restoration triggered a wave of movements for the reform of customs and morals (*fûzoku kairyô undô*). By the 1920s the state's repressive campaigns also reflected the widely held middle-class sentiment that everything challenging Japan's claim to be a modern society had to be dismissed, abolished, or repressed. It was at this time that scientists, namely medical doctors and biologists, stepped in and forcefully joined the disputes on sex and its representations. The self-appointed sexologists found allies in various segments of early twentieth-century Japanese society. On the one hand, they positioned themselves and their "knowledge" somewhere among the bureaucratic authorities that progressively tightened controls on the violation of "good manners and morals" while, on the other hand, they became increasingly interested in demographic statistics on sex-related behavior. At the same time they had links to the established medical community, which hesitated to recognize sexological theories and research for various reasons, and to a number of so-called social movements, such as the Abolition Movement, the Socialist Movement, the Women's Movement, the Birth Control Movement and the Eugenic Movement in which some of them took part. The popular print media played a no less important role in the stimulation of public discourse on sex as soon as it realized that sexual issues were a powerful means to further the industry's market.

Issues such as sexual practices, gender relations, and public health were at stake, and brought together these differently organized groups and institutions. They shared an interest in social reform but also tried to push their own agendas in accordance with their own standpoints. The state founded the Central Sanitary Bureau. It was a powerful institution with the task of accumulating data on public hygiene supported by powerful instruments such as the Special Higher Police (*Tokubetsu kôtô keisatsu*) that were meant to control hygiene and to enforce their ideas about the "improvement of the Japanese race" and public health. Social movements such as the Purity Society (*Kakuseikai*) fought for the abolition of licensed prostitution. The Japan Christian Women's Temperence Union (*Nihon kirisuto fujin kyôfukai*) merged with the Purity Society in 1926 and favored the propagation of modern gender relations based on the prohibition of extramarital sexual relationships. Medical doctors and biologists attempted to establish a new area of science that they called "sexology" (*seigaku*) or "sexual science" (*seikagaku*), while concern about the threats of venereal diseases and the potentially negative effects of masturbation among Japanese youths led some of them to enthusiastically embrace the latest sexological findings and theories of the German/Austrian *Sexualwissenschaft*. By the late 1920s more than ten popular sexological journals had been established and were spreading what was assumed to be the "scientifically correct knowledge" on sexuality. Examples include Habuto Eiji's *Seiyoku to jinsei* (Sex and Life, 1920–1922), Tanaka Kôgai's *Hentai seiyoku* (Perverse Sex, 1917–1926), Nakamura Kokyô's *Hentai shinri* (Perverse Psyche, 1917–1926), Ôta Tenrei's *Seikagaku kenkyû* (Sexological Research, 1936–1937) and Yamamoto Senji's *Sanji chôsetsu hyôron* (Review for Birth Control) that was renamed *Sei to shakai* (Sex and Society, 1925–1927). Biologists as well as doctors started to teach sex education at secondary schools and universities and undertook studies on sexual behavior of Japanese students, thus introducing sex as a topic of both scientific research and teaching.

In Search of Data

The Central Sanitary Bureau of the Ministry of Internal Affairs was the first national institution to collect data on public hygiene since the early years of the Meiji era. The reason for the authorities' concern for the physical and mental state of Japan's population lay in the widespread infectious diseases such as venereal diseases (*karyûbyô*), the high infant mortality rate and the high mortality rate of TB patients (Iwanaga 1994:79–118). Venereal diseases, mental diseases that were also believed to be infectious, and other infectious diseases were not as life threatening as the epidemics that had characterized the Meiji years but were thought to be a potential risk for social stability (Nakatani 1995). Prostitutes were perceived to be the main source of the spread of venereal diseases, and the authorities were convinced that the strict segregation of prostitutes in the pleasure quarters and regular health checks were measures that would effectively keep the society morally clean and physically healthy.

A small survey undertaken in 1914 registered an infection rate of 20 percent for syphilis and gonorrhoea (Takemura 1984:148).

Smaller systematic surveys on the potential customers of prostitutes—recruits, patients in hospitals, and male university students[8]—revealed that at least one in ten suffered from gonorrhoea or syphilis (Fujikawa 1908:29), and that at the beginning of the century venereal diseases were as widely spread as TB (Ieda 1936b). Large-scale surveys conducted by the Central Sanitary Bureau however drew a slightly different picture: whereas the number of registered prostitutes increased from 28,432 in 1884 to 54,049 in 1916 and stagnated during the years between 1920 and the 1930s (Garon 1993b:712), the number of health checks of registered prostitutes increased from 1.77 million in 1896 to 2.95 million in 1930. The same period of time saw the rate of infected cases decrease from 4.06 percent to 2.17 percent (Naimushô Eiseikyoku 1893/94–1930). Considering that medical checks were counted and prostitutes were not, these figures fail to give any indication of the actual number of infected prostitutes. Some might have undergone health checks more than once a year, others might have managed to avoid health checks altogether. The health checks furthermore became obligatory only after the implementation of the Bill for the Prevention of Venereal Diseases (*Karyûbyô yobô hôan*) in July 1926 (Murakami 1926), and even then only for registered prostitutes. The estimated several 10,000 illegal prostitutes (Kagawa 1926:8), the 48,291 (1925) barmaids and waitresses that worked in cafés and dance halls, and the 79,348 (1925) *geisha* of whom three-quarters were also believed to engage in prostitution (Garon 1993b:712), were not listed at all.

Protecting "Innocent Mothers and Children"

Doctors, activists of the Purity Society, and other social reformers concentrated on two criticisms of health tests restricted to sex workers. First, such checks did not shake the common belief that only prostitutes were infected with venereal diseases (Ieda 1936b), and second, it lulled the customers of prostitutes into a false sense of security—they believed they were safe because prostitutes underwent health checks anyway (Yûya 1916; Matsûra 1912 and 1927; Murakami 1926; Yutani 1932). In the eyes of critics the danger of infection of "innocent wives and children" was *the* open secret of the time (Komatsu 1913), and one that had to be forcefully revealed. Organized women went a step further. In 1919 and 1920 the Federation of Women's Groups of Western Japan (*Zen Kansai fujin rengôkai*), the largest women's organization of the 1920s with three million registered members, propagated their aims, namely the "elimination of evil customs" and the "reform of daily life through campaigns for the reform and purification of sexual mores of men and women" (Garon 1993a:26).

Hiratsuka Raichô, who wrote in several magazines and newspapers, was only one of the more prominent women's leaders who, from the standpoint of "human rights, individual morals, social mores and national hygiene," repeatedly criticized prostitution as the provision of females for the satisfaction of male needs (Hiratsuka 1918 cf. Hiratsuka 1983:341). Her brainchild was a bill proposed in the 1920s prohibiting marriage of males infected with venereal diseases in order to protect mothers and children. The bill included a husband's contraction of a venereal disease as a reason for divorce. Regardless of a bride's wishes, local mayors would have been required to deny a marriage permit to any man who failed to obtain a medical certificate stating that he was free of venereal disease. Women would not have had to be tested because, according to the petition, most carriers were men. The proposal forbade women from marrying or living in a de facto conjugal relationship with a man who had not obtained a marriage permit, and it stipulated the same fine (up to 300 Yen) for male and female violators. The measure would further have required any man and woman who lived together to produce a marriage permit if asked to do so by the authorities (Garon 1993a:25). Though the Diet did not institute the marriage-prohibition petition as law during the early 1920s, Hiratsuka and other women's leaders later supported the enactment of the wartime government's National Eugenics Law (1940), which aimed to prevent "those of inferior constitution carrying hereditary diseases" from reproducing (Suzuki 1989:30–33).

Sex Education on Scientific Grounds

When abolitionists of the Purity Society called for sex education they did not hesitate to involve the authorities. They were not naive enough to believe that the abolition of licensed prostitution alone would lead to the restriction of sexual relations within marital relationships, since at the beginning of the twentieth century prostitution was not the only way to violate the propagated virginity and monogamy principles. Even had they succeeded in abolishing the prostitution system, they would still have considered sex education necessary. They believed that "correct knowledge" had to be disseminated among all social groups of society, and therefore considered the implementation of sex education as socially desirable (Misumi 1920). They believed that "correct knowledge" would lead to "correct morals" (Ieda 1936a, 1936b). Only if the "truth" was revealed would young men not go to prostitutes and unmarried young women would not become pregnant (Misumi 1920). Since for the abolitionists the "truth" was the potential danger of venereal diseases for the "continued existence of the race," sex education meant teaching "sexual hygiene" (Yoshida 1923), the "strengthening of the human will" (Nagai 1919) and the "implanting of a pure soul" (Ieda 1936b). The abolitionists shared their moral perspective with most women's groups. They believed that only Christian morals could guarantee Japan's civilization, and therefore called for an "education based on purity." Purity was associated with virginity until marriage (Shikata 1939) and monogamous marital relationships (Shikata 1939; Yamamuro 1928). Purity also dismissed any nonreproductive sexual activity within the boundaries of marital relationships. While sexual activities within the boundaries of a commercial enterprise such as prostitution was one "impure practice," radicals explicitly mentioned masturbation as another (Shikata 1939).

In 1908, during one of the first public debates about whether and how sex education should be provided to prepare boys and girls for an "animal instinct" they would soon be experiencing, the newspaper *Yomiuri shinbun* discussed the same two issues: masturbation and the consumption of commercial sex. Masturbation was to be avoided because it caused unnecessary exhaustion. It also violated the spreading belief in the need to strengthen the nation through intensified procreation after the Russo-Japanese War in 1904/1905. Among bureaucrats as well as educators and doctors commercial sex was understood to be the main source for the spread of venereal diseases such as syphilis and gonorrhoea—two of the most serious diseases at the turn of the century not only in the military but also in the rapidly developing urban areas and, due to increasing mobility, in the countryside.[9] Legal public prostitution was also increasingly being understood to contradict Japan's status of a civilized nation.

The more progressive educators and physicians opposed the common view that "sex education [would] strengthen the sexual drive" (Fujikawa 1908:5). They encouraged parents to talk with their children about sexuality. They claimed that it was the parents' responsibility, not the state's, to teach, control, and take care of their children's sex education even if it were only to prevent "education" via "newspaper articles," "bad friends," or "strange novels" (Minami 1908:5). Some were not all too sure about the necessity of sex education since they believed that the sexual drive in Japanese children would not be as strong as that of Western children due to differences in diet and physical structure (Yoshida 1908:5). Others were in favor of sex education in school since they doubted that parents had received the necessary education themselves. Those who were in favor of sex education in schools were partly motivated by their lack of confidence in the parents; it was the parents in the first place who lacked the right attitude since "they were not ashamed to joyfully have sex sleeping in the same room with their children," as one of the participants in the discussion stated (Mukô 1908:5). Since parents were believed to have a rather weak "sexual consciousness" (seiishiki), less progressive educators held that it would only do harm to disclose more than absolutely necessary, and urged parents to carefully choose the appropriate words to make sure that their children shuddered at the idea of contravening their parents' advice (Mukô 1908:5).

The controversy spread into a number of other newspapers and weeklies. Three years later, in 1911, the general magazine *Shinkôron* featured various sexological themes ranging from sexual inversion, sexual ethics, and the relation between sexuality and religion to an introduction to Western sexological literature and eugenics. This set off a boom of similar publications. Women's magazines as well as popular medical magazines started featuring sexological topics. From this time the sexual urge was understood as instinct; an instinct that had to be controled. In order to control it scientific knowledge seemed to be necessary. The necessary knowledge was to be provided and disseminated by sexologists.

When Habuto Eiji, a medical doctor and extremely productive writer on sexual issues, returned from a research trip to Germany in 1913, the *Tôkyô nichinichi shinbun* reported extensively about his impressions. "In Germany," he said, "sexual questions are not only dealt with from the perspective of morals like in Japan but also scientifically. Consequently, there is hardly anyone over twenty years old who still masturbates. A tremendous amount of books on masturbation and other questions related to the sexual drive is published." He had found more than 150 books on sexual subjects written for a professional public of doctors, psychiatrists, lawyers, and scientists, many of which were read by laymen as well (*Tôkyô nichi nichi shinbun* 12 November 1913).

Arguing that there was more to know about sex than that it could lead to the spread of venereal diseases, and maintaining that sexual reform and the diffusion of sexological knowledge was a necessary part of the transformation of various institutions and customs to give Japan the appearance of a civilized country, sexologists claimed that their scientific knowledge on sexuality was the only valid one. They defamed journalists, authors of naturalistic literature, and sex-related, so-called traditional Japanese customs, such as the "superstitious phallic worship" practiced by the disciples of new religions.

The emphasis on education to control sexual activities remained especially strong in circles of educators and medical doctors throughout the twenties and thirties. Ichikawa Yoshikazu, the head of the Tôkyô furitsu daiichi kôtô jogakkô, a girl's higher school, became known for his classes on sex education. He presented his ideas on sex education in an article in *Fujin kôron* in 1921. A contemporary commentator criticized his views as those of an "unrealistic conservative" who opposed "uncontroled information on sexual matters" for youth. Ichikawa was convinced that the "poison" could only be controled by education (Nada 1970).

When a group of elementary school teachers in Kôchi started a sex education course for older pupils and presented a study of their course at a meeting of teachers in 1921, the responsible teacher was told to resign. The *Kokumin shinbun* commented that a lot of young teachers sympathized with "these ideas" (*Kokumin shinbun* 20 July 1921 cf. Furukawa 1994:117). Just as advice columns dealing with health issues in women's and hygiene magazines during the early twentieth century revealed the anxieties women had about their bodies, advice columns on sexual problems in popular medical journals and sexological journals, such as the following example, reflect the readers' concern about their sex life as well as the mainstream attitude of medical doctors toward sexual matters.

Question: I am seventeen years old and started to masturbate regularly about three years ago. Since then I have been suffering from severe neurasthenia symptoms. I have tried medicine from a number of doctors, but I am still not cured. Instead, now I am suffering from wet dreams. Please let me know, whether there is a successful treatment.

Answer: In a word, stop your bad habit! Masturbation is bad and not being able to stop leads to neurasthenia which is shameful to suffer from. As remedial measures you should do sports and sleep early at night. There is a medical cure for older people but for people at your age and considering your psychological development it is better to do without it. (*Tsûzoku igaku* 1928)

Recommending a book entitled *Science and morals* that included a chapter on venereal diseases, one of the prominent writers on sex education claimed that Japanese youths knew far too little about the relationship between the enjoyment of leisure time in the pleasure quarters and the contraction of venereal diseases. Suggesting that the book be distributed to middle school students he argued that after reading the book and learning about the cruel effects of venereal diseases, youngsters would probably kill themselves in the Kegon waterfalls, but at least by doing so there would be no persisting danger left behind. By infecting oneself and one's family however, the disease would be inherited and spread to the offspring and to society. From the nation's point of view, he continued, it might be better to kill oneself than spread the disease to innocent people (Shimoda 1908:5).

The *Tôkyô nichinichi shinbun* reported in 1922 that a spokesperson of the Ministry of Education had said that the ministry would not integrate sex education into the curriculum (Furukawa 1994:116). The fear was too strong that sex education would encourage unwelcome sexual activities. The authorities doubted that "journals and books about sex research would implant pure morals and good thoughts in youth" (Nada 1970), and their fears were largely confirmed. Researchers such as Yamamoto Senji, Yasuda Tokutarô, and Ôta Tenrei wanted to accumulate "knowledge about sex" and disseminate it among the general public via public lectures, radio programs, books, and pamphlets. Their main concern was *not* the control of what was defined as "improper sexual activities" but rather to teach that masturbation was not pathological but a perfectly normal variant of sexual activity practiced by almost 90 percent of Japanese males. Another concern were safe birth control methods to improve the living standards of the lower strata of society. Their sexological journals, most of which were founded during the 1920s and 1930s, informed middle-class urban readers in their twenties and thirties. The journals consisted of articles about sex education, translations of and reports on Western sexological research, the introduction and naming of sexological categories, the translations of German or English terms such as "pervert," "invert," "sadist," "masochist," and "fetishist." Flashbacks on the history of sex in ancient Japan and Greece were quite common as were advice columns for "sexual problems." The simple syntax, using a syllable system written with the uncommon or newly utilized Chinese characters, and explanations of medical terms in colloquial language added in parentheses, as well as illustrations for aesthetic as much as for pedagogical reasons, enabled the common readers to relate to sexological knowledge.

At the same time, the moral reformers who had long championed the modernization of gender roles and sexual mores, confronted a new modernity. By the latter half of the 1920s, "modernity" in urban Japan was no longer associated exclusively with the middle-class morality of nineteenth-century Europe and United States, but also with the casual sexuality and "modernism" of the contemporary West represented by, say, dance halls and cafés. Different from Yoshiwara and other red-light districts that provided amusement for male leisure activities, the new dance halls and cafés were associated with modernism, individualism, romantic gender relations, and most of all with light-hearted waitresses whose sex life was much harder to control than that of prostitutes. Kagawa Toyohiko was frightened by these new tendencies and blamed the state for its ignorance concerning the increasing sexual looseness (Kagawa 1936:7–8). The Cajino Fôrî in Tokyo was one place that became popular for its "erotic shows." When it became known to the police that

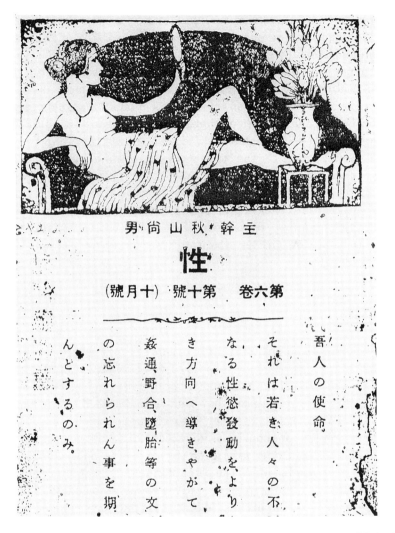

Figure 4.1   "Sei" was one of the sexological journals that were published during the 1920s (*Sei* 6/10, cover page, 1926).

female dancers would drop their underpants every Friday they stepped in and imposed restrictions in eight paragraphs, one concerning the wearing of skin-colored underpants underneath the ones to be dropped (Ishikawa 1991:82–83).

The mass media recognized "sex" as one factor that would stimulate their business. Treading the thin line between censorship and commercial advantage, they featured articles on "The story of advice for one thousand and one nights" (*Fujin kôron* 1933), or "The story of an unsuccessful wedding night" (*Tsûzoku igaku* 1934). The growing competition on the mass media market, its capitalization and segmentation as well as the professionalization of journalism, did not fail to have its effects on the contents of popular sexological and medical journals. In the hope that a readership that was enticed by a women's magazine such as *Fujin kôron* (in response to a twenty-page special report on the "true story of an unhappy lesbian love affair" that ended with an attempted suicide [*Chûô kôron* 1935]), dissemination of sexological "knowledge" by sexologists was enlivened with erotic stories of grotesque overtones featuring the visit to an "*ero*[tic] *madamu*" (*Hanzai kagaku* 1932) or with promising titles such as "The café girl as prostitute" (*Sei* 1930) or "Condom nonsense" (*Sei* 1932).

Concluding Remarks

The history of the relationship between sex and leisure in Japan shows that it has never been totally free of constraint and restriction. The substantial impact that scientific sexological writing has had on this relationship can, however, be understood only when its contextuality is seriously taken into account along with developments within the boundaries of knowledge in sexual science. A "science of sex" could only take over the discourse on sexual issues because it situated itself on the point of intersection of interests that were as diverse as their representatives were organized. Whether it was the governmental interest in statistical data on sexual behavior or the social reformist groups' growing concern for "innocent mothers and children" and the "liberation of women," whether the concern for an improvement of Japanese youth or the Japanese "race" altogether, the civilization, modernization, and scientification of sexual behavior was meant to provoke an individual as well as a social sense of responsibility for "correct sexual behavior" and to stigmatise leisure-related, nonreproductive sexual activities.

Sexologists succeeded in establishing the idea of the sexual drive as an instinct that could be controled but not denied. Confronting public awareness of venereal diseases and related "improper sexual activities," the sexologists' attempt to establish a new science merged with the bureaucrats' growing interest in data on sexual behavior that was to be used by a national body politic to improve the physical entity of the Japanese people. Perceiving Christian principles such as virginity and monogamy as the only avenue to the civilization of Japanese mores and customs, social reformist groups joined in and fought against licensed prostitution, arguing that supplying women for men's sexual leisure activities violated "human rights" and endangered Japan's status as a modern nation as well as the future prospects of a "healthy [Japanese] race."

With the late Taishô and the beginning of the Shôwa period the notion of "erotic grotesque nonsense" significantly influenced the mass media market. Sexologists and popular writers on sexual issues were confronted with a potential readership that was not only interested in education and advice on sex-related behavior but was equally attracted by entertaining erotic writing. They decided to go with the trend and increasingly provided their readership with entertaining stories, for some time managing to tread the thin line between serious sex education based on scientific theories and findings dismissing leisure-oriented sexual behavior, and the covert reintroduction of leisure-oriented sex in form of frivolous stories— thus practically inviting the authorities to repress sexual issues as a topic of public discourse altogether, whether it was "pornographic" or "scientific writing," by the end of the 1930s.

 Notes

1. This is not to say that homosexuality was ignored or denied by the authors of these journals. Whereas the long history of male–male sexual relations is well accounted for (see Furukawa 1994 and Leupp 1995a and 1995b for the most recent studies), female–female sexual practices have only very recently attracted the attention of scholars in and outside Japan (Bessatsu Takarajima 1987; Imago 1991; Robertson 1989, 1992a, 1992b, 1998).

2. He might try to marry, but this would be difficult as Edo remained a city with a large number of unmarried men till well into the eighteenth century. There were two men for every woman, few women of samurai status available, and his stipend was very likely to be too small to even attract a wealthy merchant's daughter.

3. Another option was to visit the Yoshiwara, but this also involved considerable expense. Meanwhile curfews and barrack rules might have restricted his movements to and from the lord's mansion.

4. For the politics of censorship during the Edo period see Kuwabara (1994:207–09), Tamai (1983:251–55), Thompson and Harootunian (1991).

5. *Shunga* were not only forbidden for scenes of extramarital love but also for love scenes that were perceived as "deviant," beyond rules and precautions of everyday life. Concerning the aspect of deviance, Haga suggests that "unexpected locations for improvised lovemaking" played an important role (Haga 1995).

6. However, a new edition known as the Asakuraya was published in 1909, complete with the offending section, and it was overlooked by the authorities. No public library in Japan permitted readers to see the section on the bedroom arts, but it became even more widely known as a consequence. In the 1935 edition, passages in the twenty-eighth section, dealing with positions of intercourse and sexual techniques, were left blank. Many studies of the text were made surreptitiously by Japanese researchers in the late twenties and early thirties, when there was a mania for books on sex, but the materials were only partially understood. The chequered fate of this text on the "bedroom arts" is an adequate comment in itself on the failure of the public official and the layman to make a distinction between serious studies of sex and those appealing mainly to pornographic or erotic fantasy (Ishihara and Levy 1968:10–11).

7. For an analysis of censorship of naturalistic literature see Rubin (1984:43–69).

8. Yamamoto Senji, the pioneer of sex research in Japan, undertook the first statistical survey on sexual behavior among Japanese males in 1922 and 1923 and found that 47 percent had had their first sexual contact with a prostitute. Yamamoto concluded that most of them had been persuaded to go to the red-light districts by company colleagues (Okamoto 1983:108–18).

9. See for instance the notes of Ella Lury Wiswell from her one-year stay in Suyemura in 1935 and 1936 (Smith and Wiswell 1982:95–97, 185–86).

References

Bessatsu Takarajima. 1987. *Onna o ai suru onnatachi no monogatari* (= Special Issue 64).

Chûô Kôron. 1935. *Chûô kôron* 3, advertisement section.

Frühstück, Sabine. 1997. Die Politik der Sexualwissenschaft. Zur Produktion und Popularisierung sexologischen Wissens in Japan 1908–1941 (= Beiträge zur Japanologie 34). Vienna: Institute of Japanese Studies.

Fujikawa Yû. 1908. "Seiyoku kyôiku mondai," *Chûô kôron* 23/10, 26–37.

Fujin Kôron. 1933. "Minoue sôdan senya ichiya monogatari," *Fujin kôron* 18/2, 19th October.

Furukawa Makoto. 1994. "The changing nature of sexuality: The three codes framing homosexuality in modern Japan," *U.S.–Japan Women's Journal* 7, 98–127.

Garon, Sheldon. 1993a. "Women's groups and the Japanese state: Contending approaches to political integration, 1890–1945," *Journal of Japanese Studies* 19/1, 5–41.

———. 1993b. "The world's oldest debate? Prostitution and the state in imperial Japan, 1900–1945," *American Historical Review* 3, 710–32.

Haga Toru. 1995. "Precariousness of love," (paper presented at the conference on *Sexuality and Edo culture 1750–1850* [August 1995]). Bloomington: Indiana University.

Hanzai Kagaku. 1932. "Meriken ero madamu jappu gedan ni kyôsei suru ero sâbisu," *Hanzai kagaku* 3/6.

Hiratsuka Raichô. 1983. *Hiratsuka Raichô-chô sakushû 2.* Tokyo: Ogetsu shoten.

Ieda Sakichi. 1936a. "Seichishiki to seidôtoku no kanyô," *Kakusei* 26/3, 30–31.

———. 1936b. "Junketsu Nihon no fukkô to kensetsu," *Kakusei* 26/1, 27–29.

Imago. 1991. *Tokushû: rezubian* (= Special Issue 2/8).

Ishihara Akira, and Howard S. Levy. 1968. *The Tao of sex: An annotated translation of the twenty-eighth section of The essence of medical prescriptions (Ishimpô).* Yokohama: Shibundô.

Ishikawa Hiroyoshi. 1991. "Ero guro nansensu," Tsuganesawa Toshihiro, Ishikawa Hiroyoshi et al. (eds.), *Taishû bunka jiten.* Tokyo: Kobundô, 82–83.

Iwanaga Shinichi. 1994. "Taishô-ki no eisei chôsa: Naimushô eiseikyoku nôson hoken eisei jôtai jittai chôsa ni kan suru joronteki kôsatsu," Kawai Takao (ed.), *Kindai Nihon shakai chôsashi III.* Tokyo: Keiô tsûshin kabushikigaisha, 79–118.

Kagawa Toyohiko. 1926. "Seiyoku mondai yori mitaru kôshô," *Kakusei* 16/3, 7–13.

———. 1936. "Haishô undô no konpon seishin," *Kakusei* 26/1, 7–10.

Komatsu Takeji. 1913. "Shônen to seiyoku mondai," *Kakusei* 3/2, 24–27.

Kuwabara Setsuko. 1994. "Verleger und Künstler—Zur zentralen Rolle des Verlagswesens in der Edo-Zeit," Franziska Ehmcke, and Masako Shôno-Sladek (eds.), *Lifestyle in der Edo-Zeit. Facetten der städtischen Bürgerkultur Japans vom 17.–19. Jahrhundert.* München: Iudicium, 191–210.

Leupp, Gary P. 1995a. "Male homosexuality in Edo during the late Tokugawa period," (paper presented at the conference on *Sexuality and Edo
culture 1750–1850* [August 1995]). Bloomington: Indiana University.

———. 1995b. *Male colors: The construction of homosexuality in Tokugawa
Japan.* Berkeley, Los Angeles, London: University of California Press.

Matsuura Ushitarô. 1912. "Eiseijô yori shôgi o hitsuyô to suru ya," *Kakusei*
2/4, 10–19.

———. 1927. "Sei no eisei," *Kakusei* 17/1, 4–5.

Minami Ryô. 1908. "Seiyoku mondai o shitei ni oshifuru no rigai (2),"
Yomiuri shinbun 19th September, 5.

Misumi Tamô. 1920. "Danjo no seiteki kyôiku," *Kakusei* 10/9, 30–31.

Mukô Hide. 1908. "Seiyoku mondai o shitei ni oshifuru no rigai (2)," *Yomiuri shinbun* 3rd September, 5.

Murakami Osaku. 1926. "Seibyô yobô hôan o hyôsu," *Kakusei* 16/7, 6–7.

Nada Inada. 1970. "Seikyôiku to iu na no gensô," *Fujin kôron* 55/5.

Nagai Sen. 1919. "Shônen danjo to seiteki seikatsu," *Kakusei* 9/11, 25–28.

Naimushô Eiseikyoku (ed.). 1893/94, 1895, 1897, 1900, 1910, 1930. *The annual report of the Central Sanitary Bureau.* Tokyo: Naimushô eiseikyoku.

Nakatani Yoji. 1995. "Relationship of mental health legislation to the perception of insanity at the turn of the twentieth century in Japan," (unpublished manuscript), 1–22.

Okamoto Kazuhiko. 1983. "Taishû no gaku toshite no seikagaku no tenkai,"
Gendai seikyôiku kenkyû 4, 108–118.

Robertson, Jennifer. 1989. "Gender-bending in paradise: Doing 'female' and
'male' in Japan," *Genders* 5, 48–69.

———. 1992a. "Doing and undoing 'female' and 'male' in Japan: The Takarazuka Revue." Takie S. Lebra (ed.), *Japanese social organization.* Honolulu: University of Hawaii Press, 165–93.

———. 1992b. "The politics of androgyny in Japan: Sexuality and subversion in the theater and beyond," *American Ethnologist* 19/3, 419–442.

———. 1998. *Takarazuka: Sexual politics and popular culture in modern
Japan.* Berkeley: University of California Press.

Rubin, Jay. 1984. *Injurious to public morals: Writers and the Meiji state.*
Seattle and London: University of Washington Press.

Schalow, Paul Gordon. 1990. *The great mirror of male love.* Stanford:
Stanford University Press.

Sei. 1930. "Shishoka shite iku kafê onna," *Sei* 11/9, 1st May.

———. 1932. "Kondômu nansensu," *Sei* 12/6, 28th April.

Seigle, Cecilia Segawa. 1993. *Yoshiwara: The glittering world of the
Japanese courtesan.* Honolulu: University of Hawaii Press.

Shikata Bunkichi. 1939. "Kenkô to seiyoku," *Kakusei* 29/4, 20–21.

Shimizu Masaru. 1989. *Nihon no seigaku jishi.* Tokyo: Kawade shobô
shinsha.

Shimoda Jirô. 1908. "Seiyoku mondai o shitei ni oshifuru no rigai (3)," *Yomiuri shinbun* 20th September, 5.

Smith, Robert J., and Ella Lury Wiswell. 1982. *The women of Suye Mura.* Chicago: Chicago University Press.

Suzuki Yûko. 1989. *Joseishi o hiraku.* Tokyo: Miraisha.

Takemura Tamio. 1984. *Taishô bunka.* Tokyo: Kôdansha.

———. 1986. *Kakusei kaisetsu.* Tokyo: Fuji shuppan.

Tamai Kensuke. 1983. "Censorship," *Kodansha encyclopedia of Japan.* Tokyo: Kodansha, 251–55.

Thompson, Sarah, and Harry D. Harootunian (eds.). 1991. *Undercurrents in the floating world: Censorship and Japanese prints.* New York: Asia Society Galleries.

Tokyo Nichinichi Shinbun. 1913. "Doitsu shônen no imawashii seiyoku," *Tôkyô nichinichi shinbun* 12th November.

Tsûzoku Igaku. 1928. "Eisei mondô," *Tsûzoku igaku* 6/1, 137.

———. 1934. "Kekkon shoya no shippai monogatari," *Tsûzoku igaku* 12/1, 1st January.

Yamamoto Senji. 1979. *Yamamoto Senji zenshû. Daiikkan jinsei seibutsu-gaku.* Tokyo: Sekibunsha.

Yamamuro Gunpei. 1928. "Teisô to danjo no chii," *Kakusei* 18/3, 1–2.

Yoshida Kumaji. 1908. "Seiyoku mondai o shitei ni oshifuru no rigai (2)," *Yomiuri shinbun* 8th October, 5.

———. 1923. "Seikyôiku no mondai," *Kakusei* 13/7, 7–10.

Yutani Jirôshichi. 1932. "Seibyô no tôsei," *Kakusei* 22/8, 5–10.

Yûya Jirôkazu. 1916. "Minzoku eiseiron," *Kakusei* 6/4, 4–10.

PART TWO

Sports

As is the case for many leisure activities, especially for sport and traveling, the leisure aspect involved for the consumers is work for others. Whereas in most leisure activities work and leisure assume supplementary roles, in professional sports, the same roles which are leisure for an overwhelming majority become work for a minority. The leisure activity for the majority, in those cases, changes from active participation in certain sports to passive observation as spectators. Practice is a very different category from observation.

Professional sports are not a phenomenon new to Japan; the imperial Nara and Heian courts demanded aristocratic specialists for the football game *kemari*. The most conspicuous Japanese sport which, due to its physical preconditions, can be performed only by professionals is *sumô* wrestling. Whilst performers and spectators are not all that physically different in other sports, in *sumô* they are worlds apart. It is no wonder then that *sumô* acquired the somewhat ambiguous title of "national sport." For centuries *sumô* was performed only by Japanese wrestlers prepared for the sport by a special diet. From a political scientist's point of view, T. J. Pempel tells of what happened when non-Japanese, having fulfilled the physical requirements, intruded upon the Japanese *sumô* world and began to internationalize Japan's "national sport." Recently, the Sumô Association has tried to promote global interest for this peculiar sport by travelling overseas on exhibition tours.

The internationalization of another Japanese national sport, *jûdô*, began much earlier, but few Westerners will know that this "traditional" Japanese sport only became a tradition in the late nineteenth century. Inoue Shun, one of the few Japanese sociologists specializing on leisure and popular culture, himself an active *jûdôka*, informs us that the tradition of *jûdô* was created as reaction to the Westernization and modernization of Japan in the second half of the nineteenth century.

Sumô is a sport watched by many and performed by few. *Jûdô*, conversely, is practised by many, especially during school years, and watched by few. The third sport treated in this volume, baseball, is played as much as it is watched. Although efforts have recently been made to introduce soccer as a sport to be watched by the masses, baseball has retained its throne of popularity. Seen from a quantitative perspective, baseball is the "national" sport of Japan, emphatically outdistancing soccer and *sumô*. William W. Kelly, concentrating on professional baseball, analyzes the role of ethnicity and the Japanese fighting spirit, and posits a pattern of Japanese baseball culture.

Another sport frequently seen on TV alongside baseball, soccer, and *sumô*, and therefore also probably qualified as a "national" sport, is golf, associated in the last two or three decades with a successful business career. Eyal Ben-Ari describes golf as a feature of Japanese business culture in Singapore—not as the harmless leisure activity of innocent Japanese golf-lovers. Although golf is not "proper" work, many Japanese salary men assimilate it into their workload, as they feel they are obliged to play, much as they feel obliged to drink after work with their colleagues.

S. L.

Inoue Shun

5

"Budô"

Invented Tradition in the Martial Arts

Modernizing the Martial Arts

Jûdô, kendô, kyûdô, aikidô, karatedô, and the other Japanese martial arts, generally known as *budô,* form a significant part of the leisure activities of contemporary Japan.

Budô is thought to have an ancient history but is actually a modern invention. True, the martial arts do have a long history under the terms *bugei* or *bujutsu,* but *budô* was developed in the late nineteenth century in reaction to the "modernization" begun in the Meiji period.

Of the various types of *budô,* I would like to focus on *kôdôkan-jûdô,* founded by Kanô Jigorô in 1882. Not only because he used the word *dô* (way) instead of *jutsu* (skill or art), but also due to his overwhelming success in popularizing *kôdôkan-jûdô,* did Kano play a central and leading role in the process of transforming *bujutsu* or *bugei* into *budô: Kôdôkan-jûdô* served as a model for the transformation of other martial arts.

With regard to the diffusion of *kôdôkan-jûdô,* many legendary stories of its confrontations with and victories over old *jûjutsu* schools have been handed down. They are however rather minor episodes in the earlier stages of its development. The most basic factor for its success is the fact that Kanô constructed *kôdôkan-jûdô* by modernizing *jûjutsu*. Various aspects of this "modernization" by Kanô include:

1. Kanô selected and systematized the most effective *waza* (techniques) of older schools of *jûjutsu*.

2. He introduced the ranking system (*dan-kyû sei*) to encourage trainees.

3. Concerning the method of training, he attached greater importance to *randori* (free practice or sparring) than *kata* (practice of set forms), which had been of much importance in older schools.

4. He established the rules concerning contests and refereeing.

5. He made Kôdôkan an incorporated foundation in 1909 to promote its development as a modern organization.

6. He advocated the moral and educational value of learning *jûdô*, maintaining that *jûdô* serves to cultivate people of ability who can make a contribution to the modern society.

7. He successfully placed *jûdô* in the world of discourse by untiringly lecturing and publishing on it.

8. He sought the "internationalization" of *jûdô* and tried to propagate it abroad.

9. He accepted female pupils and fostered the growth of women's *jûdô*.

10. He transformed *jûdô* into a sort of spectator sport by promoting various kinds of *jûdô* tournaments and championships.

Systematization of Techniques

Born in 1860, Kanô Jigorô was twenty-three and still a graduate student of Tokyo University when he opened the Kôdôkan. He also was an ardent student of *jûjutsu*. He not only studied the Tenjin-Shinyô school and Kitô school of *jûjutsu* under tuition of Iso Masatomo, Iikubo Tsunetoshi, and others, but also studied other schools on his own.

Kanô's greatest achievement was his critical examination and comparison of the various techniques of the many schools of *jûjutsu*, of which he selected the very best with which to form the basis of *kôdôkan-jûdô*. In a lecture in 1889, he remarked: "Following the scientific method, I selected the best elements of older schools of *jûjutsu* and constructed a new system which is most suited to today's society" (Kanô 1988, 2:102). Kanô, a rationalist, believed in the power of scientific thinking and wanted *kôdôkan-jûdô* to be grounded in science (especially in dynamics and physiology).

By theorizing about *waza* and formulating a systematic classification of them, Kanô made *jûdô* a martial art whose techniques could be communicated verbally. While the older schools disregarded verbal instruction in the belief that the arts were learned directly by experience and observation of the master, Kanô attached much importance to verbal explanation and comprehension.

The Ranking System

The introduction of the *dan-kyû* system was one of the principal factors in *kôdôkan-jûdô*'s proliferation and development. In August 1883 Kanô, the first person to introduce a clearly defined grading system into the martial arts, conferred the *kôdôkan* first grade (*shodan*) on two disciples: Tomita Tsunejirô and Saigô Shirô.

Formerly ranking had varied depending on the school, but had basically consisted of three stages: *mokuroku* (mastery of a set of techniques), *menkyo* (licence to teach), and *kaiden* (initiation in all the secrets). Kanô thought that the distance between these three steps was too great and that trainees could easily become discouraged. He therefore created a *dan* system comprised of ten steps, first to tenth grade. For trainees not yet ranked in the *dan* system, he devised a subsystem of *kyû* with six steps. This kind of ranking system gradually spread to other forms of *budô*.

Kanô's concern for encouraging trainees can be found in the fact that, in contrast to the older schools, he chose *randori* as the main component of practice rather than *kata*. One of the reasons he did this was that *randori* was more interesting than *kata* and had the advantage of not boring the trainees.

Kanô seemed to treat the trainees as clients, or even as consumers. This was something novel (or something "modern") that he introduced to the teacher–pupil relationship in martial arts.

Jûdô as Culture

Kanô was an educator holding posts successively as professor at the Gakushûin, principal of the Fifth Higher School in Kumamoto, principal of the First Higher School in Tokyo, and principal of the Tokyo Higher Normal School. This assisted him in popularizing *kôdôkan-jûdô* among higher schools.

Kanô emphasized character building in *jûdô* training. He maintained that the ultimate goal of *jûdô* training was to "perfect oneself and contribute something to the world" (Kanô 1988, 3:124). Thus *jûdô* has the educative aim to produce useful people for the community. This doctrine, acceding to the national demand that sought a new type of capable citizen, contributed to the development of *kôdôkan-jûdô*. And in the process of this development, in turn, the character-building aspect became increasingly emphasized.

In 1922 Kanô established the Kôdôkan Cultural Association (Kôdôkan bunkakai). The purpose of the Association was to contribute to society by making use of the principles of *kôdôkan-jûdô*. In its prospectus he wrote: (1) The most efficient use of energy is the secret for self-perfection; (2) Self-perfection is accomplished by helping others' perfection; (3) Mutual self-perfection is the foundation of the mutual prosperity of humankind (Kanô 1988, 9:12–14).

"The most efficient use of energy" is what Kanô thought to be the most basic principle of *jûdô*. By "energy" he means "both mental and physical power." By "the most efficient use" he implies two injunctions: first, use the mental and physical power most reasonably, avoiding waste; second, use it to promote goodness. "Goodness," Kanô defines, "is something that promotes the continuing development of collective and social lives" (Kanô 1988, 1:70–72).

Accordingly he maintained that "*jûdô* is no longer merely a martial art, but the name of a principle applicable to all aspects of human affairs" (Kanô 1988, 2:250).

He was eager to talk about the cultural significance of *kôdôkan-jûdô*. He also tried to explain all of the projects and activities of Kôdôkan. I already mentioned that he made the techniques of *jûdô* explicable, but this was not limited to the technical aspects of *waza*. He made the whole system of *kôdôkan-jûdô* "accountable," including its principles, purposes, and meanings. He was an able spokesman for *kôdôkan-jûdô*, tirelessly lecturing and publishing on it. Whenever possible, he seized the occasion to comment on, justify, and promote *jûdô*. He set up his own magazine, and devoted his energy to issuing what are now called *kôdôkan* magazines.

Kanô was not merely a practitioner of *jûdô* but also a man of letters who continued to speak about it tirelessly (now collected in *Kanô Jigorô taikei*, 14 volumes). He successfully incorporated *jûdô* into the world of discourse of modern Japan and established its raison d'être in a society without *bushi* (the warrior class). In this sense, *kôdôkan-jûdô*'s prosperity and growth can be seen, on the whole, as a triumph of the word rather than the sword.

Continuity and Discontinuity with Tradition

In this way Kanô "modernized" *jûjutsu* and stressed that *jûdô* was something different from *jûjutsu*, something more suitable to the modern world. On the other hand, he did not forget to connect *jûdô* with the old Japanese tradition of *bujutsu*.

This two-sidedness is apparent in his explanations of why he chose the word *jûdô* instead of *jûjutsu* or *yawara*. He attempted explanations on various occasions. In total he gave three reasons: first, since *bujutsu* as a whole was in decline at the time he opened the Kôdôkan, the images people had of *jûjutsu* were rather unsavory. Therefore, he thought that "at least the name should be new in order to draw pupils" (Kanô 1988, 3:123–24). Second, since the word *jutsu* refers to practical application, he chose the word *dô* (Way) to signify an underlying principle. He wanted to imply that *kôdôkan-jûdô* embodied the fundamental way and that *jûjutsu* was merely an application of it. But, why *dô*? There were many other words that refer to the principle in contrast to the application.

So, third, he emphasized the connection to tradition. Because he "didn't want the old masters' contributions to be forgotten," he selected the word *jûdô*, which had been used by some schools of *jûjutsu* (Kanô 1988, 2:103). For instance, the Kitô school, which Kanô himself had learned, sometimes used *kitôryû jûdô* or *kitô jûdô*. The diploma Iikubo Tsunetoshi awarded to Kanô in 1884 read *"Nihonden kitô jûdô"* ("Japanese-traditional Kito school of *jûdô*"), and Kanô himself, following suit, used the name *"Nihonden kôdô-kan jûdô."*

With the images of "tradition," *jûdô*, not only being a new type of martial art suitable for the changing world, became the body culture that could be associated with national identity—something unchanged in the midst of changing times. This may be regarded as a form of what Eric Hobsbawm called "invention of tradition" (Hobsbawm and Ranger 1983). This invention facilitated the development of *kôdôkan-jûdô* and often aided Kanô in his various activities. For example, young Kanô, who was quiet but basically progressive and enlightened, received the active support of such influential men of the conservative nationalist camp as Mishima Michitsune, Tani Kanjô, and Shinagawa Yajirô. This was due to the "traditional" images of *budô*, as well as to his personality. In 1910, the International Olympic Committee appointed Kanô as its first Japanese member. No doubt the fact that he was a master of the "traditional" Japanese martial arts, as well as a prominent educator (then principal of the Tokyo Higher Normal School), influenced this selection.

The Olympics and Modernization of Japan's Sports

As is well known, Kanô made persistent efforts to foster Western-style sports as well as the Japanese martial arts. The development of Western-style sports in Japan was greatly advanced by joining the Olympic games—and Kanô played a leading part in this. He established the Japan Amateur Sports Association (Dainihon taiiku kyôkai) in 1911 as the central body for selecting athletes and sending them to the Olympic games. As a result of the qualifying competition, Kanaguri Shizô (Tokyo Higher Normal School), later called "the father of Japan's marathon," and sprinter Mishima Yahiko (Tokyo University) were selected. Kanô took them to Stockholm to participate in the fifth Olympic Games in 1912, the first Olympics that Japan participated in.

Fifteen athletes were sent to the next games in Antwerp in 1920; two silver medals returned with them. In the Amsterdam games in 1928, forty-three athletes participated; both Oda Mikio in the triple jump and Tsuruta Yoshiyuki in the 200-meter breast stroke won gold medals. This was the first time that athletes from East Asia won gold medals at the Olympics. Japan's sports were thus rapidly modernized. The Japan Amateur Sports Association quickly broadened its role and became the governing body for all amateur sports.

Again, the image of traditional *budô* often helped Kanô in his activities related to the Japan Amateur Sports Association, as did his Kôdôkan operations. It provided a tacit guarantee for his activities and enabled him to gain wide support. This is a case of how the "invention of tradition" can be tied to the promotion of modernization.

In his later years Kanô made great efforts to host the Olympics in Japan. At the IOC convention in Berlin in 1936 he succeeded in inviting the twelfth Olympics to Tokyo. Though the Sino-Japanese War broke out the next year, the 1940 Tokyo Olympics were reconfirmed and officially announced at the IOC's Cairo convention in March of 1938, which Kanô attended as the head of a delegation from Japan. On the return voyage to Japan he contracted pneumonia and died on May 4, 1938, at the age of seventy-nine. He died believing that two years later the Olympics would be held in Tokyo. However, as is well known, this did not occur. In July of 1938, shortly after his death, as the clouds of war gathered, the Cabinet council decided not to host the Olympics of 1940.

The Growth and Ideologization of Budô

From the 1930s to the early 1940s, Western-style sports were rather discouraged in contrast to the growth of *budô*. As I mentioned earlier, *kôdôkan-jûdô* played a leading role in the formation of *budô*. From the late Meiji to the Taishô period (about 1910s), other *bujutsu* such as *kenjutsu* and *kyûjutsu* were transformed into "*budô*" on the model of *jûdô*: *kenjutsu* (or *gekken*) was renamed *kendô*, and *kyûjutsu* became *kyudô*.

The Japan Martial Virtue Association (*Dainihon butokukai*) played an important role in the development of *budô* as a whole, including *kendô* and *kyûdô*. The Butokukai was established in 1895 in Kyoto to commemorate the 1,100th anniversary of the founding of *Heian-kyô* (now Kyoto) by Emperor Kammu. According to the prospectus, the purpose of the association was to promote the Japanese martial arts in line with the "martial spirit" of Kammu, which formed the basis of *"wakon"* (Japanese spirit). The association built the Butokuden (Martial Virtue Hall, completed in 1899) adjoining the Heian Shrine. It organized branches throughout the country and held a Martial Virtue Festival every year in May. In 1905 it opened a training institute for martial arts' teachers, which became the Special Training College of Bujutsu in 1912. In 1919, the word *bujutsu* was changed to *budô*. This college was widely known as Busen, an abbreviation of Budô senmon gakkô.

From the 1920s to the 1930s *budô* showed a remarkable development and grew prosperous. In this process of rapid growth, however, *budô* was gradually assimilated into Japanese militarism. As the war escalated from the Manchurian Incident (1931) into the Sino-Japanese War (1937–1945) and the Pacific War (1941–1945), *budô* became closely associated with ultranationalism and the *"kôkoku shikan"* (emperor-centered historiography). It was raised to the status of *"kokugi"* (national sport) and turned into a part of the ideological apparatus for national mobilization. Under these circumstances, the Butokukai was reorganized in 1941 and placed under government control.

It was during this period that *budô* was incorporated into the school curriculum and the *"gakkô budô"* (school *budô*) was promoted. In a sense, the moral and educative value of *budô* was authorized by the state. The goal of the *budô* training, however, was no longer the same as what Kanô had advocated: "self-perfection," "contribution to society," and "mutual prosperity." Now *budô* was encouraged as a means of fostering the spirit of "self-abandonment" and "devotion to the nation-state."

In addition to the school education, such best-selling novels as Yoshikawa Eiji's *Miyamoto Musashi* and Tomita Tsuneo's *Sugata Sanshirô* played an important part in the spread of the ideologies of *budô*. *Miyamoto Musashi* appeared serially in the *Asahi* Shinbun from 1935 to 1939, and was then published in an eight-volume book edition (1939–40). *Sugata Sanshirô* was published in 1942, and brought to the screen by Kurosawa Akira the year after. Then in 1944 Tomita published the sequel, which was also widely read.

Budô versus Sports

With the progress of the ideologization of *budô*, it was increasingly stressed that *budô* had an ancient history and symbolized the traditional *wakon*. Emphasis on its discontinuity with tradition—that is, emphasis on its "modernity," which had been an important element of Kanô's dual assertion—disappeared. "Modernity" became regarded as a characteristic of the "imported sports" and as something undesirable, something to be rejected.

In the tone of argument of those days, the "imported sports" were contrasted with "traditional *budô*" and it was insisted that the former, being based on Western individualism and liberalism, should be "japanized" by the latter, which embodied the Japanese spirit. It was in this context that such doctrines as "*supôtsu dô*" (the Way of sports) and "*Nihon taiiku dô*" (the Way of Japanese physical culture) were advocated by Ôtani Takeichi, Noguchi Genzaburô, Hiranuma Ryô, Maekawa Mineo, and others (Irie 1986:181–238). They advocated, in short, replacing the Western spirit in sports by the Japanese spirit (*wakon*) of *budô*. This can be said to be an ultranationalist version of the *wakon yôsai* (Japanese spirit, Western technology) ideal. *Budô*, originally an invention of the *wakon yôsai* type, was now utilized to infuse the *wakon* into Western-type sports.

The relationship between *budô* and sports was reversed following Japan's defeat in 1945. Because of its close association with Japanese militarism and ultranationalism, *budô* was prohibited by the GHQ (General Headquarters of the Supreme Commander for the Allied Powers) and the Butokukai was ordered to be disbanded in 1946. The GHQ was especially hostile to *kendô*. *Jûdô* was treated a little more permissively. In 1948, the Kôdôkan resumed the All-Japan *Jûdô* Championships founded by Kanô in 1930, though school *jûdô* was still prohibited as was school *kendô*.

Faced with this difficult situation, the people and agencies concerned made every effort to "democratize" *budô*, that is, to recreate *budô* as a sport. In contrast to the "*budô*-ization" of sports at one time, *budô* had to be "sport-ized" to survive the postwar trends of democratization. For example, *shinai kyôgi* (bamboo-sword fencing) was contrived as a "sport-ized" form of *kendô*, and so obtained a permit from the GHQ.

From around 1950, *budô* gradually revived. The All-Japan *Jûdô* Federation (Zen Nihon jûdô renmei) and the Japan Kyûdô Federation (Nihon kyûdô renmei) were organized in 1949, and following the end of the Occupation period in 1952, the All-Japan Kendô Federation (Zen Nihon kendô renmei) was established. School *budô* was also revived: *jûdô* in 1950, and *kendô* in 1957. In 1956 the first World *Jûdô* Championships were held in Tokyo. In 1964 *jûdô* was adopted as a formal event in the Olympics at the Tokyo games.

A more detailed study of *budô*'s revival and its social context, however, is beyond the scope of this chapter.

The culture of Japan abounds with "invented traditions." *Budô* is merely one of many. I would like to touch upon another example. I already mentioned that the Butokukai was established in 1895 in Kyoto as a part of the project commemorating the 1,100th anniversary of the founding of *Heian-kyô*. This project was organized by the Chamber of Commerce and Industry of the city of Kyoto to counter the decline caused by the transfer of the national capital from Kyoto to Tokyo by the Meiji government in 1869. The project included two major events: hosting the fourth National Industrial Exhibition (Naikoku kangyo hakuranakai), and building the Heian Shrine dedicated to the spirit of Emperor Kammu, the founder of *Heian-kyô* (and beginning the *jidai matsuri* [festival of the ages] promoted by the shrine). The project thus combined "modernization" on the one hand and "invention of tradition" on the other.

Heian Shrine is now one the most noted shrines in Japan, and *jidai matsuri* is one of the major festivals and tourist attractions of the city; both, though modern inventions, are generally thought to have ancient origins. Thus Kyoto has preserved its image of and its self-identity as an ancient capital of a thousand years while adapting itself to the processes of rapid modernization and industrialization.

Many varied kinds of "traditions" have been invented in modern Japan and incorporated into all the manifold spheres of its everyday life. It is profitable, therefore, to reexamine the supposedly traditional nature of Japanese culture from the perspective of the "invention of tradition."

————————————— References —————————————

Dainihon Taiiku Kyôkai (ed.). 1946[1983]. *Dainihon taiiku kyôkai shi.* 3 vols. Tokyo: Daiichi shobô.

Futaki Kenichi, Irie Kôhei, and Katô Hiroshi (eds.). 1994. *Budô.* Tokyo: Tokyodô.

Hobsbawm, Eric J., and Terence Ranger (eds.). 1983. *The invention of tradition.* Cambridge: Cambridge University Press.

Inoue Shun. 1992. "Budô no hatsumei," *Soshiorojii* 37/2, 111–25.

Irie Katsumi. 1986. *Nihon fashizumu ka no taiiku shisô.* Tokyo: Fumaidô.

Kanô Jigorô. 1986. *Kodokan jûdô.* Tokyo: Kodansha International.

————. 1988. *Kanô Jigorô taikei.* 14 vols. Tokyo: Hon no tomosha.

Kimura Kichiji. 1975. *Nihon kindai taiiku shisô no keisei.* Tokyo: Kyôrin shoin.

Makino Noboru. 1983. *Shiden Saigô Shirô.* Tokyo: Shimazu shobô.

Oimatsu Shinichi. 1976. *Jûdô hyaku nen.* Tokyo: Jiji tsûshinsha.

William W. Kelly

6

Blood and Guts in Japanese Professional Baseball

At first glance, baseball in Japan appears to be the same game played in the U.S.—but it isn't. The Japanese view of life stressing group identity, cooperation, respect for age, seniority and "face" has permeated almost every aspect of the sport. Americans who come to play in Japan quickly realize that Baseball Samurai Style is different. For some it is fascinating and exciting; for others, exasperating, and occasionally devastating.

(Whiting 1977:v)

Patterns of (Sport) Culture

There is a widespread notion that sport is iconic of national character—that the way we play a game, and the particular game we as a people choose to play, says a lot about who we are as a people. There are countless claims, in particular, that baseball embodies something centrally expressive about America, the single most famous imperative being that of Jacques Barzun (1954:159): "Whoever wants to know the heart and mind of America had better learn baseball." This chapter is a brief examination not so much of as beyond the notion that people at play can be seen as "a people" at play. The people in question are the Japanese as fans and players of professional baseball, and in highlighting two themes—ethnicity and

95

spiritism—the chapter suggests the shape of my larger, ongoing research into the institutions and ideologies of baseball in Japan.

Despite the recent hoopla in Japan over its new J-League professional soccer, baseball remains in its century-long position as that country's most watched and most played sport. Robert Whiting is a longtime American resident in Japan and an astute and influential commentator of the sport who has become something of a Pacific Jacques Barzun by insisting that whoever wants to know the heart and mind of Japan had better learn baseball Japanese style. Not surprisingly, of course, he and most others warn that what is watched and played on the Japanese diamond is a most distinct brand of the sport, barely recognizable to American players and fans. Judging from the opening words of a recent video documentary, *Baseball in Japan* (1994), nationally broadcast on American public television, this conventional view of Japanese baseball has not changed much in the twenty years since Whiting's first book:

> Because of its slow pace, baseball fits the Japanese character perfectly. The conservative play mirrors the Japanese conservative and deliberate approach to life. Managers and coaches view baseball as a tool to teach loyalty and moral discipline—the same type of loyalty and discipline feudal Japanese lords expected from their soldiers and subjects. This samurai discipline requires endless hours of training, self-denial, and an emphasis on spirituality. So goes the Japanese approach to baseball. (Howard 1994).

We are indeed still mired in a national characterization of the sport that pits the familiar assertive Western individual against the grinding Japanese collective. As usual, too, this is not simply a matter of our own naive and condescending Orientalism. Japanese themselves, inside and outside the baseball world, have been enthusiastic promoters of a unique samurai baseball style, although they predictably give it a more positive, Occidentalizing spin. This is vividly manifest in the messiah-scapegoat cycle through which many American professional players are put during their employment by Japanese teams. All too often, they are hired and introduced as team saviors, they then meet with mixed success as the season wears on, and are eventually dismissed with loud public criticism of their laziness, selfishness, and lack of fighting spirit. These foreign players remind me of the folk remedy of *nade-ningyô*, the Taoist-inspired paper cutouts of human figures to whom were transferred, by rubbing and incantation, the ailments of a sick patient, who was finally cured when the paper figure was burned!

The linkage of sporting form and societal stereotyping is possibly even more pervasive than the national characterization of company organization, family relations, or schooling patterns. I do not want to get drawn into a critique of national character stereotyping here, except to assert what I hope is the obvious: that national character is not an *explanation* for behavior but a *substitute* for analyzing that behavior. Nonetheless, however easily we can show that both "our national pastime" and "baseball samurai style" are false representations, we can not casually dismiss these baseball stereotypes. Many people will still hold them to be true, and act in and toward the sport as if the matter was so simple. Indeed, almost every mass-entertainment sport in the modern era has been so typecast, and it is important to inquire into why this is so.

I suggest that there are at least two reasons for national stereotypes of sports. One is domestic and the other international, and both are related to the fact that the extensive organization and commercialization of sport in the modern era occurred first in Western Europe and the United States in a context of nation-state making, broadening educational hierarchies, maturing capitalist economies, and emerging mass-consumer markets.[1]

The first reason inheres in the pervasive use of mass sports to represent and manage the class, race, and gender cleavages redrawn by modern political and economic conditions within the Western nations. Among many examples, here is the American historian Michael Kimmel expressing how baseball came to be promoted as "our national pastime" in the early twentieth century as much because of as in spite of the contradictions it embodied. The early twentieth-century baseball diamond, he writes, was a "contested terrain," but,

> The contestants were invisible to both participant and spectator, and quite separate from the game being played or watched. It was a contest between class cultures in which the hegemony of middle-class culture was reinforced and the

emerging industrial urban working class was tamed by consumerism and disciplined by the American values promoted in the game. It was a contest between races, in which the exclusion of nonwhites and nonEuropean immigrants from participation was reflected in the bleachers, as racial discrimination further assuaged the white working class. And it was a contest between women and men, in which newly mobile women were excluded from equal participation (and most often from spectatorship); the gender hierarchy was maintained by assuming those traits that made for athletic excellence were also those traits that made for exemplary citizenship. The masculinity reconstituted on the ball field or in the bleachers was masculinity that reinforced the unequal distribution of power based on class, race, and gender. In that sense, also, baseball was truly an American game ... a place of both comfort and cruelty. (Kimmel 1990:109)

Precisely because they are mass public events, mixing entertainment and suspense, spectating and performing, pleasure and profit, such sports as baseball proved compelling sites for managing social differences and redirecting societal tensions.

A second set of circumstances promoting the nationalizing of modern sports can be traced to the international dynamics of their spread. Americans have always been ambivalent about our baseball diplomacy in Latin America and Japan. We have exuberantly exported the game, but we constantly worry if it can and should be played properly by those beyond the smell of hot dogs and the strains of our national anthem. And as Homi Bhabha (1994) has argued more generally, colonial and neocolonial subjects have appropriated their master's practices with equal measure of anxiety and anger. Mimicry is both a pale copy that falls short of an original and an imaginative appropriation that imaginatively exceeds the model.

The dynamics of mimicry have characterized, I believe, much of the extension of sports by the West to the non-West. They have created colonial and postcolonial anomalies: the Japanese baseball player is not unlike the West Indian cricketer, the South American footballer, the Soviet hockey player, the Kenyan marathoner, the West African basketball player, the Chinese diver.[2] "Styling" sports—Soviet-style hockey, Cuban-style baseball, Brazilian-style football—is a way of containing these categorical anomalies that our ambivalent imperialisms have encouraged.

In short, national stereotypes of sports and sporting styles reify intersocietal differences while masking intrasocietal differences. Again, they are not solely the tendency of the West, and we may draw a brief illustration from the management of ethnicity and ethnic identity in Japanese baseball—the "blood" of my title.

Purity and Polarization: Ethnicity and Postwar Civil Religion

As I have suggested above, the presence of foreign players on Japanese professional teams is one of the most remarked-about features of baseball in Japan. Some three hundred such players—overwhelmingly from North America—have played for the Japanese pro teams since the 1950s. At present, each team has a quota of three foreign players, of whom two can be on the playing roster at any one time. Their comings and goings, their heroics and tantrums are chronicled daily by the media and reported plaintively by American commentators. They are taken as constant testimony to the impermeable ethnic—and racial—barriers around the sport in Japan, and to the insularity and prejudice of Japanese society more generally.

In point of fact, the ethnic distinction between regular players (*senshû*) and foreign players (*gaijin senshû*) is not as long standing or as clear-cut as it may seem. Its ideological importance dates only from the mid-1950s. For the first two decades of pro baseball—the mid-1930s to the mid-1950s—the ethnic composition of the teams was not a major concern. The early teams had recruited among mainland Japanese who had gone to the colonies as well as an assortment of nonethnic Japanese who lived in Japan (most notably, the White Russian from Hokkaidô, Victor Starfin, who was enshrined in the Hall of Fame as the first pitcher to win three hundred games) and a number of ethnic Japanese from the States (e.g., pitcher Henry "Bozo" Wakabayashi and catcher Yoshio "Kaiser" Tanaka; see Thompson and Ikei 1987–88).

However, it was not until a decade after World War II that *gaijin senshû* became an important marked category. The first such player was actually a liminal figure: the Hawaiian-born Japanese

American *nisei* Wally Yonamine. Yonamine was signed by the Yomiuri Giants in 1951 with the encouragement of the American Occupation authorities, who were generally interested in promoting baseball as yet another democratic American practice. His Japanese descent was believed to ease his acceptance, but in fact it was often an obstacle to his popularity. He was heckled by fans and criticized by commentators who found American *nisei* like Yonamine to be the worst of both sides—neither trusted by fellow Americans nor accepted as Japanese for having been a traitor on the enemy side of the war. Yonamine had a successful career—he became the best lead-off hitter in the league, and was known for his aggressive base sliding, which had not been a tactic used in the Japanese majors before. However, his relations with the Giants club remained troubled, and he was dismissed abruptly in 1960. He went on to take revenge on the Giants, as player and manager of the Chûnichi Dragons.

After Yonamine, the players hired from American professional ranks were largely white, sometimes African American, and occasionally Caribbean. By the late 1950s, the Japan professional player rosters were bifurcated. On the one hand, there were small numbers of large *gaijin* "foreigners," recruited for publicity and power often at the end of their careers. On the other hand were the vast majority of regular "Japanese" players. Salaries, training, and other conditions of employment were determined by this distinction, which gave a moral superiority, if not financial edge or physical advantage, to the Japanese side.

This marking of ethnicity in baseball was a result of ethnicity's new role as a basis for postwar national identity. It is much remarked that, after Japan's defeat, official and mainstream versions of national identity have shifted from explicitly religious foundations (the State Shintô doctrine of *kokutai*) to more overtly ethnic bases. This "Japan Theory," as we know it most commonly, is, in Foucault's terms, a discursive formation—a loosely bounded but still powerfully conditioning field of claims, formulas, and models of ethnic markers, shared personality traits, and behavioral imperatives. In "Japan Theory," Japaneseness becomes a matter of psyche, not politics; it is an identity that we *are*, therefore you cannot *become*. It has the clear advantage of personalizing and naturalizing membership in the national community for a state whose own political character is suspected of everything from aggression to ineptitude. Winston Davis is quite correct, I think, in viewing this as Japan's civil religion (1992), manifest in a wide range of secular forms, from food and language to corporate organization and legal structure.

This is precisely what professional baseball has come to reflect and why ethnicity came to be so marked in the sport's late-Shôwa era image. Now immediately, a complication arises because, as any fan knows, Yonamine was not the last of the liminal figures. Indeed, some of the greatest "Japanese" players of the last forty years have been of mixed parentage, and a roster would include such stars as:

Kinugasa Sachio, the Hiroshima Carp third-baseman whose 2,215 consecutive games played broke Lou Gehrig's seemingly untouchable record. Given Gehrig's nickname, "Iron Man," Kinugasa was born to a Japanese mother and an African-American G.I. father.

Kaneda Masaichi, a Korean resident of Japan who leads the pitchers' record book with 400 career pitching victories and 4,490 career strikeouts. "Golden Arm" Kaneda played fifteen years with the Kokutetsu Swallows, but announced he would no longer pitch on less than three days' rest. He was traded to the Yomiuri Giants, who accepted that and other conditions. His ability to dictate such personal conditions led to his later nickname, "Emperor" Kaneda.

Harimoto Isao, another Korean resident of Japan, was a longtime star outfielder for the Tôei Flyers, setting the single-season and lifetime records for batting average. His antics and independence earned him the nickname "The Wild Man of Tôei." Harimoto too was traded to the Giants late in his career.

Oh Sadaharu, the legendary power hitter of the Yomiuri Giants and holder of the world record for career home runs, was born and raised in Japan to a Chinese father and Japanese mother. He retains his Taiwanese citizenship and remains immensely popular in Taiwan and among Taiwanese residents of Japan.[3]

Nonetheless, a conceptual dichotomy like indigenous-foreign is just that—a categorical opposition—and it allows few anomalies. Oh, Kaneda, and others could be—had to be—elided, however uncomfortably, into the Japanese category. This was done, I believe, through the understanding that whatever their blood-ethnic backgrounds, they all shared the experience of coming up through baseball in the Japanese school system. This is hardly a resolution because it directly contradicts the postwar premise that Japanese ethnicity is a matter of *being* rather than *becoming*. However, it does explain the very short ideological leash on which these mixed Japanese heroes have been kept by their clubs and the media.[4]

It also explains, I think, the peculiar fascination of such players as Oh and Kinugasa for many fans; the ambivalences of their identity have been experienced by many in the larger postwar society. Japaneseness as a tenet of national civil religion may be held to be a natural consequence of birth and blood, the intuitive expression of a homogeneous population. However, becoming this kind of Japanese for most Japanese—women, regionals, lower classes, stigmatized minorities—is always learned, incomplete, painful, vulnerable. It is precisely such mutual resonance, I think, that renders compelling such figures as Oh and Kaneda.

Historicizing Baseball and Theorizing Sport

To explain why baseball and other mass sports are so amenable to national stereotyping is *not*, of course, to explain the forms of the sports themselves. Indeed, this characterological commentary is an enormous obstacle. It has been so dominant that it has by and large foreclosed any serious scholarship on the much more complex structure of this sport and its immensely popular and potent place in modern Japan. Curiously, this has not been the case for baseball in the United States and Latin America, for football in Great Britain, and for cricket in several countries of the Commonwealth. For these sports, there is a lively and critical scholarship, both historical and social scientific, in spite of and in response to the popular stereotyping. For baseball in Japan, however, there are only a few exceptions to colorful journalism, sweeping essays, and rather anemic institutional sports history.

This is a great shame, for Japanese baseball fairly begs for scholarly attention by anyone concerned with the shape of twentieth-century Japan. Baseball began in the early Meiji elite higher schools and the First Higher School's victories over American teams in the

1890s stirred the patriotic sentiments of a population eager for parity with the Western powers. By late Meiji, baseball spread upward to the universities (especially the new private universities in metropolitan Tokyo) and downward to the middle schools. It incurred the opprobrium of the new national newspapers, until these same newspaper companies turned around and used baseball to promote sales in their fierce subscription wars. Sports journalism, new stadiums, mass transit, and radio broadcasts all made middle school tournaments, college series, and their star players into key figures of the new, commercialized, urban entertainment culture of the 1920s. In the 1930s, a professional league sparked a new level of commercial competition for spectators, readers, and listeners as well as state concern for the corrosive effects of Western cultural influences.

Throughout the postwar decades, baseball has flourished at all the levels—school, college, industrial league, and professional. The August Koshien tournament is a lightening rod for regional pride in an era of rootless mobility, for nostalgic celebrations of youth at a time of great gulfs between generational experiences, and for idealizing the purity of school sports at a time of rapidly expanding private secondary schools whose brazen player recruiting is as shameless as U.S. college football practices (see Esashi and Komuku 1994). At the professional level, baseball has been seized upon as a vehicle of corporate promotion, not only for company and product-name recognition and in-company morale, but also as a publicly visible corps of employees whose comportment will burnish the corporate image.

Thus, baseball has long been embedded in the educational system, the mass media, corporate structures, and patriotic feelings of modern Japan. Throughout the century, it has been a crucial arena where school pedagogy, corporate aims, media constructions, gender relations, and nationalism intersect. It is, in short, a significant window on to as well as a crucible for the ideologies and institutions of modern Japan.

You Gotta Have Guts

My second point in this chapter, thus, is that a critical analysis of baseball is one that situates its practices in historically specific institutional fields of power. To illustrate this briefly, I want to turn to one of the keywords in the vocabulary of Japanese baseball, "fighting spirit" or *konjô*, along with its borrowed English synonym, *gattsu*. Both pepper the conversation, exhortations, and judgments of players, managers, commentators, and fans alike. *Konjô* combines passive, stoic endurance with active, all-out drive. It is the application of effort (*doryoku*) to temper the spirit (*seishin*). The spirit—which is to say the mind/body indivisible—is honed through repetitive, imitative practice, hyperconditioning, and a tight managerial control that channels that fighting spirit into collective ends. It is the spirit of *ganbaru*, which is *not*, as it is usually glossed, doing one's best, but doing *more* than one's best. *Ganbaru*, or *gattsu*, is an ethos of overachievement and superhuman effort. Pitching day after day, the 1000-fungo drill, and other felt manifestations of fighting spirit are a reaching beyond one's normal limits and rational expectations.

To many, like Robert Whiting, "fighting spirit" *is* Japanese baseball; the modern ball field replicates the medieval battlefield, and the players are samurai with bats instead of swords.[5] My own view, though, is rather different. "Fighting spirit" has been neither a natural nor constant nor universal theme of Japanese baseball. "Guts" as an ideology of commitment, discipline, and comportment has surfaced in baseball only at certain institutional sites and during certain historical moments. I cannot here relate a full genealogy of "guts," but there have been at least three extended moments when guts was prominently foregrounded in routines of practices and imperatives of performance.

"Fighting spirit" first surfaced in mid-Meiji, in the late 1880s and 1890s, as the ethic of "muscular spirituality" self-consciously adopted by the Baseball Club of the premier higher school of the time, Ichikô, or First Higher School (Kiku 1993:84–99, Roden 1980a, 1980b). As Donald Roden has described, the head and faculty of Ichikô, one of five preparatory schools for the still-single national university, encouraged students to run their own affairs through school meetings, dormitory councils, and sports clubs. The Baseball Club became the most prominent exemplar of this rugged autonomy and self-imposed discipline. It reveled in punishing practice and a rhetoric of self-sacrifice. It no doubt saw its ethic vindicated by the considerable success it enjoyed, not only with other school teams but also against a series of American teams that it challenged through the 1890s. It is important to keep in mind, however, that this was also a time when elite youth fell under the critical gaze of a populace suspicious of their moral and physical fitness for the prestigious positions soon to be theirs. The ostentatious exertions of the Baseball Club, and their articulation of "fighting spirit" must be interpreted in that light.

Then, in the late 1910s and 1920s, "fighting spirit" found another influential ideologue—and a slightly different formulation—in the Waseda player, coach, manager, and later newspaper commentator, Tobita Suishû. Like Ichikô's club, Tobita's version stressed a spiritualized and self-sacrificing playing commitment explicitly likened to a warrior code. However, baseball clubs had now come under adult supervision, both at the university and high school levels, and not surprisingly, Tobita insisted on the unquestioned authority of the manager and his coaches in controlling the team. The lines of discipline and hierarchy were redrawn.

Although there were other coaching styles and philosophies, Tobita's proved compelling at a time, in the second and third decades of the century, when newspaper and transport companies rushed to sponsor sports events and to fan sports fever for corporate profit. Tobita's stern amateurism was used to temper this emerging commercialized popularity, especially of middle-school and Tokyo-area college baseball. Tobita's spiritualization of sport performance also dovetailed the Japanese state's efforts in mobilizing athletics to counter what it targeted as "subversive" elements among educators and university students (see Kelly n.d.b.; Kiku 1993:100–22)

A professional baseball league was organized in 1936, limped through the wartime period, and was firmly reestablished in 1950 as two six-team leagues, but "guts" really did not become ideologically central in professional baseball until it was adopted by the Yomiuri Giants during their unprecedented reign as national champion for nine consecutive years, from 1965 to 1973. Their preeminence precisely mapped postwar Japan's double-digit boom years that catapulted the country to the first rank of industrial powers. In the aftermath of the 1964 Tokyo Olympics, during the boom years of Prime Minister Ikeda's "double-your-income" policies, through the national crises of the Nixon Shocks, right up to the first Oil Crisis of 1974, the Giants were a lightening rod for national prestige and patriotic pride. The team was presented as supremely

talented, tautly disciplined, and relentlessly efficient, and its success was celebrated as a powerful synecdoche for the confident,
industrious society and competitive, resurgent economy that Japan
saw itself becoming. The Giants' "fighting spirit" was testimony to
"Japan-style management," which was now presented in a new positive light as a distinctive Japanese accomplishment. They became
the barometer of national pride.[6]

The V-9 Giants were led by two of the greatest players ever, Oh
Sadaharu and Nagashima Shigeo, and their popularity was
assured by the backing of the Yomiuri companies, by then the most
powerful news and entertainment organization in the country.
They were managed by Kawakami Tetsuharu, who had been
known during his player years as the "god of hitting." As manager,
Kawakami quickly became famous for a style of authoritarian
leadership called "managed baseball" (*kanri yakyû*). He demanded
iron discipline, arduous practices, stolid teamwork, a conservative
playing strategy. And *no foreigners*. The Giants had been the first
team in the early days of pro baseball to hire a foreigner, the above-
mentioned Victor Starfin. Then, after World War II, they were the
first team to again hire a foreigner, the Japanese American from
Hawaii, Wally Yonamine. In 1960, it was manager Kawakami who
engineered his abrupt release and declared his intention to "purify" the team, the first team to proclaim itself all-Japanese. Blood
and guts were inexorably linked.

The V-9 Giants totally dominated the league and thoroughly
reshaped the image of professional baseball. They—with the enormous power of the parent media company behind them—projected
a player image and a playing style that was coordinated, committed, and relentlessly efficient. However, as in earlier eras, the "fighting spirit" of the V-9 Giants cannot be mistaken for either a *natural* or *universal* style of playing or managing professional baseball in
postwar Japan. Indeed, a number of other professional teams had
rather different, less spiritualized formulations of training, performance, and strategy at the time.

But the Yomiuri owner Shôriki was out to forge a distinctive
identity for the team. Throughout the 1950s, his efforts to make his
Yomiuri company into a comprehensive media empire through television, newspapers, comics, and radio, were threatened by other
teams' successes. The Giants were especially embarrassed to lose

three years in a row to the Pacific League champions, the Nishi-tetsu Lions, in 1956 to 1958. The signings of Nagashima and Oh and the appointment of Kawakami as manager were aimed at reasserting its control.[7]

Moreover, "fighting spirit," however stridently it was proclaimed as the true spirit of Japanese baseball, proved to be a rather narrow description of the V-9 Giants themselves. As we have seen, their proclaimed "ethnic purity" elided such exceptions as Oh, Kaneda, and Harimoto; their dominance of league affairs and media reporting verged on intimidation; and their successes on the playing field were the result less of a tightly coordinated group effort than of the individual achievements of a few star players, especially Nagashima and Oh, who were given wide latitude in their behavior and who remained, throughout, wary rivals at best. A circle of harmony and a web of coordinated effort comprised the public team image, but it was an image that was purveyed and protected by a much more savvy deployment of individual talent, the manipulation of player egos, and the massive corporate power and media clout of the parent company.

In short, the "fighting spirit" of the V-9 Giants emblemized the spirit of Japanese baseball—or at least what most Japanese at the time wanted to imagine it to be. In so doing, Japanese both condensed professional baseball into the Giants' image and symbolized national prosperity and unique achievement with the success and style of this dominant and domineering team. A team success built on brute business strength and individual talent was allowed to stand for a sport style which in turn stood for a national distinctiveness. We need to retrace the steps in this ideological maneuver to understand both the blood and guts of Baseball Samurai Style.

Concluding Remarks

I have limited this chapter to two points, which nonetheless are of considerable importance in any serious appreciation of the position of sports in modern nation-states. First, for reasons both domestic and international, the national stereotyping of "sporting styles" is a pervasive and powerful rhetoric for reifying intersocietal differences (hence, the talk about U.S. baseball, Dominican baseball,

Japanese baseball, etc.) while masking intrasocietal differences of gender, class, ethnicity, and region. However, instead of simply dismissing such national stereotyping as just so much ideological fog, it must be treated as part of the problem to be confronted. The vast outpouring of commentary about "Japanese baseball" is a constitutive element of "baseball in Japan." A critical analysis must consider both the talk and action of baseball for their ideological effects and institutional locations.

My examples of these points have been blood as an ambivalent marker of ethnicity and guts as powerful idiom of performance. Blood and guts may be natural substances, but they are neither natural philosophies nor national characteristics. They are, rather, ideologically motivated efforts to naturalize certain distinctions and disciplines under some fairly specific historical circumstances.

Baseball in modern Japan has nationalized and pacified patriotic sentiments. It has also massified and mediated popular leisure. As Michael Kimmel argues, the baseball diamond is a contested terrain—but it is not the site of a single competition. There are many simultaneous struggles, on and off the field, that are condensed in and expressed through the efforts of the players.

Notes

1. Among many others, three recent studies that illustrate this with special reference to baseball are Kuklick (1991), Leifer (1995), and White (1996).

2. More than other sports, cricket has perhaps inspired the most penetrating analyses of the colonial and postcolonial dynamics of sport. C. L. R. James's *Beyond a Boundary* (1963) is the locus classicus. Among many others are a fascinating collection of West Indian cricket (Beckles and Stoddart 1995) and recent work by Nandy (1989) and Appadurai (1995). For broader arguments about sports imperialism and non-Western acceptance and resistance, see the contrasting positions of Guttman (1994) and Brown (1990–1991, 1991). Two books on Dominican baseball illustrate the shifting balance of domination and resistance (Klein 1991; Ruck 1991).

3. Robert Whiting's two volumes in English contain valuable sketches of these players. There is, in particular, a large literature on Oh Sadaharu, in Japanese, Chinese, and English. He has written a number of books himself; among the autobiographies, *Kaisô* (Oh 1981) in Japanese and a 1984

English-language collaboration with David Faulkner are especially valuable. I have written elsewhere about Oh (Kelly n.d. a.).

4. Kinugasa's African-American father is not mentioned in his two official biographies, and during his playing days the Hiroshima Carp front office cautioned reporters about inquiring into it. I have illustrated the restraints on Oh in my article, "Learning to Swing: Oh Sadaharu and the Spirit of Japanese Baseball" (n.d. a)

5. See inter alia his chapters on "Baseball Samurai Style" (Whiting 1976:36–67) and "The Super Samurai" (ibid.:68–82). Robert Whiting, it should be added, is an astute, informed, long-standing commentator on Japanese baseball—the most influential writer on the game in English. My skepticism about some of his generalizations does not detract from my regard for his portraits of the sport. He has also published extensively in Japanese, e.g., Whiting (1991), Tamaki and Whiting (1991).

6. Matsuzono Hisami, when owner of the Yakult Swallows, once declared that the best possible outcome would be for the Giants to finish first and his own team to finish second! This was a matter of sentiment— he was a long-standing Giants fan—but also corporate business; Yakult yogurt drink sales were said to decline whenever the Swallows defeated the Giants (Whiting 1989:7). A sense of this self-image is conveyed in the 1984 article, "Nihonjin to Kyôjin-gun," that appeared in 1984 on the occasion of the team's fiftieth anniversary (Iwakawa 1984a). It reports on a series of interviews with 102 former members of the Giants organization. A partial English translation appeared as "The Mystique of the Yomiuri Giants" (Iwakawa 1984b).

7. There were additional factors as well, including serious concerns in the late 1950s and 1960s about pro baseball's image; there was rather open player gambling and underworld influence, violence against umpires was not uncommon, as was brawling among players. Yet another key influence on the Giants' "fighting spirit" was the stirring gold-medal victory of the Japanese women's volleyball team in the 1964 Olympics, which ennobled "fighting spirit" on a national level.

References

Appadurai, Arjun. 1995. "Playing with modernity: The decolonization of Indian cricket," Carol A. Breckenridge (ed.), *Consuming modernity: Pub-*

lic culture in a South Asian world. Minneapolis: University of Minnesota Press, 23–48.

Barzun, Jacques. 1954. *God's country and mine*. Boston: Little, Brown.

Beckles, Hilary McD., and Brian Stoddart (eds.). 1995. *Liberation cricket: West Indies cricket culture*. Manchester and New York: Manchester University Press.

Bhabha, Homi K. 1994 [1984]. *The location of culture*. New York and London: Routledge, 85–92.

Brown, Bill. 1990–1991. "Waging baseball, playing war: Games of American imperialism," *Cultural Critique* 17 (Winter), 51–78.

———. 1991. "The meaning of baseball in 1992 (with notes on the post-American)," *Public Culture* 4/1, 43–69.

Davis, Winston B. 1992. *Japanese religion and society: Paradigms of structure and change*. Albany: State University of New York Press.

Esashi Shôgo, and Komuku Hiroshi (eds.). 1994. *Kôkô yakyû no shakaigaku: Koshien o yomu*. Tokyo: Sekai shisôsha.

Graczyk, Wayne. 1996. *Japanese pro baseball fan handbook and media guide, 1996*. Tokyo.

Guttman, Allen. 1994. *Games and empires: Modern sports and cultural imperialism*. New York: Columbia University Press.

Howard, Tony (producer, director, and writer). 1994. "Baseball in Japan" (video documentary). Tim Westhoven, Videographer. Produced by WBGU-TV, Bowling Green State University, Bowling Green, Ohio.

Iwakawa Takashi. 1984a. "Nihonjin to Kyôjin-gun" [Parts One and Two], *Bungei shunjû* 62/6, 132–48 and 62/9, 168–84.

———. 1984b. "The Mystique of the Yomiuri Giants," *Japan Echo* 11/3, 60–64.

James, C. L. R. 1963. *Beyond a boundary*. London: Stanley Paul.

Kelly, William W. n.d. a. "Learning to swing: Oh Sadaharu and the pedagogy and practice of Japanese professional baseball," John Singleton (ed.), *Learning in likely places*. New York: Cambridge University Press, in press.

———. n.d. b. "The spirit and spectacle of school baseball: Mass media, statemaking, and edutainment in Japan, 1905–1935," *Senri Ethnological Studies*, in press.

Kimmel, Michael. 1990. "Baseball and the reconstitution of American masculinity, 1880–1920," Peter Levine (ed.), *Baseball: An annual of original baseball research* 3, 98–112. Westport, Conn.: Meckler.

Kiku Kôichi. 1993. *"Kindai puro supôtsu" no rekishi shakaigaku: Nihon pro yakyû no seiritsu o chûshin ni*. Tokyo: Fumaidô.

Klein, Alan. 1991. *Sugarball: The American game, the Dominican dream*. New Haven, Conn.: Yale University Press.

Kuklick, Bruce. 1991. *To every thing a season: Shibe Park and urban Philadelphia, 1909–1976.* Princeton, N.J.: Princeton University Press.

Leifer, Eric M. 1995. *Making the Majors: The transformation of team sports in America.* Cambridge: Harvard University Press.

Nandy, Ashis. 1989. *The Tao of cricket: On games of destiny and the destiny of games.* New Delhi: Penguin Books.

Oh Sadaharu. 1981. *Kaisô.* Tokyo: Keibunsha.

——— , and David Faulkner. 1984. *Sadaharu Oh: A Zen way of baseball.* New York: Random House.

Roden, Donald T. 1980a. "Baseball and the quest for national dignity in Meiji Japan," *American Historical Review* 85/3, 511–34.

———. 1980b. *Schooldays in imperial Japan: A study in the culture of a student elite.* Berkeley: University of California Press.

Ruck, Rob. 1991. *The tropic of baseball: Baseball in the Dominican Republic.* Westport, Conn.: Meckler.

Tamaki Masayuki, and Robert Whiting. 1991. *Bêsubôru to yakyûdô: Nichibei-kan no gokai o shimesu 400 no jijitsu.* Tokyo: Kôdansha.

Thompson, Stephen I., and Ikei Masaru. 1987–1988. "Victor Starfin: The blue-eyed Japanese," *Baseball History* 2/4, 4–18.

White, G. Edward. 1996. *Creating the national pastime: Baseball transforms itself, 1903–1953.* Princeton, N.J.: Princeton University Press.

Whiting, Robert. 1977. *The chrysanthemum and the bat: Baseball samurai style.* New York: Dodd, Mead.

———. 1989. *You gotta have wa: When two cultures collide on the baseball diamond.* New York: Macmillan.

———. 1991. *Bêsubôru janki.* Tokyo: Asahi shinbunsha.

T. J. Pempel

7

Contemporary Japanese Athletics

Window on the Cultural Roots of Nationalism–Internationalism

Nationalism is an undeniable component of political culture in the contemporary world, and sports are an undeniable component of nationalism. Particular sports and individual athletes provide, for citizens and their leaders, a concretization of the ambiguous sentiments of nationalism and social solidarity. Such sentiments most typically take the form of collective national identification with the sport or the athlete: that's "our" team; that gymnast, runner, wrestler, or skier is "our" nation's pride and joy; that performance showed "us" as we really are, and so forth. In such formulations, the athletic or sporting accomplishments of an individual or a team become ready mechanisms for reinforcing real or imagined perceptions of national prowess: "our" team won; we're number one; "we" have always been a nation that could outlast (or outhustle, or outmuscle, or outmaneuver, or outthink) our opponents; "we" may not be good at some things but "we" sure can skate (or run, or throw the javelin, or sail boats, or whatever). And, of course, from the converse perspective, athletic failures can unwittingly carry the contrasting messages: "we" are still not up to par; "they" are still better than "us" (at this sport, all sports, life in general).

Given this power of sport as unifier or divider, it is not surprising that governments and/or political leaders often seek to utilize sports as political weapons. As African and Asian nations emerged from colonial rule during the 1950s and 1960s, and were forced to confront their internal divisions of tribal, ethnic, and/or religious differences, many of their leaders sought solace in the nationally unifying power of strong soccer teams whose membership cut across internally divisive lines and whose successes helped provide a focus of collective national emotion.

In a similar vein, during the height of the Cold War, with just a hint of détente, the United States and the former Soviet Union agreed to a track meet between the two countries. United on the abstract principle of "friendly competition" among "our" respective athletes as a means of person-to-person diplomacy (and indeed many of the athletes from each country knew and respected one another's abilities as a result of various international competitions), the two countries then fell to squabbling over how to score the meet. The debate was by no means trivial; it packed important propagandistic punch: the strength of the American team lay primarily among its male athletes while the Soviet women were generally vastly superior to their American counterparts. The Americans consequently wanted to score the male and the female competitions separately (so as to allow a declaration of the expected victory in the "really important" men's competition) while the Soviets, just as predictably, wanted the meet to be scored without regard to gender (so as to declare an expected *overall* victory). The compromise that was eventually struck was one that did both: thus the Americans consequently could proclaim that "their" men had beaten the Soviets (while simultaneously deriding the collective musculature and lack of femininity of the Soviet women) while the Soviets simultaneously announced in their papers and to the world that the unified communist team had won a stunning collective victory over "capitalism."

A more tangible personal experience of this phenomenon came during the summer of 1984 when I had occasion to be traveling in Asia. During the two weeks of the Summer Olympics, I watched television and newspaper coverage in five different countries— Hong Kong, South Korea, Taiwan, Japan, and the United States. The experience convinced me that each country's audience was "watching" a different Olympics. Sports and events that were covered heavily in one country were all but ignored in others; individual events that generated incredible international enthusiasm in the world press were often downplayed in specific countries; individual performances that were barely mentioned in the media of most countries became causes for national days of honor and celebration in others. This raised for me two big questions: what sports captivate the attention of a nation? and what sports, teams, and individuals are projected as "embodiments" of a nation's best character traits? And, more importantly, how do political and economic elites shape and draw on such sport-linked emotions?

All of this discussion is closely linked to current debates about Japan's real or imagined "nationalism" and the potentially countervailing notions of "internationalization." Japan has always been a country relatively self-confident about its own nationality and culture. With a long cultural history and lacking in the social divisions of religion, ethnicity, and language that split so many other countries, Japan's inhabitants rarely have been confused about who they are: clearly they are Japanese. Nationality, citizenship, ethnicity, and cultural identity are largely meaningless distinctions for most Japanese. Being a Japanese means identifying similarly with all such terms. Yet, precisely what it means to be Japanese has been the subject of a great deal of debate within the country, as can be witnessed by the raft of books in the *Nihonjinron* tradition, a tradition that Carol Gluck has aptly labeled the "voluminous and defensive discourse on what it means to be Japanese, as in 'how different we Japanese are from the rest of the world'" (Gluck 1992:xxix).

This sense of differentness from the rest of the world has characterized much of Japan's foreign policy over the last few centuries. Japan's historical relationship with the rest of the world has of course been multifaceted and complicated. At times Japan has seen the rest of the world as hostile and as best avoided, a pattern that prevailed during the forced closing of Japan to Western commerce for the bulk of the Tokugawa era, as well as in the xenophobic anti-Western, pro-Asian regionalism that Japan sought to advance during the 1930s and 1940s. At other times, Japan has linked its future unambiguously to the West, ranging from the country's initial welcome of Francis Xavier and Christianity, to the Tokugawa fascination with "Dutch learning" gained through the trading port of Nagasaki, through the fascination of many Meiji leaders with Western technology, to the more contemporary embrace of American jazz, Madonna, and Coke or the welcoming of Europeanism in the form of Beethoven, Picasso, and Mercedes Benz.

Throughout this dance of embrace and retreat, however, there has been a relatively strong resistance to true "internationalization," if and when such internationalization has meant an abandonment of traits seen as critical to "Japanese-ness," however defined. A strong sense of national pride and self-identity has typically pervaded Japanese culture and politics. Thus, the watchword has always been some variant of "Eastern morals, Western learning."

The debate over internationalization is once again at issue in Japan, this time primarily as a result of Japan's economic might and the challenge thereby posed for much of the rest of the world. Grossly oversimplified, the contention boils down to the following: For virtually the entire postwar period, Japan practised international relations that could best be described as deliberately low posture, but strategically oriented toward economic ends and means. In virtually all institutional forums, Japan's official presence was low-keyed; officially the country resisted any use of military power as a means of projecting international influence (Katzenstein and Okawara 1993; Sato 1989). Indeed, any international projection of Japanese power, except through economic success, was avoided as too dangerously reminiscent of the 1930s and 1940s.

Japan's postwar economic success, meanwhile, involved keeping the Japanese market largely closed to foreign penetration and using domestic market dominance by Japanese-owned firms to foster the export of Japanese manufactured goods to the far more open markets of the rest of the world. And since the massive revaluation of the yen, starting in 1971 and accelerating with the Plaza Accord of 1985, and again in the revaluations of the early 1990s, Japanese firms have moved abroad as investors and have begun to weave internationally impenetrable webs of commerce, banking, and manufacturing. Japanese manufacturing products have succeeded in international economic terms primarily because individual Japanese firms and industries have successfully met international marketing standards for the products they have produced. (In contrast, the comparative weakness of Japanese financial and security firms, as demonstrated in the collapse of the bubble economy and the *jusen* problem, can be traced in part to the failure of these sectors to be exposed to truly international competitive standards and foreign competition.)

Japan's primarily domestic orientation changed in a strategically insignificant but ideologically monumental way when Japan agreed to send Japanese military troops to participate in the United Nations' Peace Keeping Operations (PKO) in Cambodia, Mozambique, and the Golan Heights. Such moves accelerated intra-Japan debates about the merits of internationalization (Ozawa 1993). In all of these ways, Japan would appear to have been moving toward greater and greater levels of internationalization, at least when concerning Japanese activities outside of the home islands.

At the same time, Japan itself, it is argued, has been far slower to become truly international. Rather, critics contend, most efforts have been window dressing at best. Thus, Japanese governmental and private organizations have made various stabs at greater internationalization. All have been willing to examine behavior in foreign countries as a source of ideas for their actions within Japan. Many have been excellent data collectors; others were the source of numerous overseas investigative missions; most send one-half of their young career officials abroad for two-year periods. But in this context "internationalization" has meant primarily learning from abroad so as to adapt to the Japanese context; it has rarely meant substantial integration of their agencies' missions with the activities of their foreign counterparts.

As just one example of the narrow governmental interpretation of internationalization, former Prime Minister Nakasone's concept of internationalizing Japanese education meant bringing more foreign students to Japan, not to increase the exposure of Japanese faculties and students to other peoples and cultures but to teach the Japanese language and culture to foreigners. In this sense, the integration of Japan into the global community has meant, not that Japanese should become better able to deal with the world outside on the world's terms, but that foreigners should become better equipped to deal with Japan on Japanese terms (Stronach 1995: 54–55).

A similar pattern has occurred within the corporate world. Numerous Japanese corporations have moved their operations abroad, either to duck under rising trade barriers or to take advantage of cheaper land and production costs in export platforms, primarily in Asia. Other companies have entered into joint ventures, both in Japan and abroad. Within Japan, many of the previous direct barriers to trade and investment have been reduced or eliminated. Yet, to many critics of the Japanese economy, few of these changes have resulted in substantial changes in Japanese corporate behavior, the internationalization of the management staff in Japanese corporations, or the opening of the Japanese market in ways comparable to many of the smaller European countries. Rather, such openings as have occurred have resulted less in the internationalization of Japanese business and more in the Japanization of foreign production and of firms entering Japan.

As a most concrete manifestation of how "uninternational" Japan's domestic economy is, critics point to the fact that England is host to $4000 worth of foreign direct investment (fdi) per capita, Germany is the host to $1700 per capita, the United States receives $1600 per citizen, while fdi in Japan reaches the paltry sum of $96 per capita. And, it is further argued, the main losers in this situation are Japan's consumers (and many of its businesses as well) whose living standards fall well below that of most North American and European citizens, despite the high per capita GNP of the country as a whole. Only, it is argued, if Japanese society and the Japanese economy become truly internationalized, will the potential for major trade wars be reduced and Japanese citizens begin to reap the real rewards of the country's phenomenal successes in macroeconomics (Pempel 1993).

Finally, when it comes to individuals, a similar pattern has occurred. Many Japanese individuals have experienced foreign travel and foreign language study. Many others have adapted various Western ways, from American homes built by corporate executives to "black" hair styles, dress, rap music, and even skin coloring by allegedly rebellious Japanese youth (*Spin* 1993). Yet the question remains whether such adjustments really involve substantial modification of Japanese culture and lifestyles or whether they are simply quintessentially Japanese fads, in this case the fad of *kokusaika*. As one Japanese put it: "To Japanese, internationalization is like a fashionable handbag. It is worn as a pretty accessory when outside, and it may even serve a practical purpose, but once they are home, it is thrown in the closet (as quoted in Stronach 1995:55–56)." Or, as Stronach (1995:56) has put it,

> For most Japanese internationalization means such things as watching James Dean movies, being able to speak and read a little English or other European language, taking a summer holiday trip abroad, and maybe even having a foreign boy-

friend or girlfriend. It does not yet imply substantial changes such as altering domestic institutions and structures to conform to world standards or accepting foreign peoples, cultures, and institutions as equals in Japan. A Japanese man with a Western girlfriend will be the envy of his peers, but envy will turn to disdain if he marries her.

Japanese citizens are notoriously suspicious of, if not overtly hostile to, foreigners except under "safe" conditions such as offering directions in a public place. One 1984 poll showed that only 25 percent of the Japanese surveyed wanted to have anything to do with a foreigner; 38 percent would not allow a relative to marry one (*Asian Wall Street Journal* August 15, 1984). Extensive internationalization of the domestic economic and domestic society is likely to be a difficult task.

The issues that Japan confronts in economics are in many ways mirrored in the issues the country confronts in athletics. Just how "international" can or should Japan become? And what moves can the country make without endangering things perceived to have been highly beneficial to the national culture over time? Simultaneously, however, the issues are not completely for Japan to decide. The expectations of foreigners about Japan frequently reflect precisely the kinds of demands for more openness and more competitiveness that are made for automobiles, computer software, financial services, and department stores. Sensitivity to cultural differences and organizational patterns are typically less central to Western evaluations of Japanese practices.

Japan's Lack of Athletic Success in the International Arena

As countries advance economically and enhance their international prestige, they typically seek to project out their own cultural standards, in one form or another. One important feature of such projectionism for many countries involves the export of their athletic and sporting habits. This was certainly done by England in the nineteenth and early twentieth centuries, particularly with rugby and soccer (Markovits 1990). The United States sought to do the same thing with baseball, track and field, basketball, and so forth. How much has Japan sought to make similar projections and with what successes?

Perhaps the most successful examples of Japanese sports making inroads abroad involved Japan-owned golf courses world wide. The explosion of Japanese foreign direct investment during the late 1980s was marked by the rapid expansion of Japanese-owned golf courses worldwide. Many of these involved Japanese purchases of existing clubs known for their exclusivity, such as Pebble Beach in California, Old Thorns in Hampshire, England, or Turnberry in Scotland; in other cases, particularly Hawaii, Japanese developers bought agricultural land and created golf courses from scratch.

These have been truly the projection of Japanism abroad. In effect, the golf courses have created a circular economy, with Japanese citizens flying in on a JAL airliner, getting onto a Japanese tour bus that takes them to a Japanese-owned golf course while their spouses shop at a commercial village run by Japanese merchants. The closed loop in effect cuts out the local golfer, tour bus operator, merchant, and so forth (*Sports Illustrated* 1989:65).

When it comes to actual athletic competition, rather than the ownership of athletic facilities, Japan has had rather little success projecting a positive, let alone a dominant, national image. Japan has sent many teams from its "home grown" sports such as *sumô* and *jûdô* for demonstrations abroad. *Jûdô* and many of the other martial arts such as *aikidô*, *karate*, and archery have indeed had substantial influence in much of Europe and North America. In contrast, *sumô* has been treated primarily in a category akin to flower arranging and calligraphy; we Japanese can show it to foreigners, but this is so deeply an outgrowth of the native Japanese spirit that we would never expect a foreigner to learn how to do it well. We certainly could not export the activity in ways that would allow it to become popular in foreign countries.

In other, non-Japanese, sports, Japan's success has been at best mixed. Unlike the almost unbridled success enjoyed by Japanese manufactured goods world wide, or the success of such cultural exports as *karaoke*, Japan's athletes have for the most part left only scant traces of their presence in competitive international athletics. Moreover, in contrast to the rising yen or increased auto sales, with few exceptions Japan's international prestige as an athletic power has been diminishing rather than rising.

Japanese athletes have made their international mark primarily in Japan-specific sports such as *jûdô* or else in such team sports as volleyball and gymnastics. Underlying such team successes is the widespread belief in group solidarity, an allegedly strong Japanese cultural trait. A variety of Japanese teams (and a few individual athletes) have reached exceptional heights by adhering to long-honored Japanese traditions emphasizing *seishin* (spirit). Rigorous, if not cruel, training is pursued under the close tutelage of a *sensei* (master or teacher). The authority of the master is absolute and it is widely believed that the more demanding the teacher, the more valuable the training. As Smith has put it, "It is at the head of some of these groups that Japan's true autocrats are to be found." Thus, as he notes, in one television program devoted to women's volleyball, the (male) coach of the 1964 team is shown after a grueling practice walking down the file of players, pausing occasionally to administer a tongue lashing and a sharp slap to the face of a player. The collective Japanese reaction to Smith's expressions of concern was: "That's a very American reaction. Do teams with easygoing coaches win Olympic gold medals?" (Smith 1983:99–100).

The best indicator of the fact that performances by Japanese athletes have for the most part fallen far short of international standards can be found in the results of Olympic competitions, perhaps the most intense mixture of nationalisms within an international context. Japan's relatively weak performances in the recent Olympiads is surprising given the fact that a major turning point in the psychological and emotional recovery of Japan following World War II came with the Olympic Games of 1964, which were hosted by Japan and held in a dramatically refurbished Tokyo. The year also marked the introduction of Japan's world famous Shinkansen (bullet train), Japan's entry into the OECD and the acquisition of Article XIII status within the International Monetary Fund. In short, the year was a major benchmark in the international rehabilitation of Japan. The country's athletes did exceptionally well in the competition, winning sixteen gold medals, a number that placed Japan third overall, behind the United States and the U.S.S.R. Japanese athletes did particularly well in gymnastics (winning five of eight golds), *jûdô* (three of four golds), and women's volleyball (*Sports Illustrated* 1989:68).

With time, however, and in an ironic twist, Japan's national ability to produce competitive teams diminished as its economy improved. In 1976, Japan finished fifth overall with twenty-five medals (9 golds); in 1984, following a major increase in the number of events, it won thirty-two medals (8 golds) but fell to eighth place; in 1988 the country was down to fourteenth place with fourteen medals (4 gold), ranked behind countries with much smaller populations such as South Korea, Hungary, and East Germany. With twenty-two medals in 1992, Japan moved back up slightly to eleventh place, but only after it had been shocked in the 1986 Asian Games, finishing behind both China and South Korea (and seeing the latter win six of eight gold medals in Japan's most nationally prized Olympic event, *jûdô*). The 1996 Summer Games saw Japan win only fourteen medals, garnering twenty-fourth place in the national medals count.

There have been individual exceptions of Japanese stars in several "non-Japanese" sports. A number of excellent Japanese marathoners have done well in international competition, perhaps the best known being Seko Toshihiko, who won nine of ten major marathons during the 1980s. Though less dominant than Seko, Arimori Yuko made a major mark by finishing second by only 8 seconds to Russian Valentina Yegorva in the 1992 Olympic women's marathon (*Runners World* 1992:84–85). Mizoguchi Kazuhiro closed in on the world record in the javelin (*Sports Illustrated* 1989: 66–67). Ito Midori made a major mark in figure skating: "With athletic abandon . . . [she] transformed a sport where elegance once ruled" (Lubarsky 1991:40).

For the most part, individual Japanese athletes have rarely reached consistently competitive international levels, and most of those who did, including Seko, were products of the *seishin-sensei* tradition of coaching that seems emblematic of Japanese "national" traits (Seko used to bow daily before the picture of his deceased coach, Nakamura Kiyoshi, and dedicated his subsequent competitions to Nakamura after the latter's death) (*Shûkan Asahi* 1984:5). One of the more tragic stories that seems to fit Japanese cultural stereotypes is that of Tsuburaya Kokichi, a Japanese marathoner who entered the Tokyo Olympic stadium in second place, only to fall to third place and a bronze medal as he was outkicked at the finish. Several years later Tsuburaya committed suicide following years of depression after "letting his country down."

Far more rare are situations such as that of female golfer Oka-moto Ayako who has achieved consistently high and long-term competitive levels on the world golf tour and who is quick to criticize her male golfing counterparts as "too lazy and spoiled" to do well in international competition.

Also an exception is Nomo Hideo, a professional baseball pitcher with the Los Angeles Dodgers. Nomo spent five years with Japan's Kintetsu Buffaloes before bolting from his country's tightly restricted leagues following differences of opinion with his manager over what Nomo saw as overly strenuous workouts combined with the club's unwillingness to offer him a multiyear contract. Getting around the ten-year requirement to become a free agent, Nomo retired from Japanese baseball, signed for a $2 million bonus with the Dodgers, and went on to have an excellent year in 1995. He won his first six games and became the starting pitcher in the All-Star game. Nomo's "Americanisms" apparently did him little harm among the general Japanese public. Indeed, when Nomo was pitching, NHK relayed Dodger games to giant screens in major shopping centers throughout the country. But such cases remain relatively rare. Nomo, for example, was the first Japanese to have serious success in major league baseball since 1964.

Thus, unlike the widespread success of Japanese-manufactured exports abroad, Japanese athletes have enjoyed far more modest success. Japan has been able to project some of its own national athleticism abroad with sports from the martial arts, for example, but overall the impact of Japan on world athletics has been rather limited.

"Internationalization" of Athletics within Japan

Changing perspectives, it is also clear that Japan has had a mixed record with regard to "internationalization" of sports within the country. Japanese high schools and colleges have introduced virtually all major forms of athletics from rugby and ice hockey to bowling and figure skating. Just like the Big Macs, Swatch watches, and

Gucci accoutrements that are so much a part of the lives of younger Japanese, "Western" sports seem to be quickly and easily accepted and accomodated by individual Japanese.

At the same time, at least two problems deserve mention. First, for the most part, school sports do not include foreign participants or pit Japanese teams against those of other nations. Hence, Japanese national pride is rarely at stake. And, second, just as foreign food items and consumer wear do not threaten the core of Japanese financial and manufacturing success, so too high school and college sports are not at the core of "Japanese" athletics. A quite contrasting situation can be seen in more central and professional athletics.

Perhaps no single sport more typifies Japan that *jûdô*. Here the links between nationalism and sport were made most clear with the retirement of Yamashita Yasuhiro. Yamashita, the pride of the Japanese *jûdô* world, retired on June 17, 1985 at the age of twenty-nine. A gold medalist in the open weight class at the Los Angeles Olympics in 1984, Yamashita was for many Japanese the essence of the uniquely Japanese athlete. A pure amateur, he was undefeated from October 1977 until his retirement; he had a string of 203 consecutive victories. For nine years, he won the All-Japan Judo Championship. He retired at his peak, suffering no embarrassing defeats. He was seen by many as having brought back a sense of pride in *jûdô*, which had suffered in Japanese eyes during the 1964 Olympics with the incredible victories of a Dutchman, Anton Geesink. Throughout his carreer, Yamashita was never defeated by a foreigner. Mohamed Rashwan of Egypt, who finished second to Yamashita in Los Angeles, declared that he could not understand Yamashita's decision to retire since he himself was a year older and felt in truly fine shape. But Yamashita decided to go out at his peak, declaring:

> To put it simply, I felt I had reached the limits of my strength. In *jûdô*, you always have to be in top condition. You've got to be determined to give your best all the time, to really drive yourself. To tell the truth, lately I just haven't had the spiritual edge to give to it and I've been feeling as if something is missing. I've always known that when you lose your fire, when you can't do the kind of *jûdô* that you know you should, that

it's time to retire. Actually, my retirement has come as a great relief. (Chuzo 1985b:422–25)

This sense of spirituality in one's sport and Yamashita's strong devotion to Japan and its collective traditions were undoubtedly behind the decision of then-Prime Minister Nakasone to make Yamashita only the third athlete to receive the Kokumin Eiyosho (National Medal of Honor) after baseball player Oh Sadaharu and mountaineer Uemura Naomi.

Nakasone had, after all, been one of Japan's most politically nationalistic politicians. It was Nakasone, as a young parliamentarian, who called on Douglas MacArthur to eliminate Article IX from the draft Constitution being forced on Japan during the Occupation. It was also Nakasone who in calling for Japanese to become more international had suggested that in doing so they should not learn English so well as to lose touch with their essential "Japanese-ness." And finally, it was also Nakasone who had declared that Japanese economic growth was partly attributable to Japanese national character and homogeneity and that the economic demise of countries such as the United States was understandable due to their ethnic diversity, which in fact made them "mongrel" societies. Yamashita was, for Nakasone, the embodiment of what a "Japanese" athlete should be.

Questions of nationalism, foreign penetration, and cultural adjustment have also been particularly acute in two other "national" sports, baseball and *sumô*. There, for much of the 1980s, the problems of foreign penetration and/or acceptance seemed to reflect competing Japanese versus foreign standards and interpretations over just how open or how closed Japan's "market" was to anything made abroad.

Japanese baseball, as is well known, traces its roots back to the early Meiji era when a young American teacher of history and English introduced the game to his high school students. Hiraoka Hiroshi, an ardent Boston Red Sox fan, established Japan's first team, the Shimbashi Athletic Club, in 1883. Japan is one of the few places outside the United States where baseball is taken seriously as a professional sport. And Americans who have played it suggest that the game in Japan bears only a vague general resemblance to its American forebear. Thus, in contrast to the American-style game with its high-priced and highly individualistic players, Japanese baseball teams seem to embody the spiritual disciplines noted above for team sports such as volleyball and gymnastics.

Much has been written about Japanese baseball and its difference from the American game, including the season-long practices and conditioning sessions before games; the spiked seats to teach the proper position for catching; the disciplined attention to such skills as bunting and base stealing; the flexible strike zone; the few *shinjinrui* Japanese players who defied the "nationalistic" focus on the collective, such as Ochiai Hiromitsu (The Gaijin Who Spoke Japanese), and Giants pitcher Egawa Suguru who broke the draft system (Whiting 1989).

The question of international versus national focus however, is brought out most clearly in the treatment of foreign baseball players on Japanese teams. As has been widely reported, any professional Japanese team may have at most three foreigners on its roster (and with the exception of Nomo noted above, and Irabu Hideki in 1997, no Japanese players ever make it to the U.S. major leagues). What has been particularly striking about most of these foreign players, the vast majority being Americans, are the problems they have encountered in mastering the Japanese game, and simultaneously, the myriad ways in which even the best of them have floundered in the face of what seems to be the collective Japanese national reluctance to allow top honors to go to foreign players.

There are some exceptions. A number of *gaijin* ballplayers became quite popular with the fans including Randy Bass, Warren Cromartie, and Bob Horner. But Bass was closing in on the home run record of Japan's most famous ballplayer, Oh Sadaharu, and found that he was deliberately walked each time he batted during the last several games of the season. Cromartie and Horner had to deal with "gaijin" strike zones, which seemed to mean tougher calls by the umpire than were used for their Japanese teammates. As one successful ball player, Leon Lee, put it: "We're mercenaries, pure and simple. Our job is to do well and let the Japanese players have the glory and take the blame when things go bad" (Whiting 1989:263).

The situation seems to be changing with time, familiarity, and mutual adjustment; however, to Western critics (and many foreign ballplayers), the situation was remarkably similar to the selective and tentative market openings for Western imports: allow foreign goods in reluctantly; limit the quantity; and do the utmost to prevent competition on an "even playing field."

A similar isolation of foreign athletes on Japanese teams can be found in professional sports such as rugby and volleyball. In women's basketball, as well, some twenty-eight foreign (mostly American) women played on twenty corporate teams (with a limit of one foreigner on the court per team at any time) during the 1991–92 season. But following that season, the Japan Amateur Basketball Association decided to ban foreign women from all competition on Japanese teams, in what one magazine called "a kind of sportsworld equivalent of the infant-industry clause—a measure to lock out competition while nurturing Japanese basketball" (*U.S. News and World Report* 1992:12).

Even more complicated links between nationalism and sport in Japan can be seen in the contrasting treatments of foreigners in perhaps the most quintessentially "Japanese" of all sports, *sumô*. Overlaid with religious and ceremonial flourishes, it has been widely touted by officials in the closed world of *sumô*, as well as by government leaders, as a most-Japanese form of competition.

Foreign-born *sumô* wrestlers were historically rare until the 1980s and 1990s. Probably the earliest attempt by a foreigner to gain entrance to the tight-knit *sumô* society was in 1885 when a huge American wrestler approached stablemaster Urakaze, pleading to be taken on as a disciple. Astonished, Urakaze wrote to the government to inquire whether this would be possible; the government denied permission on the grounds that there was no established system for allowing foreigners to reside permanently in the country (Cuyler 1979:126). While a number of Korean-born wrestlers gained prominence during the prewar period, this was when Korea had been annexed to Japan and hence they did not really count as "foreign" in the eyes of advocates of the Greater East Asia Co-Prosperity Sphere.

The first foreign-born *sumô* wrestler was Hiragi Shoji, a Los Angeles-born Japanese American, who entered the *sumô* world in January 1935. The first foreigner actually to gain prominence was a Colorado-born Japanese American, Harly Ozaki, who wrestled under the name of Toyonishiki and who entered the top division in May 1944.

It was really Jesse Kuhaulua, a Hawaiian-born American, who became the first non-Asian to gain real fame in the *sumô* world.

Jesse, who wrestled as Takamiyama, was in many respects the perfect foreigner to penetrate the closed world of *sumô*. Of enormous size at six foot three inches and eventually over four hundred pounds, he entered the *sumô* ring in March 1964, moved into the top ranks in January 1968, and lasted a total of sixteen years before retiring at the end of 1979 to head his own *sumô* stable. Throughout his years of competition, he won affection and popularity among Japanese fans in large measure because of his diligence in following the harsh rituals of *sumô* to a tee, advancing slowly through the ranks, and eventually reaching close to the top levels. Jesse frequently beat some of the top wrestlers, and indeed in July 1972 became the first foreigner to win a tournament championship. During this time he learned the Japanese language and became popular on television and in commercial advertising. But perhaps most importantly, he never threatened to become so dominant as to challenge the general and widely held presumption that the world of *sumô* would remain the province of those who brought to it Japanese blood and the consequent Japanese spirit (Sharnoff 1990:166; Cuyler 1979:128).

There was even a brief outburst of anti-Jesse xenophobia in September 1976 when the *sumô* association announced that, since *sumô* was "the national sport, recognized as such by the government," foreign-born *sekitori* such as Takamiyama would not be eligible to become *sumô* elders after retirement. Following massive press criticism, another ruling was issued that exceptions would be made for Takamiyama (and for Kaneshiro, a wrestler of South Korean descent). Eventually Takamiyama retired, became a naturalized Japanese and went on to head his own *sumô* stable.

In sharp contrast to the relatively easy acceptance of Jesse, the appearance of Salevaa Atisanoe, an ethnic Samoan born in Hawaii, unleashed a storm of controversy in the *sumô* world and a bristlingly xenophobic reaction in the vernacular press. Atisanoe, wrestling under the name Konishiki, arrived in Japan in June 1982. Of enormous size even in the bulky world of *sumô*, Konishiki soared through the ranks. In just over two years he had entered the Makunouchi division, a feat that normally takes five years or more. During the September tournament of 1984 he defeated two *yokozuna*, or grand champions (Chiyonofuji and Takanosato), and one *ozeki* or champion (Wakashimazu); in the subsequent tournament, he beat the other *yokozuna*, Kitanofuji (Chuzo 1985a:41–45).

Derided by much of the local press as a "foreign meat bomb" and a "black ship," Konishiki still managed to rise to the rank of *ôzeki* on power and number of victories. He was widely assumed to be a prime candidate for promotion to *yokozuna* as he began to dominate the *sumô* world and won two championships. This, however, the Committee on Yokozuna Appointments resisted. Takahashi Yoshi-taka, the committee's head asked what would happen to *sumô* if it were dominated by "blonds with topknots who did not understand the traditions of *sumô*." He derided Konishiki as nothing but a "brute force" and announced that if sheer power was to be the cri-terion for promotion "why not bring in lions and bears to perform?" (Sharnoff 1990:168).

Less venomous and drawing more heavily on the cultural roots of *sumô*, Kojima Koburo, a member of the same committee, wrote a long article in *Bungei Shunju* announcing that Konishiki lacked *hinkaku* (or dignity), pointing out that the bylaws of the *sumô* asso-ciation set out the criteria for promotion as explicitly involving not just demonstrated ability in the ring but also *hinkaku*. Kojima argued further that

> *Sumô* is still distinctively Japanese. All professional sports played in Japan are foreign imports except *sumô* which origi-nated here. It has been around since time immemorial and survived centuries of tumultuous social change, preserved by devotees in more or less its ancient form. ... With its long ties to the Shinto religion and the Imperial family, *sumô* is a part of the Japanese ethos. That's why it has survived and become the national sport. (Kojima 1992:373)

He went on to declare that the Vienna Philharmonic Orchestra is known for its exquisite sound, and to retain it the orchestra bans female and foreign musicians. No other orchestra, he wrote, has such restrictions. "To charges of discrimination, the Vienna Phil-harmonic responds that it would be physically impossible for women to endure the long hours of practice and that foreigners can-not play in a style so quintessentially Austrian. Japanese can appreciate this insistence on cultural autonomy" (Kojima 1992:373).

Kojima further argued that, in contrast to other sports where a "tough punk" can become champion if he wins enough bouts or leads the league in home runs, *sumô* was different since "even if *hinkaku* could be translated into other languages, it would remain a uniquely Japanese concept" (Kojima 1992:377).

He concluded by declaring that it would be a mistake to promote foreigners to *yokozuna* just to demonstrate that Japan is a part of the global community for "relations among nations must be based on the assumption that each has its own distinct culture and institutions. ... History teaches us that cultural decay, not defeat in war, is the primary cause of a nation's decline. If *sumô* compromises its standards, it will be no better than pro boxing" (Kojima 1992:376).

Foreigners were amazed at this apparent articulation of hyper-nationalism, seemingly disguised as cultural protection. To the American press in particular the Konishiki-*sumô* problem was little more than an athletic reflection of the problems in trade and foreign direct investment: a purported Japanese proclivity for declaring the country open in principle but then being closed in practice to the most serious foreign competition. To many in the nationalistic world of *sumô*, in contrast, Konishiki represented all that was wrong with America. As a foreign giant, he seemed to threaten the entire pyramid of the *sumô* world. Konishiki himself certainly did little to endear himself to advocates of *sumô* as a spiritual pursuit by his comment that he hoped to wrestle for ten years, make a lot of money, and retire to Hawaii (Chuzo 1985a:44).

Eventually, Konishiki resolved the situation inadvertently by becoming injured and eventually losing his competitive edge. Fortunately for nationalists in the *sumô* world he never again won another tournament and drifted slowly down in the ranks, thereby obviating for the time the problem of whether or not a foreign wrestler was culturally fit to serve as the embodiment of Japanese cultural norms as defined by the world of *sumô*.

Yet, even the generally nationalistic world of *sumô* eventually gave way to foreign entrants with the success of Akebono and to a lesser extent Musashimaru. Both men were born in Hawaii and were recruited by Japanese *sumô* stable masters. Akebono made his debut in Japan in March 1988; entered the *jûryô* division in January 1990, becoming only the fifth foreigner to enter these ranks. By spring 1991 he had become a *komusubi* and in summer of the same year he was promoted to *sekiwake*. He won his first championship in summer 1992 and was rewarded with promotion to the second highest rank, *ôzeki*. After two subsequent tournament victories he became the first foreigner to gain the rank of *yokozuna*. Musashimaru also had considerable success, and as of summer 1996 held the rank of *ôzeki*.

In striking contrast to Konishiki, both men depend far less for their success on sheer size and brute force. And, perhaps more importantly, both gave strong evidence within the *sumô* world of at least quasi-Japanese temperaments that might be credited with proximity to *hinkaku*. Not at all coincidentally, a truly Japanese *yokozuna*, Takanohana, was also wrestling at the time of their successes, and Takanohana still managed to finish most tournaments with the largest number of victories and the Emperor's Cup. The result was that foreign inclusion, even at the highest ranks, did not mean automatic national defeat or an end to the predominantly Japanese characteristics and national symbolism in the sport.

Japan: Between Nationalism and Internationalism

What does the above material suggest about the nature of Japanese culture and, more importantly, its ongoing struggle to position itself between the polls of nationalism and internationalism? It would be wise to begin with Japan's apparent "failure" on the competitive international circuits, most especially the Olympics.

Many have argued that Japan's comparative decline in competitive athletics during the postwar years has been the result of the country's rigid educational system, which has stressed test scores and the academic path to success while downplaying competitive athletics, particularly at the high school and college levels (with baseball as the big exception). In effect, the criticism goes, Japan as a country has focused so much single-minded attention on maximizing national economic growth that its younger citizens rarely take time out from academic pursuits to develop their athletic potential, as individuals or on team sports. Consequently, in the Seoul Olympics of 1988, only 5 percent of the Japanese team were students, compared to roughly 40 percent on most European teams. There are some exceptions, and a talented baseball player or volleyball player who has gone to a mediocre high school or college can often land a job at a prestigious company anxious to capture his or her athletic talents for the company-sponsored team.

But for the most part, school teams are weakly encouraged and the base for Japanese competitive athletics is narrow, weakening the entire national athletic pyramid at the level of intense international competition.

While the weakness of collegiate athletics in Japan is undoubtedly a major factor in the relatively low levels of success achieved by Japanese teams in international competition, it is perhaps more politically salient to note that the Japanese government (until very recently) has made little systematic effort to counterbalance this weakness. There has been no substantial government effort to build up collegiate sports or to create a Japanese national sports machine such as those developed and maintained by the United States, the former Soviet Union, Cuba, many East European countries, China, and even Kenya. Why has Japan not done so? I believe the answer lies in the relative strength of Japanese national identity and, by extension, the relatively uncontested nature of the country's international self-image. In effect, Japan's leaders saw the country as needing athletic prowess far less than economic prowess.

What is most interesting about the relative national success of countries making huge government investments in creating internationally competitive athletes and teams is the fact that in almost all cases, "national identity" or "international self-image" is problematic. The development and maintenance of top-level national athletes and national athletic teams is one way for national governments to paper over internal divisions about race, ethnicity, regionalism, language, class, and the like. It also helps such governments to project themselves to the rest of the world as strong and internationally "relevant"; as I suggested earlier in the chapter, sports success becomes a vehicle for projecting a more comprehensive image of a nation's "successfulness."

The "failure" of Japanese athletes to measure up to the standards set by countries whose athletes are products of such national sports programs suggests less that Japanese athletes are somehow "less talented" than others. Rather, it reflects the fact that the Japanese government has not, for the most part, felt it politically necessary to mobilize athletics as a means of unifying the Japanese people or of projecting a particular image of Japan onto the rest of the world. This contrasts, for example, the tremendous efforts made by the Japanese government during the Olympics of 1936, and even those made in 1964. In effect, the downplaying of international athletic competition by Japan was a quite logical corollary of the tremendously strong and relatively unproblematic character of Japanese self-identity—and also the international prominence Japan has achieved through the export of its cameras, automobiles, and electronics goods.

The situation of foreign athletes in Japan, however, suggests a more problematic insecurity about Japanese nationalism. Allowing foreign competitors onto Japanese teams has frequently meant that Japanese athletes in the same sports have emerged as somewhat more pallid, less glamorous (and not insignificantly, less well paid). To the extent that foreign athletes shine, Japanese athletes look less invincible. From such a perspective, the "uncompetitiveness" of Japan and the "weakness" of "the Japanese" become reinforced in the public mind.

In this regard, the organization of a particular sport is important. When a sport is under a truly international body, the national Japanese organization must adhere to a variety of internationally determined standards. This has been true of *jûdô*, where despite the Japanese-ness of the sport in its beginnings, it has now become sufficiently international that non-Japanese *jûdô* players are invited to Japan to coach Japanese teams and to provide clinics for athletes. Indeed, Japanese *jûdô* players may soon find that the white uniforms so long a standard in *jûdô* have been replaced by various colorful substitutes to enhance the ease of competitor identification on television, a move pushed against a reluctant Japan by the international body. Nationalism and chauvinism are by no means eliminated, but the standards by which national pride is measured must be truly international. To do well means to do well even when foreigners compete in your backyard.

However, in sports where Japanese national organizing bodies still retain control, such as in baseball and *sumô*, the willingness to subject Japanese athletes to open competition from abroad has been far more problematic. Rather, as was suggested above in regard to women's basketball, Japanese officials seem to project their nationalistic feelings onto the sport and to insist on a "protectionism" that mirrors the Japanese manufacturing market. There may be more in common between *sumô* and semiconductors than originally meets the eye.

At the same time, two recent moves suggest that there may be some movement away from past conceptions of closed Japanese nationalism in sport, and the converse opening to more internationalization. The first of these involves recent moves by the Ministry of Education to increase the budget for the Japan Athletic Sports Association. Along with this increase would come a stipend system to pay for training and housing of the country's top athletes. In addition, Keio and Tokai universities have been given budgets to develop research programs on nutrition and dietary supplements aimed at producing stronger and larger Japanese athletes.

Not to be outdone within the arena of bureaucratic competition, the Ministry of International Trade and Industry in 1990 issued a report entitled "A Vision of Japanese Sports in the 21st Century." This report calls for creating tax breaks to stimulate the construction of facilities, tapping research groups for "next generation" technologies, and establishing databanks to create a "human resources" registry of former Olympic athletes and top instructors. Most of the MITI effort, however, appears aimed more at the sports industry itself than at the development of competitive athletes. On the other hand, international athletics has become, among other things, big business. To the extent that the Japanese sports industry becomes valued, so must its products be enhanced (and if foreign ingredients enhance the overall quality and marketability of the product, internationalization is inevitable).

In these ways, the Japanese government has moved to create a stronger sports system. It remains to be seen whether the slight shift in government policies will have the desired effect or whether cultural attitudes will have to change along with funding.

Even more intriguing, however, has been the introduction of professional soccer into Japan. In a matter of a few years, Japanese soccer has gone from being a poorly attended club sport, whose principal sponsors were Japanese corporations, to being a very well-funded and highly profitable professional association. Soccer matches in the newly formed J. League now systematically draw more fans in both the stadiums and on television than many baseball games (Tomiya and Hazama 1993:86).

Furthermore, but for a last-minute draw won by the Iraqi team, Japan's national team would have made it to the 1994 World Cup, an unexpected and almost miraculous performance. The Japanese home audience for the games from Qatar was well over 30 percent with more than 50 percent of Tokyoites watching the final part of the last game. Clearly, soccer has added an entirely new dimension to Japanese athletics.

Moreover, Japanese soccer has been far more hospitable to foreign players than either baseball or *sumô*. While not all the foreign players who were recruited fit in smoothly, most did, and many of the latter made substantial contributions to their teams (Ushiki 1993). Of the seventeen goals scored in the J. League's first five games, foreign players accounted for thirteen (Tomiya and Hazama 1993:87). Moreover, many were responsible for significant changes in tactics and style of play. Furthermore, there seems to be a willingness by soccer officials to recognize that the foreigners can and will make a substantial contribution to the improvement of the Japanese game. The experiences of the J. League and Japanese soccer reinforce the importance of recognizing the national or international character of the sports organization overseeing the sport in question.

The 1996 decision of the international governing body of soccer to award the World Cup jointly to Japan and Korea for 2002 was a mixed blessing. In part, it reflected the tremendous growth in the popularity of soccer within Japan; in part it represented extensive lobbying efforts by the Japanese government as well as localities and corporations that would benefit from hosting such a prestige event. At the same time, this was the first time two countries were chosen to host the World Cup, and many involved in Japan's lobbying effort saw the decision as a loss of prestige for Japan. But Korea, despite the fact that it lacks Japan's international economic prowess, had been the country that had gone to the 1994 World Cup ahead of Japan.

All of this leaves the questions of nationalism and internationalism in Japan quite open. Just as has been true of economic matters, Japan's moves to open itself up to greater foreign participation have been largely reluctant, isolated, and half-hearted. At the same time, it would be a mistake to assume that somehow Japan is unique in this regard. Few countries are quick to reorganize at their core simply to demonstrate commitment to some broad abstraction such as "internationalization." Rather, most moves toward internationalization come as a result of recognized self-interest and/or inevitability. This seems to be taking place in several areas of late. But the tightness of Japanese society generally, and of specific organizations such as the baseball association or the *sumô* association, along with the various *keiretsu* and *dango* practices, are unlikely to be scrapped quickly in the pursuit of the ephemera of *kokusaika*. More plausibly, the openings will be slowly advanced and only when those seeking access can either adapt to existing Japanese practices or else convince key Japanese allies of the merits of their demise.

Acknowledgment

The author wishes to thank Scott R. Seyman for valuable research assistance.

References

Anderson, Benedict. 1983. *Imagined communities: Reflections on the origin and spread of nationalism.* London: Verso.

Asian Wall Street Journal, August 15, 1984.

Chuzo Kazuo. 1985a. "Sumô enters a new age," *Japan Quarterly* 32/1, 41–45.

———. 1985b. "Yamashita Yasuhiro: Pride of jûdô," *Japan Quarterly* 32/4, 422–25.

Cuyler, P. L. 1979. *Sumô: From rite to sport.* Tokyo: Weatherhill.

Gluck, Carol. 1992. "Introduction," Carol Gluck and Stephen R. Graubbard (eds.), *Showa: The Japan of Hirohito.* New York: Norton.

Katzenstein, Peter J., and Okawara Nobuo. 1993. *Japan's national security: Structures, norms and policy responses in a changing world.* Ithaca, N.Y.: Cornell East Asia Series.

Kawabuchi Saburo. 1993. "The J. League's chairman speaks of his goals," *Japan Echo* 20/4, 78–81.

Kojima Noboru. 1992. "'Gaijin yokozuna' wa iranai," *Bungei Shunju* 70/4, 372–78.

Kokuseisha. Nihon kokusei zue. Tokyo: Kokuseisha.

Kuhn, Anthony. 1994. "Ping-pong politics: Table-tennis mutiny spurs sports-ethics debate in China," *Far Eastern Economic Review* 8, 44–45.

Lubarsky, Jared. 1991. "Power skating," *New York Times Magazine*, March 12, 40–52.

Markovits, Andrei S. 1990. "The other 'American exceptionalism': Why is there no soccer in the United States?," *The International Journal of the History of Sport* 7/2, 230–64.

Ozawa Ichiro. 1993. *Nihon kaizô keikaku.* Tokyo: Kodansha.

Pempel, T. J. 1993. "From exporter to investor: Japanese foreign economic policy," Gerald Curtis (ed.), *Japan's foreign policy: After the Cold War: Coping with change.* Armonk, N.Y.: M. E. Sharpe, 105–36.

Runner's World. 1992. "Long slow distance," *Runner's World*, 84–85.

Sato Hideo. 1989. *Taigai seisaku.* Tokyo: Tokyo daigaku shuppan.

Sharnoff, Lora. 1990. "Foreigners making their mark in sumô," *Japan Quarterly* 37/2, 164–70.

Shûkan Asahi. August 31, 1984. "Rosu kara kikokushi," 5.

Smith, Robert J. 1983. *Japanese society.* Cambridge: Cambridge University Press.

Spin. October 1993. "Black like me," 74–78.

Sports Illustrated. August 21, 1989. "Japan: Coming on strong."

Stronach, Bruce. 1995. *Beyond the rising sun: Nationalism in contemporary Japan.* New York: Praeger.

Tomiya Tetsuya, and Hazama Koichi. 1993. "The dramatic debut of professional soccer," *Japan Echo* 20/4, 86–88.

U.S. News and World Report. August 3, 1992. "Outlook: Sports, a tip-off," 12.

Ushiki Sokichiro. 1993. "Imported talent on the soccer field," *Japan Echo* 20/4, 82–85.

Whiting, Robert. 1989. *You gotta have wa.* New York: Macmillan.

Eyal Ben-Ari

8

Golf, Organization, and "Body Projects"

Japanese Business Executives in Singapore

In this chapter I examine the variety of golfing encounters in which Japanese business expatriates participate in Singapore. Proceeding from Plath's (1989:72) suggestion that we study selfhood in environments defined by time, I examine these interactions from a "life-course" perspective. My main contention is that participation in golfing occasions should be understood as part of people's notions about, and actualizations of, long-term strategies for their lives. In terms of an individual's life course, such occasions are intersections of two long-term and interrelated processes of personal advancement: careering at the workplace and the cultivation of a certain kind of leisured lifestyle. In and around these occasions, managers pursue and carefully create opportunities for promotion in their organizations and meticulously cultivate themselves as embodiments of prevailing images of senior executives. On a theoretical level, I attempt to systematically relate patterns of consumption—treated as aspects of more general strategies for the establishment or maintenance of selfhood and identity—to studies of Japanese business firms and examinations of life courses in Japan.

My contention is that the life-course approach allows us to link history, organization, and individual action, and to formulate empirical and theoretical questions best answered by examining Japanese business people in the period of their overseas assignments. First, given the continuous expansion of various Japanese corporations into countries around the world in general, and in Asia in particular (Yoshikawa 1991), an overseas assignment is gradually becoming a prerequisite for advancement into senior managerial posts in many companies. Studies of returning executives and their wives (White 1988) and investigations of returning schoolchildren (Goodman 1991; Kobayashi 1978) have been published in recent decades. But while these studies further our understanding of the problems that people face upon returning to Japan, as of yet, apart from scattered scholarly comments and some journalistic observations, no extended study of Japanese expatriates in their host country has ever been carried out. My inquiry aims to fill this gap.

Second, stints abroad—in the framework of Japanese companies—tend to make much more visible certain features of the formal and informal dimensions of Japanese workplaces. Because such overseas assignments involve a change of organizational responsibilities and a significant increase in income, Japanese expatriates tend to exercise the kind of organizational power and to live out a luxurious experience that in Japan is limited to senior executives. Thus relatively junior managers have the opportunity to learn and to cultivate both the work habits and the personal lifestyles of organizational members senior to them in Japan. In this context the interrelated patterns of work and leisure that figure in personal advancement in business firms may be more amenable to investigation.

This chapter is part of a wider study of the Japanese expatriate community in Singapore. I chose that country because I thought that it would be a suitable venue for examining the social and cultural implications of the "globalization" of Japanese business. I carried out my study between June 1992 and February 1994, primarily through interviews and participant observation. Of my ninety-three interviewees, sixty people were related to business (they were overwhelmingly men). Reflecting the general patterns of the Japanese presence in Singapore almost all of these people were white-collar organization men posted to the country for periods of three to five years at the end of which they would return to Japan. It is about these people that I report.

The Background: Japanese Capitalism and Southeast Asia

Spurred by strong governmental support, during the last three decades Singapore has become a hub of business headquarters and manufacturing facilities for all of the ASEAN, Southeast Asian and, in many cases, South Asian countries (Choy and Yeo 1990). Whereas the large-scale movement of Japanese business interests out of Japan began in the late 1960s, the shift to Southeast Asia only began in the early 1970s. Originally this movement was comprised mostly of production and servicing facilities, but in the last decade or so it has increasingly come to include banking, securities, and other financial services. Concurrently, while the first moves into the area were carried out by large firms, in recent years an increasing number of small- and medium-sized companies have followed in their wake. In this context, Singapore stands at the forefront of Japan's move into Southeast and South Asia. A plethora of Japanese production facilities, headquarters, and sales and financial centers are now located in this small country, and by some estimates as much as a quarter of Singapore's GDP is generated by Japanese companies (Cronin 1992). The Japanese expatriate community, which now numbers over twenty thousand, is overwhelmingly comprised of business people and their families.

Japanese business people brought with them not only management, production, and service methods but also certain leisure activities such as tennis, swimming, newspapers and books, and above all the pursuit of golf. At the beginning of the 1970s golf had been played only at local country and golf clubs. But the entry of the Japanese into these clubs coincided—as it did throughout the Southeast Asian countries—with the growth of a significant and rather forceful Singaporean upper middle class. This group of people have relentlessly applied political pressure since the 1970s for the establishing of new golf clubs and for renovating older ones. Whereas other expatriate business communities added to this pressure, according to local testimonies the Japanese community was always the most forceful. Later, during the early 1980s, golfing tourism—again mainly Japanese—provided the additional impetus for the development of new golf courses and the upgrading of existing ones. By 1992 Singapore had twelve private and two small public golf clubs, and three more were to be opened in the next few years (*Business Times* 7 May 1992). As in Thailand, golfing has shifted from private members' clubs to profit-making enterprises based on integrated leisure complexes entailing golf courses, tennis courts and swimming pools, conference and convention facilities, business centers, and dining and drinking sites (Cohen n.d.:7).

The various pressures exerted by the burgeoning local upper middle class, the expatriate communities, and the tourist golfers finally came to a head over the issue of foreign membership. As the Japanese secured membership in all of the local clubs, and as more and more tourists appeared on the scene, Singapore government officials, club members, and managers and entrepreneurs realized that they must undertake some action unless they were to be completely inundated by Japanese members. Public outcry and press reports about the "pincer movement" of Japanese tourists and business expatriates taking over the local clubs began to appear (*Straights Times* 3 February 1990). Starting with the largest and most prestigious club—the Singapore Island Country Club—the number of members became limited and a quota was determined for foreign membership within each club (in effect, this meant corporate membership). In a characteristically Singaporean solution, in the early 1990s a law effectively limiting foreign membership in any one club was passed. Today, all clubs that want to take advantage of the opportunity of paying only half the yearly land lease to the Singapore government (thirteen of the fourteen local clubs do so) must limit foreign membership to no more than 30 percent of the total number of memberships they issue.

At the same time, because club memberships were made transferable, two markets in memberships emerged: one for locals and one for foreigners. Given the strength of the mainly Japanese expatriate firms and the power of the new upper-middle class, the price of both kinds of club membership has steadily increased. This situation implies that there are actually two price ranges for transferable memberships. For example, in one club that I visited, local membership may be bought for about Sin$150,000 (U.S.$100,000), a foreign membership can be purchased for around Sin$250,000 (about U.S. $170,000). Moreover, the preoccupation with these markets has led to the emergence of agents, advertisers, and middlemen who specialize in selling, speculating, and investing in club memberships.

Yet the continued pressure exerted by locals and by foreigners seeking access to golfing facilities has led—in Singapore as it has throughout Southeast Asia (Cohen n.d.:9)—to a movement of new clubs and resorts out to the country's periphery. In Singapore the peripheral areas where land is both available and economically feasible for development of golfing resorts are the Johor Bahru area of Malaysia (a short drive across the causeway linking the two countries) and Indonesia's Bintan and Batam islands (a brief ferry ride from Singapore harbor) (*Business Times* 7 May 1992). Today, golf clubs in the Singapore area are manifested in a hierarchy of prestige: at the top of the hierarchy are the older and larger Singaporean clubs located close to the city's center and the lower end of the status pyramid consists of newer clubs located further away on the island or in neighboring Malaysia and Indonesia. Other elements that add to the status of a club are its number of courses (a club with only nine holes is considered inferior while a club with two eighteen-hole courses is considered more prestigious) and the availability of more and newer leisure facilities in and around the golfing amenities.

Patterns of Play

The popularity of golf in Japan owes as much to the active pursuit of the sport by an aspiring upper-middle class as it does to a whole industry of real estate developers, equipment manufacturers, public relations and media representatives, and transport and tourist agents. Yet despite the construction of over two hundred courses throughout Japan in the past twenty years, it is still difficult to play regularly: golfers must book rounds months in advance, often drive for several hours to get to the courses, pay heavy user fees, and purchase memberships at prices commonly in excess of U.S.$400,000 (*Straights Times* 7 December 1991). It is no surprise then, that given the accessibility, price, and proximity of clubs in Singapore, that the local Japanese expatriate community, as one person told me, is "*gorufu kureiji*" ("golf crazy").[1] A few indicators of the patterns of play and participation in Singapore bear out this point.

It is difficult to get a good estimate of the numbers of active Japanese golf enthusiasts in Singapore, but the following one is

rather conservative. According to professional and journalistic estimates, there are about 30,000 active golfers in Singapore (this figure
includes foreigners but excludes tourists and occasional business
visitors). Of these active golfers, roughly 10 to 15 percent are
Japanese (about half of the foreign members of any given club). Thus
by estimates given to me by local club managers there seem to be
between 3,000 and 4,500 Japanese individuals who regularly play
golf on the island (even more play in Malaysia and Indonesia). These
figures imply that about one in every two or three Japanese adults
habitually indulges in golf. These estimates suit my findings and
impressions. Of the sixty business people that I interviewed, twelve
did not play golf although five of them had tried to play while in
Singapore, and another two were occasionally invited to play with
friends or associates. Although I did find out that many women also
play golf regularly, I was not able to obtain an even remotely reliable
impression of their numbers.

Frequency and duration of play.   People who reported playing
regularly said they joined meets or outings anywhere between once
or twice a week and once or twice a month. At the same time however, these patterns, I was told, may change for individual players
according to personal inclination or the burden of business and
family affairs. In contrast to Japan where a golfing excursion can
take a full day (primarily because of commuting time and rules
stipulating a lull between the first and second nine holes), in Singapore they usually take about half a day. Typically such an outing
includes about four of five hours of play, followed by showers,
drinks, and food. Some people reported that a primary reason for
playing so often was that because outings took only half a day they
could frequently be added on to the end of a working day.

Membership.   Corporate memberships, which are in principle
open to any company registered in Singapore, are the only real
means by which Japanese individuals secure regular entry into local
clubs. Such memberships differ primarily in the number of nominees
that a specific company can designate (the greater the number of
nominees the more expensive the club affiliation). Those designated
are named individuals and not "empty" slots to prevent the membership from being swapped among the members of the company—

they are assigned to specific individuals for the duration of their stay in Singapore. The larger companies very frequently hold corporate memberships in a number of clubs (because of rules forbidding an unlimited number of nominees). Thus for example, Sumitomo Corporation has corporate memberships in the Sentosa, Singapore Island, Tanamera, and Raffles country clubs in Singapore, and in two Malaysian clubs. Out of the twenty-four Japanese expatriates who serve with the corporation in Singapore twelve are full-time members and a few of the others are regularly invited by their colleagues. Similarly, at one of the Sanyo factories on the island, out of twenty-two Japanese expatriates ten are members of various clubs. At Nissho-Iwai ten out of the twenty-one Japanese managers are members of clubs. The steep prices of membership imply, in turn, that only the bigger companies have affiliations with local clubs, and that the bigger the company the greater the likelihood of belonging to the more prestigious clubs. Conversely, medium-sized companies tend to be affiliated with the less prestigious clubs in Singapore, or with golf resorts in Malaysia or Indonesia. Japanese managers of small companies almost never belong to a golf club.

Individuals and membership.   From a strictly organizational perspective, the move of any individual Japanese manager to Singapore (as indeed to almost any foreign assignment) implies a sort of "promotion." Because companies situated outside of Japan are like "daughter companies" (*kogaisha*, although their exact legal definition may vary), people who were department heads (*kachô*) in Japan become division heads *(buchô)* in Singapore and section heads (*kakarichô*) become department heads. This "promotion" has direct implications for the accessibility of the golf clubs. Corporate membership is provided both in Japan and in Singapore for individuals who are above a certain level in the organizational hierarchy. At Nissho-Iwai for instance, all heads of department are eligible to become nominees. But because almost everyone is placed at a higher level in Singapore (they usually go back to the "normal" stream of promotion after their return to Japan), many people who had little or no access to clubs in Japan play regularly in Singapore.

At the same time, just as there is a differentiation between the larger and smaller firms in terms of membership, so is there a distinction between juniors and seniors in terms of where they play.

The more senior managers play in the more prestigious courses, whereas their juniors play in the less prestigious and more peripheral clubs in Johor Bahru and Batam and Bintan. A lower-level manager in Toyota's trading company, to clarify this by way of example, who had played once in two months in Japan, now plays golf twice a week (he sports a nice suntan), but does so in a Malaysian resort. Finally, my impression is that people who are in general management or in the marketing side of business tend to play golf to a greater degree than do engineers or production specialists.

The Life-Course Approach

How are we to understand the place of golf in the lives of Japanese business expatriates against this background? My suggestion is that the life-course approach may help us unravel the complexity of golfing encounters because it forces us to examine organizations and people's lives in dynamic terms. It is my contention that if we conceptualize the stint abroad as a stage in individuals' careers then we will be able to understand how people use golf both as part of their workplace strategies for constructing reputations and securing promotion and as part of their schemes for cultivating a personal lifestyle considered peculiar to senior management.

David Plath, the most forceful and eloquent scholar to suggest the utility of the life-span or life-course approach, proposes that it is through two dimensions *and* the tension between them that Japanese individuals develop and mature: life at the workplace and cultivation of social relations among family and friends. Evoking the image of the "commuter" as one of the great archetypes of the industrial lifestyle, Plath (1983:1) states that his "master tempo of activity revolves around a daily shuttle from home to workplace and back again. Each of these two centers of activity is ordered by its own rhythm of long-term conduct: work and home each involve us in different, often contradictory, career timetables." The essence of a career is that it is a predictable sequence of movements, a relay of roles set up to normalize the potentially turbulent flow of persons through an organization. But whereas from an organizational point of view careers are predictable, from an individual point of view, as Skinner (1983) reminds us, they are uncertain. Given the numerical limits on promotion, only some people will be able to advance up the organizational hierarchy. In terms of social relations, "the Japanese archetype of human growth (to put this very simply for brevity's sake) seems to give first priority to the cultivation of emotional capacities for relatedness" (Plath 1989:83). But development too is a rather indeterminate business, as individuals constantly face the need to reconcile the claims of others in one's inner circle of human attachments (Plath 1989:88).

But what of leisure pursuits? I would propose a third pole or dimension of movement within the time span entailed in the term *life course*: work, family and social ties, and what perhaps may be termed a "consumption career," a passage through roles and positions distinguished by different uses of goods and activities. While the first two dimensions of the life course have been dealt with in the literature on Japan, there has been very little conceptual or empirical work done on how individuals become "leisured," on how they assume a certain lifestyle. Thus, along with Plath's studies, the last decade or so has seen a number of works on such matters as promotion at work (Aoki 1988:chap. 3), family composition (Coleman 1983), long-term family educational strategies (Rohlen 1983: chap. 3), and the organization of women's life courses (Brinton 1992). All of these studies commence from the recognition of two interrelated things: the first is a view of change over time that involves individual perceptions, active strategizing, and historical circumstances. The second are the cultural guidelines, or scripts, by which people appraise themselves and are appraised by others in terms of their movement in time. An individual "guides himself by cultural standards that define goals, competence, and achievement; and he is guided by other persons around him who have the power to interpret the general standards as applied to his life's particulars. The standards are articulated in an array of pathways, routes and timetables that provide for continuity in an individual's conduct" (Plath 1983:3). Thus the implication for our analysis is to relate these cultural standards or guidelines to the actual life strategies and movements of an individual within an organizational and institutional timetable.

In moving the discussion toward consumption, Plath again provides a helpful suggestion. He notes that a great deal of research has been carried out "in the humanities on the material

products of artistry and on articulations of the [Japanese] spiritual heritage. The difficulty, in terms of life course analysis, lies in
moving from these public recipes for mastery as collective representations to their fabrication into the sphere around the ordinary
self" (Plath 1989:86). Yet some work has been done in relating the
"public recipes for mastery" to the sphere of ordinary lives. Kondo's (1990) study of the discipline required by artisans or Moeran's
(1984) investigation of the folk potters of Onta spring to mind.
Interestingly, both of these studies carefully relate the analysis of
the personal cultivation involved to concrete formations of authority and social positions. Theoretically, therefore, they signal a
move of studies of "cultural" phenomena to issues of class and
power, and the position of the media and other entrepreneurs
within these processes.

   It is against the background of this rather extended theoretical discussion that I set my thesis. Golf represents *one* of the main
practices through which juniors who are on the managerial track
of large Japanese firms are socialized to the roles of senior executives. This socialization entails a wide array of active strategies,
long-term investments, and concrete negotiations over the contents and the manner of assuming these senior positions. Actions
that center on golf involve matters directly related to the workplace and more distant concerns related to lifestyle. Moreover, the
process of emulating the lifestyle of senior executives involves
learning a certain body etiquette (stance and posture as well as
clothes and style) by investing time, attention, money, and physical effort. These personal processes, in turn, are undergirded by a
set of industries that provide both the material conditions for these
long-term investments *and* (especially through the media) portray
the ideal lifestyle.

"Careering":Information, Trust, and Reputation

In a not untypical text on Japanese management, we learn that the
"national obsession with golf means that courses are crowded and
the better clubs incredibly expensive. Furthermore, the distance
from home or work to a golf course is often great. Two hours in a car,
or on a crowded bus or train, is not considered prohibitive, because

playing golf is seen as a prerequisite for one's successful career development" (Whitehill 1991:191). What is the problem with careering? And why is golf a prerequisite for advancement? Careering is problematic because there are limits on the ability of any organization to promote individuals into more prestigious, powerful, and remunerative roles. While it has by now become a commonplace notion that in the much-vaunted lifetime employment system (applicable to men in large corporations) one can find job security, what is much less appreciated are the uncertainties concerning promotion that mark this system. "In the literature on organizations in Japan there is a recurring tendency to assume that the security offered by 'permanent employment' also means a career of increasing responsibility and authority as employees move through their years of association with an organization" (Skinner 1983:68). But, in effect, many middle-level positions are limited and a series of job movements may be undertaken without advancement.

As a consequence it is not surprising to learn that individuals find themselves constantly monitoring their progress and assuming various traits in the hope of being promoted. Studies that have reported on "typical" career paths in Japanese organizations usually present seniority and work performance as the major factors in determining career progress. Because of this emphasis, an employee's relationships with others in the organization (or with related firms and with clients) are either neglected or presented as having comparatively little influence on his or her career. It is in this light that golf should be seen. It figures prominently in two interrelated aspects of cultivating workplace ties: entertaining guests and clients (*setai*) and socializing with colleagues (*tsukiai*). Through both activities white-collar workers strive to create a proper organizational reputation so that they are perceived to have the required qualities for advancement.

At the most general level, participation in golf should be perceived in the context of wider patterns of entertainment including drinking, dining, and *karaoke* (Ben-Ari 1994). In the context of Singapore, entertainment may also include accompanying guests on sightseeing tours of the island. These activities may be undertaken jointly (as in a whole-day affair in which golf is followed by dinner and a visit to a night club) or separately (although golfing occasions invariably include at least one drink). The choice of which of these events to include is almost always left to the visitor (who can be either a senior manager from Japan or an important client). A manager at Nissho-Iwai (the general trading company) told me that in Singapore entertaining guests and clients is split more or less equally between golf and *karaoke*. The manager from the furniture maker that I cited before told me that "It takes a lot of time, what with the eighteen holes, the beer afterwards, and maybe dinner. It can take a half day of your time, a long part of your working day. But if a client wants to, and especially if it is an important client for the future of the company, then I go with him to play." Playing golf with guests or clients from outside Singapore is often related to the image and actual facilities that the island is perceived to offer for Japanese. For many guests, a business trip to the island—as to many places around the world—is frequently combined with a short golfing vacation. A number of people told me that senior managers flying down from Japan for routine meetings will often schedule their visit to include all or part of the weekend so that they can play golf. From the perspective of the Japanese expatriates hosting them, the situation implies that they make an effort to make the stay in Singapore as impressive as possible for the visitors. As a manager from one of the smaller trading companies told me: "In Japan you also have opportunities to go out with clients, but here you have them for a few days. It's a special place that they remember when they go back to Tokyo. And then they think back and say, 'Ah, that Yamamoto, he is a good guy; he organized a nice visit for me.'"

Socializing with colleagues (rather than with guests and clients) also involves a variety of drinking and golfing occasions, although golfing is seen to be a very easy method of combining socializing with healthy physical exercise. Because all of the Japanese business expatriates live on the island, they often participate in tournaments organized by companies, associated companies, the Japanese Association, or the Japan Chamber of Commerce. I was told, for example, of many occasions in which "going away" parties (*owakare-kai*) assumed the form of golf tourneys rather than dining dates or drinking sessions.

What do people talk about while golfing? In both kinds of encounters—*setai* and *tsukiai*—almost nothing is said directly about business dealings, although there are general discussions about such issues as the Singaporean business environment or the conditions of Japan's economy. The emphasis, as many informants told me, is predominantly on the creation of trust. The director of Sumitomo Bank told me: "When you return to the office the next day it is easier to talk." A lower-level administrator in Toyota's trading company said that these are opportunities for "making contact and building relationships; so we tend to talk only about golf and not about business because the aim is to create a relationship." The director general of Fujikura reported that he likes to discuss hobbies and music and the social habits of people in Singapore, but only occasionally to converse about company matters. The head of Tomen corporation observed: "...We talk about the economic situation in Japan, the management systems of different companies ... about my home, I come from Okayama, about the quiet there, about the mountains, about the rivers. And about the good and bad things about Singapore. I have friends who served for example in Indonesia and they compare it to Singapore." Other people noted that, when playing golf with colleagues or with relatively close friends from Japan, a lot of information about office politics is exchanged: prospects for overseas assignments, new ventures and projects, the establishment of new offices and departments, and the successes and failures of certain individuals are some of the concerns people said they gossiped about. Thus for example the personnel manager at Sumitomo noted that he and his friends often talk about their families, friends, and about "what happens at the office."

A closely related issue—but one that came up openly in only three of my interviews—entails the character uncovered during play and the way in which it forms part of doing business. I asked the manager of a local country club about how golf is related to business. Giving a short chuckle, he answered that golf is

> a real test of character. ...So if you want to find out your potential business partner you play golf with him: see whether he is reliable. So that is why a lot of business starts on the golf course. Directly but also indirectly in the sense that if you are not sure of your partnership with this person, you invite him for a game of golf. ...You cannot hide in the game of golf: the body language, the way you play the game, the way you react

to a bad shot, the way you react to a good shot, this shows up everything. So golf reveals your character.

Yet for all of this, a word of caution should be sounded at this juncture. One must be wary of attributing a too-steady, coherent, or fully conscious ambition or motivation to golfing behavior (as to other organizational actions). I state this point because the whole attitude toward golfing encounters is permeated by fluctuations and ambivalence. Just as the workplace is sometimes marked by periods of disquiet, fatigue, or strain, so it is with golf. The deputy manager of a Japanese business hotel mentioned that though he enjoyed playing golf and socializing, he often felt that it is "hard, just like work." A deputy manager at Komatsu said that at times he felt that he could not simply decline to join such occasions because they were part of his job. The general manager of Fujikura rather candidly registered his feelings: "I am only human and sometimes I don't feel like going to play golf but would rather stay at home and rest. But I feel that I have to go because golf is part of work."

Finally, and I encountered this attitude only twice throughout my fieldwork (although it may be a portent of things to come), two younger men—one from Marubeni Trading Company and one from a company dealing with processing oil products—mentioned that they did not like to participate in golf. We were discussing the relatively new term *shinjinrui* (new human being) (Linhart 1988:288), which is used to characterize younger members of organizations, when the Marubeni manager said that maybe such a term characterizes him: "Take my boss here in Singapore, if you ask him then he doesn't know whether playing golf is business or something private. I don't like this in-between feeling, of not knowing what it is that I am doing."

Yet the words of this last young man are very much the exception. Because of the self- and organizational selection of managers assigned to overseas postings one would, I suggest, find very few dissenting voices. For the vast majority of Japanese business people in Singapore, the master script connecting golf, entertainment, and work involves the creation of a reputation: what is said or believed about their abilities and qualities within their organization. Skinner (1983:65) points out that in any organization with a fairly stable work force, reputations become widely known, and that much of a person's behavior can be attributed to attempts to shape how others view him. Over the long term, the "kind of relationship a person has with any of his co-workers can become the content of gossip which directly affects superiors' decisions about reassignments. Any act or statement may become part of the body of information making up a person's reputation" (Skinner 1983:69).

To sum up this section then, reputations are created in and around golfing in both direct and indirect manners. Reputations are created directly by displaying desired characteristics, building trust, or concocting a memorable experience that will be remembered upon a return to Japan. Indirectly, a person can make a name for himself (very rarely for herself) by using golfing opportunities to lay the ground that will help in clinching deals that will be perceived as part of his reputation. In both cases playing golf is part of careering in the sense of making organizational moves aimed at future promotion.

But there is yet another dimension to golf which, while being analytically distinct from, is related to the long-term movement of people within their organizations and social groups.

Leisure: Lifestyles, Relaxation, and Mastery

Japan is no different from other industrialized societies in the manner by which people use goods and activities to create social bonds and distinctions. What kind of distinctions does golf mark in the context of Japan and in the framework of the Japanese community in Singapore? It marks a careful differentiation between larger and smaller firms, and, more pertinent to our analysis, within organizations it distinguishes subordinate managers from senior executives. This specific distinction is related to the more general differentiation between sporting activities. Bourdieu (1984:21) suggests that the most important property of the popular sports is that they are tacitly associated with youth and are abandoned in early adulthood, very often upon entry into marriage. By contrast, "the common feature of the 'bourgeois' sports, mainly pursued for their health-maintaining functions and their social profits, is that their 'retirement age' is much later, perhaps the more so the more prestigious they are (e.g., golf)" (Bourdieu 1984:21). Sports like golf are practiced in exclusive places (private clubs), at the times players choose, with selected partners, demand relatively low physical exertion, and are, in the context of "highly ritualized competitions, governed, beyond the rules, by the unwritten laws of fair play" (Bourdieu 1984:218). Moreover, the sheer physical size of the space this sport occupies may be seen as a measure of the social space occupied by its players.

While these elements of distinction are clear, golfing practices actually involve more dynamic components that are only implicit in Bourdieu's analysis. These factors are disclosed most apparently by the life-course perspective: golfing practices entail long-term investments through which juniors aspire to become seniors. Featherstone (1991:18) proposes that we need "a theoretical framework drawing attention to patterns of investment over the life course which makes such class-related [or class fraction-related] differentiation of time use possible." He suggests that these long-term stakes are found in informational acquisition and cultural capital. But the point as I see it is not only in regularly and actively garnering information or gathering cultural capital (as in artistic pursuits), but in the ways that these processes are related to investment in disciplines of the body.

Golfing practices involve a set of processes that may be termed—to borrow from Norbert Elias (Elias 1978)—a "civilizing process." While Elias focused on the manner by which the body was historically rationalized—through table manners, norms of good conduct, and etiquette—I suggest that learning "to golf" involves methods of turning subordinates into "civilized" superiors. But the matter is not one of simply emulating superiors. The process is much more subtle and involves an embodiment of organizational seniorship. As Bourdieu (1984) intimates, "the signs of the dispositions and classificatory schemes which betray one's origin and trajectory through life are also manifest in body shape, size, weight, stance, walk, demeanor, tone of voice, style of speaking, sense of ease or discomfort with one's body etc." (Featherstone 1991:20). Let me outline these points in greater detail.

First of all, golf involves disciplining and mastering one's body in a certain manner so as to be able to perform gracefully under the pressure of the game. In other words, to be a golfer implies harnessing certain physiological needs and desires, physical capabilities, and potentials toward the inculcation of body postures and movements that are considered both "proper" and of a minimal level of achievement. This can best be understood via the pressure put on those unfortunate individuals who have not been able to learn the bodily techniques needed for competent golfing. In order to play on a golf course, an individual must be able to complete eighteen holes in a minimal number of shots (this is the handicap). Thus, even if a person has the requisite membership in a club, without a handicap certificate he cannot play on the club's course. As a consequence would-be players start off using driving ranges, practicing putting and, very often, taking lessons from golf pros prior to taking the handicap test. Moreover, because the standards at the peripheral clubs in Malaysia or Indonesia are lower (they are more lax in regard to handicaps), many beginners commence play at these resorts and then progress to play in Singapore clubs. A number of interviewees told me of how they were working on improving their playing techniques in order eventually to play on the courses of the prestigious clubs.

A second and closely related point is related to "ease." "We know from social psychology that self-acceptance (the very definition of ease) rises with unself-consciousness, the capacity to escape fascination with the gaze of others" (Bourdieu 1984:213). One example I encountered in the field may clarify this statement. A man who had given up golf told me how he had made great efforts during the first two years of his stint in Singapore to learn the game, but had failed. When playing with his colleagues and guests he had always fumbled and hit the ball in various directions. He recalled how uncomfortable he had felt and how he sensed that the others were always standing there waiting for him while he took his shots. He decided to quit. It is due to these circumstances that numerous managers sacrifice so much of their time, attention, and effort to achieve the mastery needed for playing with ease. Moreover, golf is played in an atmosphere of repose: the sporting exchanges take place as highly controlled social transactions. They exclude all physical or verbal violence, all anomic use of the body (shouting or wild gesturing, for example), and all forms of direct physical contact between the opponents. Coupled with the effects of these practices on the body—the suntan, the muscles, which are only discreetly visible, and the posture—golf works toward reinforcing the distinction of seniors.

Third, the equipment and clothes deemed necessary for play are not only relatively expensive (out of the price range of most people) but must conform to accepted notions of fashion and suitability. Singapore has a market of golfing equipment, clothing, and accessories that serves only the Japanese community. The outlets where Japanese business people buy these items—if they do not bring them from Japan—are the many Japanese department stores (Daimaru, Takashimaya, and Isetan, to mention but a few), which invariably have a golfing section separate from the sports department. According to a Japanese manager at Daimaru the overwhelming majority of golf customers are Japanese.

Fourth, Japanese business people in Singapore (as in Japan) are constantly exposed to a host of publications (and to a lesser degree television programs) about golf. The Singapore outlets of Kinokuniya and Maruzen (large Japanese bookstore chains) contain open stacks of books and magazines—in Japanese and English—about the subject, while the Japanese dailies (two are printed in Singapore) contain detailed reports on golf in their sports and business pages. Every day one can spot men reading and buying these publications in the branches of these stores. The magazines contain reports about famous professional players (and their tips and advice), presentations of new resorts and courses (in Southeast Asia and around the world), and advertisements for things like the newest clubs (irons, woods, and putters) and golf balls. Well aware of the body practices involved in the game, these ads contain explanations about the kinds of body weight and height different sets of clubs fit, and the technology involved in their production. In addition, there are announcements about related accessories such as bags for the clubs, golf cleats, and playing gloves. Other items, no doubt related to the lifestyle that these magazines would like to promote, include clothes, cars, watches, pens, wines, and sunglasses.

Finally, golf outside of the clubs and resorts figures as a topic of conversation that signals both belonging to an exclusive group *and* the ability to master the right information. As Featherstone (1991:13) observes, our enjoyment of goods "is only partly related to their physical consumption, being crucially linked to their use as markers; we enjoy, for example, sharing the names of goods with others (the sports fan or the connoisseur)." An especially perceptive

Japanese woman—she is a real estate agent specializing in Japanese expatriates—told me that golf is the number one topic of conversation among her co-nationals in Singapore. Other men often told me that when they meet to drink or socialize, golf is very often a favorite subject of discussion. In sum then, the implication of the combination of body mastery, ease of comportment, and acquisition of the right equipment and clothes is that the mastery of the cultured person entails a seemingly natural mastery not only of information but also of how to use and consume appropriately and with natural ease in every situation (Featherstone 1991:17).

My emphasis on careering and the inculcation of social and bodily practices involved in golfing does not imply that individuals do not enjoy the game or that they undertake it only for a variety of utilitarian ends. Almost all of the regular players that I talked to emphasized how much they relish the opportunities Singapore offers them to play and the satisfaction they gain from improving, meeting challenges (through bets or tournaments) or simply fraternizing with other people. What I do want to emphasize is that such enjoyment takes place within socially defined and constructed spaces in which individuals invest considerable resources and which they use to further their own personal ends.

Conclusion

In this chapter, my argument has been that golfing among Japanese business expatriates in Singapore may be understood in terms of its position in people's life courses. I showed how golf is a means to build one's organizational reputation and enhance opportunities for promotion, as well as a method for investment in embodying some of the ideals of senior management. To reiterate a point made earlier, I do not dismiss the contention that the game offers enjoyment and relaxation. But to exaggerate the diversionary dimension of golf is to lose sight of its social relation to a specific class fraction, a set of capitalist industries promoting and maintaining it, and the long-term investments necessitated by personal participation. Along these lines, the choice of golfing locations and clubs, clothes and equipment, playing style and partners is canalized by a negotiation between self-definition (or self-expectations) and images of senior managers, and the array of possibilities offered by the capitalist market. By way of conclusion let me briefly emphasize three points.

Consumption and the life course.   The theoretical innovation of my study (if you allow me a slight exaggeration) lies in linking the conceptual frameworks that we have developed for studying Japanese companies on the one hand, and the analytical structures developed for examining Japanese life courses on the other, to a set of processes centered on consumption. "Consumption" is treated as an aspect of a more general set of active strategies for the establishment or maintenance of selfhood and identity. As I showed, consumption patterns are related both to strategies for building organizational reputations and to investments in emulating and cultivating the lifestyles of senior managers. A "consumption career" then, is an operative set of steps one takes over time and that is related both to the organizational formations of power and conflict and to the set of practices embodied by senior executives. Following Frühstück (1994:1; also Featherstone 1991) the cultivation of the physical side of golf can also be seen as a "body project": "Modern persons consciously or unconsciously accept that their body's size, shape and even its contents are potentially open to reconstruction in line with the designs of its own." While diet, exercise, and plastic surgery are probably the most radical forms of such reconstructions, less drastic practices—like the ones involved in golf—should also be understood in this light. The underlying point is that, in this view, "bodies become malleable entities which can be shaped and honed by vigilance and hard work of their owners" (Frühstück 1994:1). Leisure pursuits in Japan, to put this somewhat starkly, often represent hard work.

The democratization of golf.   For all of the heightened development of golf complexes around the globe, the readability of the game as a sign of elite status does not seem to be in danger. Given the spatial limits on the development of clubs and the exorbitant price of memberships in clubs around the world, golf is unlikely to undergo a process of democratization in the near future. It seems likely to remain a sign of distinction and differentiation commanding considerable social, organizational, and personal resources.

Theory and the study of Japan. The wider thrust of my analysis, however, lies in the contention that in order to understand contemporary Japanese society one has to "go international" in a theoretical sense. In this regard, I urge us to question the assumption lying at the base of many studies of Japan, that there is an isomorphism between the geo-political boundaries of the state and its social and cultural limits. My contribution should be seen as proposing a first step toward a reconceptualization of Japanese culture. This culture—without assuming too much about its unitary nature—could be understood not only along the lines proposed by most social scientists who have studied Japan but also as a set of negotiated symbols and meanings that travel *across* national boundaries (Creighton 1991). To put this by way of example, just as it is possible to gain a richer appreciation of the variety of experiences entailed in being Japanese through accompanying various tour groups to Europe or the United States, or visiting their hangouts in Thailand, so it may be possible to learn something about "Japaneseness" in contemporary Singapore.

Notes

1. Golf, as will become evident through my analysis, tends to be limited to people who belong to the managerial track in the large firms. Consistent with the differentiation between ranks, lower-level workers partake in other sports such as volleyball, softball, basketball, and baseball, and in a related manner in the company's annual sports day (Linhart 1988:291).

References

Aoki Masahiko. 1988. *Information, incentives, and bargaining in the Japanese economy.* Cambridge: Cambridge University Press.

Appadurai, Arjun. 1986. "Theory in anthropology: Center and periphery," *Comparative Studies in Society and History* 29, 356–61.

———. 1990. "Disjuncture and difference in global cultural economy," *Public Culture* 2/2, 1–24.

Ben-Ari, Eyal. 1994. "Sake and 'spare time': Management and imbibement in Japanese business firms," *Papers in Japanese Studies* 18, Department of Japanese Studies: National University of Singapore.

Bourdieu, Pierre. 1984. *Distinction: A social critique of the judgement of taste.* London: Routledge.

Brandt, Vincent R. 1986. "Skiing cross-culturally," Takie Sugiyama Lebra and William P. Lebra (eds.), *Japanese culture and behavior: Selected readings.* Honolulu: University of Hawaii Press, 188–94.

Brinton, Mary C. 1992. "Christmas cakes and wedding cakes: The social organization of Japanese women's life course," Takie Sugiyama Lebra (ed.), *Japanese social organization.* Honolulu: University of Hawaii Press, 79–107.

Choy, Chong Li, and Caroline Yeoh. 1990. "Multinational business and Singapore society," Chong Li Choy et al. (eds.), *Business, society and development in Singapore.* Singapore: Times Academic Press, 102–106.

Cohen, Erik. 1977. "Expatriate communities," *Current Sociology* 24/3 (complete volume).

———. n.d. *Golf in Thailand: From sport to business.* Hebrew University of Jerusalem: Department of Sociology and Anthroplogy. Manuscript.

Coleman, Samuel. 1983. *Family planning in Japanese society: Traditional birth control in a modern urban culture.* Princeton, N.J.: Princeton University Press.

Creighton, Millie R. 1991. "Maintaining cultural boundaries in retailing: How Japanese department stores domesticate 'things foreign,'" *Modern Asian Studies* 25/4, 675–709.

Cronin, Richard P. 1992. *Japan, the United States and prospects for the Asia Pacific century.* Singapore: Institute of Southeast Asian Studies.

Elias, Norbert. 1978. *The civilizing process: Volume 1—The history of manners.* New York: Pantheon.

Featherstone, Mike. 1991. *Consumer culture and postmodernism.* London: Sage.

———. 1991. "The body in consumer culture," Mike Featherstone, Mike Hepworth, and Bryan S. Turner (eds.), *The body: Social process and cultural theory.* London: Sage, 170–96.

Frühstück, Sabine. 1994. "'Body projects' in contemporary Japan." Paper presented at the European Association of Japanese Studies, Copenhagen.

Goodman, Roger. 1991. *Japan's international youth: The emergence of a new class of schoolchildren.* Oxford: Clarendon.

Hannerz, Ulf. 1990. "Cosmopolitans and locals in world culture," Mike Featherstone (ed.), *Global culture.* London: Sage, 237–352.

Kobayashi, Tetsuya. 1978. "Japan's policy on returning students," *International Education and Cultural Exchange* 13/4, 16 and 47.

Kondo, Dorinne. 1990. *Crafting selves: Power, gender and discourses of identity in a Japanese workplace.* Chicago: University of Chicago Press.

Linhart, Sepp. 1988. "From industrial to postindustrial society: Changes in Japanese leisure-related values and behavior," *Journal of Japanese Studies* 14/2, 271–307.

Moeran, Brian. 1984. *Lost innocence: Folk craft potters of Onta, Japan.* Berkeley: University of California Press.

Plath, David W. 1983. "Life is not just a job resume?" David W. Plath (ed.), *Work and the lifecourse in Japan.* Albany: State University of New York Press, 1–13.

———. 1989. "Arc, circle and sphere: Schedules for selfhood," Yoshio Sugimoto and Ross Mouer (eds.), *Constructs for understanding Japan.* London: Kegan Paul, 67–93.

Roberston, Roland. 1992. *Globalization: Social theory and global culture.* London: Sage.

Rohlen, Thomas. 1983. *Japan's high schools.* Berkeley: University of California Press.

Skinner, Kenneth A. 1983. "Aborted careers in a public corporation," David W. Plath (ed.), *Work and the lifecourse in Japan.* Albany: State University of New York Press, 50–73.

White, Merry. 1988. *The Japanese overseas: Can they go home again?* Princeton, N.J.: Princeton University Press.

Whitehill, Arthur M. 1991. *Japanese management: Tradition and transition.* London: Routledge.

Yoshikawa Akihiro. 1991. "Globalization and restructuring the Japanese economy," Harry K. Kendall and Clara Joewono (eds.), *Japan, ASEAN, and the United States.* University of California at Berkeley: Institute of East Asian Studies, 31–46.

PART THREE

Travel and Nature

Japanese tourists are a well-known sight world wide, and they alone merit a reconsideration of the "work-only Japanese" stereotype. A number of Japanese and Western researchers have tried to link the popularity of traveling abroad to the highly developed religious traveling culture of premodern Japan, thereby aligning one of the "typical" Japanese features with an unbroken tradition. Susanne Formanek investigated Edo pilgrimages to a minor religious center, the Tateyama in Etchu province, and cautions not to overemphasize this argument, especially considering that much early traveling in other countries was also religiously motivated.

Many leisurely sports activities (golf and skiing for instance) and much traveling takes place in the countryside, the theme of Nelson H. H. Graburn's contribution. He notes three interesting developments taking place in contemporary Japan: traditional rural activities are being replaced by new service industries; the rural life of their ancestors has become remote, even exotic, to the urban population; and there has been a nostalgic reevaluation of country life.

Emiko Ohnuki-Tierney deals with an outdoor leisure activity called "(cherry) blossom viewing"—originally a religious, rural activity, eventually becoming an urban practice. What to non-Japanese might seem to be a simple activity turns out, in the course of Ohnuki-Tierney's chapter, to have not only religious and recreational but also political, economic, and symbolic dimensions. We can speculate that, despite its religious origins, cherry blossom viewing is one of the oldest and most typical leisure activities of the Japanese.

This part of the book concludes with a contribution on one of the most spectacular and fascinating developments in the modern Japanese leisure and tourist market, the construction of amusement parks, theme parks, and resort parks. Angelika Hamilton-Oehrl finds in the visitors to such parks a very active leisure behavior, which is in sharp contrast to a leisure pattern that stressed recreation for work. These leisure parks might be truly evaluated as an important element of Japan's postindustrial leisure culture.

S. L.

Susanne Formanek

9

Pilgrimage in the Edo Period

Forerunner of Modern Domestic Tourism? The Example of the Pilgrimage to Mount Tateyama

Outline of the Problem

In recent years, the phenomenon of Edo-period pilgrimage has increasingly attracted scholarly attention, having been discovered to be, in substance, a forerunner of present-day Japanese tourism.[1] Not only is pilgrimage by laymen described as a principle element of the overall increasing horizontal mobility in early modern Japan, but the practices that developed within the context of the Tokugawa-period pilgrimage are also held to account for some of the main characteristics of modern Japanese tourism, especially those frequently considered unique.

Indeed, the Edo period saw an extraordinary increase in horizontal mobility,[2] and where this horizontal mobility was not the product of commercial transport or of politically motivated travel (such as that within the *sankin kōtai* system or transfers from one domain to another), a large proportion of the travelers was constituted of pilgrims on their way to one of the big religious centers. The pilgrimage to Ise, for instance, illustrates how the masses would thus be mobilized. If we are to trust the reports of the town magistrate of Ise Yamada to the Bakufu, between 1717 and 1736 no less than 100,000 people made their way to this sanctuary per annum, in some years the pilgrims even amounting to several million (Kanzaki 1994:11–12). As the population in this period is estimated at 25 million, this would imply that in the years of greatest affluence at least one of twenty-five persons undertook the pilgrimage, and since, for reasons I will explain later, the individual pilgrims were likely to differ from one year to another, the chances are that almost everybody experienced this pilgrimage at least once in their lifetime—as is illustrated by the contemporary saying: "Once a month to the family shrine, once a year to Taga Shrine, and once in a lifetime to Ise Shrine (*tsuki ni ichido no ujigami-mairi, toshi ni ichido wa o-Taga-sama, isshô ni ichido no Ise-mairi*)" (Kanzaki 1992a:68, 1992b:248). This, of course, implies an extraordinary amount of travel experience for a preindustrial society.

Yet the travel experience, as far as it could be made within the context of such mass pilgrimages, naturally had very specific characteristics, which have been interpreted by Graburn (1993:50ff.), Kanzaki (1992a:69) and others, as the origins of certain features of today's Japanese tourism:

1. Traveling in the Edo period was hampered by the many barrier stations or checkpoints between the feudal domains (*han*) that had to be passed, and it was therefore easier to travel in groups of pilgrims. This would be one of the reasons for the present-day Japanese fondness or preference for group travel.

2. For many of the pilgrims in the Edo period it was only possible to raise the money necessary to set out on their tour because groups called *kô* had developed, which would collect donations from its members and then every year determine by lot one or more that were to be dispatched to pray for all *kô* members at the holy site. This would be the basis of the deep bond of the Japanese tourist to his in-group at home. As a corollary, it was of great importance that the pilgrim, on his return home, bring back material proof that he really had been where he had been sent to, since the costs of his journey had been borne by all members of the *kô*. Out of these *omiyage*, originally, literally, "charms issued by the sanctuary," there developed the well-known—and often smiled at—custom of buying local products in large numbers as souvenirs for those left at home.

3. At each sanctuary there usually existed an organization of affiliated lay priests, who would tour the country on determined routes of *danna* or patrons of the sanctuary, and would exhort the local population to undertake the pilgrimage. These *oshi* or *sendatsu*, the forerunners of modern travel agents, would offer their services to the prospective pilgrim, securing lodgings and serving as guides. This would help explain the fondness of the Japanese for the conducted tour or package tour and their reliance on travel agents and agencies (Kanzaki 1995). As these *oshi* had to make a living from these activities, they were paid for their services. Also, the donations required at the sanctuaries and the purchasing of charms accustomed the Japanese to the idea that sightseeing implies monetary expenditure. Hence, another characteristic of present-day Japanese tourism that may be inherited from early-modern pilgrimage is its high degree of organization, institutionalization, and commercialization.

4. Pilgrimage in the Edo period had lost much of its ascetic, individualistic character. The pilgrims sought sites of national importance or at least such sites that were officially recognized and known throughout the country. From there would stem the tendency of Japanese tourism to be of the "nostalgia" type, as opposed to the "serendipity" type often considered typical of Western middle-class travel. The contemporary Japanese tourist would, just like his ancestor in the Edo period, seek to visit places cognitively familiar to him, instead of looking for the unknown Other, the adventure, the not-to-be-found-at-home-authenticity (Graburn 1993:62). Or, in the words used by Foard (1982:247–48) concluding his study of the early modern Saikoku pilgrimage, pilgrimage in the Edo period impressed on the pilgrim "that he belonged to a nation—that he was a Japanese and the Japanese tradition was his—just as through modern domestic tourism throngs of Japanese encounter the Japanese national past and each other as Japanese."

5. Last but not least, pilgrimage in the Edo period had begun to undergo a process of secularization that ultimately made it bear strong resemblance to a recreational trip (Vaporis 1994:236–42). Although varying in degree, contingent upon the destination, a certain tourist outlook upon pilgrimage is not only hinted at by the sheer numbers of pilgrims—of whom it is difficult to believe that

each and every one had a personal, religiously motivated incentive for the pilgrimage—it was also decried in a number of contemporary sources. In his *Kiyû shôran* of 1830, Kitamura Nobuyo, for example, lamented: "Nowadays people [living around Edo] are fond of going to tour Kyoto, Osaka and Nara, but they never go to visit the Kashima Shrine [one of the famous shrines in the vicinity] for worship. They are going to visit many shrines and temples, but it is only the nominal purpose. The true aim of the travel is absolutely for pleasure. Of course, they visit the Ise Shrine, but only because it is just on the route of the popular tour to Kyoto, Osaka and Nara" (Kitamura 1929:176). Consequently, the alleged goal of the journey, namely to visit a holy spot in order to satisfy a religious need, is often seen to have served merely as a pretext to circumvent the restrictions on mobility enforced by the authorities, imbuing what in actuality was a pleasure trip with a transcendental purpose. As a possible consequence of this practice, even currently, when traveling for its own sake is no longer officially frowned upon, the Japanese tend to intimate that whatever trips they make serve a higher goal than just fun, styling them *kenshû ryokô* (study tours), *shôtai ryokô* (journeys at somebody's invitation), and so on (Kanzaki 1994:19–20).

Much of what has been said until now refers to the Ise pilgrimage, which is partially justified as this pilgrimage center attracted more people than any other during the Edo period. On the other hand, given the national importance of the deity enshrined in Ise and the very specific characteristics of those pilgrimages to Ise that involved the biggest numbers of pilgrims (i.e., the *okage-mairi* or the *nuke-mairi*, which seem to pertain to the more liminal side of pilgrimage rather than to its structured, institutionalized form, which, in turn, is the one thought to have given birth to the travel customs still prevailing among the Japanese), pilgrimage to Ise may be a rather special phenomenon. Furthermore the phenomenon of mass pilgrimage to Ise seems to have declined since the middle of the Edo period, apart for a few very large *okage-mairi*, which occurred until the Bakumatsu period (Davis 1992:48). The number of the Ise Outer Shrine visitors' lodgings, for instance, declined after the middle of the Edo period: of 615 lodgings in 1724, only 357 were left in 1792 (Shinjô 1982:758). Tourism and/or pilgrimage in Japan at that time entered into a second stage with more diverse tourist attractions (Ishimori 1989:185). It is therefore worthwhile to take a closer look at what pilgrimage to these other centers was like in the later half of the Edo period, if we are to obtain an understanding of its further development.

The Pilgrimage to Mount Tateyama

I must confess that the example I have chosen to treat at further length here, the pilgrimage to Mt. Tateyama, may not be the best example, not being one of the best known, but it may transpire not to be the worst. The development of Mt. Tateyama as a pilgrimage center for lay people all over the country falls precisely, as we shall see, into the aforementioned period of diversification of tourist attractions.

Located in today's Toyama prefecture, the volcanic massif of the Tateyama, part of the Northern Japanese Alps, rises from the plain of Toyama through several plateaux (Senjugahara, Bijodaira, and Tengudaira) to the three peaks of the Jôdosan, the Oyama, and the Bessan at altitudes of approximately 3,000 meters. As can be gathered from the place names with Buddhist connotations, the Tateyama once was a center of *shugendô*, the Japanese Buddhist mountain religion. Since the Antiquity the mountains were thought to be the temporary abode of the gods or of the souls of the ancestors, and as such the Tateyama is the subject of poems in the *Manyôshû* (cf. poem nos. 4000 and 4001, NKBT 7:229–31). With the introduction of Buddhism, its much more refined cosmology was projected onto the mountains, some of which began to be seen as earthly representations of the Buddhist cosmos. Out of the amalgamation of shamanist ascetic practices common to the mountains and these Buddhist ideas, there developed *shugendô*. Its adepts, the *yamabushi*, through ritual ascent of the holy mountains, sought to experience a journey to the other world, thereby acquiring the magical power to subdue malevolent spirits. As Carmen Blacker (1986: 218–33) pointed out in her vivid description of the autumn retreat of the *yamabushi* to Mt. Haguro (*akimine*), the rituals performed during these ascents were mostly designed to enable the *yamabushi* to experience rebirth in the Ten Realms of the Buddhist cosmos (*jikkai*) on a symbolic level, starting with Hell (*jigoku*), the

Realm of Hungry Spirits (*gakidô*), of Animals (*chikushôdô*), of the Fighting Spirits (*shuradô*), of Men (*ningendô*), and of the Heavenly Beings (*tenjô*), until the four realms outside of the cycle of rebirth were reached—that is, the World of the Buddhas, Boddhisattvas, the *engaku,* and the *shômon.* The Tateyama itself seems to have been used by the *yamabushi* in this way since the tenth century, as can be gathered from findings of pieces of *shakujô,* staffs used by the *yamabushi,* which date back to this period (Toyama-ken Tateyama Hakubutsukan 1991a:36). In the *Heike monogatari* of the thirteenth century it is listed as a center of *shugendô* of equal importance to the otherwise better known Ômine-san, Haguro-san, and Fuji-san (cf. NKBT 32:356).[3]

What makes the Tateyama interesting for our purposes is that, from the seventeenth century on, the *oshi* affiliated with one of the two temples at the foot of Mt. Tateyama, the Ashikuraji and the Iwakuraji, began to promote a ritual ascent of the mountain by laymen.[4] They employed an instrument for the proselytization and popularization of the Tateyama cult already successful with other sanctuaries and holy places—that is, the *etoki,* or "explanation of pictures," in this case the *Tateyama mandara* (cf. Figure 9.1). Thirty such pictures are preserved to this day. While the oldest ones date back to the seventeenth century, their production reached its peak during the nineteenth century.[5] During the rest season of agricultural activity in winter, the *oshi* toured the country with these *mandara* in their luggage, exhorting the local population to visit the Tateyama and join in its ritual ascent or *zenjô.* A textbook used for the explanation of the picture is extant, namely the *Tateyama tebiki gusa.*[6] Both kinds of material enable us to gain a fairly precise understanding of how the *oshi* proceeded.

The pictures emphasize the role of the mountain as an earthly representation of the Other World. Thus on the flanks of the mountain there are depicted the various Buddhist Hells, as described in such canonical works as the *Ôjô yôshû* (985), alongside others of which the idea had developed only at the end of the Middle Ages, such as the *sai no kawara,* the Little Children's Hell, and a series of hells closely connected to the female life course such as the Hell of the Barren Women (*umazume jigoku*) and the Blood-Pond Hell (*chi no ike jigoku*), all of which corresponded to one or other real feature of the mountain's landscape. On the summit, conversely, an

Figure 9.1   *Tateyama mandara* (Daisenbô A-hon, early nineteenth century) (reproduced in Toyama-ken Tateyama hakubutsukan 1991b:14, Pl.14).

Amida raigô scene, symbolizing the Pure Land, awaited the visitor. Accordingly, the *oshi* promised the laymen that by ritual ascent of the mountain, with the concomitant physical exhaustion, they would experience the torments of hell already during their lifetime and thereby reduce the weight of their sins. After having toured the Hells they would reach the *zange-zaka*, or Penitence Slope, where, by confessing, they would further reduce their sins, until they would finally reach the summits where they would experience the Pleasures of the Pure Land and thereby obtain the promise of being reborn there. Besides this personal profit from the ritual ascent, one could also help female relatives: by having a copy of the *Kechibongyô*[7] thrown into the so-called Blood Pond on top of the mountain one could make sure they would be saved from suffering in Blood-Pond Hell.

As in the case of most holy mountains, this ritual ascent was forbidden for women. The *oshi* nevertheless managed to attract many women through the so-called *nunohashi kanjô*, the Ceremony of the Cloth Bridge. This ritual, held at the Ashikuraji at the foot of the mountain, was also invariably depicted on the *Tateyama mandara*, at least those of Ashikuraji filiation: the participating women were gathered in the Enma-dô, clothed in the attire of the dead, and blindfolded. From the Enma-dô and across a bridge, a path of white cloth was laid out to the Uba-dô. The women would then be made to cross the bridge, and it was thought that those with a heavy load of sins would be unable to cross and fall into the river below where serpents and demons awaited them. They would also encounter the Datsueba, the Cloth-Stripping Crone, who, according to popular Buddhist lore, awaited the dead at the *sanzu no kawa*, the River of the Three Fords, in order to strip them of their clothes, which would be hung from a tree to obtain a first measure of the weight of their sins. After this ordeal, the women would be led into the dark interior of the Uba-dô. Then, at a particular moment, the doors would be flung wide open, bathing the women in light, who would thereby experience rebirth in the Pure Land. Thus, on an even more symbolic level, women could have the same experiences through the *nunohashi kanjô* as their male counterparts did during the *zenjô*.

How many people were the *oshi* actually able to attract in this way? In the Bakumatsu period around 6,000 are said to have climbed the mountain yearly (Shinjô 1982:985). In addition to these one must count the women participating in the *nunohashi kanjô*, whose number is said not to have fallen below the mark of 3,000 even in years of bad harvest (Toyama-ken Tateyama Hakubutsu-kan 1991a:46). Nonetheless, the number of visitors to the site will not have surpassed 10,000 per year, not very impressive when compared to the numbers visiting Ise. But within the cluster of smaller-sized pilgrimage centers, that, in the latter half of the Edo period, was able to attract at least as many people as the Ise Shrine, the Tateyama does not occupy such a bad position.[8] Of course it ranks behind those easily accessible centers in the plains such as the Zenkôji (up to 200,000) and the Konpira Shrine, or those with the advantage of being on the route to Ise or at least within easy reach of it, such as the Kôya-san (40–50,000), and some others, such as the Akiba-san (25,000), or even such regional shrines and temples as Narita-san, Nikkô, Tsushima, and Itsukushima Shrines, the Izumo taisha, or the temples of the "pilgrimage courses" (*junrei*), such as the *Saikoku junrei* (including Kumano) and the *Shikoku henro* (20,000, respectively). However, pilgrimage to and ritual ascent of holy mountains (*reizan*), although the times of the year during which one could visit them were rather limited due to their altitudes, accounted also for a good part of the overall mobility,[9] altogether attracting 100,000 to 150,000 persons a year. Within this group of *reizan*, approximately the same numbers as for the Tateyama hold true for better-known places such as the Fuji-san or the *Dewa sanzan*. The time when the annual number of pilgrims to the Tateyama rose to the aforementioned 10,000 falls precisely, as stated earlier, within the period of diversification of tourist attractions in the latter half of the Edo period. From a document of 1801 it can be gathered that the number of lodgings (*shukubô*) of the Ashikuraji rose from six to thirty-three somewhere around the middle of the eighteenth century, when mountaineering pilgrimage in general reached a peak, and the same probably holds true for the twenty-four lodgings at Iwakuraji temple. The same document makes it clear that the *oshi* of the various *shukubô* at Mt. Tateyama had the right to proselytize in determined provinces respectively, disclosing thereby that they actually promoted pilgrimage to their mountain all over the country[10] (Toyama-ken Tateyama Hakubutsukan 1991a:58). On the whole they had *danna* in fifty-three provinces, and thus were effectively part of the series of "religious salesmen" who competed with each other in the villages.[11]

Travel Diaries Relating the Pilgrimage to the Tateyama

Contemporary sources already speak of the pilgrimage to the Tateyama as also having partly lost its meaning as a religious act and having become a kind of tourist mountaineering, of sport, of *monomi yusan*, thus attracting several thousand visitors every year (Shinjô 1982:730–31 and 757 n.39). The extant pilgrimage accounts clearly convey the institutionalization and commercialization of the pilgrimage and reveal the *oshi* and monks to be at least as eager to earn money as to bring about the religious edification of the pilgrims. Interesting in this respect is the account left by a *shugenja* from Hyûga in his *Nihon kuhô shûgyô nikki*: he arrived at Iwakuraji on the fourth day of the sixth month in 1816, only to find that the mountain was still closed to the public, opening only on the tenth of the month. He relates how the *oshi* gathered, and, faced with some more early arrivals, decided that for an additional fee of one *bu* (ca. 1000 *mon*), the normal fee being 238 *mon* per person, they would consent to declare the mountain open (Hirose 1992:123–24, for a translation cf. Rotermund 1983:99). Another account, the one left by Kaneko Banka in his *Tateyama yûki* from 1844, illustrates the competition between the various groups involved in the organization of the *zenjô*. They were a party of two, and since entering the region of Toyama had encountered many peasants on the road begging to be hired as guides. They had indeed hired one, who was of course principally responsible for carrying their luggage. They met the proprietor of a lodging at Ashikuraji, who informed them that this was not the proper way to act. They were to ask which lodging they would be assigned to, and hire a guide there. At the Iwakuraji, instead, where they bought a *Kechibongyô* for 12 *mon*, they were required to pay a mountain ascent fee (*sansen*) of 150 *mon* each. They were handed a receipt and were told to hand this over as a proof to the monk at the Murodô up in the mountain where the central part of the *zenjô* started, otherwise they would have to pay a second fee on arrival[12] (Hirose 1992:127).

One could also hire a guide at the Iwakuraji, as did a *samurai* from Owari *han*, who, in 1823, finally was able to fulfill his wish to climb Mt. Tateyama, Mt. Hakusan, and Mt. Fuji, for which he was given forty days. He hired his guide after having received detailed information about where he had to pay what amount of money for what kind of services and where he was to purchase what kind of materials necessary for the ascent, as related in his *Mittsu no yama meguri* (Takeshita 1989:32).

The account left by the painter Ike no Taiga in *Sangaku kikô* of his visit to the Tateyama in 1760 gives a good picture of the normal schedule of the *zenjô* and the expenditure involved. They were a party of three painters, and left Toyama on the tenth day of the seventh month. They had lunch at the Iwakuraji for 100 *mon*, where they also bought new straw sandals, a map of the region, and a *Kechibongyô* for 68 *mon*. Thus equipped they reached the Ashikuraji in the evening of the same day, where they had supper for 32 *mon*. They spent the night in the Kenkyôbô lodging, threw 30 *mon* in the offering boxes along the way, had a break at a tea house (*chaya*) in Kuwagaya, where they had *konbushiru* (tangle soup) for 24 *mon*, and in the evening reached the Murodô, where they stayed overnight. On the next day it was raining and they stayed in. The day after they obviously climbed at least one of the summits, and paid 1,212 *mon* for the necessities in the Murodô, offerings and a round trip to the Bessan, 100 *mon* as offerings at the Murodô, and an additional 300 *mon* as mountain ascent fee. On the fourteenth they returned to the Ashikuraji, where they paid one *bu* for the lodging at the Kenkyôbô and 150 *mon* on offerings, and bought *ofuda* (temple charms) and a copy of the *Kechibongyô* (Suganuma 1938) before leaving the mountain for another destination.

Kaneko Banka's aforementioned account is also very interesting in that it illustrates how much this kind of *monomi yusan* travel had lost of its original asceticism. Thus we find Banka complaining several times about the lack of comfort on the ascent of the Tateyama, which prompts him in the final pages to advise the prospective pilgrim of a number of things he should better bring with him. He complains about the coarse food and about the crowded *chaya* where he had lunch with one hundred or two hundred other people all trying to get served at the same time. He also laments the bad night he spent in the Murodô: its air was polluted by the smoke and the exhalations of so many people, and it was not even safe to go out for some fresh air because in the dark one risked stepping into human excrement (Hirose 1992:129).

The travel accounts of pilgrimages to the Tateyama also all attest in one way or another to a rather ludic approach even to the main features of the cult. It even seems possible that this ludic approach is not due only to the visitors, but that the *oshi* themselves invented some of its ingredients to make the ascent more attractive. There are, first of all, the amusing names given to the different hells seen during the pilgrimage. As stated earlier, they were held to represent the *hachinetsu jigoku*, the Eight Hells of Heat, as they had been expounded in religious writings, but in the travel records, other names given to the same sites occur, occasionally even prevail, which play on the similitude of certain suggestive features of the landscape with the requisites of popular professions. Let us consider for example the *Tateyama-dô meisho*, a hand-written account of a pilgrimage to the Tateyama composed by an obviously not all too well-educated man (if we are to judge from the many errors in his use of *kanji* or even *kana*), probably in the first half of the eighteenth century (published in Gorai 1983:450–53), in which "the author seemingly wrote down the explanations his guide gave him" (Hirose 1983:734). This text mentions a *hariya jigoku*, or Needle-Maker Hell, a *sakaya jigoku*, or Sake-Brewer Hell, a *konya jigoku*, or Dyer Hell, a *kajiya jigoku*, or Blacksmith Hell (cf. Figure 9.2), an *imoji jigoku*, or Foundryman Hell.[13] The Realm of the Hungry Spirits was also given a rather amusing and inventive interpretation. The sight of holes on the plateaux, filled with water the whole year long because of the geological formation, was enjoyed as the *gaki no tanbo*, or Rice Fields of the Hungry Spirits, because there grows in the holes a plant resembling rice, but that never ripens to bear grains. They are alluded to in the aforementioned *Tateyama-dô meisho* as the *shôrai no tsukuru ta*, "fields cultivated by the souls of the dead."

Finally, each and every feature of the landscape was commented upon and explained by reference to some legend or other that had virtually no connection with the intrinsically religious purpose of the ascent. The most prominent one is of a nun and the two young maidens accompanying her, who had transgressed the interdiction of climbing the mountain imposed upon women. Much attention was thus paid to the *zaibokusaka*, a slope scattered with oblong rocks, which were interpreted as timber that had turned into stone under the footsteps of the women, to the *kamurosugi* and the *bijosugi*, two impressive cedar trees, into which the two maidens were said to have been transformed, and, finally, to the *ubagaishi*, the Crone Stone, into which the old nun was turned. This kind of interpretation apparently appealed to the male visitors, and the painter Ike no Taiga, in his *Sangaku kikô*, besides jotting down the expenses of his journey in detail, dedicated most space to extemporizing about the *shikaribari*, a rivulet thought to have originated when the old nun urinated in anger when she realized she would not be able to climb the mountain (Suganuma 1938:14), as did his fellow pilgrims in the already mentioned *Tateyama-dô meisho* and in *Etchûdô no ki Tateyama* (1841) (published in Gorai 1983:543–47). Most parts of the landscape were thus mapped out, and people could and would buy what in modern tourist phenomenology would

Figure 9.2   Jigokudani (Hell Valley) on Mt. Tateyama: the so-called *kaji-ya jigoku* ("Blacksmith Hell"), a natural chimney of sublimated sulphor.

be called "on-site-markers," in this case printed maps of the mountain on which the names of the most important sites were given (cf. the woodblock print published in Toyama-ken Tateyama Haku-butsukan 1991a:54).

The religious purpose of the ascent and the *monomi yusan* attitude remained intrinsically intertwined. Ike no Taiga's rather profane approach did not prevent him from spending some money on the offertors along the *zenjô* route or from buying *ofuda* or the *Kechibongyô*. Thus, along with the *Shikoku henro* and some others, the

Tateyama has to be counted among those pilgrims' destinations where the original religious meaning remained strongest. But the alpine landscape of the site, though it prevented the development of an entire amusement industry in the immediate surroundings entailing shops with local products, restaurants serving refined local cuisine, and even theaters or red-light districts—as they mushroomed around the better-known centers in the plains like Ise or the Zenkôji and which so eloquently tell us about the leisure character of Edo-period pilgrimage (cf. Vaporis 1994:236–40) had pleasures of its own to offer. Accordingly, the *monomi yusan* attitude is writ large in most of the accounts, and the religious meaning often played only a secondary role. In some instances it offered material for intellectual play,[14] in others, where the travelers were indeed mainly interested in the beauty of the landscape,[15] it heightened the thrill of the journey by providing it with a transcendental background.[16]

Points of Discussion

What I have hitherto tried to summarize, borrowing from the extant pilgrimage and/or travel accounts of visits to Mt. Tateyama, corroborates the idea of a highly institutionalized and commercialized form of pilgrimage in the Edo period, for which sightseeing and pleasure seeking was at least as important, if not more important than the religious goal.

On the other hand, if it is true that people sought out the place because it was well known, it is obvious that it was not mere "nostalgia" driving them. Certainly, the legends surrounding Mt. Tateyama that the pilgrims were told—either when they heard the *etoki* of a *Tateyama mandara* or during their visit to the holy mountain— confronted them, in the persons of the emperor of a remote past, who had dispatched a new governor to the province, and the son of this nobleman, who was to reveal the holy nature of the mountain, with personalities of the Japanese past, who made the pilgrims aware that the history of Japan was their history, much in the same way as did the various legends surrounding the thirty-three temples of the *Saikoku junrei*, as described by Foard (1982). Also, the mountain as an earthly representation of the Buddhist cosmos gave people from all social backgrounds the opportunity to "revisit" some of the approved tenets of official religion in an experiential way.

But the search for thrills that would free them of their everyday worries and in face of which class and status differentiations became meaningless was probably also a major incentive for pilgrims to journey to Mt. Tateyama. On the one hand, the *zenjô* and the *nunohashi kanjô* were organized so as to provide thrilling experiences[17]: they brought participants face to face with the Last Things and conveyed to them that, as Japanese, after their death they would all have to confront the judgment of Enma, who would measure the load of their sins and assign to them their place of rebirth accordingly, whatever their status during their lifetimes. On a more profane level, despite the help received from the guides, the ascent of the mountain had its frightening side, and those willing to gather the necessary physical resources and strength of mind were certainly not devoid of a sense of asceticism. It should be noted that although, as we have seen, the authors of the diaries complained of the discomfort of the journey, it was mainly the man-made "unamenities" they lamented, especially those overcrowded ones. Conversely, they seem to have welcomed those that confronted them with realities in the face of which elemental feelings would surface, such as the impressive natural phenomena or dangerous features of the landscape. Thus, for example, the peasant couple from Gifu to whose diary, the *Zenkôji Tateyama sankei tabi nikki*, I will return later in some more detail, while bitterly complaining, for example, about an inn (ironically bearing the name of Edoya suggestive of the comfort of life in the capital) that failed to provide enough mosquito nets, welcomed the tempests encountered during the journey and praised them in *waka* songs. The Fujihashi bridge near the Iwakuraji at the foot of the mountain is another case in point. This bridge was thought to represent the crossing of the River of the Three Fords that, according to Buddhist lore, the dead had to traverse before reaching the other world; this was also the first ordeal they were faced with right upon death. This Fujihashi bridge and its deplorable state significantly enough did not occasion complaints; on the contrary, most of the diaries' authors praised it for having given them the opportunity to experience being on the verge of death (cf. Hirose 1992:116, 121, 123–25, 132). This search for thrills and their equalizing quality might become all the more clear at a place like Mt. Tateyama, which was explicitly thought to represent the Other World, but it may not have been totally alien to other pilgrimages and/or recreational travels.[18]

What the pilgrimage accounts also do not corroborate is the hypothesis of the preeminence of the conducted tour and of group travel. The guide was only used on location, he was not responsible for arranging the whole tour. Additionally, when the traveler was not alone, the parties of travelers assembled freely, not at the instigation of a guide, and were mostly constituted of two or three close friends or relatives.[19] This may be due to the fact that most of these accounts, although not all, were written by educated, well-to-do men who could afford and were accustomed to more individualistic forms of travel. However, it is interesting to note that the same applies to the last account of a pilgrimage to the Tateyama I use as an example, the *Zenkôji Tateyama sankei tabi nikki* (published in Gifu-ken 1971:541–46), remarkable for its being written by a couple of well-to-do farmers from a village in today's Gifu prefecture for which the other tradition would be likely to apply. Although there is some reason to believe that they had heard about the Tateyama from one of the *oshi* during his round trip to their region, they started their journey, as they state in their diary, rather abruptly, without any companions. Having long considered the pilgrimage, they suddenly made up their minds one summer in the seventh month of the year 1863, and waited for a lucky day to depart. It is interesting to note how it was precisely the good infrastructure developed by this time that allowed them their rather improvised manner of traveling. They had planned to stay overnight in the station of Mieji on the Nakasendô, but hearing that there was flooding there, they changed their route at short notice and went instead to Sunomata station on the Mino-ji. They were not part of a group of pilgrims, nor had they planned their travel route by making reservations of any kind. Of course, in these years at the very end of the Edo period, restrictions upon travel had probably loosened, and the rather naive attitude of our peasant couple toward barrier stations is enjoyable reading. It is unclear whether they had a travel permit at all, but from what they write it becomes clear that they did not have one for all checkpoints they had to pass. Interestingly enough they do not seem to have worried too much about it, and they were able to cross all of them, once by paying somebody for advice about a *nukemichi*, a loophole, once by bribing the watchman with sweets. This may not be a representative example,[20] but at least it shows how easily people would, under certain circumstances, shift from conducted group travel to a more individualistic form of traveling once the most important barriers fell—that is, once they had enough money to do so and once the frontiers between the domains disappeared. It is only a short step from there to think that, within the same process of development, the Japanese would have opted for even more improvised forms of traveling after railways were constructed that could bring them more rapidly to different places. At this point it should be noted that even for some of the pilgrimage centers for which *kô* existed, the mere existence of these organizations did not necessarily imply that people would indeed be traveling in groups, and that the existence of the *kô* therefore cannot be held responsible for the preference for package tours in present-day Japan. Studies of the *Shikoku henro*, for example, reveal that although there were many *kô* organizations that helped the pilgrim to travel freely and in a state of *communitas* (LaFleur 1979), the overwhelming majority of pilgrims undertaking the *Shikoku henro* did not travel in groups, but singly, until the 1930s—the prevalence of group travel apparently being a fairly recent phenomenon (Reader 1987:138), at least as regards this pilgrim route. I propose that we will therefore have to take a closer look at the development of domestic tourism in and after the Meiji period if we are to understand why this development did not take place. It seems to me that the Edo-period tradition alone is not enough to explain the course that domestic tourism took afterward.

As the extremely short periods that today's Japanese usually spend on holidays (especially when they choose a domestic destination) is one of the most conspicuous and most commented-on features of Japanese tourism, a few remarks should be added at this point regarding the duration of Edo-period "leisure pilgrimages." If we assume—as do all theories directly linking present-day touristic phenomena to traditional ways of travel—that the early-modern experience of leisure pilgrimage commonly shared by the Japanese of the Edo period still continues to shape how today's Japanese envision a recreational journey and, therefore, how they organize their touristic activities, there arises a series of interpretational problems as to the duration of the journey. Due to the fact that for the vast majority of eighteenth- and nineteenth-century Japanese traveling implied walking, it is obvious that it would take them a long time to reach their destination, at least when measured by modern standards. This is all the more true for the pilgrimage to the Tateyama, which was rather out of the way and not within easy reach of the most densely populated areas. Indeed, from the diaries it becomes clear that most of the pilgrims spent at least one month, and many even much longer, on their round trip to the holy mountain and back to their home towns and villages. Of course one could argue that they spent only as much time as it took to get there and back and that, therefore, once railways and other modern means of transportation were established, a one- or two-day trip became the modern equivalent of a month's trip in Tokugawa Japan. Indeed, it is conspicuous that leisure pilgrims in the Edo period usually spent exactly the "prescribed" amount of time at the sanctuary they visited. The *Tateyama zenjô* is no exception to this rule: it could be "done" in a two-day/one-night trip, and the diaries reveal that all pilgrims stayed exactly that amount of time on the mountain— except those whom heavy rainfall compelled to stay indoors another day, which they never fail to mention as though an excuse were needed for having stayed longer. This clinging to a fixed time to spend on a certain activity seems surprisingly close to the present-day tight schedules of Japanese group or package tours, where every minute seems to be filled with organized activities that do not allow for even the slightest alteration of the program. It should be noted within this context that in the Edo period the authorities in general and the various domains in particular, although unable to completely deny permission to set off on a pilgrimage, tried to minimize the amount of time the pilgrims would be away from their homes—and their work and duties—by setting a fixed number of days to be spent on a specific pilgrimage tour (see the example of the *Mittsu no yama meguri* mentioned above), which did not allow for much longer stays at one and the same place. Continuous monetary demands the pilgrims were faced with from the service providers in what was an emerging tourism industry may also account for their propensity to make efficient use of their time.

On the other hand, travelers and/or pilgrims in the Tokugawa period showed a marked tendency to visit several destinations in one trip. This was echoed by the authorities who regulated the amount of time one was allowed to spend on specific combinations of destinations.[21] In the case of the Tateyama the combination of the ascent of the so-called Three Holy Mountains—Mt. Tateyama, Mt. Hakusan, and Mt. Fuji—was very much in demand,[22] but other combinations also took place, as in our peasant couple's case, who combined Mt. Tateyama with Zenkôji temple.

Furthermore the diaries make it clear that the pilgrims stopped at every noteworthy sight they passed, even if it had virtually no connection with the ultimate goal of their journey; stops at *onsen* on the way were also already popular,[23] of which one could at least argue that they were necessary for one's health. The peasant couple from Gifu was no exception to this rule—they stopped at Asama to take the baths.

These factors combined to ensure that the early-modern Japanese tourist/pilgrim would be away from his home and his everyday duties and roles for a rather protracted period of time, with the result that the journey would be transformed into a life-time experience, even if people were to undertake more than one pilgrimage and/or recreational trip in their lifetime. This seems to sharply contrast with the present-day situation[24] and despite the alleged authoritarianism of the Tokugawa regime, commoners in early modern Japan seem rather to have had more than less free-dom in making use of their leisure than the modern salarymen, at least as far as duration and timing is concerned. Additionally, cov-ering the distance between home and destination on foot provided Edo-period pilgrims with ample opportunity for fresh discoveries. Hence there was much "serendipity" in the way the peasant couple from Gifu, for example, stopped to visit sites of which they appar-ently had not heard before, simply because these aroused their interest as they passed by.

The Tateyama Today or the Lost Tradition

Pilgrimage to the Tateyama in the described form was discontinued in the Meiji period, when, in the course of the anti-Buddhist *haibu-tsu kishaku* movement, many buildings connected with the Bud-dhist forms of the Tateyama cult were destroyed as they also were elsewhere.[25] The modern development of Mt. Tateyama began in 1952, the cable car that brings one to the first plateau of Bijodaira within nine minutes completed in 1954, and the bus route to the Murodô, where the main route of the *zenjô* once began, in 1964. But the Tateyama Kurobe Arupen Rûto, connecting by tunnel the Murodô with the Kurobe dam and from there with the railway sta-tion in Ômachi in Nagano was completed only in 1971. Up until very recently advertising for this tourist attraction mainly mentioned the beautiful scenery and how the Tateyama Kurobe Arupen Rûto guaranteed a trip into an alpine landscape without too much physical exertion. The former religious significance of the place was hardly ever mentioned, not to speak of the fact that the modern means of transportation make the visitors neatly pass by many of the once so effectfully commented upon features of the landscape without even noticing them. Thus, when we talk about the Japanese visiting traditional sightseeing spots, we should be aware that there is also a tradition from which they have been severed.

Only recently has the prefectural government of Toyama remembered the religious past of the mountain and, in compliance with the national policy of emphasizing idealistic values rather than the ever-growing material affluence, built, in 1991, the Toyama Prefecture Tateyama Museum close to the former location of the Ashikuraji, designed to document the history of the region (cf. Figure 9.3). The famous architect Isozaki Arata was invited to design not only the very impressive main building but also an annex in which films about the nature and culture of the Tateyama are shown. The plans for the final development are even more ambitious—at the former location of the Uba-dô a kind of Paradise Playground is planned. I am very skeptical as to whether this will be accepted by the public. When I visited the spot in 1994, there were hardly any tourists to be found in the area in and around the museum. *Shugendô taiken* as it is promoted today at the *Dewa sanzan* for example, is a new form of ascent of these holy mountains that has been thoroughly cleansed of its religious—or, at least, Buddhist—implications, which was easier there than it would be at Mt. Tateyama. It appeals mainly to a public of foreigners and female Japanese visitors (up to two million per annum), for the latter significantly enough under the newly minted name of *miko shugyô*, reminiscent of shamanism (Bachmayer 1994:7–8), the Japanese too deeply inculcated with a sense of shame about the concepts of Hells and others connected with the Buddhist view of the Other World.

Concluding Remarks

On the one hand, the example of the pilgrimage to the Tateyama corroborates the view that conceives of Edo-period pilgrimage as a

Figure 9.3   Main building of the Toyama Prefecture Tateyama Museum (Toyama-ken Tateyama Hakubutsukan) at the foot of Mt. Tateyama, designed by Isozaki Arata and inaugurated in 1991.

forerunner of modern-day Japanese tourism; on the other hand it hints at discontinuities along this line of development. Continuities include the recreational character and the high degree of institutionalization and commercialization shared by both phenomena, with the concomitant competition between the various service-providing groups involved in a tourist industry and the need on the part of the pilgrims or tourists to keep to schedules. A major and obvious discontinuity lies in the fact that while the Tateyama was a well-known, albeit not all-important pilgrimage center during the Edo period, it is no more than a place of very minor interest within today's domestic Japanese tourism. Less obvious but of perhaps greater importance is another fracture, namely the trend toward individualistic forms of travel as detected in some of the extant sources related to the pilgrimage in its early modern form, and that does not seem to lead directly to the present-day prevalence of the group travel or the package tour and heavy reliance on travel agencies. I therefore feel that the concept of an "all-pervasive tradition" is sometimes overemphasized,[26] especially when it is set against what is seen as a completely divergent development in other countries. Pilgrimage also played an important part in the emergence of tourism in many countries other than Japan,[27] and in Catholic Europe, for example, many of the popular "Wallfahrten"—guided and arranged mass pilgrimages to popular centers of faith—had also early assumed forms anticipating the package tour.[28] As for tourism in Japan itself, one should not forget that though it is true that the sites visited are mostly the same today as they were in the Tokugawa period, journeys to these culturally sanctioned centers through which people today seek the "nostalgic" confirmation of their cultural landscape may well have occasioned very different feelings among Edo-period travelers who probably experienced them in a more adventurous and serendipitous way.

 Notes

1. For a general approach cf. for example Kato (1994).

2. This prompted Engelbert Kaempfer to the following statement in his diary relating his visit to Japan in the years 1691–1692: "It is scarce credible, what numbers of people daily travel on the roads in this country, and ... the Tokaido ... is upon some days more crowded, than the publick streets in any [of] the most populous town[s] in Europe," cited after Vaporis (1994:15).

3. During these early stages of its history, outside the circles of the *yamabushi*, Mt. Tateyama was known for being directly connected to Hell. Legends in the *Konjaku monogatari* [cf. for example *Konjaku monogatari* 17/27 (NKBT 24:541–42)], but also Nô plays such as *Utô* (NKBT 41:341–45), recount how a monk would meet the emaciated figure of a woman on the mountain, who, after confessing that she was indeed dead and had fallen into Hell, would beg him to ask her relatives to make some of the sacrifices necessary for her future salvation.
   For earlier reviews of the Tateyama cult with special emphasis on the religious salvation of women cf. Seidel (1992–93; 1996–97).

4. Since the Tateyama is close to the Hokurikudô, a certain number of travelers visited the mountain as early as the Middle Ages. For instance, the monk Chôgen from the Tôdaiji pilgrimaged to Zenkôji, Tateyama, and

Hakusan at the beginning of the Middle Ages, as is documented in his *Namu Amidabutsu sakuzenshû*, and in the Kannô era (ca. 1350) priests from the Yasaka Shrine on their way to the Zenkôji ascended Mt. Hakusan and Mt. Tateyama (cf. *Yasaka jinja kiroku*). In 1486 Dôkyô and others from the Shôgoin on their tour through the Eastern provinces visited the Tateyama, which may also have been due to the facilities of travel (cf. *Kaikoku zakki*). It seems as though in the Muromachi period the *sendatsu* of Kumano, when visiting their *danna* in the Kantô and Tôhoku region, also took the Hokurikudô, as did the pilgrims they had encouraged to undertake a pilgrimage to Kumano, both thus passing near Mt. Tateyama. Increasing numbers of pilgrims to the Tateyama are also hinted at by the fact that the Bakufu in 1484 lifted the barrier stations along the Tateyama pilgrimage road (Shinjô 1982:588–89).

5. These *Tateyama mandara* have been extensively published in recent years by Nagashima (1983); for an overall explanation and description of the surviving specimens cf. Toyama-ken Tateyama Hakubutsukan (1991b).

6. Published in Hayashi (1984:49–88).

7. An apocryphal sutra expounding that women who had caused pollution by dint of their menstrual or parturition blood were bound to suffer the torments of the Blood-Pond Hell after death and how they could be saved.

8. The following numbers of yearly visitors to the various pilgrimage centers are rough estimates based on the findings of Shinjô (1982).

9. The Hikosan in Buzen (Fukuoka prefecture) for example attracted up to 40,000 people per year, but it seems that these numbers were mainly made up of inhabitants of Kyûshû who experienced difficulties leaving their island.

10. The Senzôbô for example controlled the regions of Tôtômi and Kai (today's Shizuoka and Yamanashi), the Daisenbô Yamato and Kawachi (Osaka and Nara), the Gyokusenbô Shimôsa and Awa (Chiba), the Ryûsenbô Sagami and Suruga (Kanagawa and Shizuoka), the Kinsenbô Iga and Kawachi (Mie and Osaka region), the Tôkakubô Mutsu (Aomori), and so on.

11. For the village of Kagiyamura in Owari in the vicinity of today's Tôkai-shi (Aichi prefecture), for example, the visit of *oshi* from Tateyama is recorded at some time around 1850, besides the ones from, first of all, Ise, but also from the Atsuta Shrine, from Tsushima, from the Kinbusen, from Kôya-san, from Kumano, from the Taga Shrine, the Atago Shrine, and Mt. Hakusan (Shinjô 1982:768).

12. During the conference Prof. Graburn advised me that this kind of competition between the various groups involved in the organization of the pilgrimage/tourist travel was very much like the one he had observed during his own fieldwork on the *furusato*-style resorts being developed in Japan today (cf. his contribution in this volume), suggesting that the urge to clearly delimitate the various services performed by people involved in tourism industry might very well be another feature in which the Edo-period experience still lingers in present-day domestic Japanese tourism.

13. Cf. also the *Mittsu no yama meguri*, which gives detailed explanations as to how these analogies worked, the Dyer Hell for example being a hole in the rocks filled with bubbling blueish water (Takeshita 1989:36).

14. As in the case of Kaneko Banka who was very skeptical about the orthodox explanations of the monks, whom he accused of being money-grubbing. He felt compelled to note that Blood Pond actually was not filled with blood, but that it was sulphur that produced the red color. He nevertheless purchased a *Kechibongyô* and had it thrown into the lake.

15. As in the accounts of travel-loving men such as Satô Gessô (*Tateyama kikô*, 1798) or Ôtsuka Keigyô, a scholar of Toyama (*Tateyama ni noboru no ki*, 1840), described by Kumahara (1959:83–87) as early-modern pioneers of Japanese mountaineering.

16. As already pointed out by Linhart (1990:42–44), even in the case of this pilgrimage, it is impossible to subscribe to Carmen Blacker's (1984) view that tries to explain the conspicuous increase in the number of lay pilgrims during the Edo period with a kind of religious escapism people turned to in the face of the many political and social restrictions imposed upon them by the *bakufu* and the various *han* administrations. Although, on a general level, it may be true that ordinary men, finding their day-to-day life too cramped and confined and the burdens they were expected to bear as respectable human beings intolerably great, may have increasingly felt the urge to leave home, and that this may be part of the explanation for the overall infatuation of Edo-period commoners with travel, the accounts certainly do not reveal feelings on the part of the pilgrims of having slipped into the "historically long-established figure of the *yûgyôsha*, or religious traveler," as this theory would have it.

17. This is so conspicuous that I feel compelled to reproduce here Aramata's (1988) perhaps somewhat too essayistic coining of Mt. Tateyama as an *ano yo no yûenchi*, or Other-World Playground.

18. Foard (1982:239), on a more general level, has similarly described travel in the Edo period as a great equalizer and the road as a marginal space in which structures broke down, exposing both danger and freedom.

19. It should be noted within this context that the well-known expression *tabi wa michizure* ("travel spells companionship") did not mean that one would travel within a preestablished group, but that on a journey one might come to know people one would never have met or had contact with if one had stayed at home.

20. Note on the other hand that Vaporis's (1995:28–29) remarks concerning the constraints upon travel in Tokugawa Japan seem to indicate that those had been enforced only very loosely well before the Bakumatsu period. Unlike the *sekisho tegata*, issued by designated *bakufu* officials for passage through a particular station, the *ôrai tegata* were not only very convenient, since they allowed one to pass as many checking stations as needed, but were also rather easy to obtain, as they were issued at shrines and temples or by village officials and even innkeepers. Vaporis also mentions that, as is evident from a number of contemporary travel diaries, it was rather common to travel without any permit, as our peasant couple from Gifu probably did, bypassing the checking stations illegally. People were apparently aided by the officials themselves who became increasingly reluctant to enforce the law.

21. E.g., at the end of the eighteenth century the domain of Saga issued decrees on the maximum number of days to be spent on pilgrimages combining various destinations, ranging from combinations such as Ise and Zenkôji (150 days), Ise and the *Shikoku henro* (180 days) to such comprehensive forms as Ise, Saikoku, Zenkôji, Shikoku, Nikkô, and a stop at Enoshima (280 days) (Shinjô 1982:818–19).

22. As exemplified by the round trips made by the authors of the above-mentioned *Mittsu no yama meguri* and *Sangaku kikô*.

23. Cf. Vaporis (1995:26) or Walthall (1991:66).

24. Statements like the following are occasionally to be found: "This evolution towards a many-sided touristic element in pilgrimages took a great leap forward with the construction of the first railways. Shrines and temples and areas with hot springs as well as sites with historic significance or scenic attractions became complex centers of tourism supplementing one another. ... Nonetheless the actual time expended for excursions and recreational journeys remained limited to the span of a few days" (Schöller

1980:135–36). Here one cannot escape the feeling that the continuity of Edo-period practice and modern domestic tourism is somewhat exaggerated.

25. Shinjô (1982:989–90) suggests that already after the middle of the eighteenth century there was a decline in the number of pilgrims visiting Mt. Tateyama and that out of the thirty-three lodgings at the Ashikuraji many became impoverished and fourteen managed to make a living only by additionally cultivating mountain fields or finding an employer. I was not able to corroborate this view, especially in what concerns the timing of the decline. As with most of the holy mountains, ascents to the Tateyama continued as a kind of rite of passage, of *seinenshiki*, youth had to go through before they could voice a desire to marry, but this became restricted mainly to the districts nearby. Thus, despite the destruction, in 1878 Osugi Fukudô still lamented not having been able to sleep in the Murodô because it was filled with several hundred people (Hirose 1992:327).

26. As in some of the lines by Kanzaki (1994), who has done a great deal to uncover the roots of modern Japanese tourism in the Edo period and even before.

27. Cf. for example a recent collection of essays with the suggestive title "Travel Culture: From Pilgrimage to Modern Tourism" (Bausinger, Beyrer, and Korff 1991). Within this context I should not withhold from the reader a reminiscence of my own childhood: whenever my family and I went on a trip together, we used, on the instigation of my mother, to visit every church in the neighborhood, my mother not even refraining from searching out the priest when a church turned out to be closed. This would have seemed to me to be the natural course of sightseeing had not my father been there to complain once a while about this state of affairs and ask why we did not spend only a small amount of the energy we used in church-sightseeing to look more closely at some splendid secular buildings. This turned my attention to the fact that for my mother, and I think for most Austrians who had a Catholic upbringing (at least in her generation), sightseeing consisted mainly of visiting churches or other holy places.

28. Cf. e.g. Hengstler and Stocker (1994).

References

Aramata Hiroshi. 1988. "Ano yo no yûenchi e. Tateyama jigoku meguri to nyonin ôjô," *Jigoku hyakkei*. Tokyo: Heibonsha 1988 (= Bessatsu taiyô Nihon no kokoro 62), 76–81.

Bachmayer, Eva. 1994. "Dewa sanzan—die heiligen drei Berge. Zu Besuch bei den *Yamabushi*, den legendären Bergasketen Japans," *Minikomi. Informationen des Akademischen Arbeitskreises Japan* 4/1994, 4–8.

Blacker, Carmen. 1984. "The religious traveler in the Edo period," *Modern Asiatic Studies* 18/4, 593–608.

———. 1986. *The catalpa bow: A study of shamanistic practices in Japan.* New Edition. London: George Allen & Unwin (1975).

Bausinger, Hermann, Klaus Beyrer, and Gottfried Korff (eds.). 1991. *Reisekultur. Von der Pilgerfahrt zum modernen Tourismus.* München: Verlag C. H. Beck.

Davis, Winston. 1992. *Japanese religion and society: Paradigms of structure and change.* Albany: State University of New York Press.

Foard, James H. 1982. "The boundaries of compassion," *Journal of Asian Studies* 41/2, 231–51.

Gifu-ken (ed.). 1971. *Gifu kenshi. Shiryô-hen. Kinsei 7: Kôtsû, shôgyô kankei shiryô.* Tokyo: Gonnandô shoten.

Graburn, Nelson. 1993. *To pray, pay and play: The cultural structure of Japanese domestic tourism.* Aix-en-Provence: Université de Droit, d'Économie et des Sciences, Centre des Hautes Études Touristiques (1983) (= Cahiers du Tourisme, Série B, n. 26).

Hayashi Masahiko. 1984. *Nihon no etoki. Shiryô to kenkyû.* Enlarged Edition. Tokyo: Miyai shoten.

Hengstler, Wilhelm, and Karl Stocker. 1994. *Wallfahrt. Wege zur Kraft.* Steiermärkische Landesausstellung, Stift Pöllau, 30. April bis 30. Oktober 1994. With the participation of Joachim Heinzl and Angelika Thoen. Graz: Kulturabteilung des Amtes der Steiermärkischen Landesregierung.

Hirose Makoto. 1983. [Annotations to *Tateyama-dô meisho*] Gorai Shigeru (ed.). 1983. *Shugendô shiryô shûsei 1.* Tokyo: Meicho shuppan 1983 (=Sangaku shûkyôshi kenkyû sôsho 17), 733–34.

———. 1992. *Tateyama no ibuki: Manyôshû kara kindai tôsan kotohajime made.* Toyama: Shî Ê Pî (Toyama raiburarî 2).

Ishimori Shûzô. 1989. "Popularization and commercialization of tourism in early modern Japan," Umesao Tadao, Mark W. Fruin, and Hata Nobuyuki (eds.), *Japanese civilization in the modern world IV: Economic institutions.* Osaka: National Museum of Ethnology (= Senri Ethnological Studies 26), 179–94.

Kanzaki Noritake. 1992a. "The travel-loving tradition of the Japanese," *Japan Echo* 19/4, 66–69.

———. 1992b. "Monomi yusan no shûzoku no saikakunin," *Chûô kôron* July 1992, 245–50.

———. 1994. "Hitobito wa naze ni yama ni asonda no ka," *Mahora* 1, 8–20.

———. 1995. "A comparative analysis of the tourist industry," Umesao et al. 1995, 39–49.

Kato Akinori. 1994. "Package tours, pilgrimages and pleasure trips," Ueda Atsushi (ed.), Miriam Eguchi (transl.), *The electric geisha: Exploring Japan's popular culture.* Tokyo, New York, London: Kodansha International, 51–59.

Kitamura Nobuyo. 1929. *Kiyû shôran: Ge.* Tokyo: Yoshikawa kôbunkan (= Nihon zuihitsu taisei dai2ki bekkan ge).

Kumahara Masao. 1959. *Tôsan no yoake.* Tokyo: Hôbundô.

LaFleur, William. 1979. "Points of departure: Comments on religious pilgrimage in Sri Lanka and Japan," *Journal of Asian Studies* 38/2, 271–81.

Linhart, Sepp. 1990. "Verdrängung und Überhöhung als Probleme beim Verständnis von Freizeit und Unterhaltung am Beispiel der späten Edo-Zeit," Ernst Lokowandt (ed.), *Referate des 1. Japanologentages der OAG in Tokyo.* München: Iudicium-Verlag, 29–51.

Nagashima Masatada. 1983. *Tateyama mandara shûsei.* Tokyo: Bunken shuppan.

NKBT 7, 24, 32, 41. 1970–71. *Nihon koten bungaku taikei.* Tokyo: Iwanami shoten.

Reader, Ian. 1987. "From asceticism to the package tour—The pilgrim's progress in Japan," *Religion* 17, 133–48.

Rotermund, Hartmut O. 1983. *Pèlerinage aux neuf sommets: Carnets de route d'un religieux itinérant dans le Japon du 19ᵉ siècle.* Paris: Édition du CNRS.

Schöller, Peter. 1980. "Tradition und Moderne im innerjapanischen Tourismus," *Erdkunde. Archiv für wissenschaftliche Geographie* 34/2, 134–50.

Seidel, Anna. 1992–93. "Mountains and hells: Religious geography in Japanese *mandara* paintings," *Studies in Central and East Asian Religions* 5/6, 122–33.

———. 1996–97. Descente aux enfers et rédemption des femmes dans le Bouddhisme populaire Japonais—le pèlerinage du Mont Tateyama. *Cahiers d'Extrême-Asie* 9, 1–14.

Shinjô Tsunezô. 1982. *Shinkô Shaji sankei no shakai keizai shiteki kenkyû.* Tokyo: Hanawa shobô.

Suganuma Teizô. 1938. "Taiga no *Sangaku kikô*," *Bijutsu kenkyû* 73, 9–27.

Takeshita Kazumasa (ed.). 1989. *Mittsu no yama meguri: Zen.* Gifu-ken, Kôrikami-gun, Shiratori-chô, Maetani: Takeshita Kazumasa.

Toyama-ken Tateyama Hakubutsukan (ed.). 1991a. *Jôsetsu tenji sôgô kaisetsu.* Toyama: Toyama-ken Tateyama Hakubutsukan.

———. 1991b. *Tateyama no kokoro to katachi: Tateyama mandara no sekai. Kaikan kinen-ten.* Toyama: Toyama-ken Tateyama Hakubutsukan.

Umesao Tadao, Harumi Befu, and Ishimori Shuzo (eds.). 1995. *Japanese civilization in the modern world IX: Tourism.* Osaka: National Museum of Ethnology (= Senri Ethnological Studies 38).

Vaporis, Constantine N. 1994. *Breaking barriers: Travel and the state in early modern Japan.* Cambridge, Mass., and London: Harvard University Press (= Harvard East Asian Monographs 163).

————. 1995. "The early modern origins of Japanese tourism," Umesao et al. 1995, 25–38.

Walthall, Ann. 1991. "The life cycle of farm women," Gail Lee Bernstein (ed.), *Recreating Japanese women, 1600–1945.* Berkeley, Los Angeles, Oxford: University of California Press, 42–70.

Nelson H. H. Graburn

10

Work and Play in the Japanese Countryside

This chapter is concerned with the development of the Japanese countryside into a site for recreation. I have entitled it "Work and Play" because the countryside was, until a few decades ago, the site of work for the majority of the population and because, in the past two decades, the growth of tourism and recreation in the countryside has in part been planned specifically to provide work opportunities for the population whose previous occupations—farming, forestry, and fishing—have encountered serious declines.

The chapter consists of three parts: first, a consideration of what the countryside is and the ways in which it may be conceived; second, an account of the planning of nonagricultural developments and of which recreational and tourist activities take place there; and third, a consideration of the discourse of new meanings of the countryside in contemporary Japanese culture.

The Japanese Countryside

The landscape of Japan, though penetrable (by tunnels or winding roads), consists of steep and often volcanic mountains covering nearly three-quarters its area. There are many narrow valleys, but the few densely populated fertile plains contain most of both the agricultural and the urban areas. In Japan, land usage follows topography: according to the *Japan statistical yearbook* (Statistics Bureau 1993:505, 526) 77 percent of the surface of Japan is forested (over 10 percent of the mainly forested areas are now incorporated into National, Quasi-National, and Prefectural Parks), only 14 percent is farmed and cultivated, while 2.6 percent is given over to residential areas and less than 1 percent to industry.

As the focus of this chapter is play or recreation (*rejâ*) in the countryside, we are given pause when we think of the Japanese term for it—*inaka*, as expressed by the two kanji that might otherwise be pronounced *ta* (rice field) and *sha* (household or house), that is, "fields and houses" for short. In her recent *Rice as Self* Ohnuki-Tierney (1993:92–93), following Gluck (1985), states that *inaka* was and still is an urban construction, encompassing those parts of Japan likely to be visited by urban people when they leave their towns and cities. What about the other 77 percent, the relatively uninhabited landscape? This might be thought of as *hikyô*, the hidden or unexplored (i.e., uninhabited regions), or *henkyô*, the frontier, in the historical sense of not yet settled regions, or even *arechi*, waste or good for nothing land where humans could never settle.

The conception of *inaka* may have undergone change as less and less of Japan's land is cultivated, and the former dominant occupation in the largest area, forestry, has become a moribund industry. On the other hand, new uses for the land, such as skiing, trekking, and golf, may have revived, or brought into habitation, or at least into familiarity, areas that were otherwise "empty" or unknown. Thus it is likely that the countryside where the recreation now takes place is not exactly the same *inaka* where farmers live and where so many urbanites once had their *furusato*s, their home communities.

Japan has long been a relatively urban, densely populated nation, with the metropolis of Edo (Tokyo) reaching more than 1,000,000 people even before the end of the Tokugawa era. The power to define categories of life and land, and hierarchies of moral value, lay with the powerful and the *literati* and showed remarkable continuity until the last few decades. Though *inaka no hito*, the people of the countryside, might have been looked down upon, ambivalence was expressed because in the official moral hierarchy it was the farmers who were placed after the *samurai* and noble elite, above the craftsmen and business people of the towns and cities.

The relation of the countryside to the cities began to change in the Meiji era of Western-inspired industrialization (1868–1912). Then, and again particularly since World War II, the inhabitants of the rural areas have flocked to the bright lights and the many jobs proffered by the cities (Nakamura 1993). By 1930 the rural population, *inaka no hito* (engaged in agriculture, forestry, and fisheries) dropped below the 50 percent mark, and in the 1950s rural unemployment was higher than 10 percent in many areas. By 1970 only 25 percent of Japan's population lived in the rural areas.

In recent years, and I only have figures from 1990, it was claimed that the farmers make up 23 percent of the population, but only 10 percent of them actually make more than 50 percent of their living from farming—the rest are "weekend farmers" who have full-time jobs, usually in nearby towns and cities. In fact, the burden of farming has increasingly fallen on the women who now do the weeding and other less heavy jobs all week long. This has led to a serious rural problem—that few local women want to be farmer's wives as this involves as much work as ever, along with the increasing responsibility to do it alone. Many young heirs cannot find brides, as women would much rather marry a man with a regular 8 A.M. to 8 P.M. job or move into town and work part-time themselves until marriage. Farmers have tried to overcome this problem with financial promises to wives, with promises of modern machinery and utensils—they increasingly engage agencies to find them foreign wives from, for instance, the Philippines or Southeast Asia, where women are "not afraid of hard work" and where even the rural life in Japan seems unimaginably affluent. Sadly, even these efforts only rarely lead to success.

Many kinds of rural occupations have diminished or disappeared. There is little need for anyone to keep farm animals such as bullocks and horses, as these have been replaced by motorized vehicles. Charcoal makers were important in forestry before the arrival on the scene of kerosene and electricity. Even though Japan has done a wonderful job in restoring its forest areas since their devastation in World War II, lumberjacks are a dying breed because they are hardly needed now that Japan relies on the much cheaper wood from much larger trees that it harvests or buys in foreign countries such as Burma, Borneo, and the New Hebrides.

The national spotlight, however, is on rice farmers and the disappearance of rice-growing acreage. The Occupation-ordered land reform of the late 1940s put farmers in charge of their own land, motivating them to switch to other crops for greater profit. This was soon supplemented by biological, chemical, and herbicidal advances that doubled pre-World War II yields. By the 1960s, Japan was not only able to feed herself with rice but also to produce large surpluses that forced the central government to find storage and begin price supports. The government then started a financial incentive scheme to rotate the rice paddies, always leaving some fallow.

One often sees a notice in a field saying that it is fallow according to a certain timetable (probably the farmer wants no one to think he is too lazy to sow the field). With fewer fields in use, with industrial and housing developments encroaching upon rural areas, coupled with increasing numbers of farmers farming only part-time or weekends, rice production has actually fallen in recent years. In 1965 farmers planted over 3 million hectares of paddy to produce 12.4 million tons of rice, but by 1991 these figures had dropped to 2 million hectares and 9.6 million tons, representing an increase in productivity but an overall decline in production.

However, rice consumption has also dropped. Japanese want more variety in their diet and increasingly look toward bread, pasta, and such substitutes. Government-distributed rice is, even with a subsidy, at least five times more expensive in Japan than on the world market. Even government school lunches include rice only two or three times a week. Certain segments of the populace and the government have always claimed that they want Japan to be self-sufficient in rice even if only at uneconomical prices—following the experience of starvation after World War II—and their fears were borne out in the summer of 1994 when the rice crops failed massively and Japan was forced to buy foreign rice from Southeast Asia, the United States, and other countries.

I was in Japan during that time, and I was amazed at how many people—family and friends—told me (coming from California) with great glee that they each had a sure supply and didn't have to eat that *gaimai*, that foreign rice! As Ohnuki-Tierney's *Rice as Self* (1993) stresses, it is not the monetary cost (which is not expensive to the affluent Japanese) nor the nutritional value of rice (which is on a par with other available foods) that concerns Japanese, it is the key symbolic value of rice: rice as bright green in watery terraces, rice loaded with golden grains, rice as *sake*, the drink of the gods, rice as the earth, rice as the water, rice as the labor of the hardworking Japanese countryman. As former Berkeley graduate student Michael Foster suggested (1994), we should perceive Japan's sentiments toward rice and rice farming as an art form central to their heritage, not as an industry.

Planning Recreation in the Countryside: Making Work

At the national level there have been two kinds of plan to boost the economy of the lagging Japanese countryside: First are Tokyo-generated plans for the decentralization of industry by attracting plants to the countryside, *kigyô yûchi* (Knight 1993; Tatsuno 1986), plans for new recreational areas, resort areas, and even considering moving the capital from Tokyo to the hinterlands (Tabb 1995: 169–97). The former type of project, the dispersal of Japanese industry, has not been as successful as hoped, major industry and, hence, highly trained workers, are still attracted primarily to the metropolitan zones (Keener 1992; Tabb 1995). However, to examine this process would be marginal to the present project because it turns countryside into urban areas. This process often leads to widespread loss of "rural character" and a proliferation of ugly sights. Due in part to historical patterns and in part to the American influences of the Occupation period, Japan has very weak zoning laws. For instance, farmers generally hang on to their land as long as possible, both for sentimental reasons and because it is subsidized, but when they do sell their land—and many have become very rich doing so—they can sell it to a factory, a *pachinko* parlor, to a supermarket, to practically any enterprise. Thus lovely rural valleys often sprout haphazard development in all directions (the converse also occurs, tiny enclaves of farming may remain in the midst of a huge city).

Second, there has been a redistribution of national (and later prefectural) tax moneys specifically to village and *mura* governments along with a growing nostalgia for *furusato* "old/home village" culture, with the assumption that somehow the core of the "real Japan" lies in peripheral, rural communities (cf. Martinez 1990).

This is expressed in a national and regional—economic and ideological—*mura okoshi* "village revitalization" movement: this "pro-countryside" movement has real adherents, with strongly moral and ecological principles—there are meetings, national organizations, and somewhat antiestablishment schemes—as well as governmental status. Prime Minister Takeshita created a "Furusato Foundation" to give 100,000,000 Yen (approximately $700,000 at that time) to each village as *mura okoshi* development grants. The villages were, however, free to choose in what way they would spend this money.

Villages all over Japan chose to spend their money differently: improvement of roads and road signs, improvement of schools and health clinics, building of facilities for the recreation and care of the growing population of old persons, advertizing of resort attractions, loans or grants to improve inns, campgrounds, hot spring resorts, and so on. But the most famous and financially rewarding was a village in Hyogo-ken (near Kobe) that turned its cash into a solid gold ingot that was put on display in the community hall. Locals and visitors were challenged to pick it up (under the eye of guards)—a clever idea that brought in reporters, TV crews, and tourists in large numbers.

The central government passed the "Law of Development of Comprehensive Resort Areas," which came into effect in June 1987 (*Japan Times* 20 February 1990). In turn regional governments began applying for this funding, and by 1991 over eighteen schemes had been approved. The purpose of this law is, like the title of this chapter, twofold: to foster the construction of resorts and leisure facilities in order to revitalize regional economies *and* to provide more leisure opportunities for the workaholic Japanese. Approved schemes benefit from lowered corporate and real estate taxes along with low-interest loans.

For instance, one scheme was the Nagano Prefectural government's proposal, called the Fresh Air Shinshû Chi-Kumagawa plan. It called for the construction of seven golf courses on 180,000 hectares of mountainous land. This provoked a reaction from the locals who feared that these recreational facilities would lead to the pollution of sources of drinking water (more on this later).

Another scheme, in cooperation with the Forestry Agency, is called the "Human Green Plan," which proposes more flexible use of the national forest to include resort areas and sports facilities such as ski runs, golf courses, tennis courts, botanical gardens, and bird sanctuaries, as well as tourist accommodations. It encourages private investment in these public lands.

In the past three decades, Japan has developed superb albeit expensive urban and interurban public transportation systems. However, outside of the urban areas the infrastructure is relatively inadequate. Great effort and expense has been forthcoming in an attempt to supply this missing infrastructure so that the urban population will venture into the local countryside for recreational purposes. Unfortunately sometimes the building of roads cannot keep up with the growing number of cars. In 1978, Ronald Dore, in describing the rural valley that led to the village of Shinohata, wrote (Dore 1978:17):

> Ten years ago, when the trunk road was first completely metalled all the way to the next prefecture, there were express buses, but no longer. Now the roads are so crowded that express would be a mockery. No society in history has been so rapidly motorized, and few societies have had such trouble adapting to the motor-car, as Japan with its dense population and tightly packed settlements.

By 1992, 78 percent of Japanese families owned a personal car, and that number rose to over 87 percent in rural areas (Statistics Bureau 1992:50, 305).

Domestic mass tourism has a long history (Ishimori 1989; Vaporis 1995) and has now reached more than 300 million overnight trips a year (Graburn 1983a). The task of the government has been to open up means of communication from the dense metropolitan areas and to encourage the provision and publicity of rural tourism and recreational facilities which, in turn, should employ local people. In the past two decades, the government has instigated an extensive national road-building effort, both for expensive intercity toll roads (and bridges) and into previously isolated hinterland areas. The recent abundance of cars and the national highway and bridge construction program have made more accessible some of the more remote country areas and consequently visitor numbers have risen dramatically in the past decade.

Attractions of the Hinterlands

There is a vast range of attractions for visitors to the Japanese hinterlands. Some are historically traditional like pilgrimages to famous temples and shrines; most of them are newly installed and thoroughly secular. It is convenient to divide these recreations into two
kinds: *rejâ* and *kenbutsu*—that is, active and passive forms of
tourism. The former appeals to younger people and the latter to
older people, each having different conceptions of the countryside.
Class and gender are also significant factors.

For instance, the mildly active sport of golf is one of the more
popular rural recreations but nearly all players are upper-middle-
class professionals and only 15 percent are women. Golf, which has
an annual turnover of over 2 trillion Yen and has over 12 million
players in 2,000 clubs (1990 figures), was also one of the first issues
resisted by locals because of the metropolitan planning for outlying
recreation and resorts (Yamada 1990a, 1990b). The spate of building golf courses, even by leveling mountain tops, for the sake of relatively rich, middle-aged men, has threatened the landscape with
pollution and change. Golf courses now occupy more than 1.25 percent of Japan's *total* landscape, an area larger than Greater Tokyo,
which is home to 30 million people! Due to lavish use of pesticides
and herbicides, run-off pollution often threatens nearby fishing
areas and water supplies.

Hot spring (*onsen*) bathing is popular with all ages but does
not quite fit the "do" versus "see" classification; it is passive rather
than active, but the senses involved are feeling and smell as much
as sight. The past twenty years have seen an *onsen bûmu* (hot
spring boom) in resorts, most of which were formerly used by local
rural people or a few upper-class visitors (Graburn 1995; Hotta
and Ishiguro 1986; Osaki 1988). Though the natural waters were
often said to have curative, or at least recuperative powers, most of
the eighty million Japanese who annually partake of *onsen* do so
purely for relaxation.

Skiing is also a major rural recreational activity that is growing
fast and appeals to the younger generation. It is another trillion Yen
plus business, with 800 resorts by 1987 and many more planned.
Space prevents little more than a listing of other popular recre-

ational activities; for younger people, these include hiking, camping, climbing, exploring caves, diving, surfing, kayaking, and so on; middle-aged people are likely to dominate sport fishing and sea boating, while walking, cycling, swimming, fresh-water fishing and driving—the third most popular recreational activity in Japan (after eating out and domestic tourism)—are enjoyed by adults of all ages.

Domestic tourism, with over sixty million participants and three hundred million trips a year, supplies the countryside with some of its active and most of its passive visitors. Many of the attractions, in contrast to the ones mentioned above, are site specific—that is, people go to particular, well-known, often historical places. Famous natural scenery, equal in popularity to *onsen* bathing (Prime Minister's Office Survey, 1992), is even more popular than visiting famous man-made attractions. But we must not forget that all attractions are man-made in the sense that they have been socially constructed and validated as attractions (MacCannell 1976; Berque 1986). These culturally certified natural features most prominently include mountains, volcanoes, waterfalls, cliffs, caves, and shores, most of which are the habitations of powerful *kami* (gods), with shrines for praying to the *kami* usually to be found nearby. Other natural attractions are less site specific, such as river boating, whale watching, and, of course, the seasonally appropriate viewing of nature—cherry blossoms, wild azalea, autumn maples (see Ohnuki-Tierney, this volume).

Historical sites of many kinds have long formed the backbone of Japanese domestic tourism (Graburn 1983a; Ishimori 1989; Vaporis 1995). In addition to the famous shrines, temples, and castles, which are often found in urban or urbanized rural areas, specifically rural attractions are becoming very popular: most of these are obsolescent or obsolete structures, including archaeological sites, old farm houses such as *minka* (folk houses) (Ehrentraut 1993), either *in situ* in villages or, more often, brought together in "old house parks" somewhat similar to European eco-museums. Some are made more appealing for a wider range of people by including restaurants or traditional crafts activities and sales of souvenir *omiyage*. One of the most spectacular is the fairly new *Yu-no-kuni-no-mori* in Kanazawa-ken, a group of restored thatched *minka* brought together in a landscaped park, each hosting a traditional crafts activity such as lacquer ware, pottery, paper making, country cooking, and so on. This was erected at great cost a few kilometers from a popular *onsen* resort by the wealthy owner of the local taxi companies.

Some whole villages, lucky enough not to have been "modernized," remodel themselves on traditional styles but not as museums. Chiran, the lovely tea-growing village south of Ibusuki, combines the nostalgic attractions of thatched houses, manicured gardens, and neat rows of tea bushes, with the, for some, equally nostalgic national memorial to heroic Kamikaze pilots and their selfless widows. This makes the very important point that any particular tourist trip may well not be limited to one type of attraction: one often finds the old with the new, the familiar with the strange, or "nature" and culture in interesting combinations.

Rural Recreation and Japanese Culture: Making Hay (Play)

In this final section, I shall consider the factors in contemporary Japanese society that have impelled the population into rural recreation and tourism, and how it has been done. Using the model of recreation and tourism as a ritual of reversal, we infer that the attractions are pull factors that appear to provide relief or liminal compensation (Graburn 1977; 1983b) for some push factors in contemporary urban living, and that the advertizing and publicity systems (Ivy 1995:29–65) make the actors aware of either the potential relief and pleasure to be enjoyed or of some kind of pain (or guilt) engendered by city life—for example, not tending to family graves back in the *furusato* village.

It has been suggested that contemporary urban populations feel an ever-decreasing experience of Japanese-ness as valued in both nature and culture (cf. Kelly 1986). Thus many harried white-collar workers live in cramped conditions in city apartments and hanker for the spacious facilities and leisurely pace of rural holidays. I have also suggested a gendered dimension to this urban malaise (Graburn 1995), whereby the man leaves the family and goes out to battle the modern (Western-style) world, while the wife, even with a part-time job, takes care of the home and the children and provides traditional security. I further suggested that for these people, the city could be seen as a male, alien world; whereas the countryside, especially the *furusato*, could be a female counterpart.

Lebra has recently noted (1993:13) that internationalization, *kokusaika*, is a phenomenon that many Japanese feel has been thrust upon them, causing distaste, if not anxiety (perhaps paralleling the feelings of many white Americans about "affirmative action"). Internationalization is more apparent in the modern city, increasingly in the form of swarthy guest workers and other foreigners. After World War II and the end of the Occupation, the overwhelming presence of foreigners subsided, but the urban way of life became increasingly "foreign," that is, at least superficially more Western. The Tokyo Olympics in 1964 brought in many foreigners and coincided with the relaxation on buying foreign money. This, in turn, allowed Japanese tourists to go abroad in increasing numbers, itself a self-imposed *kokusaika*, but the vast majority did not go abroad. *Kokusaika* had become a more insistent policy by the 1970s. Lebra (1993:13) claims that this spurred attempts at retrenchment by self-discovery: This threat to national identity was soon countered by domestic tourism. As Ivy (1995:40–48) shows, the JNR [at that time the government still ran the national railway], tied up with Dentsu, the world's largest advertising agency, began the "Discover Japan" campaign in 1970. Actually this followed the decade older but smaller commercial campaign by JTB (Nihon kôtsû kôsha [Japan Travel Bureau] 1960).

Part of the effort to get citizens to travel out from the metropoles was the *furusato* campaign of the 1970s, which urged urbanites to travel *back* to the villages and small towns from which they or their families had migrated. *Furusato* is an inherently nostalgic concept implying alienation, which I have translated as "old/home village" (for further discussions of this concept, see Ivy 1995: 103–108; Knight 1993:210–11; Robertson 1995:89–91). As Ivy points out, the idea of *furusato-mairi*, going back to the old/home village, parallels the common appellation of the "Discover Japan" campaign—*Nihon no saihakken*—which literally means "*Re*discover Japan."

This campaign depended on the idealized construction that all Japanese families had or ought to have had a cozy rural or small-town community of origin. The campaign was probably not aimed at youths nor was it particularly effective for them. However, for those who do maintain contact with relatives back home, there are at least two annual occasions when they should return home for family/ritual purposes. These are *oshôgatsu*, the week starting with the New Year's Eve visit to the local Shinto Shrine, and *obon*, the Buddhist mid-summer "All Souls Day." Family members are supposed to worship and to care for the graves on these occasions and at the time of the spring and autumn equinoxes.

As the reality of *furusato-mairi*, the annual pilgrimage home has become less compelling for families who have lived in cities for generations—or has been replaced by the desire to go elsewhere, even abroad—the metaphor of *furusato* itself has broadened and the travel to them has become less personal. *Furusato* has been promoted as a cultural conception that might be devoid of "real" historical or genealogical links. Trips out of the city may be aimed at "*furusato*-like" places, places that look and feel "homey" to the urban middle classes. The resulting cultural construction of *furusato* has resulted in a major rural industry. There is even a *Furusato Fair* now in Tokyo.

One might suggest that the end of the "Discover Japan" campaign, which was replaced by "Exotic Japan" according to Ivy (1995: 48), perhaps coincided with the point when the possibility of having a "real" *furusato* faded and gave way to the rise of a multiplicity of possible socially constructed *furusato*s. Although Ivy focuses on the new campaign's attempt to find and promote the exotic or foreign in Japan and on the claim that Japan itself is foreign (as marked, for instance, by the use of *katakana*) (Ivy 1995:50), we could also say that the countryside was foreign and exotic rather than "home" for a majority of Japanese. Thus, the countryside has become an exciting place to explore, just like a foreign country, in multitudes of promotional television programs.

This idea that rural/*furusato* is in some ways "foreign" to younger, urban Japanese, is strengthened by Rea's (1996) insightful discussion of the significance that at least two *foreign* rural places have been labeled *furusato*—Anne of Green Gables' (*Akage no Ann*) "home" country and that of her author Lucy Lord Montgomery in Prince Edward Island, Canada, and Hill Top Farm in the Lake District, the former abode of Beatrix Potter, the writer of "rural" children's books and founder of the National Trust in England. According to Rea, the words and actions of the thousands of Japanese tourists who go there—crying, meditating, feeling the soil—lead one to believe that for many the "real" nostalgic moral center may no longer lie in the Japanese countryside but in someone else's.

John Knight's recent "Rural *kokusaika*" paper (1993) shows how one rural area in Oku Kumano has invented new traditions (cf. Hobsbawm and Ranger 1983) in its relation to the city. Among other things, it has a campaign to get footloose urban folks to "adopt" the village as their *furusato*. Urbanites regularly receive packages of country produce and a newsletter. The illusion is further instilled by visiting and, possibly, even planning to retire there.

But the ideology of *furusato*, originally a national advertising campaign, reached its peak when Prime Minister Takeshita (1987) loosed the idea of *furusato* from its country and small-town moorings and declared that every place in Japan—city districts, suburbs, small towns, or villages—should become *furusato*—that is, communities with sentimental relationships of long-term loyalty based on face-to-face interaction. This has achieved a partial success, for instance among groups of mothers who "naturally" gather to send their children to school together, as well as in community recreation and health centers, playgrounds, sports and hobby groups, as well as in government-instigated "fake" (nonreligious) *matsuri* festival days, which bring all the adults together (Robertson 1991).

Dozens of surveys in the past decade found that tourist travel within Japan (summer, winter, hot springs, etc.) was the second-highest-ranked leisure activity of the Japanese (Yano 1994:302), second only to eating out. Though I agree with Kanzaki (1992) that the Japanese have always liked to travel within their country, my point is that increasingly recreational travel is to places that were previously too bucolic, too remote, or previously unmarked on road maps. We have to ask the question: If these displacements result from urban alienation, what do the attractions of the countryside mean? Most of the above-quoted writers suggested that if the city is modernity, then the countryside must denote the traditional past.

Ohnuki-Tierney (1993:120) gives us a clue. "A crucial dimension of rice symbolism in Japanese culture is the rice paddies that stand for agriculture, the countryside and the past—all symbolizing nature with its soil and water and, ultimately the Japanese nation and its people." I contend that it cannot be just the rice paddies but the whole way of life that can provide the "antidote to urban civilization."

There has been a further tipping of the moral hierarchy, ironically instigated by the Western-influenced romantics like Yanagita, Yanagi, and Hamada (Foster 1994; Moeran 1984). One might summarize this as an ideological shift from the idea "rich city/poor village," to "poor city/rich village" (Knight 1993:211). This ascendency in things rural representing tradition has coincided with a parallel trend toward the "natural" in food and drink, in "greenery" (cf. Hanahaku Expo '90 in Osaka), and in the countryside—for example, the emphasis on fresh, locally available foods such as *sansai* (mountain vegetables).

Not surprisingly, an analysis of representations in the advertising for these domestic tourism institutions does suggest the elimination of "modern/Western" phenomena—a kind of ideological ethnic cleansing and, conversely, the nostalgic highlighting of the condensed symbols of Japanese-ness (Moeran 1983).

Conclusions

To fill these recreational amenities and to provide the income and employment for the people of the rural areas, the "supply side" must be considered, the opportunities for urban people to use them. Even today, most Japanese have very short vacation periods, scattered fairly evenly throughout the year, many of which workers do not take. Adult's and children's vacations often do not coincide. There has been a rapid increase in the affluence and an ageing of the population. There has also been some increase in leisure time available to residents in urban and suburban areas—spurred by the government's effort to reduce the work week (to five and a half days) and to increase the length of vacation time *actually taken*.

But young unmarried adults are one group that has increasing free time and spending money. They often travel to the countryside in peer groups—OLs (Office Ladies) living at home, particularly, have money to spare.

Older people, especially older women, are a growing segment. They have the money and the freedom. I would suggest that older people have a modern conception of the countryside *inaka* and its *furusato*, and that the urban youth might have the more recently "culturally constructed" set of conceptions discussed in this chapter.

What can we learn, then, about Japanese culture through an examination of leisure activities in the countryside?

First, at the economic/demographic level, we have seen an exchange in which traditional rural activities are increasingly replaced by new service industries serving tourism and recreation. The rural population crash accelerated the depopulation of many rural communities and the growth of urban and suburban areas. Moon's (1989) account of a Tôhoku ski resort illustrates a successful example of tourism development countering population loss.

Second, at the cognitive level, for the urban population the country life of their ancestors has become increasingly remote. Actual attachments to particular places, *furusato*, and to their rural populations have increasingly been replaced by simulations that have been manipulated by the national and local authorities in pursuit of the policies outlined above. At the same time, the mental conception of the countryside itself, *inaka*, has expanded, especially for younger, urban people whose parents were no longer able to talk about their upbringing and life in the countryside. *Inaka* has expanded to include many formerly uninhabited areas, where recreational activities such as skiing, river boating, surfing, and trekking now take place.

Third, at the moral level, there has been an increasing, sometimes nostalgic, appreciation of the value of country life, of the countryside, and of "nature" (*shizen*) itself. As I have stated here and in a previous work (Graburn 1995), managed nature has come to represent tradition in a very positive sense. Not only are (both traditional and novel) "natural foods" increasingly popular, but there is a new appreciation of natural phenomena for their own sake, building in part upon positive aspects of the ambivalent spiritual framework of Shinto. Modern urban "separation from nature" is now deemed to be like a disease, to be countered at the private level by increasing tourism and recreation in the countryside, and at the governmental level, by the creation of camps and schools in the countryside where cycles of urban children attend a few days at a time to learn at first hand "what nature is like."

―――――――――――――― *References* ――――――――――――――

Berque, Augustin. 1986. *Le sauvage et l'artifice: Les Japonais devant la nature.* Paris: Gallimard.

Dore, Ronald. 1978. *Shinohata: A portrait of a Japanese village.* New York: Pantheon.

Ehrentraut, Adolf. 1993. "Heritage authenticity and domestic tourism in Japan," *Annals of Tourism Research* 20/2, 262–78.

Foster, Michael. 1994. "Yanagita and Yanagi: An exploration into some of the ideas of two of Japan's folklorists." Berkeley, Manuscript.

Gluck, Carol. 1985. *Japan's modern myths: Ideology in the late Meiji period.* Princeton, N.J.: Princeton University Press.

Graburn, Nelson H. H. 1977. "Tourism: The sacred journey," Valene Smith (ed.), *Hosts and guests: The anthropology of tourism.* Pittsburgh: University of Pennsylvania Press, 17–32.

―――. 1983a. *To pray, pay and play: The cultural structure of Japanese domestic tourism.* Aix-en-Provence: Centre des Hautes Etudes Touristiques.

―――. 1983b. "The anthropology of tourism," Special Issue of *Annals of Tourism Research* 10, no. 1.

―――. 1987. "Material symbols in Japanese domestic tourism," D. Ingersoll and G. Bronitsky (eds.), *Mirror and metaphor: Material and social constructions of reality.* Lanham, Md.: University Press of America, 15–27.

―――. 1995. "The past in the present in Japan," R. Butler and D. G. Pearce (eds.), *Change in tourism: People, places, processes.* London: Routledge, 47–70.

Hobsbawm, Eric, and Terence Ranger (eds.). 1983. *The invention of tradition.* Cambridge: Cambridge University Press.

Hotta, Anne, and Yoko Ishiguro. 1986. *A guide to Japanese hot springs.* Tokyo: Kodansha International.

Ishimori Shuzo. 1989. "Popularization and commercialization of tourism in early modern Japan," Umesao Tadao et al. (eds.), *Japanese civilization in the modern world IV: Economic institutions.* (= Senri Ethnological Studies 26). Suita: National Museum of Ethnology, 161–78.

―――. 1995. "Tourism and religion: From the perspective of comparative civilization," Umesao Tadao et al. (eds.), *Japanese civilization in the modern world IX: Tourism.* (= Senri Ethnological Studies 38). Suita: National Museum of Ethnology, 11–24.

Ivy, Marilyn J. 1995. *Discourses of the vanishing: Modernity, phantasm, Japan.* Chicago: University of Chicago Press.

Kanzaki, Noritake. 1992. "The travel-loving tradition of the Japanese," *Japan Echo* 19/4, 66–69.

Keener, Christopher R. 1992. *Grass roots industry in the town of Sakaki: An alternative perspective of the Japanese post-war miracle.* University of California, Berkeley: Ph.D. Dissertation in Anthropology.

Kelly, William. 1986. "Rationalization and nostalgia: Cultural dynamics of the new middle-class Japan," *American Anthropologist* 13, 603–18.

Knight, John. 1993. "Rural *Kokusaika*: Foreign motifs and village revival in Japan," *Japan Forum* 5/2, 203–16.

———. 1996. "Competing hospitalities: Japanese rural tourism," *Annals of Tourism Research* 23/1, 165–80.

Lebra, Takie S. 1993. *Above the clouds: Status culture of the modern Japanese nobility.* Berkeley: University of California Press.

MacCannell, Dean. 1976. *The tourist: A new theory of the leisure class.* New York: Schocken.

Martinez, D. P. 1990. "Tourism and the *Ama*: The search for the real Japan," Eyal Ben-Ari, Brian Moeran, and James Valentine (eds.), *Unwrapping Japan.* Manchester: Manchester University Press, 97–116.

Moeran, Brian. 1983. "The language of Japanese tourism," *Annals of Tourism Research* 10, 93–108.

———. 1984. *Lost innocence: Folk craft potters of Onta, Japan.* Berkeley: University of California Press.

Moon, Okpyo. 1989. *From paddy field to ski slope: The revitalization of tradition in Japanese village life.* Manchester: Manchester University Press.

Nakamura Hachiro. 1993. "Urban growth in prewar Japan," Kuniko Fujita and Richard C. Hills (eds.), *Japanese cities in the world economy.* Philadelphia: Temple University Press, 26–49.

Nihon Kôtsû Kôsha (JTB). 1960. *Rural life in Japan.* Tokyo: JTB.

Ohnuki-Tierney, Emiko. 1993. *Rice as self: Japanese identities through time.* Princeton, N.J.: Princeton University Press.

Osaki Norio. 1988. "Beaten tracks to secret spas," *Japan Quarterly* 35/3, 275–78.

Rea, Michael. 1996. *A Furusato away from home.* Berkeley: Manuscript.

Robertson, Jennifer. 1991. *Native and newcomer: Making and remaking a Japanese city.* Berkeley: University of California Press.

———. 1995. "Nostalgia, tourism and nation-making in Japan," Umesao Tadao, Harumi Befu, and Ishimori Shuzo (eds.). 1995. *Japanese civilization in the modern world IX: Tourism. (=* Senri Ethnological Studies 38). Suita: National Museum of Ethnology, 89–104.

Statistics Bureau (Japan). 1993. *Japan statistical yearbook.* Tokyo: Statistics Bureau, Management and Coordination Agency.

Tabb, William K. 1995. *The postwar Japanese system: Cultural economy and economic transformation.* Oxford: Oxford University Press.

Takeshita Noboru. 1987. *Subarashii kuni Nihon: Watakushi no "furusato soseiron."* Tokyo: Kondansha, Showa 62.

Tatsuno, Sheridan. 1986. *The technopolis strategy: Japan, high technology and the control of the 21st century.* New York: Prentice-Hall.

Vaporis, Constantine. 1995. "The early modern origins of Japanese tourism," Umesao Tadao, Harumi Befu, and Ishimori Shuzo (eds.). 1995. *Japanese civilization in the modern world IX: Tourism.* (= Senri Ethnological Studies 38). Suita: National Museum of Ethnology, 25–38.

Yamada Kunihiro. 1990a. "The triple evils of golf courses," *Japan Quarterly* 37 (3), 291–97.

——. 1990b. *Gorufujo Bokokuron.* Tokyo: Fujiwara Shoten (Save Our Planet Series).

Yano Tsuneta Kinenkai (eds.). 1994. *Nihon kokusei-zue '94 / '95.* Tokyo: Kokusei-sha (no. 52).

Emiko Ohnuki-Tierney

11

Cherry Blossoms and Their Viewing

A Window onto Japanese Culture

For the purpose of understanding Japanese culture through its leisure activities, I have chosen to describe the Japanese cultural activities surrounding the cherry blossoms, *sakura*—its appreciation in a number of ways, including the cherry blossom viewing, *hanami*. In order to discuss the Japanese behavior surrounding this flower adequately, it is essential to understand the symbolism of the cherry blossom—its multivocality and historical changes.

On the one hand, I shall attempt to interpret the symbolism of cherry blossoms and their viewing, while, on the other, I shall explore broader sociopolitical dimensions of the leisure activities. I shall try to demonstrate why the cherry blossoms and their viewing, which have always been enormously important for the Japanese, should be understood as a "total social phenomenon." While following the original suggestion by Mauss (1966), I expand the concept to refer to a cultural institution that serves as a window onto the significant features of a culture. As such, any cultural institution that serves as a "total social phenomenon" is enormously complex and eludes unidimensional classification.

First I shall briefly outline both the changing symbolic meanings of cherry blossoms *and* the changing nature of cherry blossom viewing in a historical perspective. This chapter represents only a preliminary attempt, since my project on cherry blossoms is still in its beginnings.

Cherry Blossoms in Japanese Culture: A Historical Sketch

Cherry Blossoms in Agrarian Cosmology

In agrarian cosmology cherry blossoms are the spring counterpart of rice crops in the fall. Many scholars interpret the term *sakura* (cherry blossoms), which derives from an ancient term, *kura*, to mean the seat of *sa*, the spirit of the deity (Wakamori 1975:179–81), or, more specifically, the Deity of Rice Paddies (*Ta-no-Kami*). The identification of cherry blossoms with rice is embedded in the agrarian cosmology in which the Deity of the Mountains comes down from the mountains to become the Deity of Rice Paddies, returning to the mountains after the rice harvest in the fall (Yanagita 1982); cf. Ohnuki-Tierney 1987:43–44). The mountains, where the deities are believed to reside, are the most sacred place in the universe, and the Mountain Deity has always been the most important deity in the pantheons of Japanese folk religions (Blacker 1975; Yanagita 1982; Yanagita 1951:642–44). Cherry trees in ancient times were all mountain cherry trees (*yamazakura*), therefore cherry blossoms symbolized the mountains. Since the Mountain Deity's duty during the warm season was to look after rice plants as the Deity of Rice Paddies, cherry blossoms, like rice, were thought to embody the divine spirit. The way cherry blossoms bloomed during the spring was read as a "sign" forecasting the nature of the rice crop in the fall—if petals fell prematurely, it was an inauspicious sign (Orikuchi 1975). Since the petals embodied the Deity of Rice Paddies, the tree itself was regarded as sacred. In the ascetic mountain practice of *shugendô* the cherry tree is the sacred tree (Blacker 1975; Miyake 1978:160–68). Still today many shrines, without connections to the *shugendô*, are famous for their cherry trees, especially for those that are old and nevertheless still have beautiful blossoms (Wakamori 1975:180).

Although definite evidence for the above belief is found only during the eighteenth century (Miyata Noboru, personal communication), Wakamori and others believe that it was held by the ancient Japanese. Consequently, cherry blossom viewing (*hanami*) originated as a religious ritual (Wakamori 1975:180–81). The drinking of rice wine (*sake*) that accompanies this ritual—the quintessential part of cherry blossom viewing throughout history—derives from a sacred ritual in which deities and humans drank the sacred wine together, as an act of commensality. At times cherry blossom viewing served as an occasion for farmers to establish a ritual kinship as brothers, with the Deity as their witness (Wakamori 1975:181).

The agrarian meaning of cherry blossoms as the spring counterpart of the fall's rice crop is found in folk songs (*hanamiuta*) in rural Japan today (Wakamori 1975:178; see Sakurai 1974:80). It is also expressed in rituals for cherry blossoms at established temples, such as Yakushiji in Kyoto. During the *hana-e-shiki* (ritual for flowers, i.e. cherry blossoms), monks chase away demons and pray for a good rice crop in the fall (Nihon hôsô kyôkai 1988).

The aesthetics of the cherry blossom, including its viewing, has also been an urban practice. The political elite, including the imperial family, adopted the aesthetics of the cherry blossom and developed it into an elaborate affair for display of their cultural sophistication and political power.

Cherry Blossoms in the Earliest Written Sources of Japan

The two earliest records of Japan are the *Kojiki*, dated 712 A.D. and the *Nihonshoki*, dated 720 A.D. They were commissioned by Emperor Tenmu (r. 672–686) who intended to have compiled an official history of the imperial system. Both works show the process whereby folk agrarian cosmology was transformed into an official cosmology for the imperial household (for details, see Ohnuki-Tierney 1993). They also indicate a strenuous effort by Emperor Tenmu to establish a Japanese identity in order to distinguish it from the Chinese, whose culture was engulfing Japan at the time. This he did by adopting an oral folk tradition in which rice, introduced from the Asian continent, was appropriated as indigenous to Japan. Thus, a foreign element was turned Japanese *sui generis*.

There is no question that rice occupies a central place in these myth histories (see Ohnuki-Tierney 1993). The appearance of cherry blossoms, in contrast, is fairly limited. Therefore some scholars, such as Saitô (1985) (see below), dismiss altogether the significance of cherry blossoms in these myth histories. I, however, think that many of the major themes associated with cherry blossoms in later history are already present in these myth histories, even if they are not as articulated as they became in later periods.

First, the aforementioned symbolic association between rice and cherry blossoms is expressed in the marriage of Ninigi-no-Mikoto, the grandson of Amaterasu (Sun Goddess), who is central in the agrarian cosmology expressed in these myth histories. The Sun Goddess, ancestress of the Imperial Family, however, did not in fact acquire her importance until the imperial system became established (for details, see Ohnuki-Tierney 1991, 1993). When one day Ninigi-no-Mikoto encountered a beautiful woman, his wife-to-be, and inquired who she was, she was identified as Konohana-no-Sakuya-Bime. This episode appears both in the *Kojiki* (Kurano and Takeda 1958:131) and the *Nihonshoki* (Sakamoto et al. 1967:154). Although the *Kojiki* and the *Nihonshoki* contain many of the same episodes, the *Kojiki* contains records that contradict one another, indicating its earlier date of publication as well as a lesser amount of control in the process of compilation. Although some scholars object to interpreting the term *sakuya* in her name to mean *sakura* (cherry blossoms) (see below), I think there is enough evidence to assume that *sakuya* means *sakura* and therefore to conclude that the female deity represents cherry blossoms.

The first evidence comes from a later passage in the *Kojiki* (Kurano and Takeda 1958:133), which explains that, although emperors are supposed to live for a long time, because of Ninigi-no-Mikoto's marriage to this female deity whose name includes the word *sakuya* (that is, the cherry blossom whose major characteristic is a short life), emperors' lives are also short. In the *Nihonshoki* version, the union of these two deities is the reason why humans in general do not live long.

Some flowers have even shorter lives than cherry blossoms. However, the short life has been the major characteristic attributed to cherry blossoms in Japanese culture throughout history. Therefore, I interpret that the term *sakuya* refers to cherry blossoms, and not to any other flower, although Saitô (1985:39) argues that it simply means any flower. I also think that the episode offers evidence for the cultural association of the cherry blossom with its short life as early as the eighth century—the short life becoming a rich repository of symbolic meaning in later history.

Other evidence for an interpretation of *sakuya* as cherry blossoms comes from the agrarian cosmology in which cherry blossoms are symbolically associated with rice crops. In the episode of the *Kojiki* after the Sun Goddess, Amaterasu Ômikami, was established as the ancestral deity to the imperial family, the Sun Goddess is the mother of a grain soul whose name refers to the ear of the rice stalk ("Masakatsu Akatsu Kachihaya Hiame no Oshihomimi no Mikoto" [Kurano and Takeda 1958:111, 125]). She sends her grandson, Ninigi-no-Mikoto, to rule the earth. His other name is "Amatsu Hiko Hiko Ho no Ninigi no Mikoto," which portrays rice stalks with succulent grains (Kurano and Takeda 1958:125). Before his descent to earth Amaterasu gives her grandson the original rice grains that she has grown in the two fields in Heaven (Takamagahara) from the seeds of the five (i.e., many) kinds of grain (*gokoku*) given to her by Ukemochi no Kami, the deity in charge of food (Kurano and Takeda 1958; see also Murakami 1977:13). The grandson of Amaterasu transforms a wilderness into a country of rice stalks with succulent ears of rice (*mizuho*) and abundant grain of five kinds (*gokoku*), thanks to the original seeds given to him by Amaterasu. This is one version of Japan's creation myth.

In other words, Ninigi-no-Mikoto plays a pivotal role in the agrarian cosmology in which rice and rice agriculture were central. It seems a logical extension that he should marry a woman embodying the cherry blossoms that are thought to be the spring counterpart of the rice crop in the fall.

This episode also suggests that during the eighth century the cherry blossom was already a metaphor used for a woman by a man in love—a theme recurring throughout history.

The symbolic association between rice cum emperor and cherry blossoms also explains the next episode involving Emperor Richû. In the *Nihonshoki* (Sakamoto et al. 1967:425–26), when Emperor Richû stages a party in a boat on a lake, a single petal of a cherry blossom falls into the emperor's *sake* cup. Since it is not the time for cherry blossoms (November of the lunar calendar), the emperor is curious and sends his servant to locate the tree. The emperor is so delighted when the servant brings him a branch of the cherry tree that he names his palace "Waka-*Sakura*-no-Miya" (Palace of Young

Cherry Blossoms). In addition, he gives titles, using the term *young cherry blossoms*, to the servant who poured wine into his cup and to the one who fetched the cherry tree branch. In the *Kojiki*, although the episode of a petal falling into his cup does not appear, both the name of the palace and those of his servants appear (Kurano and Takeda 1958:283, 289).

I believe that since lunar November is the time for the rice harvest ritual (Ohnuki-Tierney 1993), the Emperor Richû episode provides additional evidence that rice and cherry blossoms were already symbolically affiliated at the time. Even without a direct reference to rice crops, this passage testifies to the symbolic association between cherry blossoms and the emperor who symbolizes rice. The episode is also a testimony to the establishment of the association between cherry blossom viewing and drinking at this time.

Another significant reference to cherry blossoms in the *Nihonshoki* involves Emperor Ingyô (Sakamoto et al. 1967:442–44). Although he had just taken a wife, he fell in love with a woman called "Sotohoshi-no-Iratsume." On his way to visit her in 419 A.D., he passed by a cherry tree with beautiful blossoms and lamented that he had not met her earlier—that is, before his marriage. This episode again demonstrates that the cherry blossom was a metaphor for a woman in the mind of a man in love. Furthermore, it also stands for a woman in an illicit relationship, foreshadowing its role as metaphor for the geisha in much later times.

The above passages show that most of the major symbolic themes involving cherry blossoms in later history were already present in the myth histories, although some were only in inchoate forms. These themes include: (1) cherry blossoms as the spring counterpart of the rice crop; (2) the drinking of *sake* as an integral feature of cherry blossom viewing; (3) cherry blossoms as an epitome of a short life; (4) cherry blossoms as a metaphor for a woman in the mind of a man in love; (5) cherry blossoms as a metaphor for a woman, for the man having an illicit love affair with her. Saitô (1985:39–42) dismisses the importance of cherry blossoms in these myth histories. He claims that the term for cherry blossoms is found only in the names of places and people and never as the object of aesthetic appreciation. Saitô's argument is puzzling, considering that in order to be in the names of people and places cherry blossoms had to be important for the people.

Cherry Blossom Viewing among the Elite

Although the Japanese, especially the elite, took pains to establish their own identity, as demonstrated by the compilation of the afore-mentioned myth histories, the Chinese were the significant Other for the Japanese elite who were in awe of their Han and Tang civi-lizations, adopting everything from their writing system to their metallurgy, city planning, and so on. This wholesale adoption inclu-ded the Chinese plum blossom aesthetics. Hence, in the oldest col-lection of poems in Japan, called *Manyôshû*, references to cherry blossoms occupy the eighth position in frequency of appearance of all flowers, and are far outnumbered by the references to plum blos-soms. The *Manyôshû* contains some 4,500 poems composed over 400 years until 759 A.D. References to cherry blossoms appear in poems by unknown poets and poets from rural Japan, indicating the importance of cherry blossoms among these people at a time when the upper-class Japanese were still embracing the imported aes-thetics of plum blossoms (Saitô 1985:41–43; Wakamori 1975:172–73). Praise for the beauty of cherry blossoms by less well-known poets may be interpreted as a satirical commentary on the court life in Kyoto (Wakamori 1975:172–73).

Despite cherry blossoms being overshadowed by plum blossoms in the mid-eighth century *Manyôshû*, in 812 A.D. the imperial fam-ily hosted, for the first time in history, a cherry blossom viewing party (*kan'ô-kai*) (Nihon hôsô kyôkai 1988). By the mid-ninth cen-tury, the plum tree planted on the left-hand side of the main build-ing (*shishinden*) of the imperial palace in Kyoto was replaced by a mountain cherry tree (Nihon hôsô kyôkai 1988), indicating that the association of cherry blossoms with the imperial household was firmly established. It was only in 1868 that the Meiji government decided that the sixteen petal chrysanthemum should be the impe-rial crest and began restricting the use of the crest or anything resembling it by other Japanese (Murakami 1977:179–82).

Cherry blossom viewing among the aristocrats developed into an elaborate affair accompanied by drinking, feasting, and later by masquerades. Most important, however, was the composition and reading of poems about cherry blossoms by the hosts and guests. Cherry blossom viewing became *the* occasion for the literati to demonstrate their ability in *bun*, which refers to the refined qualities of being "cultured" (the opposite of *bu*, might or excellence in warfare). By the same token, these lavish aristocratic cherry blossom viewings were also occasions for the hosts to display their political power and wealth.

By the time of *Kokinwakashû*, a collection of poems compiled in either 905 or 914 A.D., cherry blossoms were decisively at the center stage of love and aesthetics. The most frequent motif was cherry blossoms as a metaphor for beautiful women used by the male poets.

In addition to the written sources, the visual arts provide a wealth of material on the cherry blossom and its viewing in different periods of history. Cherry blossoms appear quite frequently in the *yamato-e*, which is the Japanese style of painting established during the latter half of the ninth century in opposition to the Chinese style painting (*kanga*) that had dominated Japanese art until then. Again we see that cherry blossoms were chosen as a symbol of the Japanese and Japanese art, as opposed to Chinese art. The *yamato-e* tradition focused on the depiction of the four seasons and each month of the year, all of which were represented by flowers and other features of nature (Shinbo 1982).

The tenth to twelfth centuries saw the development of scroll paintings reach its peak. Called *e-makimono*, these paintings told famous stories by means of lavish illustrations depicting critical scenes. They are an enormously rich source of information on cherry blossoms and their viewing. Numerous versions of the *Genji Monogatari E-maki*, scroll paintings of *The Tale of Genji* by Murasaki Shikibu, are the best-known examples, especially the one painted by Tokugawa Reimeikai during the first half of the twelfth century (Shinmura 1990:770). A number of scenes from *The Tale of Genji* depict cherry blossoms. *The Tale of Genji* was instrumental in establishing *mono no aware* (pathos as an important theme in the Japanese ethos). Indicating that the *aware* appears 1018 times in *Genji Monogatari* (The Tale of Genji), Morris (1979:207–208) explains *aware*:

> The accepted pattern of sensibility that was so highly valued in Murasaki's time is summed up by *aware*, one of the many untranslatable ... words that are used to define Japanese aesthetics. ... its [*aware*'s] most characteristic use in *The Tale of Genji* is to suggest the pathos inherent in the beauty of the

outer world, a beauty that is inexorably fated to disappear together with the observer. Buddhist doctrines about the evanescence of all living things naturally influenced this particular content of the word, but the stress in *aware* was always on direct emotional experience rather than on religious understanding. *Aware* never entirely lost its simple interjectional sense of "Ah!"

Cherry blossoms whose delicate petals fall to earth after a few days could not have been more appropriate for symbolizing the aesthetics of pathos, based upon the realization of the fragility of all beings (see Shinbo 1982). *The Tale of Genji*, however, does not directly link *aware* with cherry blossoms.

It seems clear then that the aesthetics of cherry blossoms developed hand in hand with the *cultural nationalism* of the Japanese elite at that time, who were anxious to establish their own identity as distinct from the Chinese after several centuries during which they whole-heartedly had embraced the Chinese civilization, including the aesthetics of the plum blossom. During the late ancient period and throughout the medieval period, the aesthetics of the cherry blossom, as depicted in the visual arts, praised in poems and prose, and viewed during elaborate rituals, became the hallmark of aristocratic culture. The plum blossom continued to be an object of aesthetics, especially in the *sumi-e* (ink paintings by brush strokes) and various other representations, but there is no question that the cherry blossom had become far more important.

The blossom's importance and centrality is, in a somewhat ironic way, disclosed by a famous cherry blossom viewing hosted by Toyotomi Hideyoshi, a sixteenth-century warrior of unknown origin, who was the first person to conquer and unify Japan. He hosted two elaborate cherry blossom viewing spectacles complete with poetry recitations, one in 1594 at Yoshino and the other at Sanpôin of Daigo Temple in Kyoto in March 1598. The latter was held shortly before his death and was the last of his spectacles (Ogawa 1991:114–24; Yamada 1993 [1990]:220–22).

I believe that the *bu* (might) was not enough to convince Hideyoshi of his worth, and that the ultimate validation of his worth had to come from *bun* (culture). If so, Hideyoshi's cherry blossom viewing spectacle was highly significant in demonstrating that at that time the cherry blossom stood out as the antithesis of, and was superior to, military aggression—a hierarchy that was reversed during the later military periods.

It should also be noted that during the medieval period, *chigo*—young boys at temples who were frequented by older priests—were also said to be as beautiful as cherry blossoms (Matsuoka 1991).

Cherry Blossom Viewing among Common People

As with most historical records, information concerning the common people is less available than information concerning the elite (see Ohnuki-Tierney (1987) for a detailed discussion of the "common people" in relation to the development of "Agrarian Japan"). However, during the Keichô and Genwa periods (1596–1624) a number of paintings emerged that depicted the leisure activities of both commoners and elite. There are a number of scroll paintings in which cherry blossom viewing by common people is depicted. Although the aristocrats held their own private cherry blossom viewing parties at their manors, they also visited places famous for cherry blossoms and shared the pleasure with the common people, albeit often demarcating their area with curtains (Harada and Yamana 1983).

As portrayed by Ono (1992), cherry blossom viewing among common people reached its zenith during the Edo period (1603–1868) when common people in Edo (Tokyo) developed a tradition of cherry blossom viewing that became their major annual event—an event complete with costumes and feasting, as well as with their own genre of poems called *senryû*.

There are two forms of art—one visual and one performance—that played a crucial role in the development of the symbolism of cherry blossoms in Edo, and later in most of Japan. They are the *ukiyo-e*, or the woodblock prints, and the *kabuki* theater. Both art forms were developed by the emerging merchant class (*chônin*). Woodblock prints became the major medium for propagating the symbols of Japanese cultural nationalism (such as Mt. Fuji, rice and activities related to rice agriculture, cherry blossoms, and *sumô* wrestlers), although most masters of woodblock printing may not have had political motivations. Woodblock prints provided a close association between specific locations and cherry blossoms, so that people would identify and relate to, for example, a temple with a famous old cherry tree. Most influential were series such as *Edo Meisho Hyakkei* (One hundred famous sites in Edo) by Andô Hiroshige (1797–1858), and *Edo Meisho Zue* (Illustrated book on the famous sites in Edo) illustrated by Hasegawa Settan, edited by Saitô Sachio, and published between 1829 and 1836.

Of particular importance is the association propagated by these woodblock prints between "night cherry blossoms" (*yozakura*) and *geisha*, through their depiction of Yoshiwara Nakano-chô, the famous *geisha* quarters in Edo. The "mysterious seductiveness" of cherry blossoms at night became very different in implication from that of cherry blossoms against the blue daytime sky, echoing the old association between cherry blossoms and an illicit love affair of Emperor Ingyô, and suggesting another dimension of this complex field of meaning.

The *kabuki* theater was equally, if not more, influential in the propagation of cherry blossom symbolism. Famous plays, such as *Yoshitsune Senbonzakura* (Yoshitsune and One Thousand Cherry Trees) and *Sakura-hime Azumabunshô* (Cherry Blossom Princess) effectively used the motif of cherry trees and cherry blossoms. For the purpose of this project, the most decisive development was the staging of the *Kanadehon Chûshingura* on the Kabuki theater (by Takemotoza) in 1748. It was an adaptation of a play of *jôruri* (puppet theater) based on the famous story of the forty-seven warriors who, in 1703, took revenge on their master (Asano Naganori) who was humiliated and ordered to commit suicide. (See Maruya [1984] for the importance of this story for the Japanese.) Used in the production was a proverb, *hanawa sakuragi hito wa bushi* (Cherry blossoms are the flower among flowers and warriors are the human among humans). This is a saying of unknown origin that until this time had been used only occasionally. The *kabuki* play established the association of cherry blossoms with the warrior class. It also popularized the proverb that became familiar to almost all Japanese, and still is today (Ogawa 1993:15–16; Saitô 1985:53–54; Yamada 1993:96, 215–16, 224–25, 440–41, 452). Thus, during the mid-Edo period, while the people in Edo developed cherry blossom viewing into a full-blown folk festival, the association of cherry blossoms with warriors got underway.

Cherry Blossoms in Later History

Although most of the activities related to cherry blossoms may be regarded as "leisure" activities, those that took place during the height of militarism were far from being leisure activities. The military government used the association between cherry blossoms and a short life as a symbolic weapon to urge soldiers to die for their country.

In contemporary Japan, some still remember the morbid associations of cherry blossoms during the war. However, immediately after the end of World War II, the Japanese took up cherry blossom viewing again. Today cherry blossom viewing is enormously popular among people from all walks of life. In fact, the whole nation seems to go into a frenzy over cherry blossoms. At the end of March they wait in anticipation, with newspapers and other mass media offering daily forecasts. They draw a map of Japan, from Okinawa to Hokkaido, on which are charted the expected dates for cherry blossoms to bloom. The map, that looks like a map indicating the approach of a typhoon, is referred to as *sakura zensen*. When they start to bloom, television covers cherry blossom viewing in each region as well as numerous festivals associated with cherry blossoms. The season for cherry blossoms coincides with the Buddhist flower festivals commemorating the birth of Buddha on April 7.

The beginning of April is the start of the school year, the fiscal year, and the time of new hiring at companies. Hence April is the beginning of the new year, vibrant with excitement and hope for new life. The whole nation celebrates the new beginning with flowers, especially cherry blossoms.

As if to express the social mosaic of contemporary Japanese society, each social group has its own cherry blossom viewing. Although the activities are all referred to as cherry blossom viewing (*hanami*), each has a different meaning depending upon the viewer. Women and family members go during the daytime to view cherry blossoms at nearby locations, such as along the river banks, with their lunches. On weekends, they go with the father, who is considered to do "family service" (*kazoku sâbisu*) for the family since he is often absent from their daily life on weekdays. Pupils from kindergarten to high school go on school trips to view cherry blossoms. College students go with friends, or view at their own universities, some of which are well known for their cherry blossoms.

It has also become a major event for most companies, especially for medium-sized and small companies (*chûshôkigyô*), and small branches of large companies. Early in the morning each section of the company sends their most recently hired employee, usually a male, to spread a mat to secure a good place so that the rest of the people in the section can go there with food and drink after work. He demarcates an area with a plastic spread and hangs pieces of paper on which are written the company name and the time their feasting shall commence. He then waits all day, taking naps or reading. From around 6:00 P.M., the rest of the company members arrive. On these occasions "bosses" in the company do not want to dampen the atmosphere with their presence; it is considered appropriate for them to offer money or food and drink instead. Eating and especially drinking continue to be the most important ingredient of the occasion. Most are equipped with barbecue grills or portable stoves, and cook their *oden* and other foods that are traditional at cherry blossom viewings. Another common feature is *karaoke*. One used to bring one's own equipment for the *karaoke*, but now one usually rents the equipment from a company who sends a man with the *karaoke* equipment on a bicycle who cycles from one firm to the next in the same area. The event used to last until late into the night. Now, however, policemen, a ubiquitous presence at Ueno and other places renowned for drinking parties, turn off the lights and with loudspeakers tell people to leave at 8:00 on week nights and a little later on weekends. Many continue their party (*nijikai*) at local bars, which the policemen continue to watch for possible violence, as policemen at Ueno Park explained to me.

There is a clear spatial pattern for different kinds of cherry blossom viewing. Thus, certain places, such as Shinjuku Gyoen or Jindaiji Temple, are for noneating, nondrinking viewing. Some individuals are avid photographers equipped with fancy cameras. Others gaze at the beauty of the flower. Many family members, young and old, visit together—Jindaiji, for example, draws people of all ages—whereas other places, such as Shinjuku Gyoen, are for the younger population. Other sites, such as Ueno Park and Mukôjima, are known for nocturnal company feasts under night cherries. I have seen the physically handicapped, escorted by the officials of their facilities, visit various sites of cherry blossoms, but only during the daytime.

Discussion

My cursory sketch of the significance of cherry blossoms in Japanese culture and history excluded, for reasons of length, many findings about cherry blossoms and their viewing that generate further complexity in their cultural meanings and their historical transformations. Although I find the information I have gathered to date dazzlingly complex, I have, needless to say, only scratched the surface of this enormously complex topic that has been at the core of Japanese culture throughout history.

In the remainder of the chapter, I offer some explanations for the fascination of cherry blossoms that Japanese have, who are not simply following or reproducing the "tradition," but have actively reappropriated and recreated this leisure activity.

Symbolism of the Cherry Blossom

The Polysemic Cherry Blossom

The cursory review of the cherry blossom and its viewing in historical perspective proves that it stood for a host of enormously different referents. They were women in the minds of men in legitimate relationships as well as *geisha* whose relationships with men were illicit, albeit culturally sanctioned at the time. Conversely, they represented warriors and soldiers, men among men. Furthermore, they stood for homosexual temple boys.

Some revered cherry trees are old trees. The term *ubazakura* (elderly women cherry blossoms) refers to a type of cherry whose blossoms come out before its leaves emerge, which differs from the mountain cherry blossoms that bloom simultaneously with the leaves' emergence. Since the pronunciation *ha* is a homonym both for leaves and teeth, the cherry is called *uba*—elderly women without teeth. It should be noted that the term *uba* conveys a positive image of elderly women. At the same time, as we saw earlier, young cherry trees, *wakazakura* (young cherry blossoms), are also praised.

We saw that one of the principal meanings of the cherry blossom is its short life. It is important to realize that the concept of a short life represents both life and death, since death is preceded by a short life. In fact, Yanagita (1970a, 1970b) indicates the rural practice of planting cherry trees, especially young ones, in cemeteries. He took special note of the importance for rural people of drooping cherries whose branches fall to the ground, for they believed that the soul of a deceased person traveled through the blue sky and down to the ground through these cherry trees. Again we see that cherry trees represent both life and death.

Even in urban areas cherry blossoms are closely associated with cemeteries. When the Meiji government took over the manors of feudal lords, they converted them into Tokyo's large municipal cemeteries, some of which, such as Aoyama-bochi in Aoyama and Somei-reien near Sugamo, are famous for their cherry blossoms and attract many people in their season.

Cherry blossoms only superficially represent mere categories of people and phenomena. At a deeper level they represent relationships and processes. Thus, cherry blossoms do not represent women in abstract, but women in relation to men in love. The same holds true in the case of the temple boys. In short, cherry blossoms are symbols par excellence of the bonds between "humans," which, in Japanese, are written with two characters—*nin* (human, person) and *gen* (among). In other words, for the Japanese a society consists of *interdependent* individuals. In short, cherry blossoms represent the most fundamental notion of social persona in Japanese culture (for a detailed account of "personhood" in Japanese culture, see Ohnuki-Tierney 1981, 1987).

Similarly, cherry blossoms represent the cyclical process of life and death: life leading to death and death predicated upon life and followed by rebirth.

Association of Cherry Blossoms with the Principal Theme of the Japanese Ethos cum Cosmology

The meaning of cherry blossoms becomes even more complex when we examine it in the context of Japanese cosmology. Geertz

(1973), in his well-known distinction between world view and ethos, emphasized the complementarity of a world view, the cognitive dimension of our behavior, and ethos, the affective dimension. Geertz (1973:126) writes: "the ethos is made intellectually reasonable ... [by] world view ... and the world view is made emotionally acceptable by [ethos]." His point is that sacred symbols "relate an ontology and a cosmology to an aesthetics and a morality; their peculiar power comes from their presumed ability to identify fact with value at the most fundamental level." I suggest that Geertz's point applies to all evocative symbols, and not just sacred symbols.

A dominant characterization of cherry blossoms throughout Japanese history is its short life, its fragility. It appears as early as the eighth-century myth histories. Throughout subsequent periods, the fragility of cherry blossoms was chosen as the major symbolic expression of *mono no aware*—the aesthetics of pathos, which has been one of the core principles of the Japanese ethos *cum* world view, at least of the elite. In my view thoughts and feelings are inseparable in practice, that is, in our behavior, including perception and conceptualization. In fact, I believe that the inseparability of the two dimensions is the source of power of symbols in all cultures. The *mono no aware* represents *feeling* (pathos) about the *thought* (the fragility of life). The two are embodied in cherry blossoms that, therefore, serve as what Langer (1980 [1942]:79–102; see also Langer 1953) calls a presentational symbol.

Aesthetics of Symbols and Symbolic Actions

Most importantly, the source of evocation (see Turner, esp. 1975a [1974]; 1975b) of the cherry blossom lies in its aesthetics, which simultaneously evokes both thought and feeling, and plays a significant role in real action, as in wartime (see Burke 1966 for the concept of symbolic action).

As is evident from the historical survey presented above, the aesthetics of the blossom underscores every major meaning of cherry blossoms. In the agrarian cosmology, cherry blossoms were the seat of the Deity of Rice Paddies. In Japanese folk shintoism, as in most religions, deities were assigned the value of purity, which in turn is assigned an aesthetic value (Ohnuki-Tierney 1993). Whether as a symbol of pathos, or that of a warrior's or a soldier's death during the subsequent periods, cherry blossoms have always been portrayed as beautiful.

The aesthetics of the cherry blossom may seem too obvious to point out. However, the crucial importance of the aesthetics becomes evident when we consider how the *sensory* beauty of the flower is transferred to various referents of this symbol, even to warriors' and soldiers' deaths. The transference of the notion of the fragility of life from the flowers to a human life was achieved in the film productions of *Chûshingura* during the Meiji period when the suicide of the master was enacted through a spectacular cascade of cherry blossoms falling onto the stage. The play further promoted the significance of warriors as the human among humans, just as cherry blossoms are the flower among flowers. The play paved the way for the association of soldiers and cherry blossoms during later military periods. Like cherry blossoms, the voluntary death of soldiers was meant to be beautiful. *Death acquires an aesthetic quality as a result of transference of the sensory beauty of cherry blossoms* (see Mosse [1975:19, 20] for political significance of aesthetics).

Aesthetics as the source of symbolic evocation also explains why cherry blossoms symbolize such desperate referents as they have done in the historical perspective: women, men among men (warriors and soldiers); death as well as life; etc. The common denominator for all is aesthetics—they are all perceived as beautiful.

Conclusion

The complexity of the symbolic representation of cherry blossoms poses a challenge to the way anthropologists have often viewed symbols and their referents. First, the meaning and poetic functions of symbols should never be interpreted without reference to those who use them, since the meaning depends upon the agent who uses it (Ohnuki-Tierney 1990). Through their concept of "indexicality" (Burks 1948–49; Peirce 1960) Peirce and his followers have emphasized the importance of agents. Cherry blossoms demonstrate the importance of agents. That is, they do not represent women per se; they represent women only in relation to men who use cherry blossoms as the metaphor for the women with whom they are in love.

Second, it defies any simplistic notion of multivocality or polysemy, which hitherto considered a symbol as having a limited set of meanings. The cherry blossom has an almost infinite number of meanings, some of which are diametrically opposite to each other, for example, women and men.

Thirdly, the richness and complexity of the meanings of the cherry blossom urge us to establish levels of abstraction for each meaning—a task necessary for any complex symbol, as I elaborated in an earlier work (Ohnuki-Tierney 1981). At the first level, cherry blossoms represent women, men, life, and death. At another level, they represent the relationships and processes between categories—men and women, life and death.

At another, yet higher level of abstraction involving the Japanese world view and ethos, cherry blossoms stand for *mono no aware*—pathos. Ultimately, however, it is the aesthetics of cherry blossoms that is not merely the cognitive and emotive dimensions of the flower but also the source of its evocative power.

Cherry Blossom Viewing as Social Activity

The Cherry Blossom as a Symbol of a Social Group

Although an important meaning of cherry blossoms involves love— the bond between two individuals—cherry blossoms have also been a metaphor representing a particular social group. It has been the flower for farmers, urbanites, imperial families, aristocrats, warriors, men, and women, with each group appropriating and then reconstituting its meaning and aesthetics. As the spring counterpart of the rice crop, cherry blossoms were important for the farmer, just as they were to the imperial family whose ideological foundation rested on an agrarian cosmology. The aristocrat praised its beauty in poems and literature and staged spectacular cherry blossom viewings. The aristocratic culture was emulated and adopted by the upper-class warriors who aspired to be "cultured." The blossom, having been adopted by the upper-class city dwellers, was embraced also by the urban common people who created their own version of aesthetics and appreciation of the flower. During the military period, the symbolism of cherry blossoms was re-invented by the military government and the leaders of the time. Today, cherry blossom viewing is a major annual event for Japanese from all strata of society.

The various social groups not only appropriated cherry blossoms as a metaphor of their own groups, they actively used the occasion of cherry blossom viewing as an opportunity to strengthen intragroup bonds by commensality. It is due to this reason that the annual cherry blossom viewing is of enormous importance for companies. In fact, in some companies it is almost impossible for the members not to participate in the event, lest they be ostracized.

Most importantly, cherry blossoms were from the very beginning *marked* as the flower to represent the Japanese collective self. Thus its birth as an important symbol took place *in the discourse with the Other—with the Chinese.* This was accomplished by replacing, at least partially, the Chinese aesthetics of plum blossoms, which the Japanese had initially embraced, *and* by establishing the cherry blossom's symbolic association with rice. As I wrote in some detail in my book (Ohnuki-Tierney 1993), rice and rice paddies became the major metaphor for the Japanese, as opposed to other peoples, throughout history. As mentioned earlier, cherry blossoms became a major motif of the *yamato-e* tradition of art, which was developed in opposition to the Chinese style of art. The emergence of the association between the cherry blossom and the Japanese self during their respective early histories is of enormous importance as it planted the possibility for later periods to transform the flower into various expressions of cultural and political nationalism.

Cherry Blossom Viewing and Social Stratification

The representation of a social group by cherry blossoms and their viewing is, however, far more complex than the same flower representing each and every social group. From the perspective of class structure, cherry blossom viewing defies any "trickle down" theory, which has often been used as an explanatory model. With his central concern with class structure, Bourdieu uses the notion of *symbolic violence*, which he defines as "the gentle, invisible form of violence" that imposes the ideology and lifestyle of the dominant class upon the working class (Bourdieu 1977:192). In Japan, white rice diffused from the upper class downward (Ohnuki-Tierney 1993), just as white bread did in England (Thompson 1971) and white sugar did in England and elsewhere (Mintz 1985). These are only some examples of the general pattern in which an upper-class taste trickles down to the people.

Not so with cherry blossom viewing. The diffusion of the symbolism of the cherry blossom is complex. It involved an upward diffusion of agrarian ideology from farmers to the political elite including the imperial family. On the other hand, there is no question that the symbolism of the cherry blossom and its viewing, as evolved by the elite, trickled at least partially downward in later history, just as much of the agrarian ideology of the elite, including the symbolism of rice, did.

However, we noted that the urban common people of the Edo period were not simple emulators of the elite culture. They created their own aesthetics of the flower and of the viewing. In fact, in relation to the subsequent periods, especially to the military uses of cherry blossoms in the 1930s, the merchant-class culture was far more influential, as we saw, than the aristocratic culture of early times, although, as Marx's (1989 [1852]:320) insightful remarks would have it, the artists involved in the production of woodblock prints and *kabuki* theater certainly did not shape history as they had intended.

Another important point on the relationship of the cherry blossom viewing with social stratification is that it is not predicated upon the presence of different social classes, as almost all spectator entertainment in Japan (and elsewhere) is. As detailed elsewhere (Ohnuki-Tierney 1987), almost all street entertainment was performed by those so-called "outcast." Even the *kabuki* originated as performances by the members of this social class. Thus, any performance involved members of both the "outcast" and other social classes.

Cherry blossom viewing represents leisure activities in Japan in which members of the same social group participate. To conclude, however, that these leisure activities represent communitas, as Victor Turner did in his ritual analyses, is too hasty. The company cherry blossom viewing is embedded in the stratification within the company. The most recent employee procures a place for the rest of his colleagues. Bosses often donate money, or food and drink, but they do not participate.

Summary

Cultural meanings assigned to cherry blossoms and their viewing offer a powerful lens through which we can look at most significant dimensions of Japanese culture throughout history. The flower has represented every social group, has represented social relationships as well as the life-cycle process.

I suggested in the beginning that we view the complex involving the symbolism and appreciation of cherry blossoms as a *total social phenomenon* (to use Mauss's term), which entails many dimensions. In ancient Japan, cherry blossoms and their viewing were of religious significance, just as all leisure activities were. Orikuchi (1976:62) points out that during the ancient time the term *asobi* (play) referred to the dance performed to placate the soul of the guardian deity of the nation or the household. Similarly, Akima (1972; 1982:498–500) argues that the term *asobi*, whose literal meaning today is to play, denoted music making rather than playing in general. During this early period in history, the term referred to merry-making—singing, dancing, and drinking.

But, to single out a religious dimension is to misrepresent the phenomenon in that any total social phenomenon simultaneously entails multiple dimensions—the religious, the recreational, the political, the economic, the symbolic, and so forth. Even today a visit to a temple or a shrine for healing often involves not only medical and religious dimensions but also social and recreational elements—going with one's family members or friends and eating and shopping for foods known in the area (see Ohnuki-Tierney 1984 for a detailed discussion on the topic).

Given their complexity and multiple dimensions as well as their evocative power, cherry blossoms and their viewing have provided opportunities for various historical agents to *re*-create meanings of cherry blossoms and the event of their viewing.

References

Akima Toshio. 1972. "Shisha no uta—Saimei Tennô no Kayô to Asobibe," *Bungaku* 40/3, 97–112 (337–52).

————. 1982. "The songs of the dead: Poetry, drama, and ancient rituals of Japan," *Journal of Asian Studies* 41/3, 485–509.

Blacker, Carmen. 1975. *The catalpa bow: A study of shamanistic practices in Japan.* London: George Allen & Unwin.

Bourdieu, Pierre. 1977. *Outline of a theory of practice.* [Original publication in French in 1972] Cambridge: Cambridge University Press.

Burke, Kenneth. 1966. *Language as symbolic action.* Berkeley: University of California Press.

Burks, Arthur W. 1948–49. "Icon, index, and symbol," *Philosophy and Phenomenological Research* 9, 673–89.

Geertz, Clifford. 1973. *The interpretation of cultures.* New York: Basic Books.

Harada Tomohiko and Yamana Yûzô (eds.). 1983. *Kinsei fûzoku zufu 2, Yûraku.* Tokyo: Shôgakukan.

Kurano Kenji and Takeda Yûkichi (eds.). 1958. *Kojiki Norito.* Tokyo: Iwanami shoten.

Langer, Susanne, K. 1953 [1942]. *Philosophy in a new key: A study in the symbolism of reason, rite and art.* Cambridge, Mass.: Harvard University Press.

————. 1980. *Feeling and form.* New York: Charles Scribner's Sons.

Maruya Saiichi. 1984. *Chûshingura to wa nanika.* Tokyo: Kôdansha.

Marx, Karl. 1989 [1852]. "Excerpts from the Eighteenth Brumaire of Louis Bonaparte," Lewis S. Feuer (ed.). *Basic writings on politics and philosophy: Karl Marx and Friedrich Engels.* Garden City, N.Y.: Doubleday, 318–48.

Matsuoka Shinpei. 1991. *Utage no shintai—Basara kara Zeami e.* Tokyo: Iwanami shoten.

Mauss, Marcel. 1966. *The gift: Forms and functions of exchange in archaic societies.* [Original publication in French in 1925] London: Cohen & West.

Mintz, Sidney W. 1985. *Sweetness and power: The place of sugar in modern history.* New York: Viking.

Miyake Hitoshi. 1978. *Shugendô—Yamabushi no rekishi to shisô.* Tokyo: Kyôikusha.

Morris, Ivan. 1979 [1964]. *The world of the Shining Prince: Court life in ancient Japan.* New York: Penguin Books.

Mosse, George. 1975. *The nationalization of the masses: Political symbolism and mass movements in Germany from the Napoleonic Wars through the Third Reich.* Ithaca, N.Y.: Cornell University Press.

Murakami Shigeyoshi. 1977. *Tennô no saishi.* Tokyo: Iwanami shoten.

Nihon hôsô kyôkai (ed.). 1988. *Nihon no bi: Sakura.* Video. Tokyo: Nihon hôsô kyôkai.

Ogawa Kazusuke. 1991. *Sakura no bungakushi.* Tokyo: Asahi shinbunsha.

———. 1993. *Sakura to nihonjin.* Tokyo: Shinchôsha sensho.

Ohnuki-Tierney, Emiko. 1981. "Phases in human perception/cognition/symbolization processes: Cognitive anthropology and symbolic classification," *American Ethnologist* 8/3, 451–67.

———. 1984. *Illness and culture in contemporary Japan: An anthropological view.* Cambridge: Cambridge University Press. 4th reprinting in 1989.

———. 1987. *The monkey as mirror: Symbolic transformations in Japanese history and ritual.* Princeton, N.J.: Princeton University Press.

———. 1990. "Monkey as metaphor? Transformations of a polytropic symbol in Japanese culture," *Man* (N.S.) 25 (1990), 399–416.

———. 1991. "The emperor of Japan as deity (*kami*): An anthropology of the imperial system in historical perspective," *Ethnology* 30/3, 1–17.

———. 1993. *Rice as self: Japanese identities through time.* Princeton, N.J.: Princeton University Press.

Ono Sawako. 1992. *Edo no hanami.* Tokyo: Tsukiji Shokan.

Orikuchi Shinobu. 1975 [1928]. "Hana no hanashi," *Orikuchi Shinobu zenshû* 2, 467–93. Tokyo: Chûôkôronsha.

———. 1976 [1947]. "Nihon bungaku no hassei," *Orikuchi Shinobu Zenshû*, vol. 7, 44–72. Tokyo: Chûôkôronsha.

Peirce, Charles S. 1960 [1932]. "The icon, index, and symbol," *Collected papers of Charles Sanders Peirce*, vols. I, II. Charles Hartshorne and Paul Weiss (eds.). Cambridge, Mass.: Belknap Press of Harvard University Press, 156–73.

Saitô Shôji. 1985 [1979]. *Shokubutsu to Nihon bunka.* Tokyo: Yasaka shobô.

Sakamoto Tarô, Ienaga Saburô, Inoue Mitsusada, and Ono Susumu (eds.). 1967. *Nihonshoki* 1. Tokyo: Iwanami shoten.

Sakurai Mitsuru. 1974. *Hana no minzokugaku.* Tokyo: Yûzankaku.

Shinbo Tôru (ed.). 1982. *Yamato-e no shiki: Kachô-ga no sekai* 1. Tokyo: Gakushû kenkyûsha.

Shinmura Izuru (ed.). 1990 [1955]. *Kôjien.* Tokyo: Iwanami shoten.

Thompson, E. P. 1971. "The moral economy of the English crowd in the eighteenth century," *Past and Present* 50, 76–136.

Turner, Victor. 1975a [1974]. *Dramas, fields, and metaphors: Symbolic action in human society.* Ithaca, N.Y.: Cornell University Press.

———. 1975b. "Symbolic studies," *Annual Review of Anthropology* 4, 145–61.

Wakamori Tarô. 1975. *Hana to Nihonjin.* Tokyo: Sôgetsu shuppan.

Yamada Takao. 1993 [1990]. *Ôshi.* Tokyo: Kôdansha.

Yanagita Kunio. 1970a [1930]. "Shidare-zakura no mondai," *Yanagita Kunio-shû* 22. Tokyo: Chikuma Shobô, 213–19.

———. 1970b [1930]. "Shinanozakura no hanashi," *Yanagita Kunio-shû* 22. Tokyo: Chikuma shobô, 220–27.

———. 1982 [1947]. "Yamamiya-kô," *Yanagita Kunio-shû* 11. Tokyo: Chikuma shobô, 299–358.

——— (ed.). 1951. *Minzokugaku jiten.* Tokyo: Tôkyôdô.

Angelika Hamilton-Oehrl

12

Leisure Parks in Japan

Since World War II leisure parks in Japan have developed into a socioeconomic phenomenon that has advanced beyond the image of mere "children's entertainment" and must now be recognized as an important economic factor as well as a sophisticated service industry. Their layout can even be regarded as an indicator of the general patterns in leisure pursuits.

This chapter aims at approaching leisure parks from three different angles. First it will examine their economic importance and, second, their role in politics—these two factors are closely related—to demonstrate how important the leisure industry in Japan has become. Finally it will consider the implications of the development of leisure parks by looking at the changing trends of the industry.

The term *leisure park* is used very broadly and denotes a wide variety of facilities with very differing layouts. In Japanese one finds such terms as *rejâ rando*, *famirî rando*, *gorakuen*, or *yuenchi*. Their main common feature is that they are commercially operated enterprises, an important distinction from public leisure institutions such as museums or zoological gardens with primarily a cultural or educational background (Agricola et al. 1986:69).

This chapter will concentrate on three main types of leisure parks, which I classify as amusement parks, theme parks, and resort parks. Amusement parks have the character of static fairs, whereas theme parks such as Disneyland go a step further by organizing their attractions according to a certain theme. Resort parks are of the "Euro Disney Resort" type—parks that provide facilities and incentives for a longer and recreational stay in addition to the thrill of the rides.

There is in Japan a thriving leisure park business that exceeds even that of North America. The total number of leisure parks in Japan is estimated at being well above 250. In 1992 their total number of visitors was over 60 million and sales in the parks reached 415 billion Yen (Hasegawa 1993:148).

Tokyo Disneyland is by far the most successful of the four Disneyparks world wide with a record of 16.14 million visitors in 1991. It is followed by Toshimaen and Nagasaki Oranda Mura, each with about 4 million visitors per year (Gekkan Rejâ Sangyô 1992: 144–45). It is, however, not only the huge turnover from the tickets and sales that make the leisure parks an important economic factor. Quite unique to Japan are the extensive cross links between the leisure parks and the other economic sectors beyond the leisure industry. These intertwine the leisure park business with the general development of the economy.

The most traditional investors in Japanese leisure parks are railway companies. Although by the turn of the century many amusement facilities had developed on sites traditionally visited by people for recreational purposes, such as public parks, famous historical and religious sites, *onsen* and flower and foliage viewing spots (Fichtner and Michna 1986:160), the most crucial stage of development began with the expansion of the urban excursion traffic. Private railway companies played a dominant role in promoting domestic tourism and founded amusement parks along their lines to increase the number of passengers. The most famous example is the Takarazuka Familyland founded by the Hankyu-Line in 1923 (Schöller 1980:145). The spectrum of investors in leisure parks broadened after World War II when, in the wake of the leisure boom, the number of leisure parks increased dramatically. 90 percent of today's parks were opened after 1950. Not only banks and insurance companies discovered that leisure parks could be profitable investment opportunities for surplus capital—oil companies, media groups, and toy manufacturers also emerged as shareholders or entrepreneurs.

When the oil shock slowed down the Japanese economy it brought to the park business many new investors who had left the energy-consuming heavy industry and now sought to strengthen the service industry.

Nagasaki Oranda Mura, for example, has 250 shareholders from all branches of the economy—from the Industrial Bank of Japan to Yamaha Motors and Kirin Brewery—many of whom seek to promote their products through association with leisure parks (NHV Material A).

In addition to the diverse background of the investors, leisure parks also multiply their links with other economic branches by diversifying their own economic activities. Korakuen, for example, did not only incorporate congress centers and exhibition halls but also set up hotels, supermarket chains, and financing agencies to spread the financial risks.

With such a broad basis of business activities leisure parks naturally have an enlivening impact upon the regional economy. The establishment of a leisure park not only creates jobs, but accompanying its construction there are improvements in the area's infrastructure. Since the decline of many industries, such as ship building, and the move away from heavy industry to service industry, the implementation of leisure parks has given some towns valuable incentives to shift the economic structure of the region to the tourist industry and thus make up for the lost jobs. Not only did this reduce the migration into towns, but the introduction of leisure industry instead of heavy industry curtailed the pollution threat from the latter (NHV Material A).

Along with the growth of their economic significance the support of leisure parks has increasingly been taken into account in policy making.[1] In the course of the trade dispute in 1987, caused by Japan's export surplus, the support of the leisure sector was an important factor for discussion during international economic negotiations. In the face of strong international criticism of Japan's "unfair" trade strategies, the Japanese government was pressed to shorten the yearly working hours, which were still far longer than in other countries, and to increase the domestic consumption of goods and services. The government promoted the extension of the leisure infrastructure as well as the beneficial use of free time to prove that Japan was on its way to becoming a "superpower in quality of life" (*seikatsu taikoku*) and thus counterbalance the negative image of the Japanese as "workaholics" (Chua Eoan 1993:42).

A so-called resort-law (*rizôto-hô*, full name: *sôgô hôyô chiiki seibihô*) was passed that granted major tax relief for projects in economically weak regions. This triggered a massive resort construction program all over Japan. However, the government's hopes that the leisure industry would revive structurally weak regions have not been fulfilled in every case.

This resort boom came to an abrupt end at the beginning of the nineties because of the continuing recession and the collapse of real estate prices. Numerous projects faced difficulties due to insufficient technical know-how and unreliable financing. Even though the number of visitors did not drop, many companies withdrew from new investments (Zenkoku Rejâ Bijinesu Sôran 1992:88). In addition to that, new resort projects faced increasing opposition from environmental organizations complaining about the devastating side effects of excessive golf-course and ski-slope construction. Of the 2,200 projects that were planned for the construction stage in 1992 over 60 percent were cancelled or postponed (NHV Material A).

Of course the growth of the leisure sector and the boom of leisure parks was not only a result of political support and economic investment interests, but was mainly a reaction to the growing demand within the Japanese population for a wider range of opportunities for spending one's spare time.

The large increase in the number of leisure parks after World War II can be traced back to the so-called leisure boom (*rejâ bûmu*).[2] Drastic reductions in working hours combined with increasing incomes caused a "leisure fever" that swept through all social strata. For the increasing number of car owners leisure parks proved to be the perfect idea for a day's excursion; they could be visited in one day, they offered a wide-ranging program that pleased most members of the family.

In the years that followed the initial onset of the leisure boom the character of leisure parks changed considerably. Most of the early leisure parks can be categorized as "amusement parks" (e.g., Korakuen). They resembled static fairs in that they offered a wide spectrum of entertainment on more or less crowded grounds and were very often sited in urban areas. With a growing demand from the clientele for more sophisticated types of leisure during the 1970s and 1980s leisure parks altered their appearance. It was the theme park concept developed by Walt Disney that dominated the leisure park market from the late seventies and had its final breakthrough with the success of Tokyo Disneyland. Disney's secret was that he added a whole new dimension to the layout of a leisure park.

Annoyed by the chaotic and dirty atmosphere of American amusement parks Disney developed the concept of a park where everything (from fancy rides to the dustbins) is laid out according to a comprehensive theme. By creating a unique atmosphere in the park he took the visitor into a dream world that contrasted sharply with his everyday surroundings (Fichtner and Michna 1986:14; Luyten 1991:24). As well as the largely physical excitement of the rides the visitor escaped into a happy world that had nothing in common with the problems of his work and home environment and was thus offered a satisfaction that mere amusement parks could not provide.

Soon this concept was imitated all over the world. The attractiveness of the contrast world that a theme park can offer seems to rise with the degree of urbanization. As a general rule, there is a proportionally higher demand for leisure parks and resorts in highly urbanized areas than in the countryside. To a large extent the high population density and the crammed living conditions explain the popularity of theme parks in Japan (Fichtner and Michna 1986:170).[3]

Another major distinction between amusement parks and Disney's theme parks is that the latter target a much broader audience. Whereas in traditional amusement parks there was seldom anything for parents to do but to watch their children, Disney parks were designed to attract all age groups. A major objective of the Japanese leisure park companies was to attract not only parents with children but the well-paid, unmarried, young Japanese women and men as well (Gekkan Rejâ Sangyô 1992:140).

Since the opening of Tokyo Disneyland the majority of Japanese leisure parks called themselves theme parks (*têmapâku*). For a long time the set-up and the facilities of the Disneypark were merely copied, but in recent years the companies have realized that such a standardization will in the long term harm the business and therefore now strive for a more individual profile. A lot of effort is spent on the creation of different fantasy worlds with unique attractions (Nikka 1992:35). In the face of increasing competition, parks have not only had to continuously add new facilities to make people return but have also had to be in vogue with the latest trends in the leisure industry. Companies were thus constantly on the hunt for new and trendy themes and had to be willing to change their own as fashions changed.

Looking at the most common themes in Japanese leisure parks it appears that the simulation of foreign worlds is the most popular idea, along with entertainment through high-tech facilities. The wide range of foreign-country themes may be interpreted as a reflection of the growing interest in travel abroad. Most attractive seem to be the European countries and North America—they are more "exotic" than the Asian neighbors—and so we find Holland, Spain, Switzerland, Scotland, Denmark, Germany, and Canada on the leisure park map. Many country themes are closely connected to fairy tale worlds, such as Grimm's tales for Germany and Andersen's *Little Mermaid* for Denmark, or to children's books like *Heidi* for Switzerland and *Ann of Green Gables* in the case of Canada. The preference for countries that are known in Japan by their fairy tales is explained by the high percentage of children among the visitors (Fichtner and Michna 1986:160). In addition, the images of fairy tales and romantic worlds can be exploited by the parks to attract young couples (Gekkan Rejâ Sangyô 1992:140).

Another range of theme parks, those which simulate historic scenarios, reflect a great interest in Japan's history. Parks like Edo Mura or Meiji Mura take visitors back to the Japan of the sixteenth to the nineteenth centuries. Simultaneously, the multitude of historic themes indicate a new trend in the conceptualization of the parks. Many try to create an image of sophisticated entertainment with a highly educational value (Nemoto 1992:45), and often increase their attractiveness with life-size copies of historical buildings. Arita Voc and Dairiseki Mura offer exhibitions with themes one would expect in a museum. Arita Voc displays the history of porcelain and has recreated the complete Dresdener Zwinger (Nagasaki Shinbun 1 January 1993). Dairiseki Mura has exhibitions on the subject of stone and had 600 tons of granite imported to reconstruct a Scottish castle (Nippon Kôgyô Shinbun 4 January 1993).

A rejection of "mere entertainment" is also signaled by the adoption of themes such as nature, ecology, and health. Since the 1980s a longing for unspoiled nature is reflected in the trends of all sectors within the leisure and tourist industries. Ecology trips have been profitable since 1985, and so-called ecology camps (*ekorujî-kyanpu*) have sprung up, where visitors may learn about their natural environment (Gendaiyôgo 1992:1297). "Unity with nature" (*shizen to jibun no ittaika*) and "learning through experience" (*taiken gakushô*) are slogans of leisure parks that are trying to create a new image for themselves. Mongoru Mura, for example, uses the association with the nomad world and claims that the health education of the youth and the youth's contact with nature is its major concern (Nagasaki Shinbun 13 January 1993). The theme of New Zealand, represented surprisingly often, works along these lines, evoking images of endless farms and familiar contact with animals.

Nowadays, even parks whose original theme had nothing to do with ecology try to catch the spirit of the times by assuming a green cloak for the occasion. The fairytale park Harmony Land tried to promote "unity with nature" by building Japan's first alternatively fueled roller coaster and consequently used this as an excuse to set up *taiken gakushu* seminars with the topic "the quest for alternative energy sources" (Nikkan Kôgyô Shinbun, 27 November 1992).

Along with the trend toward health and recreation, the parks altered their layout into forms that would persuade visitors to prolong their stay. A numbers of parks changed into resort parks, altering their facilities in such a way that they would be visited not only for day trips, as amusement and theme parks tend to be, but also for longer periods of time. To allow for this they added housing facilities and offered entertainment with a more relaxing and recreational value. Among the standard facilities of such parks are golf courses, and the element of "water" became cumulatively important as the fitness and health deluge flooded over Japan in the eighties. Many parks include elaborate swimming pools and other amenities such as beauty parlors. Realizing the rising popularity of water sports in the 1980s many parks integrated marinas into their layout—the biggest one, Wakayama Marina City, offering berths for 1,100 yachts (Nippon Kôgyô Shinbun 18 January 1993).

With the shift from amusement park to theme park and resort park one observes three simultaneous changes:

1. Due to the kind of activity resorts offer, they require more space than other kinds of leisure parks. Whereas the thrill rides of amusement parks can afford to be situated in the middle of towns, theme parks, and especially resorts, tend to move into the countryside where land is cheaper. A rural setting also increases the attractiveness of those parks, which are geared toward sport and recreation. With

increasing urbanization the contrast world gained even more importance, and this was enhanced by the use of a natural environment.

2. In addition to that, a stay in a resort park implies a fundamental change in the traditional patterns of domestic Japanese tourism: characteristic are short-term group excursions—not more than two or three days, spending one night in each place (JNTO 1992:5). This manner of traveling suits amusement parks very well, but resorts are suited less for the group and more for the individual—and, particularly, for longer holidays.

3. Finally, one can observe a change in the leisure pattern that a park visit stimulates. A visitor in an amusement park has, during the few hours of his stay, a full-time program provided for him. He may saunter from one ride to the next and let himself be entertained. He has no need of inventing activities of his own—especially when visiting the park as part of a group. In a resort where one stays a longer period of time in a relaxed manner, it is more difficult to provide the customer with a minute-to-minute program. The resort is not mere comsumption of entertainment provided by someone else—the visitor is expected to be more creative and to take advantage of the educational and sports facilities. There is more effort put into making use of the facilities (e.g., boating) and into structuring one's time.

The recent development of leisure parks is illustrated by the example of a theme park resort project that includes all the described tendencies, and furthermore claims to know and show the way into the future. The Huis Ten Bosch park of the Nagasaki Oranda Mura was opened in 1992 and belongs to the generation of parks that are situated at a distance from urban areas. Not only in terms of investment and size is it twice as big as Tokyo Disneyland, but its concept also reaches way beyond that which any leisure park has ever aspired to. Not only does the company want its visitors to stay for more than a day, but it desires that people should live in the park, ultimately transforming it into a living city with more than 30,000 inhabitants (Kaminogo 1992). If one studies the plans closely they appear to be a publicity stunt—their realization will not occur in the near future. However, a closer look at the concept is interesting as it is forecasting future trends and indicates the crucial preconditions for further development.

The makers of Huis Ten Bosch have completed the creation of an escapist dream world by extending a fantasy into the time dimension. The layout of Huis Ten Bosch is that of a complete Dutch town. Its geography shows the phases of development of a European town—complete with its own fake history. Huis Ten Bosch denies that it has any similarity to the "mindless entertainment" of the Disney Parks. "Screaming-type fun" is rejected, there are no rides of the normal kind in the park. It is totally geared toward highly educational value and historical correctness—during the construction a whole block of houses was torn down again because the bricks turned out to be 2 mm too big (Kaminogo 1992:44). However, Huis Ten Bosch aims to be more than a mere open-air museum. In addition to all that a normal city entails, such as shops, restaurants, museums, even a police station, it offers luxury hotels and villas, a health center, a marina, and even a branch of Leiden University where twenty students per year may follow their normal university curriculum. It claims to be the city of the twenty-first century, a model of how Japanese can learn to spend their leisure in fulfillment. Its attempt is to introduce a new leisure pattern into Japan—that is, to teach people how to spend more time away from work and how to pass their time individually, not by following a group around, but by going off and exploring the town by themselves. The thematic concept is described with the following slogans: "A new city where man and nature can coexist," "City of Greenery and Water," "Transmittence of Dutch Culture," "City of Comfort and Relaxation," "City for Mingling and Communication among People," and "Pursuing true Richness" (*honmono no yutakasa o oimotomeru*).

Apart from the health and ecology trends (which can also be found in other parks), two aspects are interesting: the orientation to a European model of a living environment and the promise of satisfaction on a more spiritual level.

Both aspects would seem to be related to the discussion on "true affluence" that, in the media, accompanied the government's declaration to make Japan a "superpower in quality of life." A number of newspaper articles remarked that the Japanese seem, despite their

economic power, not to perceive themselves as a truly "affluent society" (Iwata 1992:10). A high income alone was deemed to be insufficient for a high quality of life. In addition to the long working
hours and a lack of social security the crammed housing conditions
were among the reasons most blamed for the lack of satisfaction.
With an increase of free time the home environment had to meet
more demands than being merely a shelter in the work cycle. In the
search for higher living quality the comparison with Europe seemed
of importance, as Japanese towns are conceived as ugly in comparison: the power cables lie above the earth—the towns are often
overdeveloped and lack orchestration (NHV Material B).

Apart from demands for more free time (equated with affluence) there was also observed a growing consciousness of the value
of turning this free time into "true richness"—the quantity-into-
quality conversion. A number of government surveys (Sôrifu 1990;
News and Views 1992:7) in the nineties described the phenomena
as a search for spiritual satisfaction beyond the mere material satisfaction of needs. The definition of wealth was increasingly extended to an ineffable emotional level. Claims were made that the
Japanese had not been able to reach this emotional satisfaction in
their leisure time—the "hedonistic pursuit of pleasure exists side
by side with ... a hollowness and emptiness of spirit" (Koseki 1989:
122). With a surprising disregard for Japan's entertainment traditions, opinions were vociferated such as: "The Japanese merely
chased after the latest trends without any true satisfaction because
the fast economic development had left no time to develop the classic style and sense for luxury which they so much admire in Europe" (Fujioka 1989:28). Huis Ten Bosch thus appears to personify
an ideal contrast world that offers an intellectually satisfying way
of spending free time, and whose luxurious design, which is perceived as sophisticated because it takes the European town as its
model, makes it the prototype of a living environment based on
affluence and leisure.

However ambitious and fashionable a concept as Huis Ten
Bosch may be, there are, besides the recession, some concrete obsta-
cles that put the long-term success of resorts in question. Of the
aforementioned characteristics of Japanese domestic tourism—
group travel and short-term stay—only the first shows distinct signs
of changing. Group travel is still an important traditional form of

tourism, but the number of people who travel independently and make no use of package tours rises constantly (Sôrifu 1989:52).

Long-term holidays on the contrary have still not become common in Japan and the length of a stay seldom exceeds two to three days. When asked how long they would like to go on holiday, a time span between three and seven days proved most popular. How to structure longer holidays seems to be a formidable problem—the majority of people asked could not imagine a European-style week-long stay in one place, they perceived it as boring (Sôrifu 1989:47). The fact that the Japanese Tourist Organisation even offers seminars for *sararîman* who have more spare time but do not know what to do with it, seems to point in the same direction (Gendaiyôgo 1992:1310).

In addition, the reduction of work hours has ceased lately, and fundamental changes in the organization of work time, in the economy, and the reform of some economic structures would be necessary to make these long holidays at all feasible. In addition to lacking legislation, the organization of work in many offices (which puts an extra workload on the colleagues if someone goes on holiday and thus makes him even more reluctant to go) as well as the just-in-time delivery system makes it hard for companies to close down separately for holidays.[4]

Summary

Looking at the changes in the layout of parks in the last twenty years one notices a clear shift from the mere search for entertainment toward a use of leisure time that stimulates the intellect and has recreational value. That shift may be defined at several levels: from *asobi* to *rejâ*, from a passive leisure pattern to an active leisure pattern, or from perceiving leisure as being "free time as time for recovery between work" to being "free time as time for self-improvement"—the repeatedly claimed characteristic of the development of Japanese leisure (Linhart 1988). Trying to prove that Japan is not a nation of "working bees," the Japanese Tourist Organisation states that the term *rizôto* denotes a growing emancipation of leisure. Resorts offer an environment that is independent from work and a living environment where free time can be enjoyed free of the obligations of daily life. It is no longer bound to a specific purpose, be it recovery of work power or self-improvement, but as "pleasure in its own right" (JNTO 1992:30).

In any case the development of leisure parks relates to a question that has been raised in the discussion of Japanese work and leisure patterns: Is Japan turning into a postindustrial leisure society?[5] On a theoretical level a resort town such as Huis Ten Bosch, which actually aspires to become a home for people, can be regarded as the prototype of a "leisure society." Here leisure has an active and individual pattern, has a positive value and is an essential part of everyday life[6]—but it remains to be seen how much that commercial utopia resembles the future.

Notes

1. For a more detailed analysis see Linhart (1989).

2. For a first analysis of the leisure boom see Plath (1964).

3. A further factor for the popularity of leisure parks in Japan is certainly the high ranking of domestic travel among the favorite pastimes of the Japanese compared with the still low rate of overseas travel. Fichtner and Michna (1986:170) also suggest that the aptitude of leisure parks for group visits is a reason for their success in a culture like Japan, whose leisure pattern he calls "group-oriented."

An interesting topic for further studies is the question of whether the success of leisure parks is related to a different attitude in Japan toward "artificial worlds" and toward "nature." Keeping in mind how much the dreamworlds of Disney have been criticized by American intellectuals and even more so in Europe as an "allegory of what is fake" (Eco 1985:50), it is surprising how little prejudice there seems to be in Japan against such "unreal reality" as Huis Ten Bosch.

4. For a detailed analysis of the work-time issue see Herold (1990) and Weber (1989).

5. See, e.g., Weber (1989) and Linhart (1988).

6. These are mainly the criteria Linhart (1988:277) established for the definition of a postindustrial leisure pattern.

———————————— References ————————————

Unpublished Sources

NHV Material. Data of Nagasaki Oranda Mura, made available through the liaison office in Den Haag, Nagasaki Holland Village Nederland B.V.
A   Data on Huis Ten Bosch.
Data for the meeting of the advisory board of Nagasaki Holland Village.
B   Nagasaki Oranda Mura Tokyo Puresu Informajon Ofisu, "21 seiki no machi zukuri fôramu." Nagasaki.
Oranda Mura PR katsudô hôkoku 4/5, 1992; report about PR-activities 12. 10. 1991—14. 3. 1992.

Published Books and Papers

Agricola, Sigrid, Hartmut Lüdtke, and Uwe Karst (eds.). 1986. *Methoden der Freizeitforschung*. Opladen: Leske + Budrich.
Chua Eoan, Howard. 1993. "Welcome to the great indoors," *Time Magazine* 2 August 1992, 31, 42–43.
Eco, Umberto. 1985. *Apokalyptiker und Integrierte: Zur kritischen Analyse der Massenkultur*. Frankfurt: Fischer Taschenbuch Verlag.
Fichtner, Uwe, and Rudolf Michna. 1986. *Freizeitparks: Allgemeine Züge eines modernen Freizeitangebotes vertieft am Beispiel des EUROPA-PARK in Rust/Baden*. Freiburg.
Fujioka Wakao. 1989. "Heisei gannen gurêdo appu e no michi," *Chûô kôron* 4, 204–18.
Gekkan Rejâ Sangyô. 1992. "Rejâ rando keiei no genjô," *Gekkan rêjâ sangyô* 11, 141–74.
Gendai yôgo no kiso chishiki. 1992. "Ryokô yôgo no kaisetsu," Tokyo: Jiyû kokuminsha, 1310–17.
Hasegawa Mina. 1993. "Leisure," *Japan economic almanac 1993*. Tokyo: Nihon keizai shinbunsha, 146–47.
Herold, Renate. 1990. "Japans langer Weg in die Freizeitgesellschaft," *Aus Politik und Zeitgeschichte* B39/90. Bonn: Bundeszentrale für politische Bildung, 27–35.
Iwata Kikuo. 1992. "Relative richness," *Look Japan* 10, 9–11.
JNTO. 1992. *Tourism in Japan 1992*. Tokyo: Ministry of Transport/JNTO.
Kaminogo Toshiaki. 1992. *Hausu ten bosu monogatari*. Tokyo: Porejiden-tosha.

Koseki Sampei. 1989. "Japan: Homo Ludens Japonicus," Anna Olszewska (ed.), *Leisure and lifestyle: A comparative analysis of free time* (Sage Studies in International Sociology 38). London: Sage Publications, 115–42.

Linhart, Sepp. 1988. "From industrial to postindustrial society: Change in the leisure-related values and behaviour," *The Journal of Japanese Studies* 14/2, 271–307.

———. 1989. "Die Anwendbarkeit des Freizeitbegriffes auf Japan," *Leviathan* 2, 204–15.

Luyten, Paul. 1991. "Probleme und Chancen: Freizeitparks in der Europäischen Gemeinschaft," *Amusement Industrie* 80. Paderborn, 24–29.

Nagasaki Shinbun. 1993. "Saigen sareta Zuingâ kyûden," 1 January 1993.

———. 1993. "Mongorumura shigatsu kaison," 13 January 1993.

Nemoto Yûji. 1992. "Daijôbu? Kaigyô & kensetsu keikakuchû. Têmapâku 104 no seisaku," *Shûkan Daiyamondo* 15, 22 August 1992, 40–45.

News and Views from Japan. 1992. "Japanese recognize that all work and no play makes Jack a dull boy," *News and Views from Japan*, 4 May 1992. Brussels: Information Center of the Mission of Japan to the European Community, 4–6.

Nikka Kojin. 1992. "Natsuyasumi—Nihon no rejâ," *Shûkan Daiyamondo* 15, August 1992, 36–37.

Nikkan Kôgyô Shinbun. 1992. "Atorakushon shinsetsu," 27 November 1992.

Nippon Kôgyô Shinbun. 1993. "Sukottorando kôjô fugugen ga kyûbichi," 4 January 1993.

———. 1993. "Temupâku 22 nichi chakkô," 18 January 1993.

Plath, David. 1964. *The after hours: Modern Japan and the search for enjoyment.* Berkley: University of California Press.

Schöller, Peter. 1980. "Tradition und Moderne im innerjapanischen Tourismus," *Erdkunde* 34, 134–50.

Shûkan Daiyamondo. 1992. "Tôkyô dizunîrando kaigyô ikô ni kaisetsu sareta têmapâku," 15, 22 August 1992, 41–42.

Sôrifu. 1989. *Kankô hakusho—Heiseigannen-han.* Okurashô insatsukyoku.

———. 1990. *Kankô hakusho—Heiseini-han.* Okurashô insatsukyoku.

Weber, Claudia. 1989. "Arbeitszeit und Freizeit in Japan," *Leviathan* 2, 217–25.

Zenkoku Rejâ Bjinesu Sôran. 1992. "Zenkoku rejâ bijinesu sôran," 12, 88–97.

PART FOUR

Theater and Music

The emergence of a distinct consumer culture during the late Taishô and early Shôwa periods brought major challenges to popular entertainment. New forms of popular theater and music that evolved during those years and the adjustment of traditional forms were more than mere reflections of their times. They appear to have been among the earliest factors in twentieth-century life that contributed to the transformation of traditional Japanese society into one of mass consumption and mass culture. Certainly the mass production and consumption of popular entertainment helped to generate consciousness of a new culture among a mass nationwide audience. Although some of these forms of entertainment preserved traditional and even local modes and tastes, they helped to form the consciousness of that changing society out of which they were born.

All of the four chapters in Part 4 are concerned primarily with the audience of either theatrical or musical performances or both. In her chapter on popular theater Annegret Bergmann begins from the Edo period, when *kabuki* was closely linked to the so-called pleasure quarters. After the Meiji Restoration however, several organizations were founded to further the reorganization of *kabuki* as a national theater in accordance with what were perceived as "western standards." Bergmann investigates how *kabuki* itself as well as related forms of entertainment for the audience, have changed since then, despite the fact that the foundation of a national theater was only accomplished about a hundred years later.

As opposed to the predominantly male *kabuki*, Roland Domenig and Jennifer Robertson deal with the history of the all-female theater troupe Takarazuka, which enjoys great popularity up to this day among an overwhelmingly female audience. While Domenig focuses on the multitalented innovater and founder of Takarazuka and his ideas about a "theater for the masses," Robertson is concerned with a different set of questions. Analyzing the state's strategies to organize and rationalize leisure and entertainment in wartime Japan, she forcefully argues that the Takarazuka theater was one of those entertainment institutions that were deployed as an influential agent in controling leisure-consuming people.

While both kabuki and Takarazuka started out as forms of entertainment for the masses and managed to a large degree to preserve their popularity, Eckhart Derschmidt tells us a quite different story about jazz music in Japan. Looking at various types of jazz cafés, from the postwar era when live concerts were still rare events up to the present, he describes how Japanese jazz cafés had to adjust to new challenges in order to survive, such as access to canned music or changes in the lifestyle of every new generation of listeners. Thus, these cafés fulfilled a variety of functions. The present decline of jazz cafés however, is among other indications expressed in a clearly backwardly directed preoccupation of the audience with the original, the pure, and the authentic. Consequently, Derschmidt concludes, the days of the Japanese jazz café are numbered.

S. F.

Annegret Bergmann

13

From Pleasure to Leisure

Attempts at Decommercialization of Japanese Popular Theater

The semiannual report for 1994 of the Center for the Development of Leisure, *Yoka kaihatsu sentâ*, a MITI affiliated institution founded in 1972, barely mentions theater attendance in its statistics (Yoka kaihatsu sentâ 1994). It would, however, be wrong to conclude that theater attendance is not a popular leisure activity.

Actually, Japan's commercial theaters are nearly always sold out. Apparently the term *leisure* simply does not apply to going to the theater, which is seen more as a cultural and educational activity.

In this chapter, however, I will present the attempts of transforming the popular theater, which has always been commercial, into a government-subsidized cultural institution, modeled on western standards.

This chapter consists of three parts. The first part will deal with the popular theater, *kabuki*, as a pleasure activity during the Edo period. The second part will deal with attempts to get rid of the "adult" side of the popular show business since the Meiji Restoration. The third and final part will focus on the result of these efforts, concentrating on the popular theater of Japan since the end of World War II.

Kabuki, the popular theater of Japan during the Edo period, has always been theater to enjoy. A trip to the theater implied not only attending a performance but also drinking and chatting—having fun. For those with more money to spend on *asobi*, on playing around, the theater visit might have been followed by a party with friends, geishas, or actors.

In contrast to the *nô* theater, *kabuki* never enjoyed the sponsorship and protection of the ruling class during the Edo period. *Kabuki*, therefore, has never been produced for the sake of its artistic value alone or as l'art pour l'art, but for the very down-to-earth reason of making a living. That applies to the so-called founder of *kabuki*, Okuni, the founders of the first theaters in Edo, the stars on stage at the Tokyo Kabuki-za, as well as to the producer of Shôchiku K.K., the biggest theatrical enterprise in the present world.

Since its earliest years *kabuki* had to circumnavigate the strict censorship of the authorities in order to survive. This censorship did not only target the contents of the plays but also the character of the theater itself, due to the side business of its actors, namely prostitution. The artistic performances of *onna kabuki*, women *kabuki*, and *wakashû kabuki*, young men's *kabuki*, at the beginning of the seventeenth century, were "side shows" (Raz 1983:149) or commercials to promote the main business line of the dancers, for whom the audience actually came. To avoid an undermining of the government-imposed social hierarchy by prostitution, the government prohibited *onna kabuki* in 1623 and its substitute, the *wakashû kabuki*, in 1652.

By no means did these bans on *kabuki* put an end to the "water trade" side of the Edo show business, for which the *yakusha hyôbanki*, actors' critiques, give vivid testimony. Especially in the early days of *kabuki* the actors' sex appeal was given much more attention than their acting talents.

Since 1659 these critiques were published yearly, modeled on the early Edo-period courtesan critiques, the *yûjô hyôbanki*. Mature male *kabuki*, *yarô kabuki*, was the form that survived the prohibition of *wakashû kabuki*. All actors had to shave their attractive forelocks and rely more on acting than on sex appeal to attract an audience. The actor's shaved head, *yarô atama*, gave it its name.

However, *yarô* as well as *kagema* and *iroko*, were terms for male prostitutes during the Edo period. Until the beginning of the Meiji period *yakusha kai*, "to buy an actor," was an expression as familiar to the people as *jorô kai*, "to buy a prostitute," or *geisha kai*, "to buy a *geisha*" (Gunji 1956:70–71). Yoshizawa Ayame and Segawa Kiku-nojô, famous *onnagata* of the Genroku period, had both started their career as *iroko*, as "sexy boys." *Iroko* who also appeared on stage were called *butaiko*, "stage boys." In the Kyôhô era (1716–1736) the *iroko* reached the peak of their popularity and, at least until the Tempô era in the middle of the nineteenth century, every theater had its own group of *iroko*, who were "managed" by either the owner of the theater or popular actors, musicians, reciters, or by theater teahouses or *irokoya*, brothels for male prostitutes (Gunji 1995:54).

Kabuki was as popular among the common folks of Edo as the cinema was in its heyday. The main attraction for the commoners were not so much the three big licensed theaters, Nakamura-za, Ichimura-za, and Morita-za, but more the small theaters around the corner, mostly built within the compounds of shrines and temples. A visit to the big theaters was quite expensive and extremely time consuming, especially since the Tempô Reform in 1841–1843 banned the theaters from the center of Edo and relocated them in Saruwakachô. To travel to and from the theater and attend the show took, all in all, two days. However, the so-called small theaters or *miyachi shibai*, shrine and temple theaters, were around the corner where everybody could drop in for just one or two acts for a cheap fee.

Kabuki performances originated in the so-called *kanjin saru-gaku*, fund-raising performances at shrines and temples. With the beginning of the Edo period *kabuki* performances moved away from their "hosts" for the sake of commercial profit and finally became monopolized by a number of government-licensed theaters. The theaters at shrines and temples became illegal and of a low standard. However, in the strict hierarchy of the *kabuki* world they always provided a niche for actors who, due to their family background or other reasons, would have had no chance to become a star or even earn a reasonable living in one of the big theaters.

In terms of rules and regulations, it is also interesting to note that these shrine and temple theaters were treated as the unli-censed, privately run brothels of the temple and shrine districts, *oka-basho*. These illegal but tacitly tolerated red-light districts have always been rivals of the licensed pleasure quarter Yoshiwara (found-ed in 1617) and its successor Shin-Yoshiwara (founded in 1657).

These shrine and temple theaters were, of course, also strictly restricted and censured by the authorities, controled by the *jisha bugyô*, which issued a licence for one hundred days, generally in connection with a festival at the shrine or temple. Officially, small theaters were only allowed booth stages, while the use of the traveler curtain, *hanamichi*, and revolving stage were forbidden. During the end of the Edo period, however, it became increasingly easier for the theaters to renew their licences, so that these theaters finally became permanent institutions, with a theater building and galleries resembling the big theaters (Gunji 1956:39). At the beginning of the nineteenth century there were around thirty small theaters on some fifteen temple and shrine grounds in Tokyo, for instance at Yushima Tenjin, Kanda Myôjin, Ichigaya Hachiman, and in the Asakusa district (Gunji 1956:41–42).

Actually the Meiji-za, to which I will refer later, has its roots in one of these small theaters. Even though its sensuality was gradually replaced by mere entertainment, *kabuki* was always linked to pleasure, to *asobi*, to enjoy oneself, free of social restraints and restrictions imposed by the authorities. According to Tsubouchi Shôyô (Tsubouchi 1927:60–61) and Gunji Masakatsu, *kabuki* was too closely linked to the pleasure quarters and its character too influenced by the red-light districts to be modernized and adapted to modern society. Therefore, present-day *kabuki* can only be a traditional theater form, a nostalgic hobby (Gunji 1956:17).

Indeed, during the Meiji period a lot of attempts were made to "purify" the *kabuki* theater, to erase its pleasure character in order to transform it into a sophisticated entertainment for the well-educated and a representative for Japanese culture at its best. The ideal was to create a national theater, not only a theater building but also a representative Japanese performing art, adapted to the new ideals of the Meiji government.

One of the pioneers to adapt *kabuki* to the new social ideals of *bunmei kaika* was the actor and owner of the theater Morita-za, Morita Kanya XII (1846–1897). After the Meiji Restoration, which brought an end to the regional restriction of theaters, Kanya was the first of all theater owners to move his theater to the center of Tokyo, to Shintomichô in 1872. Several years later, in 1878, the theater was rebuilt and modernized. This new Shintomi-za was the first theater in Japan to be illuminated by gaslights and to have a number of western-style seats in the audience. In the following years a visit to a performance of the Shintomi-za almost became a must for foreigners on an official visit to Japan. Thus the Shintomi-za virtually became a kind of national theater. This was not on Morita Kanya's initiative alone. Originally, Kômyôji Mitsusaburô who had spent three years in France, from 1870 until 1873, and Saionji Kinmochi (1849–1940) had brought the idea of a national theater to the openminded and adventurous Morita Kanya. But in the end Kanya gave up the idea of a national theater modeled on Western examples, because he deemed the time not ripe. He had also incurred huge losses with the production of western plays in his Shintomi-za (Ishihara 1968:109). Kanya finally returned to the production of "good old *kabuki.*"

Nevertheless the idea of a national theater persisted. On 28 April 1878 illustrious people from politics, theater, and literature met at the mansion of Matsuda Michiyuki, then secretary of the Ministry of Home Affairs. Besides the host, Matsuda, Itô Hirobumi (1841–1909), historian Yoda Gakkai, the top *kabuki* actors Ichikawa Danjûrô IX (1838–1903), Onoe Kikugorô V (1845–1903), Nakamura Sôjûrô I (1835–1889), Nakamura Nakazô III (1809–1886), and Morita Kanya came together to discuss the future of the Japanese theater. Based on his own experiences during the Iwakura mission to Europe and America (1871–1873) and upon information from Kômyôji, Itô emphasized that, unlike in Japan, plays abroad were always logical, that the audience was well educated and that the actors did not become toys, *gandôbutsu*, of the spectators (Ishihara 1969:178). The aim of this meeting was to create a refined and purified *kabuki* according to western standards, which, of course, would leave no room for the worldly pleasures of the old *kabuki*. These ideals initiated the first western plays on the Shintomi-za stage and the so-called "living history" plays, *katsurekigeki*, of Danjûrô IX, plays based on historical accuracy.

This movement culminated in the foundation of the Engeki kairyôkai, the Association for Theatrical Reform, in August 1886 by the politicians Suematsu Kenchô (1855–1920) and Inoue Kaoru (1835–1915), the scholars Sotoyama Shôichi and Hozumi Nobushige (1856–1926), the journalist Fukuchi Ôchi, and others, supported by the influential politicians Itô Hirobumi, then prime minister, Ôkuma Shigenobu (1838–1922), Ôkura Kihachirô (1837–1928), entrepreneur and founder of the Ôkura *zaibatsu*, and Saionji Kinmochi (Ishihara 1969:179).

This association of politicians, entrepreneurs, and scholars—there were no members from the theater world—intended to abolish everything in *kabuki* that did not fit into western theater standards like the *hanamichi*, the musicians on stage and *onnagata*. Thus the reform of *kabuki* aimed at abolishing its essence and, therefore, had to fail.

Along with the reform and modernization of *kabuki*, the Association for Theatrical Reform also planned to build a national theater. Through the intermediation of Suematsu Kenchô, an Assembly for the Promotion of the Establishment of a National Theater (Gekijô setsuritsuan tôgikai) was founded on 19 August 1886 (Fujinami 1988:109). With the establishment of a national theater, the Engeki Kairyôkai intended to abolish old customs and practices of *kabuki*, like selling tickets through the theater-affiliated teahouses and eating, drinking, and chatting during the performances. Thus the Association tried to rid *kabuki* of all the peripheral entertainments and pleasures it had entailed during the Edo period and transform it into the Bildungstheater that Tsubouchi Shôyô had advocated.

The new national theater was meant to be modeled on the Opera House in Paris, hosting both theater performances and concerts. Commissioned to an English architect, overall construction costs were estimated at 250,000 Yen. But with the fall of the Itô cabinet in the following year the whole project was abandoned (Kawatake 1966:67).

The only "success" of the Association for Theatrical Reform was a *kabuki* performance in presence of the Meiji Tennô in April 1887 at the residence of Inoue Kaoru. With this performance *kabuki* officially shed not only its stigma of social outcast but became the representative theater of Japan, a status it has maintained to this day.

Part of the legacy of the Association for Theatrical Reform is the Kabuki-za in Tokyo. Originally planned under the name of "Reform Theater," it was founded by one of the members of the association, Fukuchi Ôchi (1841–1906), who eventually had to give up his reform theater project to raise funds to build the theater. At least the first Kabuki-za, opened in 1889, had a western-style facade, but its interior as well as its productions were still following Japanese theater traditions. For the sake of commercial success, performances had to be entertaining. Fukuchi, originally a journalist, was not familiar enough with the management of a *kabuki* theater and left the Kabuki-za only several years after its opening, because of disagreements with the main financier over the program.

The Kabuki-za was not the only attempt to establish a new western theater building. In 1906 the notion of a national theater was revived by a group of powerful people in politics and industry who met once under the name of Society of the Founders of a National Theater (Kokuritsu gekijô hokkininkai). But the main members of the society, the entrepreneurs Shibusawa Eiichi, Ôkura Kihachirô, and Fukuzawa Momosuke abandoned their own plans and, instead, built the Teikokugekijô, the Imperial Theater, which opened in March 1911 (Fujinami 1988:110).

According to the first managing director of the Imperial Theater, Nishino Keinosuke, there were two reasons for the promotion of a national theater: First of all, there was a need for an appropriate building to give receptions for high-ranking foreign visitors. In 1905 the Kabuki-za was used to hold a reception for some hundred marines from the English fleet who visited Japan on the occasion of the Japanese–English Alliance (Nagayama 1993:152). Approximately 50,000 Yen were used to install electric lighting and electric stage equipment just for this occasion. However, to the great embarrassment of the Japanese hosts, the lights went off two or three times during the event, convincing everybody that a national theater was urgently needed for international representation.

The second reason was to get rid of old theater customs, particularly the ticket distribution through the theater-affiliated teahouses. This was not merely an affair of ordering tickets, it was more a question of how much one was ready to spend on tips, *chadai*, for a ticket. Not surprisingly, the higher the tip, the greater the chance to get a good seat. If one did not want to squeeze into the cheap seats, going to the theater was quite a major undertaking (Ishihara 1969:110–111).

During the Meiji period, despite several initiatives to build a state-run noncommercial theater, these projects were never realized. Instead individuals took up these ideas and built theaters at their private initiative, which finally assumed representative functions.

At the end of the Taishô period, in 1921 the *shingeki* actor Sasamoto Kôgo (1896–1923) advocated a national theater. Sasamoto mainly played the partner roles of the famous female actress Matsui Sumako. After her suicide in 1919 he was hired by the Asakusa Opera. Since the end of the Meiji period, with the emergence of the first cinemas, Asakusa had become the Broadway of Tokyo, one of the busiest entertainment districts in town for hundreds of thousands of new townspeople who had moved into town following the growing industrialization. Already in 1904 Tsubouchi Shôyô had called for a new theater for the people, because the old entertainments like *kabuki* did not appeal to the "new people," *shinkokumin*, the masses of the urbanites (Tsubouchi 1977:349).

During the Meiji period so-called *Tempô rônin*, the old people born during the Tempô era, were the main supporters of *kabuki*, because for them it was still contemporary theater. Toward the end of the Meiji period these *kabuki* lovers began to vanish and new forms of entertainment conquered the heart of the people (Fukuda 1991:22).

Hence the enormous success of the Asakusa Opera, not to be mistaken for a western opera, since it was basically a show, consisting for example in 1917 of a fairy-tale comedy, a western play, a "Grand Opera," and a variety show including dances (Ishihara 1969:179–80).

Supported by the influential Upper-House member Yanagiwara Yoshimitsu and Ogasawara Chôkan, also a well-known patron of arts, as well as Lower-House member Hatoyama Ichirô (1883–1959, prime minister in 1954), Sasamoto wrote a petition for a noncommercial national theater in March 1921. He claimed that literature, fine arts, and music had all been reformed and modernized, while the theater was still out of reach for the common people due to its profit-oriented organization (Ôzasa 1986:352) .

In November of the same year the legislator Hatoyama also called for a national theater, to create a theater that reflected the present society and went beyond mere entertainment. But debate about the construction of a national theater in the Diet was finally given up at an early stage, due to the death of its promoter Sasamoto in August 1921 (Ôzasa 1986:354) and the Great Kantô Earthquake in September 1923.

In the Shôwa era *kabuki* actors and playwrights took up the idea of a national theater again. In April 1936 Nakamura Utaemon V (1865–1940), Okamoto Kidô (1872–1939), Ikeda Daigo (1885–1942), and Kawatake Shigetoshi (1889–1967) founded the Committee for the Establishment of a National Theater (Kokuritsu gekijô setchian iinkai), with Nakamura Kichizô (1877–1941) as its head (Fujinami 1988:110). In 1921 the playwright Nakamura had been opposed to a national theater, fearing that public servants, politicians, and influential investors would dominate its productions and prevent new developments in the performing arts (Ôzasa 1986: 355). Now he pleaded for government subsidies and for the construction of a national theater to preserve *kabuki* and to improve Japanese theater (Ishihara 1969:183).

With the support of powerful men from the world of politics and finance, the committee submitted to the Diet a proposal for the building of a national theater, which was approved but never realized because of the outbreak of the Sino-Japanese War in July of the following year (Fujinami 1988:110).

After World War II, the Japanese Ministry of Education earmarked funds for a national theater in all its budgets since 1947, but for decades to come, the theater project did not get beyond the planning stage. Initially rising criticism about the founding of a national theater so shortly after the war prevented the government from pushing forward with their plans. The Katayama cabinet, however, took the initiative to set up a Committee for Theater and Culture (Engeki bunka iinkai), which compiled a paper on the establishment of a national theater and a national school of acting. Once again, with the resignation of the Katayama cabinet in February 1948, all plans were dropped (Fujinami 1988:110).

During the 1950s new efforts were taken to realize a national theater. In 1955 the Council for Investigation and Study of Performing Arts (Geinô chôsa kenkyû kyôgikai) was set up within the Committee for the Protection of Cultural Property (Bunkazai hogo iinkai). In the next year this council founded the Preparatory Council for the Establishment of a National Theater (Kokuritsu gekijô setsuritsu junbi kyôgikai). Around that time the League for the Promotion of a National Theater (Kokuritsu gekijô sokushin giin renmei) was set up in the Diet. In November 1958 it was decided to build the new national theater in Miyakezaka next to the Supreme Court and the Imperial Palace, a location in the middle of nowhere, far away from the bustling center of Tokyo.

The report of the Preparatory Council had proposed a complex of four theaters for the preservation of traditional Japanese performing arts and the creation and development of new forms of performing art. Planned were a theater for traditional performing arts with 1500 seats, one for contemporary performing arts with 2000 seats, and an 800-seat theater for *bunraku*, traditional music, traditional dance, modern theater, and others, as well as a theater for *nô* and *kyôgen* with 700 seats. Four years after the original proposal, in July 1962, the plan was scaled down to two houses—a big house with about 1800 seats and a small theater with about 800 seats, after the building site was found to be too small for four theaters (Fujinami 1988:111–12).

But reducing the number of theaters, of course, meant limiting the aspirations of the national theater as well. In June 1966 the Japanese Diet passed the National Theater Bill, which said that the national theater is *mainly* to present and preserve Japanese traditional performing arts. The emphasis is on the word mainly, *omo to shite*, an expression not included in the original bill but added after harsh protests—especially from the modern theater. By adding this expression the door was at least left open for productions other than traditional ones. A Japanese National Theater finally opened on 1 November 1966, about a hundred years after it was first considered.

Originally planned in the Meiji period as a noncommercial theater for the entertainment of the upper class and high-ranking guests of state, with performances of modern Japanese theater, that is to say westernized *kabuki* or western theater plays, the National Theater that finally opened its doors to the public is an institution for the preservation of *kabuki*.

The National Theater is per definition not an establishment for the socializing of the upper class, but "a place of recreation for people who are working during daytime," as the first director of the theater, Teranaka Sakuo, claimed in 1966 (Sanuki 1966:48).

But taking into account that *kabuki* performances start at noon or at 5 P.M. it becomes quite obvious that the National Theater, apart from on the weekend, can hardly be a "place of recreation" for the average blue- or white-collar worker. But since the National

Theater has to finance its productions through ticket sales, it cannot afford to schedule only evening performances. Even though originally intended to be noncommercial, the budget of the National Theater covers only the maintainance costs for the building and the salaries of its administrative staff. Since actors are not hired on long-term contracts at the National Theater, it has to "borrow" actors from the big production companies for every production (Sanuki 1966:43, 47).

In 1966 all *kabuki* actors were either affiliated with Tôhô or Shôchiku and even though there had been plans to establish an ensemble at the National Theater, in the end it could not be realized because of Shôchiku's dominance at that time. As Kawatake phrased it in 1966—slightly polemically—"the big theater companies argued that their profit-orientated business was naturally in contrast to the government's interest (in a national theater), and when it finally opened they lacked wise and progressive sense to cooperate, so the troup could not be put together" (Kawatake 1966: 68). Actually they must have feared competition from a government-subsidized theater with different cost calculation. According to the chief producer for *kabuki* at the National Theater, due to the long oppression of *kabuki* by the authorities—censorship was only abolished after World War II—*kabuki* actors themselves had not been eager to be "employed" by the government or to be on long-term contracts at the National Theater (Orita 1995).

However, to produce a sufficient income the National Theater has to be managed almost like a commercial theater, while its productions have to live up to the aim of preserving and promoting traditional performing arts, which are mainly *kabuki*—popular "medleys" of only one or two acts of popular plays as staged at the Kabuki-za are out of question for the National Theater. At the end, even though the National Theater was finally realized, it proved impossible to sever popular theater from its commercial interests and dependencies. And that was not primarily due to the influential position of the big theater companies, which only emerged at the end of the Meiji period, but due to the lack of financial support from the Japanese government from the outset of the national theater movement in the early Meiji period. The promotion of a national theater by the government was confined to phrasing ideals; in the end the warm words were not accompanied by cool cash. Finally, *kabuki* as popular theater survived thanks to private entrepreneurs who also preserved it as a theatrical art form.

Today, *kabuki* is not the only popular theater in Japan, even though the *kabuki* stars of today are not only well known among *kabuki* fans. The critic and scholar Yasuda Takeshi (1922–1986) went as far as to say that the attempts to modernize *kabuki* during the Meiji period have taken the pleasure away from it. According to Yasuda, going to the *kabuki* theater does not imply enjoying oneself anymore, because there is no room for *asobi* anymore, only solemn admiration of the performance on stage. (Yasuda and Iizawa 1971: 13). While the National Theater is celebrating popular theater of the past to educate people about their historic theater culture, other theaters fill the gap and produce theater with an emphasis on fun and entertainment. These are the Shinjuku Komagekijô, the Shinbashi Embujô, and the Meiji-za in Tokyo, the Misono-za in Nagoya, and the Gekijô Hiten, and Shin-Kabuki-za in Ôsaka. Except for Meiji-za, Misono-za, and Shin-Kabuki-za, they are all owned by or are affiliated with big production companies. These theaters are, of course, all commercial enterprises and, until World War II, had relied mainly on *kabuki* performances.

After World War II, however, the popularity of *kabuki* declined, basically because of the booming film industry, and the theaters had to find new ways to appeal to their audience. This is especially true for the three theaters without support of a big production company. The Misono-za opened in 1897, the Shin-Kabuki-za in 1932, and the Meiji-za in 1893. They were not built at traditional theater sites but at so-called new entertainment quarters, or *sakariba*, which had sprung up in the course of rapid urbanization after the Meiji Restoration. All three theaters were managed by Shôchiku for a certain period, but have meanwhile turned into independent theater stock companies. The Meiji-za, for example, became an independent company in 1950 but still relied on *kabuki*, *shinpa*, and *shinkokugeki* performances—ready-made productions procured from production companies. In the 1960s the Meiji-za started its own productions. Due to the declining popularity of *kabuki*, there was need to substitute the old *kabuki* stars on stage. They were no longer a guarantee for commercial success. The solution discovered by the Meiji-za—as well as the Misono-za and the Shin-Kabuki-za—was to produce plays with popular film stars, mainly from historical samurai films. The so-called *star shibai* of the popular theater was born. All these new stars on stage had been famous film stars, such as Ichikawa Utaemon (1907–), Hasekawa Kazuo (1908–1984), Ôkawa Hashizô (1929–1984), and later Satomi Kôtarô (1936–), Kitaôji Kinya (1943–), and others. In the 1970s popular television stars like Matsudaira Ken (1953–) began to appear on stage.

In March 1960 Minami Haruo (1923–), an *enka* or popular ballad singer, was tremendously successful on stage at the Shin-Kabuki-za, which until a year before had relied principally on *kabuki*. The director of the Shin-Kabuki-za replaced the regular *kabuki* program in March with a performance of Minami, because he was convinced that Minami's show would attract a much larger audience. A new variety of the *star shibai* was born and eagerly copied by other commercial theaters. Even the Kabuki-za in Tokyo produced a show with Minami in August 1963 (Sanuki 1991:122–23). The programs of this *star shibai* most commonly consist of a theater play (specially written for the occasion), an episode of a television drama or a popular historical drama (often chosen from the repertoire of *shin-kabuki* or *shinkokugeki*), and a musical show that features the star in glittering costumes regardless of whether he or she is a professional singer or not. *Star shibai*, especially new plays, resemble Edo-period productions of *kabuki* performances: the star is the absolute focus of the play and therefore determines what will be performed. A production with the popular *enka* idol Itsuki Hiroshi at the Misono-za can easily cost more than 250 million Yen, which is much more expensive than a ready-made *kabuki* performance bought from Shôchiku (Shinoda 1992). However, thanks to the stars, theaters are packed, *star shibai* is still very popular, and the theater companies make profit. The problem is that there are no new stars to fill the theaters in the future, who could fascinate an audience of nearly two thousand, as neither the film nor the television industry has managed to produce real stars, in contrast to the innumerable but short-lived *tarento*.

Maybe one has to go back to the roots of the theater, to its actors, and establish a national school of acting, not only for *kabuki* but for popular theater as well. This idea is not new, it dates back to the Meiji period, but probably we will have to wait another century for the event to materialize.

─────────────────── References ───────────────────

Fujinami Takayuki. 1988. *Dentô geinô no saihakken.* Tokyo: Hakusuisha.

Fukuda Nobuo (ed.). 1991. *Taishô no engeki to toshi.* Tokyo: Musashino shobô.

Gunji Masakatsu. 1956. *Kabuki to Yoshiwara.* Tokyo: Awaji shobô.

———. 1995. "Kabuki to iroko," *Bungaku* 6/1, 50–57.

Ishihara Shigeo. 1969. *Kokuritsugekijô shuzai nikki.* Tokyo: Ôfûsha.

Kawatake Toshio. 1966. "Kokuritsu gekijô no risôzô," *Shingeki* 11, 66–77.

Nagayama Takeomi. 1993. *Kabuki-za hyakunenshi.* Tokyo: Shôchiku kabushikigaisha, Kabushikigaisha Kabuki-za.

Orita Kôji. (Chief producer at the National Theater.) 1995. Interview March 6th.

Ôzasa Yoshio. 1986. *Nihon gendai engekishi: Taishô Shôwa shokihen.* Tokyo: Hakusuisha.

Raz, Jacob. 1983. *Audience and actors: A study of their interaction in the Japanese traditional theater.* Leiden: Brill.

Sanuki Yurito. 1966. "Kokuritsu gekijô no soshiki to unei," *Shingeki* 11, 43–48.

———. 1991. "Ôsaka Shin-Kabuki-za no hensen," *Engekikai* 6, 122–23.

Shinoda Kunio. (Producer of the Misono-za.) 1992. Interview October 7th.

Tsubouchi Shôyô. 1927. "Shingakugekiron," Inoue Tatsuzô (ed.), *Tsubouchi Shôyô yôshû.* 2nd ed. Tokyo: Chikuma shobô, 344–52.

———. 1977. "Kabuki shibai no tetteiteki kenkyû," Wada Toshihiko (ed.), *Shôyô senshû daijû kan.* Tokyo: Shunyôdô, 41–93.

Yasuda Takeshi, and Iizawa Karasu. 1971. "Asobi koso engeki no inochi," *Teatoro* 9, 8–17.

Yoka kaihatsu sentâ (ed.). 1994. *Rejâ hakusho '94.* Tokyo: Buneisha.

Roland Domenig

—————— 14 ——————

Takarazuka and Kobayashi Ichizô's Idea of "Kokumingeki"

During the Taishô period music and theater were among the favorite leisure activities of the people. The Taishô period marks a turning point in Japan's theater and music history. In the Meiji period several efforts were undertaken to bring western music and theater to Japan. Most of them, however, were superficial and intended only for a small elite—for the ordinary people they were of little or no significance. The majority still preferred *kabuki* and traditional music like *gidayû*, *nagauta*, or *naniwabushi*. During the Taishô period, however, western music and theater were no longer merely copied but was adapted to Japanese conditions and transformed into new and uniquely Japanese traditions, like the *shinpa* and *shingeki* theater or popular songs such as *enka* or *kayôkyoku*.

This chapter examines one of these new traditions originating in the Taishô period, the Takarazuka Girl Opera (Takarazuka shôjo kageki).[1] In the first part of the chapter I will explore the origins of the Takarazuka troupe, its background and main influences, and in the second part I will examine the ideas of the founder of the troupe, Kobayashi Ichizô, who's ambition was to create a new national theater (*shinkokumingeki*).

The Takarazuka troupe was founded in July 1913. At the time Kobayashi was director of the Minoo-Arima-Railway Company, a small railroad company that he turned into today's Hankyû group. In Takarazuka, a small village west of Osaka at the end of the rail-

267

road, Kobayashi built an entertainment park around a hot-spring spa to entice more passengers to use the railway. At the core of the entertainment park stood a western-style indoor swimming pool, which was, however, a failure (Kobayashi 1955:6). To compensate for the financial loss, Kobayashi turned it into a theater and founded a singing troupe whose special feature was that it consisted only of girls. Kobayashi got the idea for this all-female troupe from the boy orchestra, which since 1909 had been the popular attraction of the Mitsukoshi department store in Nihonbashi.[2] The Takarazuka troupe started with sixteen girls between ten and fourteen years of age, and what began as an amateur experiment eventually developed into a professional and very popular form of entertainment.

Kobayashi admitted that at the beginning there was no concrete plan as to how to develop the troupe. Initially he himself was not very active, because his attention was absorbed by the railroad business (Sakata 1991:241). Kobayashi hired Andô Hiroshi, a graduate from the prestigious Tokyo Music Academy, to organize the troupe and to train the girls in singing and dancing. The first performance of the Takarazuka shôjo kagekidan or Takarazuka Girl Opera, as the troupe was named, took place in April 1914.[3] They performed three short plays, Kitamura Kisei's *Donburako*, Motoi Nagayo's *Ukare Daruma*, and the dance *Kochô no mai*, all of them tested pieces newly arranged for the girls.[4] *Donburako* and *Ukare Daruma* were both so-called *otogi kageki* (fairy-tale operas). Fairy-tale operas became the centerpieces of the Takarazuka repertoire until the Revue replaced them in the late 1920s.

The performance was well received, but this did not mean that the troupe's future was automatically ensured. In fact, in its first years of existence the troupe encountered many difficulties and it had to struggle for survival (Kobayashi 1955:16). Kobayashi, however, was very pleased with the first performances and began to commit himself to the future developement of the troupe, and until his death it was Kobayashi's special darling.

Kobayashi Ichizô (1873–1957), founder of the Hankyû-Tôhô-group and one of Japan's great innovators in the entertainment and leisure industry, showed an early interest in literature and theater. During his studies at the Keiô University he often frequented the theaters of Tokyo, and after his employment at the Mitsui Bank in 1893 he became familiar with the popular theater of Osaka. In 1907 he left the bank to become director of the Minoo-Arima-Railroad Company and eventually one of Japan's most important businessmen.[5]

With his commitment to turn the Takarazuka troupe into a professional enterprise, Kobayashi began to develop the idea of a new national theater—an idea he would pursue until his death. Kobayashi himself began to write plays for the troupe and, by 1918, twenty-two of his plays were performed in Takarazuka. Kobayashi's approach was very simple: he took well-known melodies, often from the song books compiled by the Ministry of Education for schools, and wrote new texts, which he then arranged into simple stories (Kobayashi 1955:14). He realized, however, that this amateur approach was unfit for turning the troupe into a profitable enterprise, and in 1918 he began to transform the troupe into a more professional venture. His first step was to hire some first-class teachers and found the Takarazuka Music Academy,[6] at which the girls received a better and more systematic training in singing and dancing. He also built a new theater that was bigger and better equipped than the old one. Of particular importance was the appointment of Tsubouchi Shikô as artistic director. Tsubouchi Shikô was the adopted son of Tsubouchi Shôyô, whose ideas were to have a lasting impact on the development of the troupe.

Tsubouchi Shôyô, one of Japan's great theater reformers, had, in 1906, founded the Bungei Kyôkai which, apart from Osanai Kaoru's Jiyû Gekijô, was the most important movement in the first half of the century to advance modern theater in Japan.

Tsubouchi perceived theater, or art as a whole, as an organ (*kikan*) of social management (*shakai keiei*), which, like religion or education, causes a powerful spiritual as well as material response. For him theater fulfilled two important functions, namely amusement (*goraku kikan*)—to entertain, comfort, and console the people—and improvement and propagation of public morals (*fûkyô kikan*) (Ishikawa 1965:101). With the Bungei Kyôkai, Tsubouchi wanted to reform the Japanese theater, which, as he thought, had lost both of these functions.

Although Tsubouchi stated that popular amusement (*minshû goraku*) should generally be carried out, judged, and regulated by the people (*minshû*) themselves, he argued that since Japan was still in a transitory phase the people were not yet ready for this task and that it was the duty of the higher classes to guide the lower classes and help them to achieve education (Ishikawa 1965:102). Although Tsubouchi adamantly opposed a moralistic theater of the traditional *kanzen chôaku* type or a theater that sought to teach controversial "new" ideas, he nevertheless believed that the ultimate goal of the theater was to enlighten society (*shakai no fûka*). The Bungei Kyôkai was thus designed to educate "enlightened" (*shikiken aru*) pioneers of the *shingeki* movement and to promote new plays and a "new theater suitable for the new age, which overcomes the ills of the traditional theater and which indirectly, through providing aesthetic experiences, works to enlighten society" (Horie-Webber 1976:158). To achieve this he set up Japan's first drama academy, in which the actors and actresses received proper training and were educated in drama and literature. Unlike the traditional theater, the *shinpa*, or even Osanai Kaoru's Jiyû Gekijô that originally still had men play female roles (Powell 1976:138), Tsubouchi thought it indispensable to cast actresses in the leading female roles. One of the actresses trained by Tsubouchi was Matsui Sumako, the star of the Bungei Kyôkai and Japan's first modern actress.

Probably the most important feature of the Bungei Kyôkai was that it was determined by the objective of searching for a new "national" theater (Horie-Webber 1976:159). The theoretical framework for this was already exposited by Tsubouchi in 1904 with his "Theory of a New Music Theater" (*Shingakugekiron*), in which he demanded the creation of a national theater (*kokugeki*) whose ideal form he believed to be a *butôgeki* or dance drama: "There is no civilized country in this world without its own national music and theater. It appeals to the people's ears and eyes, comforts and pleases their hearts and it educates and enlightens them" (Sakata 1991: 248). This national theater, Tsubouchi stressed, must not adhere to old aesthetics like the *nô*, nor should it be a realistic theater (*shajitsugeki*) like the *kabuki*. It should rather be a music drama in the form of a dramatic poem with music and dance at its center. The music, however, must not be an end in itself but a tool to emphasize the drama. Although Tsubouchi suggested the integration of western music—for example to emphasize a dramatic climax—he thought it inappropriate that western music should become national music (*kokugaku*). He therefore dismissed it as a basis for his music theater. He stressed that the Japanese music theater of the future should not be a mere imitation of western music theater but unite the strength of the traditional Japanese music theater forms (Horiuchi 1948: 164). Tsubouchi thought the *nagauta* (a dramatic music poem) the best-suited form for his dance drama (Sakata 1991:249). Tsubouchi's efforts to reform the traditional Japanese music theater may be interpreted as a reaction to the enthusiasm of many of his countrymen for western opera. Opera, particularly the work of Richard Wagner, had a strong impact on Japanese intellectuals, and at the turn of the century several efforts were undertaken to bring western opera to Japan. The first Japanese full-scale opera production was Gluck's *Orfeo et Euridice* in 1903, which was followed by other more or less successful attempts at western-style opera. Tsubouchi, himself strongly influenced by Wagner's concept of Gesamtkunstwerk (Kasaha 1990:72), was skeptical about this enthusiasm and warned that the Japanese should not merely try to imitate western opera but should better think of a way in which the traditional Japanese music theater could be reformed. With his *Shingakugekiron* he tried to present a theoretical alternative to the unreflected adoration of western opera (Komiya 1954:521).

To realize his theory Tsubouchi wrote several experimental dance dramas. One of them was *Tokoyami*, which was performed at the Bungei Kyôkai's first public performance in November 1906. *Tokoyami* tells the story of the Sun Goddess Amaterasu, who was lured out of the cave in which she was hiding by the performance of a dance. The drama was performed by forty actors and actresses, a thirty-member orchestra, and a choir of more than one hundred singers—also the reason why the performance ended in a financial fiasco.

Prior to *Tokoyami*, Tsubouchi had written another experimental dance drama, *Shinkyoku Urashima*, which, although never performed,[7] is of interest insofar as it clearly depicts the influence that Tsubouchi had on the Takarazuka troupe. The fairy tale *Urashima Tarô*, rendered at the troupe's second performance, strongly resembles Tsubouchi's play (Sakata 1991:247). It is also noteworthy that, after seeing a performance in Takarazuka in 1916, Tsubouchi remarked that much of his *shingakugeki* theory had been realized in Takarazuka (Kobayashi 1955:18).

Another crucial influence on the Takarazuka troupe came from Shimamura Hôgetsu, Tsubouchi's disciple and co-founder of the

Bungei Kyôkai. After the dissolution of the Bungei Kyôkai in 1913 Shimamura founded the Geijutsuza, which differed considerably from the Bungei Kyôkai. Unlike Tsubouchi, who was a theorist and did not spend much thought on economic matters (as the fiasco of the first Bungei Kyôkai performance clearly demonstrated), Shimamura was more concerned with and well aware of the financial limits of the theater business. Shimamura knew that in order to make successful commercial theater it is necessary to comply with the taste of the audience and he resorted to a practice that proved very successful.[8] To give the plays a more relaxed feeling, he wrote songs that were set to music by Nakayama Shinpei. The song of Katusha from Tolstoi's *Resurrection*, sung by the star of the Geijutsuza, Matsui Sumako, was an immediate success and became Japan's first modern hit song.[9] The first performance of *Resurrection* was only a few days before the premiere performance in Takarazuka, and Nakayama Shinpei's songs became a very important source of inspiration for the Takarazuka troupe (Sakata 1991:253).

When Kobayashi founded the troupe in July 1913, he called it Takarazuka Choir (Takarazuka shôkatai). In December 1913, however, the name was changed to Takarazuka Girl Opera (Takarazuka shôjo kageki).[10] The emphasis placed on the word *opera*[11] is easily understood when one knows that, aside from cinema, opera was the craze of the time.[12] First attempts to bring opera to Japan were undertaken at the turn of the century. The first opera performed by Japanese was Gluck's *Orfeo et Euridice*, staged by students of the Tokyo Music Academy in 1903. A very important step for the promotion of opera was the creation of a music division at the Imperial Theater in 1911.[13] One aim of the Imperial Theater was the performance of western music drama, and the music division was established to train professional Japanese opera singers and to instruct them in western opera music. The Italian choreographer Giovanni Vittorio Rosi was hired as director and became the central figure in the introduction of western opera to Japan. However, since there was a shortage of good singers it was difficult to perform full-scale operas. Hence the repertoire consisted mainly of lighter pieces, operetta, and musical comedies, which were arranged according to the singers at hand. The lack of trained male voices was particularly deplorable and many male roles were assumed by female singers (Masui 1990:64). This was the reason why several all-female opera groups existed at that time. During the Taishô period, Takarazuka was only one all-female opera troupe among many.[14]

In 1916, after his tenure at the Imperial Theater was not prolonged due to financial difficulties, Rosi founded his own opera house, the Royal Theater, where he continued his work. Soon, however, he too faced financial difficulties, and in 1918 had to close the theater. One reason he had to give up was that his theater was too expensive and available only to an elite audience (Masui 1990:27). Another reason was the increasingly severe competition from other opera troupes, most of which were founded by Rosi's former pupils. Today they are collectively known as Asakusa Opera,[15] because the center of their activities was the theaters in Asakusa, the amusement center of Tokyo. They were less elitist than Rosi and they shortened, rewrote, and arranged the operas according to the taste of the audience (Masui 1990:2). Therefore the operas often had nothing in common with their western original other than the title and some popular melody. This potpourri style was typical also for the Takarazuka troupe,[16] which performed regularly in Tokyo from 1918 onward. The troupe became an important part of Tokyo's music and theater scene, and in 1932 Kobayashi built them a special theater, which marked the beginning of the Tokyo Takarazuka Company, better known under the abbreviation Tôhô.

The Asakusa Opera almost disappeared at the end of the Taishô period. The main reason for this was the Great Earthquake of 1923, which destroyed most theaters in Tokyo. Another reason was that it was increasingly difficult for the opera companies to appeal to a large audience. The audience had become more demanding and difficult to satisfy, partially because of the better music education at school, and partially because they had more opportunities to compare the troupes with foreign opera troupes, which now visited Japan regularly. The coup de grace for the Asakusa Opera was the emergence of the talkie film and the rising popularity of music films.

Asakusa Operas were very important models for the Takarazuka repertoire. Many successful Asakusa Operas were shown in Takarazuka and some pieces from the Asakusa Opera's standard repertoire, like Nishimoto Chôshun's *Venice no yûbe*, were first performed in Takarazuka. It is noteworthy that, following the Great Earthquake of 1923, Kobayashi employed some leading figures from the Asakusa Opera in Takarazuka and thus reinforced the impact of the Asakusa Opera on the troupe's development.

Aside from the Asakusa Opera, which basically consisted of western standard pieces and their imitations set in contemporary "modern" Japan, there were also attempts to create uniquely Japanese operas. It suffices to mention only one, and this because Kobayashi mentioned it as a key event concerning his later commitment to the Takarazuka Girl Opera. *Yuya* was first performed in 1912 at the Imperial Theater, the text was by Sugitani Taisui after a *nô* play with the same title, the music was written by August Junker, a German professor at the Tokyo Music Academy. The opening night was a total fiasco. The audience burst into loud laughter because the music of Junker, who did not know Japanese, did not match to Sugitani's text in antique Japanese. The music, therefore, sounded very strange, especially to an audience not yet familiar with opera. Whereas the majority of the audience chortled their way through the entire opera, Kobayashi discovered a group of young people in the cheap back rows listening seriously and devotedly to the performance. Kobayashi often referred to this episode and stated that the devotion and fascination of these young people convinced him of the future prospects of opera, especially for the young generation. Later it encouraged him to pursue his *kokumingeki* ideas in Takarazuka (Kobayashi 1955:9).

In 1923 Kobayashi summarized his ideas of a new *kokumingeki* in his "Remarks on Japanese Opera" (*Nihon kageki gairon*), which may be interpreted as a continuation of Tsubouchi's *Shingakugekiron*. Kobayashi sees the origin of a national theater in the *kabuki* of the Edo period. This, however, he stressed, has to adapt to the contemporary context in order to retain its vitality and actuality. Otherwise it would become an antiquated form like the *nô* or the *bunraku*, which attracted a small and specific audience but which was not part of popular culture (Kobayashi 1955:113). Kobayashi saw *kabuki* as popular theater for the ordinary people with songs and dances at its center and, like Tsubouchi, he stressed that the basic form for a new *kokumingeki* must be a music theater. He also agreed with Tsubouchi that a new national theater should not be a mere copy of western opera. But, whereas Tsubouchi demanded a reform of the traditional Japanese music theater, suggesting a kind of "*nagauta* musical," Kobayashi advocated a harmonious merging of Japanese traditions with western music. Kobayashi was nevertheless skeptical about the integration of western music into the traditional Japanese theater dominated by *shamizen* music. Instead he demanded a paradigm change according to which western music must take the leading role. In order to transform Tsubouchi's dance drama (*kabu-geki*) into a modern, contemporary theater Kobayashi thought it necessary to replace the traditional music with "the music that 70 million Japanese learn compulsory at school" (Sakata 1991:249), implying western music. Kobayashi was a fervent critic of the so-called *karyû-geijutsu*, the traditional theater and music with its strong connection to the pleasure quarters.[17] He dismissed them as old fashioned and outdated, and stressed that a new time needed a new brand of music and theater. Kobayashi insisted that western music must form the musical basis for his propagated *kokumingeki*. On the other hand he stressed the importance of an uniquely Japanese content in the plays. Kobayashi described his ideal as "native in spirit and western in form" (*yôshikinihonryû*) and as "seven parts Japanese, three parts Western" (*washichiyôsan*) (Sakata 1991:274). These mottos held especially true for the first years of the troupe. Many of the teachers in Takarazuka came from a traditional background, which naturally determined the direction of the troupe. Until the introduction of the Revue in the late 1920s the troupe's repertoire was not particularly distinguished. It was rather a strange mixture of attempts to compromise western music with Japanese traditions. It is important to notice, however, that even if western-style revue eventually became the dominant form in Takarazuka, the troupe never excluded Japanese plays from its repertoire. Historical plays were always an important pillar of the Takarazuka repertoire.

One reason why Kobayashi rejected the traditional theater of the *karyûkai* was its orientation toward a dominantly male audience. Kobayashi intended his *kokumingeki* as wholesome family entertainment. He claimed that what had been called "entertainment for the masses" had in fact been intended almost exclusively for men. His *kokumingeki*, however, must appeal to women as well as to men, to children as well as to their parents.

In the decades after the Meiji restoration the situation of women changed considerably, especially in urban areas where women and children became major consumer groups. In the Taishô period this change led to the emergence of a new type of woman, the so-called *moga*, or modern girl, that often is presumed representative of the period of the so-called Taishô democracy. Young women, dissatisfied with the traditional forms of leisure and entertainment, were looking for new forms of entertainment, and Takarazuka offered them exactly what they were searching for, a modern theater that reflected their sense of *Zeitgeist*. Women always constituted a very important part of the troupe's audience. Currently the audience is almost exclusively female, but in the first years the troupe was especially popular among male high school students, and women were in the minority (Ashihara 1986:25). This popularity even prompted a ban on all junior high school students attending performances in Takarazuka (Robertson 1992b:174).

Kobayashi envisioned his *kokumingeki* as a central form of art of the people (*shômintaishû no chûshinteki geijutsu*) (Kobayashi 1955: 116). It had to cater to the taste of the period (*jidaikankaku*) and comply to the demands of the people (Kobayashi 1955:173). Kobayashi's vision was thus a theater for the people and, ultimately, also a theater by the people, as it was determined by the people's demands.

To understand whom Kobayashi meant by "the people" it is helpful to take a look at the heated debates during the Taishô period about the definition of the people and their relation to culture and art.[18] At the center of these discussions was the question of who represents "the people" and whether art or culture is for (*no tame*) or from (*ni yoru*) the people. The discussions were triggered by Honma Hisao's article "Meaning and value of people's art" (*Minshû geijutsu no igi oyobi kachi*), in which he maintained that the main function of art is the education (*kyôka*) of the people, which he defined as *heimin* or "common people who do not belong to the upper or aristocratic class but to the middle or lower working class" (Ishikawa 1965:103). One of Honma's main critics was the anarchist and leader of the socialist movement Ôsugi Sakae. Like Honma, Ôsugi referred to the people as *heimin-rôdôsha*, placing emphasis on the underprivileged workers' class, but he differed fundamently from Honma on the role of art. Whereas Honma conceived *minshû geijutsu* as art for the people, Ôsugi conceived it as art from the people. Ôsugi was strictly against the idea of imposing bourgeois ideas on the people on the pretext of educating them. For him *minshû geijutsu* was a self-expression of the people and their values (Yoshimi 1987:45).

These two poles also characterized the following *minshû bunkaron* and the *minshû gorakuron*. The latter discussed the question of whether amusement for the people should be controlled by the state or not. Tachibana Takahiro, a well-known film critic who occasionally worked as censor for the police, held that (1) "the people" refers not only to the unprivileged working class but to the public in general, that is, all people regardless of class, and (2) that the role of amusement must be to educate the people and to provide a tool for their recreation (Tachibana 1920:2). In this respect Tachibana agreed with Tsubouchi, who also stressed the importance of educating and guiding the lower classes. Gonda Yasunosuke, the most prominent representative of prewar leisure studies, in his early studies took the converse view that *minshû goraku* is not to be controlled from above but that it comes from within the people: "The amusement of the people does not create the people's life, but the people's life creates their amusement" (Gonda 1975:293). Gonda later changed his views and fell in line with the nationalist government, which underscored the importance of regulating and controlling the people and their leisure activities (cf. Tsurumi 1976).

Kobayashi's concept of the people comes closest to Tachibana's view, for Kobayashi intended his *kokumingeki* not for a specific audience but for all people regardless of their social background (Kobayashi 1955:171). Concerning the function of his *kokumingeki*, Kobayashi on the one hand maintained that it must comply with the demands of the people and thus be determined by the people's taste, on the other hand, however, he also stressed the importance of a morally upright and noble (*kôshô naru goraku*) entertainment[19] that must be regulated and controlled (Tsuganesawa 1991: 163). In this respect Kobayashi closely resembles Tsubouchi. Once the troupe was established and its form codified, Kobayashi put a stronger emphasis on the latter aspects and maintained that the troupe must be controlled and regulated. In the late 1930s, and especially during the war, Takarazuka was instrumentalized as a tool of propaganda, and its foremost task was to mobilize the people for the goals of the nationalistic government to which Kobayashi belonged for a brief time as minister of commerce (see Robertson's contribution to this volume). It can be argued, however, that this was also necessary for the troupe to survive and not to be forbidden by the government.

Kobayashi, as we have seen, intended his *kokumingeki* as a theater for the people. This implied that it had to be accessible not only to a rich elite but to all people—that is, the masses. To ensure that everybody could afford to visit the theater meant that the admission fees had to be kept low.[20] To make a commercially profitable theater for the masses with low admission fees required a new theater with a greater capacity. In 1923 he built a new Grand Theater with 4,000 seats in Takarazuka, at the time the biggest and most modern theater in Japan. Kobayashi's importance as reformer of the Japanese theater was less in the artistic field than in the introduction of new management methods suited for modern mass theater. Kobayashi's business philosophy was committed to three keywords: the mass (*taishû-honi*), the family (*kazoku-honi*) and entertainment (*goraku-honi*) (Tsuganesawa 1991:167). All three were combined in Takarazuka in what Tsuganesawa calls Kobayashi's "Takarazuka strategy": the creation of a new form of mass entertainment attractive to the whole family that was part of Kobayashi's overall vision of a modern consumer society.

The beginning of the Shôwa era marked another turning point in the history of the Takarazuka troupe. With *Mon Paris* began the era of the Japanese Revue and with it the golden years of Takarazuka.[21] Within little more than a decade the Takarazuka troupe had turned into a highly professional form of entertainment that enjoyed great popularity. The features that evolved during the 1930s, the golden age of the Takarazuka Revue, are still emblematic of the troupe. The most significant feature was probably the division of female-role players and male-role players.[22] There was no special distinction between these two in the first years of the troupe as was there no star system. Osanai Kaoru in 1918 was particularly impressed by the ensemble spirit of the troupe, and he pointed out that all actresses were on an equal footing and that no star dominated the troupe (Kobayashi 1955:22). The troupe started with very young girls who, in time, grew up, and so the original girl troupe matured to a troupe of young women. Parallel to this natural development the erotic attraction of the troupe became stronger and in the late 1920s a division of male-roles (*otokoyaku*) and female-roles (*musumeyaku*) was established. It was the male-role player, or *otokoyaku*, the ultimate star of the Takarazuka troupe, which prevented Kobayashi's last idea of his propagated *kokumingeki* from becoming true. Kobayashi considered the Takarazuka girl troupe only as an intermediate stage. In the long run he wanted to include males in the troupe, which would ultimately evolve into a theater in which the male and the female were equal (Kobayashi 1955:37).

Although Kobayashi tried several times to bring men into the troupe, the resistance of the troupe was too strong and eventually Kobayashi had to give up. Except for this last point, however, I think it can be said that most of Kobayashi's ideas of *kokumingeki* have been realized in Takarazuka. It should be stressed, however, that Kobayashi's idea of *kokumingeki* has to be distinguished from other attempts to create a national theater, like the *kokumin engeki* movement of the 1930s and 1940s (cf. Robertson 1991) or the attempts of the government to create a national theater (see Bergmann in this volume). While these attempts were directed at creating a theater representing the state (*kokugeki*), Kobayashi wanted to create a theater that represented the people (*kokumingeki*). In this respect, I would conclude, he succeeded, because Takarazuka developed into a very popular form of entertainment unique to Japan, which even today, after more than eighty years, still appeals to the Japanese people, regardless of age, social status, or sex.

 Notes

1. In English the troupe is generally referred to as Takarazuka Revue, but this term seems inappropriate to me in referring to the troupe in its first years of existence. The first Japanese revue was given in Takarazuka in 1927 and it was only in the 1930's and after the war that the loanword *rebyû* (revue) was used. During the war (since September 1940) the use of the foreign word "revue" was forbidden by the nationalist government (Takahashi 1974:48).

2. The first boy orchestras were founded at the time of the Sino-Japanese war and were modeled after military orchestras. They enjoyed great popularity until the end of the Taishô period (Hosokawa 1990a). There also existed girl orchestras such as the Shirokiya Shôjo Kagekidan, a predecessor of the Takarazuka troupe, founded in 1912 (Horiuchi 1948:166).

3. The first performance was part of a Wedding Expo (*konrei hakuran-kai*). To attract as many people as possible Kobayashi staged several Expos, which were very popular at the time. Kobayashi targeted especially women and children as important new consumer groups and he undertook several attempts, like Expos, to appeal especially to those groups. The Takarazuka troupe was one of these attempts (Tsuganesawa 1991:42f.)

4. *Kochô no mai* was first performed in 1911 at the Imperial Theater, *Ukare Daruma* in April 1912 by the girl troupe of the Shiroki department store in Tokyo, and *Donburako* in March 1912 at the Kabukiza Theater (Hosokawa 1990b: 110).

5. For biographical details about Kobayashi see Sakata (1991), Kojima (1986), and his autobiographies (Kobayashi 1955; 1990).

6. In January 1918 Kobayashi founded the Takarazuka Training Association (Takarazuka yôseikai) which replaced the old one that was created in 1913. In December 1918 it was officially recognized by the Ministry of Education as a private school and in January 1919 it was renamed Takarazuka Music Academy (Takarazuka ongaku kageki gakkô) (Ueda 1986).

7. *Shinkyoku Urashima* was the first play Tsubouchi wrote after his *Shingakugekiron*. Since Tsubouchi tried to combine many different traditions, like *nagauta*, folk songs, ancient *gagaku* and western music, for financial reasons it was not possible to stage the entire work. Parts of the first act were performed in 1907 as *nagauta*, and in 1914 the second act was unsuccessfully staged by Onoe Kikugorô at the Imperial Theater. In 1920 Tsubouchi wrote another Urashima play, *Chôsei Urashima*, parts of which were performed two years later (Omiya 1954:524). The complete play was first performed at the Tokyo Takarazuka Theater in March 1935. Tsubouchi died the day before the opening night on February 28th (Hagiwara 1954:100).

8. Osanai Kaoru used songs for his Jiyû Gekijô production of *Yoru no yado* in December 1910, but none of them was particularly successful (Kurata 1979:170).

9. It was also Japan's first bestselling record, selling more than 20,000 copies (Morimoto 1976:8).

10. Kobayashi's biographer Sakata Hiroo states that the name was invented not by Kobayashi but by Andô Hiroshi (Sakata 1991:196). Andô, a fervent advocate of western opera, accepted Kobayashi's offer to organize

the troupe because he believed the girl troupe to be only an intermediate stage to a final opera company of adult singers of both sexes. Andô always emphasized the importance of introducing male singers to the troupe (Sakata 1991:268).

11. In the first years, the *furigana* reading "opera" was always added to the word *kageki* (Sakata 1991:197).

12. In 1922 the Kinryûkan, the center of the Asakusa Opera, registered 512,471 visitors or 10.5 percent of the guests of all official theaters (*gekijô*) in Tokyo (not including the many *yose* theaters, which were below *gekijô* status). Masui estimates that in 1918, at the peak of the opera-boom, between 1.5 and 2 million people saw Asakusa Opera (Masui 1990:192). Few exact data exist about the Takarazuka troupe, but in 1918 about 550,000 people visited Kobayashi's hot-spring spa. In 1924, the year before the Grand Theater was opened, the figure rose to a little less than 1.2 million (Hagiwara 1951:283). Since no additional fees were charged for the theater it can be expected that most of them saw the girl troupe.

13. The Imperial Theater (Teikoku gekijô or Teigeki) was established in 1911 to promote and advance modern theater in Japan. It was Japan's first western-style theater, and the most important playground for modern and experimental theater in prewar Japan. In March 1940 Tôhô took over the management of the Imperial Theater (Hagiwara 1954:127).

14. In 1916 Nishimoto Chôshun founded the Japan Opera Association (Nihon kageki kyôkai), which performed mainly girl opera (*shôjo kageki*). In July 1916 Nishimoto's play *Venice no yûbe* was given in Takarazuka and became the biggest success so far. It later became a central play of the Asakusa Opera repertoire. Other popular girl opera troupes of the time were the Tôkyô Shôjo Kagekidan, the Asahi Kagekidan and the Tôkyô Naniwa Shôjo Kagekidan (Masui 1990:93). Later the all-female Shôchiku Kagekidan (SKD) became Takarazuka's main rival (Shôchiku Kagekidan 1978).

15. Asakusa Opera is a collective term that came into use after the war to refer to the popular opera of the Taishô period. Opera was not limited only to Asakusa, however, because most troupes toured the whole country after a new program was shown in one of Asakusa's theaters.

16. Kobayashi speaks of a "cocktail of music, dance and theater" (Kobayashi 1955:117)

17. Although in his youth Kobayashi often frequented the traditional theaters of Tokyo and Osaka and seemingly liked the plays he saw (Tsu-

ganesawa 1991:112), he later became a fervent critic of the traditional Japanese theater. His aversion went so far that in Takarazuka he prohibited the use of *shamisen* music, which he regarded as the embodiment of the traditional *karyûkai* (Sakata 1991:274).

18. The discussions are known as *minshû geijutsuron* (1916), *minshû bunkaron* (1919), and *minshû gorakuron* (1921) (Ishikawa 1965, 1981; Yoshimi 1990).

19. This is demonstrated by the motto of the Takarazuka troupe: purely, righteously, beautifully (*kiyoku, tadashiku, utsukushiku*).

20. Low entrance fees have always been a characteristic of the Takarazuka theaters. In the first years the show was actually free of charge, because everyone who paid the entrance fee for the hot-spring spa could see the show for free. In 1923 the entrance fee for the spa was 20 Sen for adults and 5 Sen for children (Ôsaka-shi shakai-bu chôsa-ka 1923:228). The first theaters were still in the traditional way with *tatami* mats. The Kôkaidô Theater, which opened in 1919, offered also some western-style seats, for which an additional fee of 20 Sen was charged. All later theaters were equipped with seats and charged admission. Takarazuka theaters were nevertheless among the cheapest forms of popular entertainment in those days (Ôsaka-shi shakai-bu chôsa-ka 1923:228).

21. The emergence of the Takarazuka Revue was the result of Kobayashi's propagation of huge theaters, because the revue was the theater form that suited the bigger stages best.

22. For a detailed description of this division and of general aspects of sexuality and gender in Takarazuka see Robertson (1992a, 1992b).

--------------------------- References ---------------------------

Ashihara Kuniko. 1986. *Waga utajinsei.* Tokyo: Kokusho kankôkai.

Beasley, W. G. (ed.). 1976. *Modern Japan: Aspects of history, literature and society.* Tokyo: Tuttle.

Gonda Yasunosuke. 1975. *Gonda Yasunosuke chôsakushû.* Vol. 1. Tokyo: Bunwa shobô.

Hagiwara Hiroyoshi (ed.). 1954. *Takarazuka kageki 40-nenshi.* Takarazuka: Takarazuka kagekidan shuppan.

Horie-Weber, A. 1976. "Modernisation of the Japanese theater," Beasley 1976, 147–65.

Horiuchi Keizô. 1948. *Ongaku gojûnen-shi.* Tokyo: Senshobô .

Hosokawa Shûhei. 1990a. "Shônen Ongakutai," *Music Magazine* 1990/2, 130–35.

———. 1990b. "Shôjo," *Music Magazine* 1990/7, 106–11.

Ishikawa Hiroyoshi. 1965. "Erîto ni arawareta minshû no imêji," Minami Hiroshi (ed.). *Taishô bunka.* Tokyo: Keisô shobô, 101–17.

———. 1981. *Goraku no senzenshi.* Tokyo: Tôsho sensho.

Kasaha Eiko. 1990. "Taishô bungaku ni okeru opera ongaku no isô," *Kokubungaku* 35/2, 69–77.

Kawasaki Kenko and Watanabe Miwako (eds.). 1991. *Takarazuka no yûwaku: Osukaru no akai kuchibeni.* Tokyo: Aoyumisha.

Kobayashi Ichizô. 1955. *Takarazuka manpitsu.* Tokyo: Jitsugyô no Nihonsha.

———. 1990. *Itsuô jijoden.* Tokyo: Tosho shuppansha.

Kojima Naoki. 1986. *Kisai jûô—Kobayashi Ichizô no shôgai.* Tokyo: PHP Bunko.

Komiya Toyotaka (ed.). 1954. *Meiji bunkashi 9: Ongaku-engekihen.* Tokyo: Yôyôsha.

Kurata Yoshihiro. 1979. *Nihon rekôdo bunkashi.* Tokyo: Tokyo shoseki.

Masui Keiji. 1990. *Asakusa opera monogatari.* Tokyo: Geijutsu gendaisha.

Minami Hiroshi. 1983. "Nihon modanizumu." Tokyo: Shibundô (= *Gendai no esupuri* 188).

Morimoto Toshikatsu. 1976. *Rekôdo hayariuta-shi [Onban kayôshi]—uta to eiga to rekôdo to.* Tokyo: Shirakawa shoin.

Ômori Seitarô. 1986. *Nihon no yôgaku.* Vol. 1. Tokyo: Shinmon shuppansha.

Ôsaka-shi shakai-bu chôsa-ka (ed.). 1923. *Yoka-seikatsu no kenkyû.* Kyoto: Kôbundô.

Powell, Brian. 1976. "Matsui Sumako: Actress and woman," Beasley 1976, 135–46.

Robertson, Jennifer. 1991. "Theatrical resistance, theaters of restraint: The Takarazuka Revue and the 'state theater' movement," *Anthropological Quarterly* 64/4, 165–77.

———. 1992a. "The politics of androgyny in Japan: Sexuality and subversion in the theater and beyond," *American Ethnologist* 19/3, 419–42.

———. 1992b. "Doing and undoing 'female' and 'male' in Japan," Takie Sugiyama Lebra (ed.), *Japanese social organization.* Honolulu: University of Hawaii Press.

Sakata Hiroo. 1991. *Waga Kobayashi Ichizô. Kiyoku tadashiku utsukushiku.* Tokyo: Kawade bunko.

Shôchiku kagekidan (ed.). 1978. *Rebyû to tomo ni hanseiki: Shôchiku kagekidan 50-nen no ayumi.* Tokyo: Kokusho kangyôkai.

Tachibana Takahiro. 1920. *Minshû goraku no kenkyû.* Tokyo: Keigansha.

Takahashi Masao (ed.). 1974. *Takarazuka kageki no 60-nen.* Takarazuka: Takarazuka kagekidan shuppan.

Tsuganesawa Toshihiro. 1991. *Takarazuka senryaku: Kobayashi Ichizô no seikatsubunkaron.* Tokyo: Kôdansha gendai shinsho.

Tsurumi Shunsuke. 1976. "Minshû goraku kara kokumin goraku e," *Shisô* 624, 278–88.

Ueda Zenji (ed.). 1986. *Takarazuka ongaku gakkô.* Tokyo: Yomiuri shinbunsha.

Yoshimi Shunya. 1987. *Toshi no doramaturugî.* Tokyo: Kôbundô.

———. 1990. "Komyunikêshon to shite no taishû bunka," *Shinbungaku Hyôron* 39, 78–105.

Jennifer Robertson

——————— 15 ———————

The Politics and Pursuit of Leisure in Wartime Japan

The general purpose of this chapter is to examine the place of theater in the mass organization of leisure in Japan during the wartime period, specifically 1931–1945. A few general comments about theater and leisure are appropriate at the outset.

The German theater historian Erika Fischer-Lichte has written that "theater is a communal institution, representing and establishing relationships which fulfil social functions" (Fischer-Lichte 1989: 19). But, as she has also pointed out, there is a dearth of work on how theatrical systems point to, embody, or influence certain "cultural systems," including, I would add, leisure.

It is useful to think of leisure itself as a cultural system insofar as it constitutes a temporal and spatial zone where controlled and legitimated activities both mark a break from and parallel the routines of wage-earning, work-related practices. This, in fact, is the way in which leisure was conceptualized by leaders in the industrial, entertainment, governmental, and military sectors in Japan during the wartime period. These persons understood that the way in which people spent their dispensable money and time was a mode of organizing their lives, and therefore, leisure was one of the concrete forms in which the social structure was manifest in action (Burns 1973:49 in Chaney 1979:98). Furthermore, the fact that leisure activities helped to form social communities based on interest rather than on neighborhood or kinship meant that such activities were an amplification of identity (Chaney 1979:98). The wartime emergency situation (*jikyoku*) prompted accelerated efforts to control leisure in ways that would mobilize and amplify a national identity around a collective awareness of New Japan, as the imperial body politic was called.

The specific theme of this chapter concerns the attempts by Kobayashi Ichizô in the 1930s and 1940s to create a leisure industry centered on theatrical entertainment. Kobayashi (1873–1957) was the founder of the Hankyû conglomerate, whose most visible holdings include a railroad company, a department store, a spa-amusement park complex, and the all-female Takarazuka Revue founded in 1913. I will focus primarily on the Takarazuka Revue; Roland Domenig has written about Kobayashi's *kokumingeki* activities elsewhere in this volume. My aim is to explore the relationship between Kobayashi and the state[1] as manifested in the promotion of the Takarazuka Revue as an ideal form of wartime entertainment for the Japanese people as a whole. But first, some background information about the Takarazuka Revue is necessary.

Takarazuka Revue

Conceived in part as a novel inversion of the all-male *kabuki* theater, Takarazuka revues from the outset included Japanese-style "classical" dramas and historical subjects, such as the *Tale of Genji*, European-style and Broadway-based performances, such as *Mon Paris*, Japan's premier revue (1927), and *Madame Butterfly*, as well as folk dances from all over the world. Generally speaking, it was during the wartime years that presentist plays, or "plays dealing with the present (emergency) situation" (*jikyoku engeki*), were staged. Whereas it was usually the case that Takarazuka Revues were set in historical Japanese settings or in exotic foreign locales, the majority of wartime dramas were set in the immediate Japanese present. Most of the revues produced during the late 1930s and early 1940s were about wartime policies and exigencies, such as the "southward advance" and colonial policy (e.g., *Saipan-parao: Waga nan'yô* [Saipan-Palau: Our South Seas], 1940), immigration to Manchuria (e.g., *Shunran hiraku koro* [When Spring Orchids Bloom], 1941), patriotic college students (e.g., *Gunkoku daigakusei* [College

Students of a Military Nation], 1939), and battlefield casualties (e.g., *Kaigun byôin* [Navy Hospital], 1940). Quite a few of these revues were written by playwrights employed by the Navy and Army ministries, who also sponsored their production.

The Takarasiennes, as the Revue's actors were nicknamed, after Parisiennes, include *otokoyaku*, or man's-role players, and *musumeyaku*, or woman's-role players. They are assigned to these gendered roles during their two-year curriculum at the Takarazuka Music Academy, founded in 1919 and from which all the actors must graduate. Like the *kabuki* actors before them, the cross-dressed actors clinched the popular appeal of the Revue among a very broad, multigenerational, mixed-sex audience.[2] I have published elsewhere on the sexual politics and gendered organization of the Takarazuka Revue and will not recapitulate that information and argument here (see Robertson 1989, 1991, 1992a, 1992b).[3] Let it suffice for me to summarize that just as gender was constructed on the basis of contrastive physical and behavioral stereotypes about females and males, so too was Japanese cultural superiority constructed on the basis of reified images of "us" and "them" also performed by the Takarasiennes—images that had especial cogency during the wartime period.

Theater and Imperialism

The usefulness of Takarazuka in creating an imperial vision of a global hierarchy headed by Japan (according to which all "nations and races" would assume their "proper place") was also linked to the structure of the revue form itself. Revues consist of a montage-like display and concatenation of different, even contradictory, images, lands, settings, peoples, and scenarios as a means of shaping and reshaping popular and national consciousness.

Takarazuka staged revues in which a range of colonized peoples in their local settings were performed for the Japanese mass public who were thereby familiarized with the cultural spread of the empire and reminded of the superiority of Japanese culture. *Momotarô* (the Peach Boy), staged by Takarazuka in 1942, is a case in point. This popular folk tale was about a miraculous Japanese boy who, in the wartime version, recruited a retinue of loyal followers from Indonesia, China, and the Philippines to help free Japan and Asia from American and European ogres (Dower 1986:253, 356).

The revue theater helped to bridge the gap between perceptions of colonized others and actual colonial encounters. By the same token, the Takarazuka Revue was also deployed as a didactic form of entertainment at home, in which audiences were strongly urged to practice frugality and correct thinking, and to be on the alert for foreign spies in their midst. For example, the revue "Ears, Eyes, and Mouths" (*Mimi to me to kuchi to*, 1941) included songs emphasizing the necessity of anti-espionage precautions in everyday living ("for spies are lurking everywhere, in trains, buses, coffee shops, barber shops, public baths, and movie theaters") (*Sekai no ichiba* 1941:77; *Mimi to me to kuchi to* 1941:26).

State ideologues regarded theater to be far more effective a didactic medium than cinema (Endô 1943:1). In theater was recognized not only a means of organizing and rationalizing the leisure of soldiers and subjects, but also the art of "claiming the people" (cf. Tsuchiya 1985:100, 97, 104; Dana 1943; De Grazia 1981; Schnapp 1993). The simultaneous interaction in theater of characters in a play with performers and spectators, produces a "performance consciousness" or a collective imaginary capacity to engage in the construction of potential worlds. The potential or possible worlds encountered in the performance are carried back by the audience into the wider— "real"—sociopolitical world in ways that may influence subsequent action (Kershaw 1992:25–29). The Japanese wartime state was particularly interested in securing a link between the potential world conjured up in the theater and the possibilities of the New World Order (*sekai shinchitsujo*) (cf. Endô 1943:1).

However, theater reformers and Japanese state ideologues also grappled with the problem of how to measure and control the "performance efficacy" of wartime theatrical productions. Once an audience dispersed and reentered the wider social realm, the twofold problem remained of how to reinforce the official text of a play, and how to measure accurately any influence that the performance may have had on the audience's behavior (cf. Kershaw 1992:2). One way of reducing the slippage between the main text and potential subtexts of a play was to include in didactic revues, such as "Eyes, Ears, and Mouths," the figure of an emcee who, at strategic intervals, explained the dominant, unequivocal meaning of the play, contextualized the various episodes, and delivered axiomatic summaries for the audience.

Takarazuka and New Japan

The relationship between the revue theater and the state was more a matter of mutual convenience and opportunism than one of seamless consensus and total state control over forms of leisure and popular entertainment. Kobayashi's interest in creating consumer citizens, along with new leisure pursuits for their edification and his profit, dovetailed with the state's interest in rationalizing and controlling people's leisure time and activities. The strategies for the mass organization of leisure employed in fascist Italy (Dopo-Lavoro, an "after work" organization), Nazi Germany (Kraft durch Freude, or "strength through joy"), and the United States (Federal Theater Project) were familiar to Kobayashi and other theater reformers of the day. And an international conference on leisure in Tokyo in 1940 doubtlessly facilitated the transnational exchange of strategies for leisure control and organized entertainment (De Grazia 1981:240). Japanese theater reformers, including Kobayashi, studied and adapted Euro-American dramaturgical methods in efforts to consolidate a transcendent and unifying "citizens' culture" (*kokumin bunka*). Theater, asserted one nationalist reformer, must become a paragon of civic morality (*kokumindôtoku to naru tehon*) that will turn audiences away from westernism (i.e., individualism) and toward a collectivist New Japanism (Iizuka 1941:47, 50).

It is worth noting in this connection that the Euro-American influenced Takarazuka Revue was an ambiguous symbol of and for the New Japan, which itself was an unstable signifier. On the one hand, the New Japan was an imagined community constructed from select artifacts of western material culture and a nation whose western inflections would, theoretically, allow it to withstand the encroachments of European and American powers (cf. Feuerwerker 1989). On the other hand, the New Japan was both the repository for and legacy of the products of Asia's ancient cultural histories, and bore the burden of salvaging Asia for the Asians. Similarly, whereas Kobayashi gave Takarazuka the positive valence of signifying the differentiation of a unique and superior Japan from Asia and the world, his critics placed a negative valence on the revue as signifying the westernization and thus corruption of "traditional" Japan (see Robertson 1995).

Kobayashi's Vision

Kobayashi's efforts to promote the Takarazuka Revue as a symbol of the New Japan included innovations in architecture and production methods. He advocated the construction of large "mass theaters" that could accommodate thousands of working and middle-class spectators to whom would be offered low-priced tickets (Kobayashi 1967:550). In 1924, Kobayashi had opened a 4,000-seat theater in Takarazuka (near Osaka) to replace the smaller original stage at the hot-springs spa. The 3,000-seat Tokyo Takarazuka theater opened on New Year's Day, 1934. These were the two largest theaters in Japan at that time. A conservative estimate of the total annual number of spectators at both the Takarazuka and Tokyo Takarazuka theaters in the 1930s and 1940s produces a figure in the millions—a significant audience that, in the eyes of the state, could not remain unclaimed.

A production schedule was planned that, from Kobayashi's point of view, precluded Takarazuka shows from catering to an elite class. Instead of staging productions twice a day, as in the case of the *kabuki* theater, daily performances were scheduled from six to ten o'clock in the evening; in addition, afternoon matinees were held on Sundays and holidays (Kobayashi 1967:126, 549, 550). Kobayashi believed that all Japanese citizens (*kokumin*) should work eight hours a day and spend four hours in the evening at rest and recreation. The theater in general, and the Takarazuka Revue in particular, was promoted by him as "one of the most edifying forms of entertainment"; a "basic life necessity" (Kobayashi 1967:130).

Audiences, he insisted, must be composed not of individuals but entire households: just as the household was defined in the Civil Code as the smallest, most indivisible unit of society, so should it be the smallest unit of spectatorship. In the daily *Osaka mainichi* (8 January 1935), Kobayashi claimed that "what has been called entertainment for the masses has really been for males specifically.

... Mass theater must cater to women as well as men. ... A married couple should attend [the theater] together." Promoted as "healthful family entertainment," Takarazuka was aimed at "the whole conjugal household (*katei*) over its constituent members (*kazoku*), the public (*kôkyô*) over the household, the masses (*taishû*)—and ultimately, the totality of 'the people' (*kokumin*) of Japan—over the public" (Kobayashi 1967:130). In short, Kobayashi envisioned concentric circles of increasingly ideal spectators, expanding outward from the household and eventually encompassing the "family state" (*kokka*). Attending a Takarazuka performance was billed as tantamount to performing a social duty and a patriotic act, and, appropriately, Kobayashi nicknamed the Tokyo Takarazuka theater the "palace of household entertainment" (*katei kyôraku no dendô*) (Kobayashi 1934:268).

Kobayashi was interested in producing plays and creating a public space that catered to and accommodated women as well as men—he criticized existing forms of mass entertainment and recreation (such as horse racing, team sports, etc.) as targeted largely for male audiences. Kobayashi acknowledged and staked a claim on the female spectator in particular if only to more effectively shape women into consumers. He developed the railroad terminal department store and encouraged female spectators especially to treat themselves to the theater of capitalism. The revue theater with its juxtaposed images and events was analogous to the miscellaneously stocked department store, where publicity campaigns emphasized the spectacular dramaturgy of selling and shopping (Iizuka 1930:44; Takaoka 1943:195). Similarly, the sumptuous sets and exotic foreign settings of the revue provided spectators with the most accessible vision of what capitalism, commodity culture, and empire meant. The 1941 revue *Made in Japan* for example, celebrated the expansion of Japanese trade into global markets and promoted silk, porcelain ware, musical instruments, bicycles, and other representative manufactured goods of the country. This same also celebrated Japanese colonial policies as well: the theme song, also titled "Made in Japan," included the lyrics, "the less advanced will join with us to revive their trade. Our fortune brings fortune to those lacking foreign currency" (*Sekai no ichiba* 1941:71).

Kobayashi's profit-oriented, commercial interest in organizing and rationalizing leisure and entertainment overlapped with the state's interest in the same. Ever the opportunist, Kobayashi promoted Takarazuka as the dramatic equivalent of the New Japan. Takarazuka, he proclaimed, represented a break with the past and captured the new, the modern, the *Zeitgeist* of the twentieth century (Kobayashi 1967:130–31). In fact, one of the salient characteristics of the revue form that the Japanese state found particularly useful was its novelty. In keeping with its etymology, the "revue" theater represented a break from "the past"; that is, a break from a fixed, singular, canonical reading of events past and present. Like photomontage, the revue offered "completely new opportunities ... for uncovering [and also making] relationships, oppositions, transitions and intersections of social reality" (Ollman 1991:34). *Kabuki,* in contrast, was derided by Kobayashi as an "antique" (*koten*) theater whose "pathetic *shamisen* melodies did not resonate with the spirit of the times" (Kobayashi 1967:130).

Not all of Kobayashi's contemporaries shared his enthusiasm for the revue form and its manifold aesthetic and political possibilities. Some regarded the 350-year-old *kabuki* theater as a venerable cultural artifact in which they could admire the past and recognize themselves as a nation. They recognized the class-cutting popularity and "awesome commercial appeal" of the Takarazuka Revue, and were impressed by both the disciplined actors and the "rationality" of Kobayashi's production methods. But these critics ultimately dismissed the revue form itself as "devoid of content"—"a fad ... which, like people's lives today, is superficial, intuitional, divorced from tradition, and without systematicness" (Iizuka 1941: 65–66, 68–69).

In an effort to organize leisure by "bringing the theater to the people," Ôyama Isao and Iizuka Tomoichirô, both prominent theater historians and critics, inaugurated the Citizens' Theater Movement (*Kokumin engeki undô*)[4] in the late 1930s. They recognized the influential reach and wide appeal of theater as a manipulatable artifact of everyday life (Fuwa 1941:2). "Citizen's theater" was defined as "a theater in which the spiritual essence of the [Japanese] people is expressed and nurtured" (Iizuka 1941:45; Ôyama 1941). The movement would facilitate the "advance of the Japanese race" (*nihon minzoku hatten*), a nationalist and imperialist agenda sanctioned by the military government (see Robertson 1991). Promoted as "wholesome entertainment" (*kenzen na goraku*) citizens' theater necessarily precluded dramas dealing with suicide, prostitution, and the "grotesque," topics that were perceived to have a deleterious psychological effect on popular audiences (*"Shinjû" no shibai kinshi* 1939; Terazawa 1943). The mass organization of leisure and entertainment was a highly contested project, and in the early 1940s, Kobayashi and his contemporaries vied with each other in claiming their theater as the rightful symbol of the New Japan.

Mobile Troupes and Industrial Drama

Kobayashi was especially astute in positioning the Takarazuka Revue as a bridge between the sociopolitical order at home and an idealized vision of empire. Moreover, Takarazuka was also a "traveling bridge," insofar as mobile troupes of Takarasiennes were dispatched, in the late 1930s, to factories, farm villages, and hospitals throughout the country. Groups of Takarasiennes even toured war fronts in China, Korea, and Manchuria in the fall of 1939 and 1942, the spring of 1943, and the fall of 1944, to provide civilians and soldiers with "wholesome entertainment" and to weave together symbolically the disparate parts of the Japanese Empire (Matsumoto 1939; Shasetsu: Engeki bunka to engekihô 1942; Takagi 1942; Toita 1956 [1950]:250–52; Uemoto 1941).[5] I should note parenthetically that these tours inspired Imperial Army soldiers to innovate soldier shows of their own in which the males performed as women (Kamura 1984:121–122; also Maruki 1930).[6] The length of these tours varied from one to three months (Hashimoto 1984:172). Recognizing the material and symbolic value of the traveling shows, the state pressured commercial theaters to organize the mobile troupes under the auspices of a national federation, the Nippon idô engeki renmei.[7]

Mobile units of Takarazuka actors were dispatched to over sixty factories in the Kansai area alone in 1942, and staged an average of between ten and thirty performances in each prefecture that they toured (Furukawa 1943:58–59). The Takarazuka Revue was among the theaters incorporated into the new "industrial drama" (*kôba (kôjo) engeki*) movement of the 1940s, which deserves mention in connection with my general topic. Factory-based theater shows and clubs were favored by the state for several reasons: to help to nurture a communal work spirit; to inject some humanity into the machinelike nature of factory labor; to elicit the proper ethnic/nationalist (*minzokuteki*) behavior from the workers; and thus to create a basis for heightened productivity in a time of war (Ôoka 1941:22). War provided an unprecedented opportunity for experimenting with adult recreation, and factory, village, and urban theater programs were seen as "pacifying agents" (cf. Tsuchiya 1985: 99, 104). As one Japanese nationalist theater reformer remarked, "War may be destructive, but it also provides an opportunity to forge a national culture"—and the mass organization of leisure was an important part of that process (Iizuka 1941:44).

Advocates of industrial drama also noted that wartime conditions had occasioned unprecedented changes for Japanese industry. Military conscription and war-related production resulted in an acute shortage of skilled labor, accompanied by longer hours and the deteriorating health of workers, absenteeism, intense interfirm mobility, and rising wages (Garon 1987:217, 224). Attention was thus drawn to the issue of leisure time, which one analyst calculated now amounted to only two hours a day at most, making it difficult for factory workers to develop an appreciation for "culture" (Ôoka 1941:18). By cultural appreciation, the analyst was referring to workers' familiarity with the Japanese Empire and the New World Order.

Ôoka Kinji, a theater reformer, expressed concern that 90 percent of factory workers had not graduated from primary school, and that those who were enrolled received no "cultural training" (1941: 18). He discussed the various solutions forwarded by state organizations, such as the Greater Japan Industrial Patriotic Association, active between 1940 and 1945, which was established as a unifying body to absorb, control, and mobilize each company's labor union and workforce according to the needs of the military state (Hunter 1984:108; Garon 1987:220–22). These attempts to raise the workers' cultural consciousness concentrated on the use of theatrical, musical, artistic, and literary materials; for example, the association invited top-flight actors and musicians, including Takarasiennes, to perform for factory workers and called for the creation of factory-based theater troupes (Ôoka 1941:19).

Ôoka noted the dearth of theatrical scripts appropriate for factory use; that is, scripts that would help nurture the consolidation of a work ethic. In this connection, he reported how, in the case of spinning mills, theater groups formed by female workers imitated the Takarazuka Revue; some of the women performed the men's roles all "too realistically," in his view (1941:21). Without any doubt he was aware of the connection certain critics had drawn between the popularity of the all-female Revue and the alleged increase in homosexual relations among girls and women, including factory workers. As I have written elsewhere, despite Kobayashi's precautions and proscriptions, the history of Takarazuka has been characterized by a tension between the dominant text of the Revue, which celebrates an ideal heterosexuality, and the subtext of the performances, which entails a homosexual subcultural style (Robertson 1989, 1991). In any case, the bad press did not stop either government ministries or the industrial drama organizers from utilizing the Takarazuka Revue as an effective vehicle of industrial policy and for imperial propaganda. The Revue's patriarchal management, strict vertical social organization, and emphasis on hierarchy determined by age, sex, and gender, as well as the rigorous discipline of the training curriculum were confluent with the social-engineering agenda of the wartime state.

Conclusion

Although Takarazuka was not alone among the theaters vying for recognition as the epitome of New Japan, state ideologues found the ambiguous hybridity of the Revue especially intriguing and useful in the wartime campaign to mobilize the people. Mainstream historiographical consensus has it that "imperialism never became a very important part of the [Japanese] national consciousness," and that "[t]here were no Japanese Kiplings, there was little popular mystique about Japanese overlordship and relatively little national self-congratulation" (Jansen 1984:76). My examination of the role of theater in the mass organization of leisure in imperial Japan focuses on the affective, aesthetic, and cultural policies of the wartime nation that have been neglected relative to the more bureaucratic, military, and political economic dimensions of imperialism. The sheer abundance of archival and dramaturgical evidence suggests that the mainstream consensus was premature; theater, including the Takarazuka Revue, was deployed as a powerful agent in controlling leisure time and in shaping a belief in Japanese cultural superiority.[8]

Notes

1. I refer to "the state" in the singular, as a thing-in-itself, for the sake of convenience. I follow Corrigan and Sayer (1985) in regarding "the state" not simply as an "organ of coercion" or a "bureaucratic lineage," but as a repertoire of agencies (sites, technologies, institutions, ministries), which collectively, albeit not without internal contradications, shape and reproduce the dominant ideology.

2. Today, Takarazuka is a small part of an enormous, multimedia entertainment industry, and, consequently, Revue audiences are now more selective and consist mostly of girls and women, and particularly married women over thirty years of age.

3. The main Takarazuka theater remains one component of an expansive "wholesome entertainment" complex which in 1943 included a hot-springs spa, a library, a botanical garden, an entomology museum, and a zoo noted for its white tiger. In 1919, Kobayashi established the Takarazuka Music Academy as part of the Revue complex and from which all actors must graduate.

Approximately seven hundred people presently enable Takarazuka to function, and the literature suggests that about the same number were employed during the wartime period: four hundred performers and three hundred specialists including producers, directors, writers, costumers, set designers, instructors, and two thirty-five-piece orchestras. The actors are divided into four troupes, established between 1921 and 1933 (see Robertson 1992a). Dividing the women into troupes facilitated organizing the growing number of actors (from twenty at the outset, to about three hundred fifty in 1931 [Hashimoto 1984:118–20]), and enabled year-round performances at different venues throughout Japan. Each troupe is overseen by a (male) member of the Revue administration appointed to that post. The internal hierarchy consists of a troupe manager and a vice-manager appointed from among the senior actors.

There were other all-female revue theaters established in the early twentieth century as well, notably the Shôchiku Revue founded in Tokyo (in Asakusa, a major working-class theater district) in 1928, which quickly became Takarazuka's main rival in every respect. Other, much smaller, Tokyo revues included the Casino Folies (opened in 1929), in Asakusa, and the Moulin Rouge (opened in 1931), in Shinjuku, a student and intellectual center at the time (see Seidensticker 1990:68–87).

4. Whereas *kokumin engeki* can be translated literally as "citizens' theater," "state theater" is a more accurate description of the movement, which was sanctioned by the military state as a means of claiming the people through the interpellative power of dramaturgy. See Robertson (1991).

5. Revue administrators briefly entertained a plan of establishing a Takarazuka-like theater in North China (Matsumoto 1939). Since, as of 1934, the 1,934 drama theaters of widely varying sizes were concentrated in cities (Monbushô goraku chôsa 1932), regional tours by commercial theater troupes were important components of national community building. The intensive activities of the mobile groups of actors further popularized theater among diverse audiences in Japan and abroad (Toita 1956 [1950]: 252) and helped to disseminate a military and imperialist ethos in the guise of entertainment.

Members of the Shôchiku Revue also toured the same war fronts and colonial outposts, and also those in Southeast Asia and Micronesia (Shôchiku kagekidan 1978:45–48).

Although mobile theater troupes have a centuries-old history in Japan, the specific use of such troupes during wartime was reinforced by the example set in fascist Italy, where the state deployed Thespian Prose Cars, basically portable stages, to bring sanctioned entertainment to the masses. Japanese theater critics were aware of such innovations in Italy and elsewhere. By 1936, over a million spectators were accounted for throughout Italy. The actual performance efficacy of the cars is another matter (see De Grazia 1981:162–63).

6. The spectacle of males cross-dressing as women was a regular feature of the mobile entertainment troupes who performed for British and American soldiers during World War II. As Fawkes and Bérubé note, the woman's-role players often were more popular and sought after than actual female actors and dancers (Bérubé 1990:67–97; Fawkes 1978:45, 53, 125, 163). Apart from recent scholarship on state-coerced and regulated prostitution (i.e., the traffic in "comfort women"), little research has been conducted on the organization of soldier entertainment in the Japanese armed forces.

7. The Japanese Federation of Mobile Theaters.

8. There is relatively little research on the ways in which theater interfaces with imperialism and colonialism (see my recent article, Robertson

1995). In the case of Japanese studies, the uses of film and radio as vehicles for the spiritual and physical mobilization of the Japanese and colonial peoples have been expertly documented and discussed (e.g., Dower 1993; Fukushima and Nornes 1991; Goodman 1991; Hauser 1991; Kasza 1988; Silverberg 1993). But there is a dearth of critical research on wartime theater, where staged performances operated as social metacommentaries on and motivators for such interconnected practices as nationalism, imperialism, racism, militarism, sexual politics, and gendered relations (cf. Bratton 1991; Pickering 1991:229). Similarly, theater-state relations are overlooked or ignored in the otherwise excellent scholarship on the Japanese colonial empire (Beasley 1987; Dower 1986; Duus, Myers, and Peattie 1989; Myers and Peattie 1984; Peattie 1988; Shillony 1991 [1981], et alia). Rimer (1974) offers a complementary overview of the New Theater (*shingeki*) movement through the career of the playwright, Kishida Kunio.

References

Beasley, William. 1987. *Japanese imperialism, 1894–1945*. Oxford: Clarendon.

Bérubé, Allan. 1990. *Coming out under fire: The history of gay men and women in World War Two*. New York: Free Press.

Bratton, J. S. 1991. "Introduction," J. S. Bratton, et al. (eds.), *Acts of supremacy: The British Empire and the stage, 1790–1930*. Manchester: Manchester University Press, 1–17.

Burns, Tom. 1973. "Leisure in industrial society," Michael Smith (ed.), *Leisure and society in Britain*. London: Allen Lane.

Chaney, David. 1979. *Fictions and ceremonies: Representations of popular experience*. London: Arnold.

Corrigan, Philip, and Derek Sayer. 1985. *The great arch: English state formation as cultural revolution*. London: Basil Blackwell.

Dana, Henry. 1943. *Drama in wartime Russia*. New York: National Council of American-Soviet Friendship.

De Grazia, Victoria. 1981. *The culture of consent: Mass organization of leisure in fascist Italy*. Cambridge: Cambridge University Press.

Dower, John. 1986. *War without mercy: Race and power in the Pacific War*. New York: Pantheon.

———. 1993. *Japan in war and peace: Selected essays*. New York: New Press.

Endô Shingo. 1943. "Nanpô no engeki kôsaku," *Engei Gahô* 37/2, 1.

Fawkes, Richard. 1978. *Fighting for a laugh: Entertaining the British and American armed forces, 1939–1946*. London: Macdonald and Jane's.

Feuerwerker, Albert. 1989. "Japanese imperialism in China: A commentary," Duus, Peter, Ramon Myers, and Mark Peattie (eds.). 1989. *The Japanese informal empire in China, 1895–1937*. Princeton, N.J.: Princeton University Press, 431–38.

Fischer-Lichte, Erika. 1989. "Theater and the civilizing process: An approach to the history of acting," Thomas Postlewait and Bruce McConachie (eds.), *Interpreting the theatrical past: Essays in the historiography of performance*. Iowa City: Iowa University Press, 19–36.

Fukushima, Yukio, and Marcus Nornes (eds.). 1991. *Media wars: Then and now*. Yamagata International Documentary Film Festival '91. Tokyo: Sôjinsha.

Furukawa Riryû. 1943. "Kansai ni okeru idô engeki no genjô," *Gendai engeki* 5/6, 57–60.

Fuwa Suketoshi. 1941. "Engekihô shimon dai'ichigo tôshin'an," *Engei gahô* 35/1, 2–3.

Garon, Sheldon. 1987. *State and labor in modern Japan*. Berkeley: University of California Press.

Goodman, Grant (ed.). 1991. *Japanese cultural policies in Southeast Asia during World War 2*. New York: St. Martin's.

Hashimoto Masao. 1984. *Takarazuka kageki no 70 nen*. Takarazuka: Takarazuka kagekidan.

Hauser, William. 1991. "Women and war: The Japanese film image," Gail Bernstein (ed.), *Recreating Japanese women, 1600–1945*. Berkeley: University of California Press, 296–313.

Hunter, Janet. 1984. *Concise dictionary of modern Japanese history*. Berkeley: University of California Press.

Iizuka Tomoichirô. 1930. *Engeki to hanzai: Kindai hanzai kagaku zenshû 15*. Tokyo: Bukyôsha.

———. 1941. *Kokuminengeki to nôson engeki*. Tokyo: Shimizu shobô.

Jansen, Marius. 1984. "Japanese imperialism: Late Meiji perspectives," Myers, Ramon, and Mark Peattie (eds.). 1984. *The Japanese colonial empire, 1885–1945*. Princeton, N.J.: Princeton University Press, 61–79.

Kamura Kikuo. 1984. *Itoshi no takarazuka e*. Kobe: Kôbe shinbun shuppan sentâ.

Kasza, Gregory. 1988. *The state and mass media in Japan, 1918–1945*. Berkeley: University of California Press.

Kershaw, Baz. 1992. *The politics of performance: Radical theater as cultural intervention*. London: Routledge.

Kobayashi Ichizô. 1934. "Taishû geijutsu no jin'ei," *Chûô kôron*, 1 (January), 268–73.

———. 1935. "Goraku yo katei e kaere," *Ôsaka mainichi*, 8 January.

———. 1967. *Takarazuka manpitsu*. Tokyo: Jitsugyô no Nihonsha.

Maruki Sato. 1930. "Aisuru senyû," *Hanzai kagaku* 11, 84–89.

Matsumoto Narao. 1939. "Pick of 13 zukettes is going to China to cheer up Nippon soldiers at front," *The Osaka Mainichi and Tokyo Nichinichi,* 9 August.

Mimi to me to kuchi to. 1941. *Takarazuka kageki kyakuhonshû* 24/3, 26–43.

"Monbushô goraku chôsa." 1932. *Tôkyô Asahi Shinbun,* 2 December.

Nakagawa Ryûichi. 1941. "Amerika no renpô engeki undô," *Gendai Engeki* 4/3, 51–52.

Niizeki Ryôzô. 1940. *Nachizu doitsu no engeki.* Tokyo: Kôbundô.

Ollman, Leah. 1991. *Camera as weapon: Worker photography between the wars.* San Diego: Museum of Photographic Arts.

Ôoka Kinji. 1941. "Kôba engeki ni tsuite," *Gendai engeki* 4/2, 17–22.

Ôyama Isao. 1941. "Kokumin engekiron josetsu," *Kokumin engeki* 1/1, 106–14.

Peattie, Mark. 1988. *Nan'yô: The rise and fall of the Japanese in Micronesia, 1885–1945.* Pacific Islands Monograph Series 4. Honolulu: University of Hawaii Press.

Pickering, Michael. 1991. "Mock blacks and racial mockery: The 'nigger' minstrel and British imperialism," J. S. Bratton et al. (eds.), *Acts of supremacy: The British empire and the stage, 1790–1930.* Manchester: Manchester University Press: 179–236.

Renov, Michael. 1991. "Warring images: Stereotype and American representations of the Japanese, 1941–1991," Fukushima and Nornes, 86–114.

Rimer, J. Thomas. 1974. *Toward a modern Japanese theater: Kishida Kunio.* Princeton, N.J.: Princeton University Press.

Robertson, Jennifer. 1989. "Gender-bending in paradise: Doing 'female' and 'male' in Japan," *Genders* 5, 188–207.

———. 1991. "Theatrical resistance, theaters of restraint: The Takarazuka Revue and the 'state theater' movement," *Anthropological Quarterly* 64/4, 165–77.

———. 1992a. "Doing and undoing 'female' and 'male' in Japan: The Takarazuka Revue," Takie S. Lebra (ed.), *Japanese social organization.* Honolulu: University of Hawaii Press, 165–93.

———. 1992b. "The politics of androgyny in Japan: Sexuality and subversion in the theater and beyond," *American Ethnologist* 19/3, 419–42.

———. 1995. "Mon Japon: Theater as a technology of Japanese imperialism," *American Ethnologist* 22/4, 970–96.

Schnapp, Jeffrey. 1993. "18BL: Fascist mass spectacle," *Representations* 43 (Summer), 89–125.

Seidensticker, Edward. 1990. *Tokyo rising: The city since the great earthquake.* New York: Alfred A. Knopf.

Sekai no ichiba. 1941. *Takarazuka kageki kyakuhonshû* 24/4, 71–86.

"Shasetsu: engeki bunka to engekihô." 1942. *Tôkyô asahi shinbun,* 22 November.

Shillony, Ben-Ami. 1991 [1981]. *Politics and culture in wartime Japan.* Oxford: Clarendon.

"*'Shinjû' no shibai kinshi.*" 1939. *Ôsaka asahi shinbun,* evening ed., 17 December.

Shôchiku kagekidan. 1978. *Rebyû to tomo ni hanseiki: Shôchiku kagekidan 50nen no ayumi.* Tokyo: Kokusho kankôkai.

Silverberg, Miriam. 1993. "Constructing a new cultural history of prewar Japan," Masao Miyoshi and H. D. Harootunian (eds.), *Japan in the world.* Durham: Duke University Press, 115–43.

Takagi Shin'ichi. 1942. "Kôba kokumin engeki juritsu e no teishin," *Gendai engeki* 5/3, 22–24.

Takaoka Nobuyuki. 1943. *Kokumin engeki no tenbô.* Tokyo: Hôbundô.

Takarazuka Kagekidan. 1943. *Takarazuka nenkan.* Osaka: Takarazuka Kagekidan.

Terazawa Takanobu. 1943. "Ken'etsukei no tachiba kara," *Engei gahô* 37/8, 3.

Toita Yasuji. 1956 [1950]. *Engeki gojûnen.* Tokyo: Jijitsûshinsha.

Tsuchiya Hiroko. 1985. "'Let them be amused': The industrial drama movement, 1910–1929," Bruce McConachie and Daniel Friedman (eds.), *Theater for working-class audiences in the United States, 1830–1980.* Westport, Conn.: Greenwood, 97–110.

Uemoto Sutezô. 1941. "Manshû ni okeru engeki seisaku ni tsuite," *Gendai engeki* 4/3, 48–50.

Eckhart Derschmidt

16

The Disappearance of the "Jazu-Kissa"

Some Considerations about Japanese "Jazz-Cafés" and Jazz-Listeners

Around the beginning of this century jazz began to develop in America. Around World War I, it began to spread overseas, to Europe as well as to Japan. This process had many more parallels than differences. For example, that jazz, at least then music of the lower social strata, was imported by and first became popular among members of the upper class. And that jazz and its adherents repeatedly faced oppression and censorship by the governments of both cultural hemispheres in the 1920s and '30s.[1] Jazz was reimported after WW II—the American army, with its radio stations and musicians sent there to entertain the soldiers, playing the most important role in the process in Europe as well as in Japan. But nowhere in Europe, and of course not in America, did an institution like the Japanese *jazu-kissa*[2] evolve, a café, whose main, and as from the middle of the fifties whose sole, function was to provide a space in which to listen to jazz. Or, to be more precise, to jazz on vinyl.[3]

In December 1993, the closing of a small café in Jinbo-chô, Tokyo, caused an enormous hullabaloo in the Japanese media and even made it onto the first page of the evening issue of *Yomiuri Shinbun* (24 December 1993).[4] The Hibiki had been one of Tokyo's most prominent *jazu-kissa* for about twenty years, known for its audiophile stereo equipment, its huge record collection, and for its master, a well-known jazz critic and author of books on jazz. With the demise of the Hibiki there are only few such places left in Tokyo, and it may not take long for this kind of café to vanish completely. There were more than a hundred *jazu-kissa* in Tokyo in the seventies,[5] but the number began to decline during the eighties. The Hibiki was only the latest and most prominent victim of that development. Economic factors like the ever-increasing commodity prices in urban areas can explain the decline only partly. By examining the functions of the *jazu-kissa*, the ways of jazz perception and listener attitudes, I will try to show that the dissipation of the services provided by the *jazu-kissa* caused a decline in guests that could not be reconciled and finally forced many shops to close.

Listening to jazz is part and parcel of the more general concept of music reception—the active process by which music is heard and processed, under circumstances to be described individually. Rösing (1994:67) delineates a "causal system of musical reception" that consists of three equal, mutually complementing and mutually influencing areas: first, the musical stimulus, or product. Second, the recipient. And, third, there are the particular circumstances in which reception takes place, which have an impact that is not to be underestimated. These three areas are related to three basic questions: Who receives, what is received, and under which circumstances? The determining areas of musical reception have to be seen and interpreted in direct relation to the respective sociocultural environment.

In the following, particular attention will be paid to the problem of availability of, and access to, media, which appears to be one of the most powerful factors in explaining consumption patterns (Shuker 1994:225) and thereby the changing role of *jazu-kissa* in the process of jazz reception.

Until recently the clientele of the *jazu-kissa* was dominated by high school and university students. Young people between fifteen and twenty-nine years of age are most interested in, and most enthusiastic about, music. They are thus most actively engaged in listening to and acquiring knowledge about music. According to a NHK study from 1982, all musical media are used most extensively by this age group (NHK hôsô yoron chôsa-jo 1982:41). This is a phenomenon independent of time, a feature related to the process of growing up. The fact that the kind of music preferred by this age group is very apparent in public, while other musical styles are well alive but less visible, is referred to as the "musical iceberg phenomenon" by the NHK study group (NHK hôsô yoron chôsa-jo 1982:74). They distinguish between prewar, war, pre-Beatles, Beatles, and post-Beatles generations, in regard to the period of time when respective listeners were between fifteen and twenty-nine years old, just as the contemporary generation may be called the "Tekkno" or "HipHop generation." Similarly I will distinguish between the pre-Coltrane or Bop generation of the fifties, Coltrane generation of the sixties, post-Coltrane or Fusion generation of the seventies, and—in the absence of a powerful leading figure—the Postmodern or Neo-Bop generation of the eighties, with regard to jazz fans. But let us now return to the fifties.

In the 1950s there were only limited possibilities to come into contact with jazz. Particularly outside of the urban centers radio programs, initially only those of the American troops, and then after 1951 those of private Japanese radio stations, were about the only means of listening to jazz. Probably the most popular jazz program of that time was Bunka hôsô's *Jazz at the Toris*, established in 1954, that featured a live band (George Kawaguchi's Big Four, the most popular band of the time) which, at the request of the audience, played popular tunes "jazz style." It was broadcasted 170 times and now symbolizes a period in which jazz was still popular music. American jazz could be heard on NHK's *Rhythm Hour* and late-night programs of the private radio stations.

Another possible encounter with jazz was via movies. Films like *Benny Goodman Story* and *Glenn Miller Story* were extremely popular, some jazz fans of the pre-Coltrane generation recall having seen these movies more than twenty times. Jazz was the soundtrack music of many films of the *nouvelle vague* in the late fifties (Iwanami 1977:49; Mihara 1991:238).

Live concerts were still rare. Live jazz, performed by Japanese musicians, could primarily be heard in night clubs and cabarets (Uchida 1976:284f.). The first American musicians (to play for Japanese audiences) were the Gene Krupa Trio in 1952, followed by Norman Granz's Jazz at the Philharmonic and the Louis Armstrong Allstars in 1953. It was not until 1961 that American top players came to Japan more frequently.

Records were virtually unavailable during the first half of the fifties. Only in 1956 did King Records begin the "King Jazz Series," which featured the Japanese bands of the time. The only way to get American jazz records was to import them directly, which was extremely expensive. As the *jazu-kissa* were among the few who could afford to do so, they were about the only places where one could listen to the latest American jazz records. Cultural critic Uegusa Jinichi once stated: "For the jazz fan, late-night radio programs and the *jazu-kissa* ... are places of research" (*kenkyû no ba*) (cit. in Mihara 1991:239). And the records were the source of research. According to Soejima (1994:4) one had to be able to tell white from black players in a recording in order to be accepted as a real jazz fan. Not very surprisingly, the *jazu-kissa* of the fifties and early sixties resembled educational institutions. Not only musicians like Watanabe Sadao or Akiyoshi Toshiko went there to learn about the latest developments in jazz (Watanabe 1994:1) but also the ordinary jazz fan. *Swing Journal* provided one page for the *jazu-kissa*, where the latest acquired records could be presented. At the Mama near Tokyo Station, the master always described the records in great detail, before he put them on the turntable. Like: "The next record I am going to play, I received by airmail[6] just a few hours ago. Billie Holiday's last pianist, Mal Waldron wrote that piece in memoriam of her. The members of the band are ...." It was just like jazz college, with the master as teacher. Even today it is not unusual for masters or jazz critics to be called *sensei* by "ordinary" jazz fans. Periodically, the masters also organized so-called record concerts (*rekôdo konsâto*), in which they themselves or famous critics presented programs, dedicated to particular musicians or styles, or just the latest releases. And the mood in the *kissa* was somewhat like that of a classroom, after the teacher has distributed the answering sheets of a test. Many of the guests took notes (Onishi 1991:207). This didactic style can also be found in the *Swing Journal*, the only big jazz magazine at the time, and has partially prevailed until today. This kind of knowledge fetishism is maybe best illustrated by MEG-master Terashima Yasukuni, who—admittedly ironically—tells of one of his employees who proposed a *nyûten-shiken*, an entrance examination,[7] for new part-timers, to "be able to preserve the level of the shop" (Terashima 1982:233). What developed here, ironically, was exactly that kind of ritual accompanying the appreciation of art that is usually associated with classical music: like these "products of high culture," jazz had to be appreciated with reverent, informed, and disciplined seriousness (Levine 1988 in Twitchell 1992:65) . But the contradiction between the kind of music listened to and the way of listening was only realized in retrospect (Shimizu 1977:172).

The sixties brought little change with regard to access to media. The evolving television did not feature jazz prominently until Watanabe Sadao was given his own program in 1969. On the radio, jazz was mainly played in late-night programs. Records were increasingly available but still too expensive to be bought with a student's pocket money. An *eâmêru-pan* (record imported by airmail) was 3,000 Yen, whereas the first monthly salary of a university graduate was about 10,000 Yen.

From around 1965, live houses began to develop in Shinjuku, providing playing opportunities for the rapidly developing Japanese jazz scene.[8] What changed fundamentally was the attitude of the students. Although Japan was in the middle of high economic growth and everybody was striving for the three C's—car, cooler, color TV—the students and intellectuals turned their backs on these developments. In the musicians of the Free Jazz movement—John Coltrane, Albert Ayler, Cecil Taylor—they found powerful allies, expressing their common experience of oppression and solitude[9] (Steinert 1992:212; Nakano 1984:86). There are several accounts of how closely the student movement and the intellectuals related the musical expression of free jazz to their own situation (e.g., Nakagami Kenji's short story *Hakai seyo, to Airâ wa itta*, or a short citation from a small literary magazine in 1970: "The New Left is New Jazz. And we are Ayler" (Kareki 1989:78). Of course it is problematic to derive political functions music-immanently from jazz, but, whatever the artist's intention, what counts in the final analysis is the audience's perception of and reaction to the work (Butler 1986:103–104).

In the mid-sixties, several new *jazu-kissa* were established. Compared to the previous generation they were darker, and the volume of the music was increased to the limits of the bearable—an unprecedented sound experience (Aikura and Aoki 1981:186). This also altered the way of listening from informed seriousness to contemplative meditation. Speaking—although impossible anyway—

became generally forbidden (see, for example, Shimizu 1977:171).
Jazu-kissa began more and more to resemble temples, as the jazz
following began to resemble Leonard's notion of "cult," by which he
means "a loose group almost without organization not so much a
brotherhood as a transient, fluctuating collection of individuals
drawn together by ecstatic experience. The cult requires little, if any
common discipline and permits other religious affiliations. It demands only loyalty to the source of attraction and appropriate rituals which may be part of a broader system or belief" (Leonard 1987:
30). The darkness, the tremendous volume[10] of the music, the
motionlessly listening guests, and the frequently strict and authoritarian master, who not only placed the records on the turntable but
also checked that his shop rules were being obeyed, all added to the
impression that one entered a very special, almost religious room
(Shin 1991:279), a completely different world (Murata 1991:159).
The quasi-religious status that was attached to the music is also
reflected in book titles like Hiraoka Masaaki's *Jazu yori hoka ni
kami wa nashi* (No gods except jazz) (Hiraoka 1971). Many accounts
of this time describe the first step into a *jazu-kissa* as a quite shock-
ing, disturbing experience:

> I first entered the Funky in Kichijôji when I was seventeen,
> and I was shocked by the big volume of the music. The huge
> speakers trembled, and even the chair I sat on trembled under
> the sound waves. Then I looked around and recognized a man,
> who shook his head with the rhythm of the music. Over-
> whelmed by his distracted expression I looked to the other
> side, and I saw a beardy guy, who listened with closed eyes, and
> some other men quietly reading their books. To me, that dark
> smoky room seemed rather unhealthy. (Oshima 1989:136)

The death of the most prominent proponents of free jazz, John
Coltrane (1967) and Albert Ayler (1970), and the defeat of the student movement in the Anpo struggle of 1970 brought an abrupt end
to this style of jazz perception.[11] The former activists graduated
from university and entered professional life, and the upcoming generation had completely different needs. With fusion music (called
jazz rock at that time) a more comprehensible and commercial style
prevailed over the outcry of free jazz. The post-Coltrane generation

was the first one that had more or less full access to media, at least from their early teens. Records were readily available, and stereo sets came within reach of the students' limited budgets. International artists frequently toured in Japan, and, with the jazz festival, a new means of jazz reception was introduced. Additionally, live-houses, where mainly Japanese artists performed, were established all over Japan.

In the area of jazz print media, the seventies saw the establishing of three new big jazz magazines, two of which, namely *Jazz* and *Jazzland*, had to cease publication within two years for the obvious reason of having opposed the prevailing trend and the demands of the post-Coltrane generation. But a look at the list of contributors makes clear that these projects were doomed to failure from the very outset: most of them were members of the previous generation, who had tried to continue the intellectual and theoretical style of the sixties.[12] The third magazine, *JazzLife*, suited the new demands: the main focus was on fusion music, Japanese musicians were featured prominently, and practical instructions for various instrumentalists were given.

With the rock and fusion boom in the seventies the *jazu-kissa*'s struggle for survival began. Although they were still the locus for the remains of the student movement until about 1973, from then on a new type of guest appeared, who demanded a different kind of music and who did not want to obey the authoritarian regime of the masters. This, obviously, was a consequence of the demands of the student movement.

The masters, many of whom were members of the Coltrane generation, had to cope with similar problems as the magazine editors. If one continued business as usual, guests would dwindle and closing down the shop would become unavoidable. Fusion boomed, but fusion was unacceptable to a real jazz fan, whose foremost exponents the masters always thought themselves to be (Terashima 1981)—a dilemma that proved fatal for many *jazu-kissa* in the late seventies.

Of course some of them adopted successfully to the new situation and to the needs of the new generation. They realized that it was no longer sufficient to provide only one kind of information (Orito and Yoshii 1981:200). Different kinds of information had to be available, and communication among the guests, but also between master and guests, had to be made possible. The volume was reduced, the black walls were repainted in brighter colors, comic books were provided (Oshima 1989), and alcoholic beverages sold—something considered a sacrilege in many *jazu-kissa* during the sixties. As a matter of course, fusion was included in the repertoire—especially Japanese fusion, considered as a standard of comparison by the young guests, many of whom played instruments themselves (Orito and Yoshii 1981:203). Due to this expansion of services to anything that could possibly attract customers, I would like to argue that the *jazu-kissa* of the seventies resembled supermarkets.

The eighties saw two major changes in the field of media: one was the explosive spread of the walkman, entering the domain of the *jazu-kissa* (the right to play music loudly); the other was the invention of the CD, which, after its appearance on the market in 1982, almost completely replaced the LP within five years (Yagyû 1995: 44). The hegemony of the jazz magazines has remained unchanged since the late seventies: *Jazu Hihyô*, the smallest in circulation, for the maniacs and remaining serious listeners; the *Swing Journal*, market leader since being established in 1947, for the mainstream jazz fan and audio maniac; and *JazzLife* for the young fan with instrumental ambitions. In summer, jazz festivals, the biggest sponsored by major companies like Budweiser and JVC, took place all over the country and attracted a completely new audience (see Takano 1989). Attending a jazz festival became a "leisure event," of which the music was only one of many attractions. *Natsu da, biiru da, jazu da!* (Summer, beer, jazz!), as a headline in *Asahi shinbun* (13 June 1990) put it.

A new kind of live-house—most notably the Blue Note Tokyo—was created, that aimed at a wealthy clientele (Iwanami 1992:10). The marketing strategy was to provide jazz performed by foreign stars in a stylish ambience. The number of bars with jazz as background music increased. Hotels began again to employ jazz trios for the background music in their bars (Baba 1992:12). Jazz had become *oshare* (chic) at last. Even jazz goods, from perfume to golf equipment, appeared on the market (Yoshimura 1992:15).

All of these developments would not have had positive effects on the *jazu-kissa*. But there was another trend that had: contrary to all the glitter and noblesse of the new bars described above, and also the nearly unlimited availability of CDs, the people began to search for "the authentic" (*honmono*), which included the original records[13] of the fifties and sixties. And these were collected in great numbers at the remaining *jazu-kissa*.[14] So the *jazu-kissa* have finally become jazz museums, giving the young jazz fans a glimpse of what jazz used to be, and providing the older jazz fan with a nostalgic ambience. This provides a stable income for the masters for the time being, but in my opinion it is rather unlikely that the *jazu-kissa* will be continued after the current masters have retired. As many of them are in their sixties already, the end of the *jazu-kissa* seems near (Hiraga 1991:277).

Schools in the fifties, temples in the sixties, supermarkets in the seventies, and museums in the eighties: the *jazu-kissa* have fulfilled various functions as they were frequented by different and subsequent generations of listeners with different demands.[15]

Notes

1. For the situation in Europe see Knauer (1994), for Japan a.o. Yoshida (1985) and Uchida (1976).

2. *Jazu-kissa* = Jazz café. *Kissa* is short for *kissaten* (café), which is defined as "a shop in which non-alcoholic beverages and snacks are served." The *kissaten* has its origins in Western Asia and spread to Europe in the seventeenth century. The first *kissaten* in Japan opened in April 1888 and a few others followed, but they were for the upper class only. It was not before the Taishô era that *kissaten* for more ordinary guests emerged. There was a distinction between *kafê*, where alcoholic beverages were available, and *junkissa* or *sabô*, where they were not (Hashitsume and Satô 1991:189). In the early twenties, some *kissaten* began to provide grammophones for the entertainment of the guests. And from the very beginning, these were distinguished by the kind of music played: *meikyoku-kissa* for classical music, *jazu-kissa*, or *tango-kissa* (Yoshida 1985:19).

3. In my opinion, there is an unusually high readiness on behalf of Japanese listeners to accept records as substitute for live concerts, a fact that would deserve a seperate study. Keil (1994:248) made a similar observation with regard to the adaption to the electronically mediated music in what he calls "mediated-and-live musical performances" (most prominently *karaoke*).

4. Writer Ochiai Keiko (1994) uses that incident in her recent short story in great detail. A newspaper article about the imminent closing of a *jazu-kissa* in Shinjuku is a clue in the story, in which four women, now in their forties, recall their youth, spent together at university.

5. Guidebooks by Jazu Hihyôsha in 1975, 1976, 1980 list 103, 113, and 178 *jazu-kissa* in Tokyo, respectively.

6. By the time, a competition between the *jazu-kissa* developed: Who was able to get the latest records first? Therefore they had to be sent by air mail. Some masters had private sources (see Iwanami 1977:59).

7. The questions to be asked included, "Which Blue Note record has the number 4001?" and "Fats Navarro's *Nostalgia* is which cut on the A side?" (on a record whose title is supposed to be common knowledge).

8. The first live-house in Tokyo, the Gallery 8, was opened in Ginza in 1964, but it had to close after only two years due to economic difficulties (Yoshida 1985:140–55). In 1965 the Pit Inn in Shinjuku was opened and it still exists today, though in a different place (for a history of Pit Inn Shinjuku see Aikura 1985).

9. Of course, free jazz was not the only kind of "oppositional" music. Probably folk had considerably more overall impact on the student movement (see Maeda and Hirahara 1993, esp. 32–36, 74).

10. About the effects of volume on the listener Walser (1993:45) writes: "Loudness mediates between the power enacted by the music and the listener's experience of power. Intense volume abolishes the boundaries between oneself and such representations."

11. Especially the sudden death of John Coltrane was an enormous shock for many jazz fans (see for example Kitamura 1986).

12. While at least some knowledge about jazz was a prerequisite in intellectual circles of the sixties, many intellectuals lost their interest in jazz during the early seventies (e.g., Aikura 1973). In 1976 the literary magazine *Eureka* brought out an issue with the topic "Has jazz burnt out?" (vol. 8, no. 1).

13. Compare note 3.

14. This fact is probably best illustrated by a comic strip, published 1986 in Big Comic Spirits. Ironically it was part of the gourmet-comic ser-

ies *Oishimbo*. The plot: Yuppie gets fed up with pop music and begins to listen to jazz again. When he comes to a "typical old" *jazu-kissa* after a long time, he hears that it is about to close down. Hereupon the main character is prompted into action and brings the story to a happy end. One main part of the dialogue is the conversation about and love for famous old jazz records (reported in *Jazu Hihyô* 53 [1986], 263).

15. One aspect that I could not touch within the limitations of this chapter is the relationship between jazz and hi-fi equipment, although it certainly has some relevance for the popularity of *jazu-kissa* from the late sixties onward. It also contributed to the decline in guests when good stereo sets became available at reasonable prices.

References

Aikura Hisato. 1973. *Jazu kara no shuppatsu*. Tokyo: Ongaku no tomo.

———. 1985. "Nihon no jazu raibu no reimei," Aikura Hisato (ed.), *Shinjuku pitto in*. Tokyo: Shôbunsha, 17–36.

———, and Aoki Tamotsu. 1981. "'Mienai ongaku' toshite no jazu," Akiyama Akio (ed.), *Ongaku no techô: jazu*. Tokyo: Seidosha, 183–97.

Baba Keiichi. 1992. "Raito na jazu ga tanoshimeru Tôkyô no shiti-hoteru no myûjikku supotto," *Bessatsu Swing Journal: Super Jazz Catalogue,* 12–13.

Butler, George. 1986. "Jazz in the contemporary marketplace: Professional and the third-sector economy strategies for the balance of the century," David N. Baker (ed.), *New perspectives on Jazz*. Washington and London: Smithsonian Institution Press, 103–12.

Hashitsume Shinya, and Satô Kenji. 1991. Headword "Kissaten," Ishikawa Hiroyoshi et al. (eds.), *Taishû bunka jiten*. Tokyo: Chôbundô, 189.

Hiraga Masaki. 1991. "Kamisama no wanpatân wa nando kiite mo saikô nan da," Jatteku Bâdo (ed.), *Oretachi no jazu-kyô seishunki: Jazu-kissa tanjô monogatari*. Tokyo: Jatteku shuppan, 274–77.

Hiraoka Masaaki. 1971. *Jazu yori hoka ni kami wa nashi*. Tokyo: Sanichi shobô.

Iwanami Yôzô. 1977. "Hanasô! Jazu no tanoshisa o!!" *Jazurando* 1, 48–59.

———. 1992. "Kaigai ichiryû âtisuto no ensô ga tanoshimeru ninki jazu raibu supotto," *Bessatsu Swing Journal: Super Jazz Catalogue,* 10–11.

Jazu Hihyôsha (ed.). 1975. *Jazu Nihon rettô 50-nenpan*. Tokyo: Jazu hihyôsha (= Kikan jazu hihyô bessatsu no. 3/1975).

———. 1976. *Jazu Nihon rettô 51-nenpan*. Tokyo: Jazu hihyôsha (= Kikan jazu hihyô bessatsu no. 3/1976).

————. 1980. *Jazu Nihon rettô 55-nenpan.* Tokyo: Jazu hihyôsha (= Kikan jazu hihyô no. 35).

Kareki Takao. 1989. "Asakusa, Ochanomizu-hen: Hiru wa Asakusa/Furamingo, yoru wa Ochanomizu/Okinawa-ken. Jazu o kiki, sake to awamori aotta roku-nin no kinô to kyô," Adoribu-hen (eds.), *Tôkyô jazu-kissa monogatari.* Tokyo: Adoribu-sha, 75–118.

Keil, Charles. 1994. "Music mediated and live in Japan," Charles Keil and Steven Feld, *Music grooves.* Chicago, London: Chicago University Press, 247–56.

Kitamura Kôichi. 1986. "Jon Korutorên ga ikite iru," *Jazu Hihyô* 55, 210–16.

Knauer, Wolfram (ed.). 1994. *Jazz in Europa.* Hofheim: Wolke (= Darmstädter Beiträge zur Jazzforschung Band 3).

Leonard, Neil. 1987. *Jazz—Myth and religion.* New York, Oxford: Oxford University Press.

Maeda Yoshitake, and Hirahara Yasushi. 1993. *Nihon no fôku & rokku hisutorii 1: 60-nendai fôku no jidai.* Tokyo: Shinko Music.

Mihara Takashi. 1991. "70-en o nigirishimete tôtta 'Daunbîto,'" Jatteku Bâdo (ed.), *Oretachi no jazu-kyô seishunki. Jazu-kissa tanjô monogatari.* Tokyo: Jatteku shuppan, 236–43.

Murata Fumikazu. 1991. "60-nendai Tôkyô *jazu-kissa* monogatari," Asaya Kôji (ed.), *JAZZ santo monogatari.* Tokyo: Swing Journal, 155–61.

Nakano Osamu. 1984. "Sonzetsu to nekkyô: Jazushiin furagumento," *Eureka* 16/1, 86–95.

NHK hôsô yoron chôsa-jo. 1982. *Gendaijin to ongaku.* Tokyo: Nippon hôsô shuppan kyokai.

Ochiai Keiko. 1994. "Kôfuku na natsu no musumetachi," *Gekkan shôsetsu* 11, 368–401.

Onishi Yonehiro. 1991. "Ofukuro no yubiwa o shichi ni irete katta 'Buraunî,'" Jatteku Bâdo (ed.), *Oretachi no jazu-kyô seishunki: Jazu-kissa tanjô monogatari.* Tokyo: Jatteku shuppan, 203–11.

Orito Yû, and Yoshii Tamotsu. 1981. "Yureugoku ongaku no naka de *jazu-kissa* ten no mirai o hanasô," *Jazu Hihyô* 37, 196–203.

Oshima Yu. 1989. "Shibuya-hen: Paruko ga ari, Tôkyû bunkamura ga dekite mo, mô Dôgensaka ni katsute no *jazu-kissa* wa yomigaeranai," Adoribu-hen (eds.), *Tôkyô jazu-kissa monogatari.* Tokyo: Adoribu-sha, 26–44.

Rösing, Helmut. 1994. "Aspekte der Rezeption von populärer Musik," *Beiträge zur Popularmusikforschung* 14, 63–79.

Shimizu Tetsuo. 1977. "Danmo-zoku datta koro," *Eureka* 9/1, 170–73.

Shin Masayoshi. 1991. "Shinkyô shûkyô ni hairu omoi o shite haitta *jazu-kissa,*" Jatteku Bâdo (ed.), *Oretachi no jazu-kyô seishunki: Jazu-kissa tanjô monogatari.* Tokyo: Jatteku shuppan, 279–83.

Shuker, Roy. 1994. *Understanding popular music.* London and New York: Routledge.

Soejima Teruto. 1994. *Gendai jazu no chôryû.* Tokyo: Maruzen.

Steinert, Heinz. 1992. *Die Entdeckung der Kulturindustrie oder Warum Professor Adorno Jazz-Musik nicht ausstehen konnte.* Wien: Verlag für Gesellschaftskritik.

Takano Hiroaki. 1989. "Manatsu no jazu kibun: Maru-jô: Kanmuri no jamu-sesshon," *Asahi Journal* Nr. 1607 (= 31/41), 107–11.

Terashima Yasukuni. 1981. "Jazu-kissaten konton monogatari," *Jazu hihyô* 37, 186–90.

———. 1982. "Nyûten shiken," *Jazu hihyô* 41, 232–34.

Twitchell, James B. 1992. *Carnival culture: The trashing of taste in America.* New York, Oxford: Columbia University Press.

Uchida Kôichi. 1976. *Nihon no jazu-shi: Senzen sengo.* Tokyo: Swing Journal.

Walser, Robert. 1993. *Running with the devil: Power, gender, and madness in Heavy Metal music.* Hanover, London: Wesleyan University Press.

Watanabe Sadao. 1994. "30-en de kiku jazu—saisentan no jifu idaku: Amerika ni fureta konton Yûrakuchô," *Yomiuri shinbun* 24, 4.

Yagyû Sumimaro. 1995. "Ôdio no hanseiki," *Aera* 11, 44–45.

Yoshida Mamoru. 1985. *Yokohama jazu monogatari: "Chigusa" no 50-nen.* Yokohama: Kanagawa shinbunsha.

Yoshimura Kôji. 1992. "'Baiku ni gorufu-kurabu ni ôdetoware etc. …' JAZZ nêmingu shôhin," *Bessatsu Swing Journal: Super Jazz Catalogue,* 15.

PART FIVE

Playing Games and Gambling

Gambling is a universally practiced leisure activity, though said to be particularly popular in Asian countries. The many edicts of the Tokugawa government against gambling is an indication of its popularity among the Japanese.

In this volume three contributions are concerned with gambling. I deal with a game which, in some of its incarnations, can be categorized as gambling, namely *ken*. *Ken* is similar to the Italian *morra*, which would also appear to have been employed as a simple gambling instrument in Europe. There are some Japanese reports of how the fist game *ken* was played in coffee shops for money before the war. My own chapter, however, is not concerned with this aspect of the game. I try to show that during the process of rationalization that accompanied Japan's modernization, the exotic forms of *ken*, played by adults, became obscure and gradually died out, while the simple, easily comprehensible *jan-ken* succeeded as a children's game and even became known all over the world.

What comes first to the minds of the Japanese upon mention of gambling is betting at horse, motorcycle, bicycle, and motorboat races. Although these forms of gambling are legal, among the general public they have long been associated with criminality and unhealthy activities. As Nagashima Nobuo shows in his chapter, a more permissive attitude toward gambling was only recently adopted, and it has come to be regarded as an activity that may be pursued during one's leisure time. Instead of heavy betting, it is turning into an entertainment with only "a mere spice of financial danger."

Interestingly, the most common form of gambling in Japan, *pachinko*, is not considered to be a gambling activity by most Japanese but rather as mere time killing or as an everyday entertainment. It has often been forecast that *pachinko* will cease to exist before long, but today it is more popular than ever before. As Wolfram Manzenreiter mentions in his contribution, a writer called *pachinko* the "king of Japanese leisure ruling over a kingdom of 30 million subjects." Unlike other Japanese machines, the *pachinko* machine has not been successfully exported, a proof of how difficult it can be for non-Japanese to understand Japanese customs, even those developed only recently, like *pachinko*. Manzenreiter concentrates on explaining the fascination this form of gambling holds for the Japanese and why it became such an almost everyday, afterwork activity for many Japanese.

S. L.

Sepp Linhart

17

From "Kendô" to "Jan-ken"

The Deterioration of a Game from Exoticism into Ordinariness

A Peculiar Memorial Stone within the Precincts of the Mimeguri Shrine

If one visits the Mimeguri shrine, just across the Asakusa bridge and then a little stroll to the North along the Sumida river in the Sumida-district of Tokyo, one might be perplexed by the great number of memorial stones to be found there. Especially one with a rather peculiar shape might well attract the special attention of the visitor, but without a good guide book, even if he is Japanese and has some knowledge of Japanese history and literature as well as of historical writing forms, he might be at a loss as to how to interpret this special stone. Rather big among the Mimeguri commemorative stones, it has a triangular shape like an *o-nigiri*, a rice dumpling, which Japanese take on outings. The *Kasshi yawa* of the famous Hirado *ex-daimyô* Matsuura Seizan (1760–1841), a peculiar documentation of information gained over his lifetime and of Matsuura's various experiences in Edo where he spent his life in retirement, recorded between 1821 and 1841, tells us what the stone is about:

319

Someone says: Sha-ô, a man from Yamanote, an authority in the *ken* game, already dead. His disciples amount to 500 people. A memorial stone for him is to be found in the precincts of the Mimeguri shrine.

Someone says: The stone in Mimeguri is of red colour, has a height of 4 *shaku* (121 centimeters) and a wideness of 5 *shaku* and 6 *sun* (171 centimeters).

The inscription on it says:

The Nagasaki-born Sha Ô came to Edo,
where he told the world how to make drinking banquets nicer,
but now he has left us.
With our poems we mourn for him.
The pleasant meetings have come to an end,
and the ten finger games became stricter.
We long for those games with the thumb,
while the poems of wine rain down on the beautiful jar.

Headnote: Sha-ô is the same person as Sha Ô, as the pronunciation of his name tells.

Tan Nanpo

Hiraku te no	The "five" of the opening hand
û wa kachi nari	means victory
ume no hana	plum blossoms
Sha Ô	

The backside of the stone bears the following engravure:

Master Nozaki Sha Ô had the common name Seizô. He was a person who knew the drinking game *ken* very well. In the year of the sheep, metal and younger brother (1811) he died on the 23rd day of the first month, 84 years old. He was buried at the Eiryûji in Honjo and given the posthumous name Shunkyôin Sha Ô Kyôshi. We have now engraved the names of the people who decided to follow his way on the back of this stone, and

Figure 17.1 The memorial stone for Sha Ô in the precincts of the Mimeguri shrine, Sumida-ku, Tokyo. Photographed by the author.

hope that it might become well-known in the world. The stone
was erected in the spring of the ninth year of Bunka, the year
of the monkey, water and elder brother (1812). We did this
hoping for a good night for a famous man.

    After this there are thirty-six names in three rows each, so
that they amount to 108 names, but since they are already
fainted and difficult to read, I do not list them here. (Matsuura
1911:8–9)

    Now the riddle is solved and we can even answer why this stone
has its peculiar shape. For a memorial stone for a master of the *ken*
game the shape of an *o-nigiri* is most appropriate, because "playing
ken" was called *ken o utsu* or *ken o nigiru*. So it turns out that a pun
is contained in the shape of this stone.[1] I find that the stone in the
Mimeguri Shrine is an important historical proof that the game of
ken, which originally developed in the world of the red-light districts, had transgressed their borders and was on its way to becom-

ing a rather respectable leisure activity, and within fifty years of Sha Ô's death it even aspired to develop into one of Japan's famous ways. One century later this development culminated in the founding of the Greater Japan Way of Tôhachi-ken Association on February 2, 1941. But after the Greater Pacific War *ken* fell into a rapid decline and was mainly preserved as the children's game *jan-ken*.

The refined world of the entertainment districts, from the Edo period's Shimabara and Shin-Yoshiwara to present day's Gion, the world of a semiholy way, and the innocent world of children, these are the three realms of the game of *ken*: born in the amusement districts, it developed both into a Way and a children's game, but today it is only the latter use which is still important, while of the others—compared to their great times—only weak impressions are still to be found in present-day Japan. *Ken* with its at least three-hundred-year-old, but probably much longer history in Japan can thus be taken as a representative form of Japanese entertainment for both sexes and for children and adults as well.

The Main Forms of the "Ken" Game and Their Exoticism

I think that at this point I have to give a short overview of what *ken* was like, when it was not yet associated with *jan-ken*, a form that appears only as late as the 1840s in the literature. The *ken* that master Sha Ô played was numbers-*ken* or *kazu-ken*. Since it is thought to be the "original *ken*" it is also called *hon-ken*, and since it was believed that it reached Japan from China en route from Nagasaki it is also known by the names *Nagasaki-ken* or *Kiyô-ken*, Kiyô being the name Japanese sinologists used for Nagasaki. In this *hon-ken* two people sit opposite each other and show a certain number with their right hands, while shouting the expected sum of the numbers shown by both players. The one who shouts the correct sum wins. If both players shout the wrong number, or if both players shout the correct result, the outcome is a draw or *aiko*. The left hands are used to count the respective wins. Since the movements are performed very quickly, one plays for three or five wins. The loser has to drink a cup of sake—which made the game very popular among those who like drinking (*jôgo*), while those who try to avoid alcoholic beverages (*geko*) are said to hate it. If one judges simply from this explanation, few people will think it an interesting game. What made it interesting for the Japanese was the way of calling the numbers. The eighteenth-century Japanese, being aware that *ken* originally was a Chinese game, called them in Chinese or in what they thought to be Chinese. As a result, they did not shout *"ichi, ni, san"* or *"hitotsu, futatsu, mittsu"* in accordance with the usual Japanese way for saying "one, two, three." Instead they counted the numbers from one to ten as *"ikko, ryan, sanna, sû, go, roma, che, pama, kwai, tôrai,"* and zero as *mute*. There even existed a *gesaku* writer representative for the Tenmei period who obviously choose his professional name from this way of counting, namely Tôrai Sanna (1744–1810), meaning Mr. "Ten Three" or "The one who wins only three out of ten games." Naturally, since there was no standardized Chinese pronunciation, there were variants. Everybody who wanted to play had to study these numbers before he could participate. Because the game was originally—from the turn of the seventeenth to the eighteenth century—played mainly in the amusement quarters, the guide booklets to the Shin-Yoshiwara included pages on which this game and especially the correct way of counting were introduced to the prospective customer. *Ken* with its elegant movements of the hands and fingers and its exotic pronunciation became a favourite diversion for the visitors of the courtesans.

In my opinion the exoticism contained in this variant of the game may be said to constitute the main reason for its popularity. We must not forget that during the Edo period Japan was secluded from the world, but well aware of the existence of the great and different cultures of China or Morokoshi, India or Tenjiku, and the Southern or Western Barbarians. China was not only the country closest to Japan, it was also the country with a highly developed culture, which the Japanese did not cease to emulate until the paradigmatic change to imitate the West took place in the nineteenth century. Ôta Nanpo (1749–1823), the man who composed the Chinese poem on Sha Ô's memorial stone, also well known as Shoku Sanjin or Yomo no Akara, is regarded as one of the finest writers of Chinese poetry during the Edo period. At the same time he was also a *gesaku* writer and a *kyôka* poet, and it is no wonder that this *bakufu* retainer with his education in Chinese culture and his predilection for the floating world was also a great lover of *ken*, the Chinese drinking game. Drawing on the homonym of the famous Chinese "seven sages in the bamboo forest" (*chikurin no shichiken*), Nanpo also wrote a *kokkeibon Shichi-ken zushiki* (A Description of the Seven-*ken*), in which he describes a numbers-*ken* variant invented by himself and his friends (Yomo et al. 1830), a variant that can also be said to be a good blend of Japanese and Chinese culture.

That the game of *ken* by the Japanese was considered something profoundly Chinese is also apparent in a revealing "model" introductory speech for referees at *ken* tournaments, contained in the 1809 *ken* instruction book *Kensarae sumai zue* by the two *ken* masters Yoshinami and Gojaku. After offering thanks to the attendants, players, and fans alike, the referee gives a short historical outline of the development of the game from the times of the wise kings in China. From China, where it served as a means to make drinking parties more interesting, *ken* spread to Nagasaki at the time when the amusement quarters of Maruyama were opened in the middle of the seventeenth century. Sometime in this period a group of Chinese held a party in Maruyama to which they invited several courtesans. They put up a precious wine glass and the eight delicacies, accompanied by Chinese songs and music. After some time they divided themselves in two groups and began to play *ken* in the proper manner by the light of fireworks. Those who had lost took two or three sips from the precious glass of red wine and retreated. It is difficult to put into words how well they behaved. They tried to select the five best players. For the winners they had prepared in advance five tiger skins, five leopard skins, five red woolen cloths, five beautiful maidens, as well as other prizes. The five maidens were positioned beside the players so that Yin and Yang were in harmony (Yoshinami and Gojaku 1809). Even though this story, recorded roughly 150 years after it is said to have happened, does not have much historical value—for example, the prizes mentioned are unbelievably expensive items; it is not understandable why a certain *ken* game of a group of Chinese should have served to introduce this game to Japan, since the Chinese still like to play this game at every party—it is important in that it conveys to us an impression of the Sinophilic influenced discourse into which the *ken* game was set after it became popular during the eighteenth century.

From the second half of the eighteenth century onward, other *ken* games, which can be classified as *sansukumi-ken*, began to appear in the literature and illustrations. *Sansukumi-ken* means "*ken* of the three who are afraid of one another," and they always consist of three patterns like in *jan-ken*, the *ken* of stone, scissors, and paper. In these *ken* games, pattern A defeats B, B C, and C A. In *mushi-ken* (*ken* of small animals), which seems to be the oldest form of *ken* to have come to Japan from China, the "frog" (*kaeru, kawazu*), represented by the thumb, defeats the slug or shell-less "snail" (*namekujiri*, little finger), the "snail" triumphs over the "snake" (*kuchinawa, hebi*, forefinger), and the "snake" defeats the "frog."[2] But while *mushi-ken* developed into a game for children, as the *Kiyû shôran* reports—"*Mushi-ken* and other *ken* are only played by children" (Kitamura 1933, 2:428)—the *ken* that eventually became most popular in Japan was a *sansukumi-ken* known by a great variety of names: fox-*ken* (*kitsune-ken*), village-head-*ken* (*shô-ya-ken, nanushi-ken*), village-*ken* (*zaigô-ken*), or Tôhachi-*ken* (*Tôha-chi-ken*). In this *ken* the fox (*kitsune*), an animal with supernatural powers, defeats the village head (*shôya, nanushi*) who is superior to the hunter or gun (*karyûdo, ryôshi, teppô*). The hunter can of course shoot a fox, and the *sansukumi* circle is closed. While *jan-ken* and *mushi-ken* are played with the right hand only, in fox-*ken* both hands are used to make more interesting gestures. In the tiger-*ken* (*tora-ken*), which seems to have been invented in Japan a short time after the fox-*ken*, the gestures are even more interesting, because the whole body is used. This *ken* probably arose through the popularity of Chikamatsu Monzaemon's play *Kokusenya gassen* (The Battle of Coxinga, 1715). In this *ken*, the half-Japanese, half-Chinese hero Watônai defeats the tiger (*tora*), which defeats Watônai's old mother (*basama*), who is in turn superior to Watônai, her son. *Mushi-ken, jan-ken, kitsune-ken*, and *tora-ken* are the main Japanese *sansukumi-ken* games, besides which there existed many others at various times and in different regions.

Whereas the tiger-*ken* contains a great portion of exoticism—there are no tigers in Japan, and Watônai/Coxinga despite his Japanese origins was a pirate in South China—the other three main forms of *ken* are no longer exotic. The frog, snail, and snake are animals known by everybody, as are stone, paper, and scissors. But while their popularity was restricted to the world of children, the most popular *ken* among adults was fox-*ken*. The fox is an omnipresent animal at the numerous Inari shrines throughout the country, as well as an animal with supernatural powers. It appears to be

Figure 17.2   *Tôhachi-ken* today. The two players at the left and the right of the *sumô* ring imitation present the poses of the "hunter (gun)" and the "village headman." The man in the center is the referee. Photograph taken by the author in February 1996 in Asakusa, Tokyo.

this quality of the fox that led to the *kitsune-ken* being favored over the numbers-*ken* some time in the Tenpô era, as I have elucidated elsewhere (Linhart forthcoming).

From Amusement to a "Way"

From a number of citations from *gesaku* literature we know that originally *ken* was an exciting amusement for the visitor to the amusement quarters, exciting because it was new and exotic, exciting because the customers played it, while drinking, with the courtesans or with the young men with whom they occasionally had sex afterwards. For many men that went to the amusement quarters it constituted a foreplay in the real sense, and from some remarks from literature it seems that it especially fulfilled this role in homosexual relations.

When the exoticism contained in its Chinese origin, tradition, and pronunciation no longer sufficed there were other means to make it interesting. In the case of *sansukumi-ken* it was easy to think of new groupings and gestures instead of the ever-present traditional *kitsune-* and *tora-ken*, thus investing the game with a new quality of creativity. In Santô Kyôden's *kibyôshi Senji kaidan hana wa Miyoshino inu wa buchi* from 1790, of course a parody of the well-known saying, *"Hana wa Miyoshino hito wa bushi,"* a dog-man finally turns into a real human being. This resulted in much gossip and in the amusement quarters people stopped to play *kitsune-ken* from this time onward and only played *inu-ken* or dog-*ken*, consisting of the three figures of "gun-shooter" which defeats the "dog" which defeats the courtesan who defeats the gun-shooter (Santô 1987:72). Even though the modern commentator says that such a *ken* never really existed, its real existence is not important. Far more important is that we can take this as a literary proof that people experimented with the *sansukumi* pattern and had fun in filling it with other than the well-known figures. Matsuura Seizan tells us that the people of Nagasaki made fun of the Tsarist envoy Rezanov when he waited in Nagasaki for the *bakufu*'s answer to his request to open trade relations between the two countries, because Rezanov seemed to have fallen in love with a Japanese prostitute provided for him by the Japanese authorities to ease the waiting time. So they immediately constructed the following *sansukumi* relation: Rezanov loses against the prostitute who of course loses against the Nagasaki *bakufu* representative who in turn loses against Rezanov (Matsuura 1930:113). *Ken* pictures of the last two decades of the Edo and the first two of the Meiji period give us good insight into this creativity.

The other method to make *ken* more interesting was to give it the shape of another activity to which it has no resemblance at all, *sumô*. I will cite Santô Kyôden again. In his *zuihitsu Kinsei kiseki kô* (Reflections on miracles from recent times, 1804) he writes:

In the Kyôhô period the people who indulged in *sake*-drinking used to play *ken-zumô*, and it was terribly popular. It is said that Tamagiku was especially skillful. This Tamagiku from the Odawara House of the New Yoshiwara introduced the decora-

tion for the hand as we know it today, which fits the hand perfectly. From black velvet she had made something like a cover
for the back of the hand, and with a golden thread she embroi-
dered the emblem on it which is shown here. This is the hand-
cover which is used when playing *ken-zumô*. (Santô 1928:784)

In Japanese this hand cover, modeled after the decorative apron
used at *sumô* contests where it is called *keshô mawashi*, was called
ken-kin or *ken-mawashi*.

The hand cover continued to be an important accessory of good
ken-players, and they tried to have it made from the finest materials available, as we can tell from a short notice, roughly 150 years
after its invention, in the *Yûbin hôchi* newspaper of October 28,
1875: Kakusai, a *Tôhachi-ken* player from the Shibatô-ren, had his
ken-mawashi made from gold-braid for which he paid seven Yen
(Shinbun Shûsei Meiji Hennen-shi 1936:2:421). This was roughly
the same price as one *koku* of rice (6.9 Yen), which is said to be
enough for one person to survive an entire year.

But the *ken-mawashi* was not the only utensil taken from *sumô*.
Almost everything was copied meticulously, as can be seen in the
1771 instruction book *Fûgetsu gaiden* (Unorthodox tradition of
nature), which was published by a club of Osaka *ken* fanatics, the
Daken enkai itchi, in Meiwa 8 (1771), and written by Kikusha Namitaka, an authority among *ken*-players: the fan (*uchiwa*) as the symbol of the important function of the referee, the wooden clappers
(*hyôshigi*), the hand cover, the wooden buckets with washing water
(*chôzu oke*), the seats for the players (*koshikake, aibiki*), the religious
ornaments for the ring, the bow for the bow-twirling ceremony to
announce the end of the tournament, and of course the ring itself, of
which the *Fûgetsu gaiden* contains, as far as I am aware, the earliest picture (Kikusha 1771). Since it even gives the measurements of
the fighting circle, we can imagine what it looked like. Its height was
about 6 *shaku* (182 centimeters), and every side was 2 *shaku* and 4
sun wide (74 centimeters), so that it probably looked quite impressive in a Japanese-style room. On *nishiki-e* I could find only one
depiction of a *ken* circle, a very small, graceful one, namely on a picture by Ryûryûko Shinsai, which also contains a *kyôka* poem by a
man with the comical name Nomiyoshi (Good Drinker) from the
Masumoto-rô (The Origin of the Drinking Cup Inn):

Ken-sumô	In the *ken*-fight
yubi ni mo gokyô	there are also five teachings for the fingers
hakohera o	the hand which breaks the *hakohera*
utsu te no kuse no	without its strange habits
nakute nanakusa	the seven grasses of spring (Narazaki 1989:257).

Special utensils for the elegant *ken* player were *kengi*, wooden sticks made from fine foreign wood and carried in a small case made from brocade. Ten in number, they were used to determine the relative strength of two players. These *kengi* can be seen in the 1830 instruction book *Ken hitori keiko* (Sanô and Ikken) as well as in Matsuura Seizan's *Kasshi yawa* (Matsuura 1911:9). It is even said that the name of the famous *gesaku* writer Jippensha Ikku (1765–1831) is derived from such a contest, meaning "Ten times played, one victory, nine losses!" (*jippen ja ikku*) (Watanabe and Mogami 1975:99).

For training purposes players were advised to use a device consisting of five sticks, which was thought to substitute the living opponent (Yoshinami and Gojaku 1809).

Another element of *sumô* transferred to *ken* has to be mentioned here, namely the *banzuke*, ranking lists of players, a common trait of many arts, sports, and entertainments. In these *banzuke* the ranks were, of course, modeled after *sumô*. The earliest designation of a famous *ken* player as *ôzeki*, then the highest rank in *sumô*, is found in the 1771 *Fûgetsu gaiden*, which states: "The bow is the prize for the *ôzeki*, while the *sekiwake* and the *komusubi* get a fan" (Kikusha 1771). From this line we can deduce that at least at this time in Osaka the three ranks of *sumô*, *ôzeki*, *sekiwake*, and *komusubi* were also used in *ken-zumô*. Therefore we are safe in assuming that ranking tables (*banzuke*) were also issued from this time onward, but the oldest one I have so far been able to locate was apparently printed during the Bunka period (1804–1818) (Linhart 1991a:161). The *Kensarae sumai zue*, an instruction book of 1809, contains lists of fifteen groups of *ken* players in Osaka, ordered by rank. There is always one *ôzeki*, one *sekiwake*, and one *komusubi*, forming the three ranks of *sumô*, while the list of players from Nagasaki in the same book is already in the later style of a real *banzuke*, with players divided into those of the Eastern and the

Western Leagues. The Nagasaki list from 1809 contains the names of 126 famous *ken* players, which might serve as an indication of the popularity of *ken* at that time.

There were two different kinds of *banzuke*: such for internal use of the group to which a player belonged, and others for a region or a city, as, for instance, for Osaka. The first ones, "small lists" or "fan lists" (*kobanzuke* or *uchiwabanzuke*), were decided upon by the head of a specific group, while the "big lists" (*ôbanzuke*) were made by consultation (*hanashiai*) of the different group leaders as well as by tournaments. In the twentieth century, people who were *ôzeki* twice became *yokozuna*, and subsequently referees. Finally, after having served as referee for some time, they were promoted to the rank of *toshiyori*, and as such were also inscribed on the *banzuke*.

Players not yet promoted to the *maegashira* rank were also divided according to strength into *tamari* (those waiting), *jô no kuchi* (those entering), *jô nidan* (second class), and *jô sandan* (third class). At the end of the list we find the names of influential people from the *ken* world, like former champions and heads of different groups. In the center of the *banzuke* are the names of the organizers and sponsors, and of the inspectors and advisors (Kubota 1941:119–21).

According to a newspaper announcement in the *Tôkyô yorozu chôhô* of January 6, 1907, after the Meiji Restoration no general *banzuke* for Tokyo had been made since the Restoration,[3] and therefore for that date a great *ken* meeting was scheduled in order to create a new list. The referee was the female owner of the restaurant Suekichi in Ushigome, in earlier times a well-known player under the name Imaharu, while the head of the Beriberi Hospital, Tôda, became an honorary member under the name Azumanobori Ôasahi (Shinbun shûsei Meiji hennen-shi 1936:13:195–96).

Certainly *ken-zumô* was a very amusing activity for the *ken* fanatics, but for people who did not belong to their world—like ourselves today—what they did must have seemed very strange, even mildly lunatic. The collection of satyric verses *Momejiku daisekku* contains this verse:

Chimanako de	With eyes blazing in fury
dôhyôiri suru	they parade into the ring—
ken-zumô	the *ken-zumô* wrestlers! (Nihon daijiten 1974:324)

Similarly a *senryû* from the collection *Takarabune*, issued in the Kamigata area in Kan'en 3 (1750), teases the *ken* players:

Shiroi te de	With soft and dainty hands
ogamasete kita	she came and made him pray,
ken-zumô	the *ken* wrestler!

But the *ken* players were also making fun of themselves. In the mentioned *Fûgetsu gaiden* we find among many others the following verses,

Toshi wasure	Forgetting her age
onna mo sunaru	this woman makes
ken-mawashi	a belt for her fist (Kikusha 1771:2: 1ura)
Furisode no	There are also wrestlers
sekitori mo ari	with long and silken sleeves:
yukimisake	*sake* while enjoying a snow scene (Kikusha 1771:2:4omote)

which transmit to us a certain feeling of self-irony, but, simultaneously, a feeling of pride.

It has often been said that many of Japan's different entertainments developed out of simple entertainments into "Ways." This type of development is also apparent in the history of the *ken* game. When the *ken* players incorporated several organizational and exterior elements of *sumô* wrestling into their game from the beginning of the eighteenth century, it was clearly for fun, in order to make their game more interesting, but in the long run this developed into a drive to make this innocent drinking game *ken* one of the famous martial arts of Japan. In the *ken* instruction book *Kensarae sumai zue* from Bunka 6 (1809) we can already detect the trend to transform *ken* into an activity valued higher than a simple game, when it says, for example, about training habits:

Those who want to become good *ken* players have to play five hundred to six hundred games a day for a period of sixty days, after which they should take a rest for ten days, before they practice again diligently as before for another sixty days, until they play without thinking about their fingers as if it were quite normal. If one reflects deeply about the pattern of one's fingers in the games after that one will quite naturally become a skilled player. (Yoshinami and Gojaku 1809:1:13ura)

It seems natural that everybody who practices like this can become a *ken* professional, but if one allots so much time to the activity it has to become something worth more than a mere game. The same instruction book also contains chapters such as "About the five stages of the heart in *ken*," and "How to abandon one's self in *ken*," which express the spirit of Zen Buddhism. I interpret these chapters as attempts to create for *ken* the kind of spiritual basis that exists, for example, in archery and other Japanese martial arts.

The preface to the instruction book *Ken hitori keiko* from Bunsei 13 (1830) by Ôsai Kisanji says that "this book [was written for] the beginners of the Way of *ken*," and "the people who play this way, get their pride from the table of rankings, and their elegance from their fist-belts" (Sanô and Ikken 1830:215). In this preface the expression "Way" is used twice when referring to *ken*.

As soon as *ken* developed into a Way, *iemoto* organizations also appeared. Such organizations apparently came into being around 1850 in connection with the *Tôhachi-ken* boom.[4] In 1906 the *Tôkyô asahi shinbun* published the following article under the headline "New and old tales about *Tôhachi-ken*":

The flourishing of *ken* groups: Subsequently there appeared a master with the name Haru-no-ie Sôgan (Kusamaru), who reformed fox-*ken* and produced *Tôhachi-ken* and formed a group of players. Especially among the *hatamoto* there were many *Tôhachi-ken* lovers, and in the Kôka and Kaei period (1844–1854) groups like the Azuma-ren, the Hide-ren, the Asahi, the Azumanobori, the Kozakura, the Musashino and other substantial groups came into existence in great numbers, and it was tremendously popular. ... In the group called Ryûô-ren there was a former retainer from the Tayasu-*han*, whose name was Kaneko Sôjirô, while his name as a player was Kigan (Onimaru). At the time of the Restoration he renamed himself into Kiô (Oni-ô), while he transferred his former name Kigan (Onimaru) to his pupil Zengyô from Iwato-chô 5, Ushigome-ku, a former *bakufu* retainer with the name Kakinuma Chôhô. He gave the name of Zengyô to another pupil from Akagi Shita-machi 52 from the same district, who was a teacher of tea and *ikebana* with the name Seihyôan Sôgetsu, while his civil name was Kurosawa Tadamasa. After that *ken* battles almost disap-peared for a time, until recently when there were attempts at a revival of the old style. Kigan (Onimaru) became Kiô (Oni-ô) II, while Kurosawa was made Kigan (Onimaru) III, and their pupil Hamamura Tetsutarô became Zengyô III. (Shinbun shû-sei Meiji hennen-shi 1936:13:160)

This means that at the end of the Meiji period the *iemoto*-organiza-tion of the Way of *ken*, which originated at the end of the Edo peri-od, was revived and continued until the end of the Pacific War. This becomes clear from the publication of the book *Kenzen goraku Tôha-chi kendô* by Kubota Magoichi in 1941. Kubota, who himself was an *iemoto* master of the Tôkensha group under the name of Tendô, stressed the fact that *ken* was not to be perceived as a game but that it was to be included among the martial arts of Japan. Around the time of the publication of his book all *ken-iemoto* came together and founded the Greater Japan Way of Tôhachi-ken Association (2 February 1941). As one can grasp from Kubota's book, at this time the *ken* of the *ken* Way had become a very difficult activity, and he tried to make an explicit difference between it and the original drinking game:

> *Tôhachi-ken* is played among the *ken* players according to very strict rules, but this is generally not widely known. Every *iemo-to* had a great amount of authority, and since it was forbidden to let others know one's *ken* name at *sake*-parties and since the better one played the more one had to restrain oneself, the gen-eral people knew it only from hearsay and imitated it out of their imagination. Therefore the *ken* which is performed by *gei-sha* at drinking parties is not the real *ken*; it is not more than an imitation with the hands. They have taken over also sever-al conventions and ceremonies of which they have heard, but

seen from the viewpoint of a *ken* player they are really amusing. A real *ken* game is not something which is done accompanied by *shamisen* and the like. (Kubota 1941:116–17)

"Ken" as Children's Game

A finger game, which might be *mushi-ken*, can be found on pictorial
scrolls of the Kamakura period, and there is another pictorial scene
from this age without written comment where perhaps this *mushi-
ken* is played at a drinking party (Masuda 1989:678), but when this
ken appears in the literature for the first time in the Edo period it
was already introduced as a children's game. *Jan-ken*, which resembles *mushi-ken*, is similarly referred to from its first appearance in
the literature as *kodomo no jan-ken* (the children's stone-*ken*). Compared to these two kinds of *ken*, numbers-*ken*, tiger-*ken*, and fox-*ken*
were apparently defined as belonging to the world of adults. Therefore the author of the essay *Asukagawa* from Bunka 7 (1810) complains that the children these days very often play a game that
clearly belongs into the closed adult world of amusement districts:

> In former days children used to play red-shell-horse-riding, or
> they fought with the shells of mussels. Of today's children
> nobody knows these games. The games which children play
> when they come together are "The old man goes to the moun-
> tain to cut wood, while the old woman goes to the river to
> wash" like in former times, but now they play also *mushi-ken*,
> fox-*ken* and original *ken*. How funny! (Shibamura 1929:419)

Children are likely to imitate everything that adults do, and, according to Shibuzawa Seika's book *Asakusakko*, children from Asakusa were, at the end of the nineteenth century, even imitating the
chonkina-strip-game of the adults, a game of forfeits based on *kitsune-ken*.

> *Chonkina, chonchon kinakina, chon* on the rape flower, *cho-
> chon ga yoiyasa*." Two children, standing opposite to each
> other, after having put together the palms of their hands right

and left as well as alternately, finally make one of the postures of fox, hunter or village headman to decide a winner. The loser has to put off a piece of what he is wearing every time, until one of them is stark naked. To see the little children on cold winter days trembling, because one after another piece of cloth was stripped them off is a strange scene which can no longer be seen today. This game is a special element of downtown. (Shibuzawa 1966:10–11)

After the transformation of the various *ken* games into the "Way of Tôhachi-*ken*" in the 1840s, *ken* was able to retain its popularity right into the enlightened years of the Bunmei Kaika movement during the Meiji period. In 1876 *Tôhachi-ken*, along with billiards, a lemonade drink called *ramune*, and artificial hot springs in the city, was considered one of the four most popular things of the year (Asakura and Inamura 1965:140). And on September 16, 1876, the *Yomiuri shinbun* wrote satirically about the *ken* boom:

> *Chikagoro wa dôken toka jishu no ken toka minken toka iu koto ga ryûkô suru yue, hakuchi renchû ga nandemo ken to sae ieba bunmei kaika da to omoichigai, Asakusa, Kanda, Shiba, Akasaka, Honjo Fukagawa doko e itte mo Tôhachi-ken ga ryûkô de.*
>
> (Recently equal rights, the rights of the individual and people's rights are en vogue, and the stupid ones think fool-ishly that if they only say *ken* that it would be civilization and enlightenment. Wherever you go, to Asakusa, Kanda, Shiba, Akasaka or Honjo Fukagawa, Tôhachi-ken is popular.) (Shin-bun shûsei Meiji hennen-shi 1935:3:53).

If we use the aforementioned logic that children are impressed by grownups and tend to imitate what they do, we can speculate that *kitsune-ken*, the basic form of *Tôhachi-ken*, should have been rather popular among children during the late Edo and early Meiji period. But adults played *ken* just for fun while drinking (the loser had to drink), and in the amusement quarters with their sexual partners as a kind of foreplay to the sexual act, and they transformed the inno-cent game into a Way—three possibilities usually not open to children. Therefore children combined the game with other games, especially with card games and other paper games, commonly known as *menko*, a game in which the winner gets the cards of the losers. Let me try to give some historical evidence for this development.

When Philipp Franz Siebold (1796–1866) left Japan after his first stay in Deshima from 1823 to 1828 he brought with him not only a huge collection of Japanese books but also a collection of various things for daily use, which are still preserved in the National Museum of Ethnography in Leiden. Among them there are eight wooden plates, 6.0 centimeters long and 3.7 centimeters wide, with depictions of the three figures of *kitsune-ken* (Leiden Museum collection no. I-2633), which were most likely a kind of children's toy, although we do not know how it was used for playing. Since three plates depict the *shôya* and three the hunter yet only two the fox, we can assume that one of the plates has been lost. Among the possessions of the Austrian photographer Michael Moser, who went to Japan forty-five years after Siebold in 1869 and stayed there until 1876, working some time for the Japanese government as a foreign employee, there is also a similar plate with the picture of a hunter, twice as big as the plates from the Siebold collection, but we can assume that it is a plate for the same game.[5] These *ken* plates or *ken-fuda*, as we might call them, can well have been used like the later *menko*—that is, to throw one on top of the other or throw one against the other to drive it away.

Although today very little can be found in the literature about *kitsune-ken* dolls, such dolls existed at least in the late Edo period, in the year 1859, and we can assume that they also were used for various games. *Kitsune-ken* dolls are also to be found on the title page of a small *ken* instruction booklet from 1909 called *Ken no uchiburi* (Konishi 1909). A catalogue of an exhibition of items collected by the Association for the Promotion of Things for Daily Use by Children with its seat at the Mitsukoshi Gofukuten in Tokyo— the exhibition held at the time of the International Exhibition of Hygenics in Dresden, Germany, in 1911—contains as number 63 "Three enemies," namely snake, frog, and slug, all made of earthenware. The head of the snake contains a small piece of iron, that of the frog a positive magnet, and that of the slug a negative one. Therefore the frog attracts the snake while the snake flees from the slug. Put together the three animals cannot move. The cata-

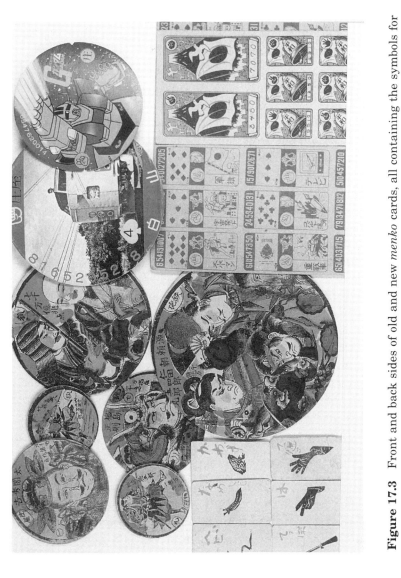

Figure 17.3 Front and back sides of old and new *menko* cards, all containing the symbols for playing various *ken* games. From the author's collection.

logue also mentions that this game, which corresponds to the *mu-shi-ken*, has been known in Japan since the eighteenth century (Mitsukoshi 1911:15).

In an interview at the end of the 1970s about children's games in the Meiji period, Mr. Furuya from Osaka, born in 1892, had this to say:

> What I played frequently as a child is *shôya-ken*. We used to call it *shôya-ken*, namely pictures cut out from paper, and then *bettan* (*menko*). ... They were circular. We did not have square ones. On the front side there were drawn pictures of samurai, but there were also others with armour, or helmet. But there were no pictures of generals, because this was before the Russo-Japanese War. We stuck two or three on a piece of cardboard, and tried to make them as thick as possible, in order to win. You had to throw yours towards the ones of the others, and if you managed to turn them over, you won and could take them.
>
> I really was good in that game. Therefore I had several hundred of them which were about so many (shows a height of 30 centimeters with his hands). For those who lost, it was expensive to buy them in a shop, and therefore I sold them mine for far more cheaper money. Well, 20 cards I gave them for about two *ri*, and if I lost one, they were overjoyed. ... (Since he was made fun of by his wife sitting next to him:) No, I gave them to them for nothing, since I had several hundred and therefore was rather proud and could afford to help them. You see, this was not really a problem of money! (Fujimoto 1986: 306–307).

Although it is rather difficult to explore the history of children's games, because they usually leave only very sporadic traces, I think there are enough of them to construct a comprehensive picture. The *kitsune-/Tôhachi-ken* boom of the last Edo years obviously stimulated the commercial talents of entrepreneurs in various fields. According to Sakai (1933:842), at the end of the Bunsei period around 1830 a cake maker in Osaka had started to insert small copper plates with the *ken* numbers on them into Japanese crackers, which he called *Azuma meibutsu kentô senbei* (or Famous

Eastern Guessing Cakes), with a pun on words contained in the expression *kentô*, in which *ken* refers to the word *see* as well as to *fist* or *ken* game. They are said to have become very popular. People just shouted the guessed number and then looked into the cracker for the result. Another field in which the *ken* boom left traces was that of publishing.

In the wonderful collection of *omocha-e*, woodblock prints intended as playthings for children, owned by Ann Herring, there is a game called *Shinsei kitsune-ken omoshiro hyôshi* or Newly Developed Interesting Expression of Fox-*ken*, dated 1859, eleventh month. Designed by Kunisato and published by Wakabayashi-dô, it consists of five sets of three figures—the fox, the village headman, and the hunter, the same three figures as children, as young women, as mature women, and finally as *kabuki* actors. The cover of the game shows three *kitsune-ken* dolls, also a field for an entrepreneur wanting to profit from the *ken* boom, and a twig with plum blossoms—the symbol of *ken*, because the plum blossom has five petals like a hand has five fingers.[6] Interestingly this game was, according to the rules, played for cakes, and depending on the set one assembled one got one to five cakes. For me this seems to hint that this was intended rather to be played at home or among children than in an amusement quarter, where it probably would have been played for *sake*.

This game seems to be one of the earliest examples of the game later called *shôya-ken*. In this game the word *ken* was later to be written not with the character for "fist" but for "ticket." In a recent article Ebashi (1993) analyzed how this game together with other games developed into *menko*, the most popular game among boys from the late Meiji period until after World War II, as the research of Hanzawa (1980) in the late seventies has convincingly proven. Even today one finds on every *menko* card the symbols of *jan-ken* as well as those of *kitsune-ken*, even though they are often no longer recognized by the children of today.

Ken, thus, through the medium of *menko*, influenced generations of Japanese. It is no wonder that it was also adapted for other games, like *sugoroku* or even *shôgi*, in which the conventional figures were replaced by *jan-ken* figures. That *jan-ken* is an important part of many children's games and enjoys great popularity has recently been shown in the results of a field survey by the National

Museum of Japanese History in Sakura, Chiba prefecture (Kokuritsu Rekishi Minzoku Hakubutsukan 1991), as well as by the NHK
TV program "Kotoba terebi," which broadcasted a special program
"Sagatte tadotte jankenpon" on November 18 and 25, 1994 (Kajiki
1995), and there is no necessity to repeat the findings here.

Final Remarks:
The Importance of "Ken" in Japan's Leisure Culture

Ken was in existence in the Edo period from at least 1700 onward
and served as an innocent drinking game or as a kind of foreplay in
the amusement quarters, but *ken* lunatics took it further from
there, invented *ken-zumô* and finally tried to turn it into one of
Japan's famous Ways, *dô* or *michi*, in the form of *Tôhachi-ken-dô*.
Children, imitating their parents, quickly followed the footsteps of
their fathers or mothers, and, during the Meiji period, with the help
of some entrepreneurs from the publishing trade, established their
own *ken* culture, namely on the paper cards called *menko*, as well
as in many orally transmitted games. At the same time *jan-ken*
seems to have established itself as a game universally known and
played by Japanese children and grownups, equally usable as a
simple game with several variations and extensions and as a means
of decision making.

   I think that even though *ken* is more or less restricted to *jan-ken*
today, it played an enormous role in the leisure life of Japanese
adults and in the world of children's play for at least 250 years, but
it underwent a very significant change when it turned from num-
bers-*ken* to *sansukumi-ken*, and then from fox-*ken* to *jan-ken*, or, in
other words, from exotic to ordinary. With children it was always the
second variant that was popular, never the exotic one. The question
to be solved is why that was so, and why the most common or most
ordinary or least interesting form of the simpler *sansukumi* game
survived, namely *jan-ken*. Compared to the other once-popular
forms of *sansukumi-ken*, the poses in *jan-ken* are boring: paper,
stone, scissors—things without life, things with which it is difficult
to identify. How different are Watônai, his mother, and the tiger, the
fox, the village headman, and the hunter, and even the snake, the
frog, and the slug! I think the simplicity of *jan-ken* gives the answer.

It is universally understandable, it contains nothing to be afraid of like a tiger or a fox, it contains no moral rule such as is contained in Watônai's mother or the village headman and it gives us no shiver like we might get when thinking of the snake or the slug. It is almost a perfect abstraction of the *sansukumi* principle, universally appealing, and the spread of *jan-ken* is a good demonstration for this.

In her book *Japanese society*, Nakane (1973) speaks of a primitive egalitarianism that permeates Japan. Similarly, Kreiner (1969) gave proof of a basic egalitarian principle to be found in the Japanese village structure in his study of the *miyaza*. If this is true, this way of egalitarian thinking has to be implanted into the Japanese at some point in their early childhood. Perhaps *jan-ken*, a word every Japanese from the age of two is supposed to know according to the Sanseidô dictionary for children (Ôkubo 1971), gives us at least a partial answer to how the successful implementation of this egalitarian thought is effected.[7]

─────────────── *Notes* ───────────────

1. All over Japan one can find gravestones or memorial stones for deceased *go* or *shôgi* masters that have the shape of a giant *go* or *shôgi* stone, but to my knowledge this is the only stone of its kind for a *ken* master.

2. In Shibuzawa Keizô's index of depictions of the common people's life on *emakimono* there are two depictions of what he calls *jan-ken*, but I think that these pictures are illustrations of *mushi-ken*. The first one is from the *Ishiyama-dera engi emaki* (Shibuzawa 1965–1968:vol. 3:228–29), and the second from the *Hônen shônin eden* (Shibuzawa 1965–1968:vol. 5:20–21).

3. This statement cannot be applied to Osaka. I was able to find four *honken banzuke* for Osaka from the years 1884, 1885, 1887, and 1888, each containing between 229 and 270 names of players.

4. *Tôhachi-ken* is a more complicated variant of *kitsune-ken*. It is said to have been named after the medicine peddlar Tôhachi, who sold his pills calling: "Tôhachi, gomon, kimyô!" meaning "Tôhachi pills, for five mon only, very effective!" According to another explanation this variant of the game is named after a male entertainer (*hôkan*) from Shin-Yoshiwara who invented it. It is not yet clear where the name *Tôhachi-ken* originated. Since there is an interesting *nishiki-e* by Kuniyoshi from 1852, in which he

makes fun of the people devoting themselves to this entertainment, we can assume that it originated some time after the Tenpô period.

5. The collection is owned by the grandchild of Moser, who told me that he remembers that there were also other plates, among them at least one with a funny-looking animal, with which he used to play as a child but which are now lost. I assume that the "funny-looking animal" was a white Japanese fox, an animal not easily identifiable for a Central European, for whom a fox has to be red-brown.

6. The plum blossom (*ume*) also has the reputation of being Chinese and is seen in contrast to the Japanese cherry blossom (*sakura*). See the contribution by Ohnuki-Tierney in this volume.

7. In writing this article I made use of some portions of previous articles on the subject of *ken* (Linhart 1991a, 1991b, 1995a, 1995b).

―――――――――― References ――――――――――

Asakura Haruhiko and Inamura Tetsugen (eds.). 1965. *Meiji sesô hennen jiten*. Tokyo: Tôkyôdô shuppan.

Ebashi Takashi. 1993. "Shôya-ken, kami-menko no tanjô ni tsuite," *Katachi, asobi: Nihon ningyô gangu gakkai shi 3*. Tôkyô: Nihon ningyô gangu gakkai, 14–26.

Fujimoto Kônosuke. 1986. *Kikigaki Meiji no kodomo: Asobi to kurashi*. Tokyo: Honpô shoseki.

Hanzawa Toshirô. 1980. *Dôyû bunka shi*. 5 vols. Tokyo: Tôkyô shoseki.

Kajiki Minako. 1995. "Kotoba terebi 'Zenkoku janken mappu' kara mieru koto—shichôsha sanka ni yoru hôgen shûshu no kokoromi," *Hôsô kenkyu to chôsa* 2, 44–51.

Kikusha Namitaka. 1771. *Fûgetsu gaiden*. 2 vols. Osaka: Daken enkai itchi Meiwa 8. Used copy owned by Kokuritsu kokkai toshokan, Tokyo.

Kitamura Nobuyo. 1933. *Kiyû shôran*. 2 vols. Tokyo: Seikôkan shoten.

Kokuritsu rekishi minzoku hakubutsukan shiryô (ed.). 1991. *Hakubutsukan shiryô chôsa hôkokusho 3: Minzoku shiryô-hen 3-shû*. Sakura: Kokuritsu rekishi minzoku hakubutsukan.

Konishi Katô Suishi. 1909. *Ken no uchiburi*. Tokyo: Shunkôdô.

Kreiner, Josef. 1969. *Die Kultorganisation des japanischen Dorfes*. Wien: Braumüller.

Kubota Magoichi. 1941. *Kenzen goraku—Tôhachi-kendô*. Tokyo: Seishin kagaku shuppansha.

Linhart, Sepp. 1991a. "17, 18 seiki no Nihon ni okeru ken—sake no sakana kara gakumon no taishô e," Fujii Jôji and Yokoyama Toshio (eds.), *Antei-ki shakai ni okeru jinsei so shosô: Shigoto to yoka*. Keihoku: Kyôto zeminâru hausu, 142–63.

———. 1991b. "Die Popularität des *Ken*-Spiels im 18. Jahrhundert—Nachweis und Erklärungsversuche," Eva Bachmayer, Wolfgang Herbert, and Sepp Linhart (eds.), *Japan von Aids bis Zen: Referate des achten Japanologentages vom 26. bis 28. September 1990 in Wien*. Wien: Institut für Japanologie (= Beiträge zur Japanologie 29-I), 254–75.

———. 1995a. "Rituality in the *ken*-game," Jan van Bremen and D. P. Martinez (eds.), *Ceremony and ritual in Japan: Religious practices in an industrialized society*. London and New York: Routledge 1995 (The Nissan Institute/Routledge Japanese Studies Series), 38–66.

———. 1995b. "Some thoughts on the *ken*-game in Japan: From the viewpoint of comparative civilization studies," Umesao Tadao, Brian Powell, and Kumakura Isao (eds.), *Japanese civilization in the modern world XI: Amusement*. Osaka: National Museum of Ethnology 1995 (= Senri Ethnological Studies 40), 101–24.

———. forthcoming. "Interpreting the world as a *ken* game," Massimo Raveri (ed.), *Japan at play*.

Masuda Yasuhiro et al. (eds.). 1989. *Asobi no daijiten*. Vol. 1. Tokyo: Tôkyô shoseki.

Matsuura Seizan. 1911. *Kasshi yawa. Zokuhen 2*. Tokyo: Kokusho kankô-kai.

———. 1930. *Kasshi yawa: Ge no kan*. Tokyo: Nihon zuihitsu taisei kankô-kai (= Nihon zuihitsu taisei 3rd installment, vol. 8).

Mitsukoshi Gofukuten. 1911. *Beschreibung der Gegenstände ausgestellt vom Verein zur Förderung von Gebrauchsgegenständen für Kinder auf der Internationalen Hygienischen Ausstellung*. Dresden.

Nakane Chie. 1973. *Japanese society*. Rev. ed. Harmondsworth: Penguin Books.

Narazaki Muneshige (ed.). 1989. *Hizô ukiyoe taikan 8: Parî kokuritsu toshokan*. Tokyo: Kôdansha.

Nihon daijiten kankôkai (eds.). 1974. *Nihon kokugo daijiten*. Vol. 7. Tokyo: Shôgakkan.

Ôkubo Ai (ed.). 1971. *Yôji no kokugo e-jiten*. 6 vols. Tokyo: Sanseidô.

Sakai Yasushi. 1933. *Nihon yûgi-shi*. Tokyo: Kensetsusha.

Sanô Renren, and Ikken Yôshô. 1830. *Ken hitori keiko*. Bunsei 13. Used copy: privately owned. Modern editions: *Zatsugei sôsho*. Vol. 1. Tokyo: Kokusho kankô-kai 1915, 119–30. Matsuda Osamu, Moriya Katsuhisa, and Yoshida Mitsukuni (eds.), *Nihon shômin bunka shiryô shûsei 9: Asobi*. Tokyo: Sanichi shobô 1974, 215–23.

Santô Kyôden. 1928. "Kinsei kiseki kô," *Nihon zuihitsu taisei*. 2nd install-ment, vol. 3. Tokyo: Nihon zuihitsu taisei kankôkai, 671–796. Modern edition of the text published in Bunka 1 (=1804).

———. 1987. *Shiriizu Edo gesaku Santô Kyôden*. Nobuhiro Shinji and Yamamoto Harufumi (eds.). Tokyo: Ôfôsha.

Shibamura Morikata. 1929. "Asukagawa," Nihon zuihitsu taisei kankôkai (ed.), *Nihon zuihitsu taisei*. 2nd installment, vol. 5. Tokyo: Nihon zuihit-su taisei kankôkai, 411–28.

Shibuzawa Keizô (ed.). 1965–1968. *Emakimono ni yoru Nihon jômin seika-tsu ebiki*. Vols. 3 and 5. Tokyo: Kadokawa shoten.

Shibuzawa Seika. 1966. *Asakusakko*. Tokyo: Zôkeisha.

Shinbun shûsei Meiji hennen-shi hensankei (ed.). 1936. *Shinbun Shûsei Meiji Hennen-shi*. Vols. 2, 3, and 13. Tokyo: Rinsensha.

Watanabe Shinichirô, and Mogami Ryotarô. 1975. "Ken," Satô Yôjin (ed.), *Senryô Edo no asobi*. Tokyo: Shibundô (= Special volume of the journal *Kokubungaku kaishaku to kanshô*, No. 519), 95–114.

Yomo no Akara et al. 1830. *Shichi-ken zushiki*. New edition, Edo: Nishimura Genroku, Bunsei 13. First edition: An'ei 8 (=1779). Used copy owned by Kokuritsu kokkai toshokan, Tokyo.

Yoshinami and Gojaku. 1809. *Kensarae sumai zue*. 2 vols. Edo: Murataya Jirôbê, Ôsaka: Kawachiya Taisuke, Bunka 6. Used copy owned by Jinbun kagaku kenkyûsho, Kyoto University. Reprint published in 1941 by Bun-shôdô.

Nagashima Nobuhiro

18

Gambling and Changing Japanese Attitudes Toward It

Gamble Races and the Concept of Leisure

The main purpose of this chapter is to investigate those features of Japanese society and culture that emerge from its gambling. This theme covers, however, a very broad range of phenomena, and for that reason I shall first be concerned with *kôei kyôgi* (officially managed races), those races with a licence for betting that are managed by administrations or special foundations under the control of a particular ministry, to which the Japanese word *gyanburu* usually refers.

There are four kinds of *kôei kyôgi*, namely, *keiba* (horse racing), *keirin* (bicycle racing), *kyôtei* (motorboat racing), and *ôto-rêsu* (auto-motorcycle racing). In terms of organizations, horse racing is divided into two different bodies. One is Chûô keiba, organized by the JRA (Japan Racing Association) under the control of the Ministry of Agriculture, Forestry, and Fishing. It owns ten race courses sited from Hokkaidô to Kyûshû, thus making it a nationwide organization. The other is called Chihô keiba with thirty race courses, each under the control of a local government, locations ranging from prefecture to city to the special ward in Tokyo, the last of which comprises twenty-three ordinary wards (*ku*). Chihô keiba is not a unitary body but rather a category, although there is a federation type of organization for public relations called NAR (*Chihô keiba zenkoku kyôkai*). Keirin Association (fifty courses) and Ôto Association (six courses) are under control of the Ministry of Technology and Industry, and Kyôtei Association (*Nihon senpaku shinkôkai*) with twenty-four courses is under control of the Ministry of Transport. The Ministry of Home Affairs observes all four races. Apart from horse racing, the races were founded, or "invented," just after World War II, to increase revenue for central and local governments. What is important in relation to the theme of leisure is that these "gamble" races were regarded not as a form of leisure but as a "necessary evil," useful only for their financial purpose.

It is only in the last decade or so that gamble races started to be openly talked about as "leisure," although they have long been classified as such for statistical purposes. It might therefore seem absurd to relate the gambling of the past with leisure, but there is an important linguistic-cultural factor that directly connects the two—the word *asobi* and its almost unchanging meaning throughout Japanese history. Its basic image is one of "a free and unbound activity" and its dictionary meaning may be translated as "no work," "play," "travel," "leisure," "prostitution," and "gambling." Indeed, the word *asobite* (literally "player"), in the sense of a gambler, appears in the decree prohibiting gambling issued by Jitô Tennô, an Empress, as early as 697 (Kida 1966:12). The main meaning of the word *asobinin* is a "gambler," although it also denotes a person without a fixed job (not unemployed).

The reason gambling, traditionally deeply associated with leisure, was not wholly regarded as such in recent times is because the foreign concept of leisure seemed for the majority of Japanese to exclude such a shameful activity as gambling. It is partly due to the use of the English word *leisure* in a Japanese way.

The Current State of Gamble Races

The extent to which participants in respective gamble races spend money on bets is shown in Figure 18.1. The total turnover of gamble races in 1993 was more than 9,000 billion yen. Compared with that of 1984 it had increased by more than 180 percent. Horse racing of JRA leads the market, its growth in ten years an impressive 260 percent. Kyôtei and Keirin halfway kept up with JRA, whereas

	1982	1983	1984	1985	1986	1987	1988	1989	1990	1991	1992	1993
1. Game	567	871	987	1,087	1,130	1,161	1,258	1,424	1,543	1,701	1,838	1,884
(1) *Pachinko*	477	769	887	980	1,014	1,060	1,153	1,312	1,426	1,576	1,699	1,750
(2) *Mahjong*	29	29	32	36	34	33	31	31	29	28	27	25
(3) Game Center, Game Corner	33	34	35	30	25	24	26	29	35	41	49	43
(4) TV Game, Game Soft	28	39	33	41	57	44	48	52	53	56	63	66
2. Gamble	534	527	510	540	572	616	678	774	899	957	964	936
(1) Horse Races, national JRA	142	144	151	165	180	197	221	256	310	343	361	374
(2) Horse Races, regional	74	69	60	68	61	65	71	82	94	98	92	82
(3) Bicycle Races	120	116	110	111	122	130	144	161	184	193	192	179
(4) Motorboat Races	152	150	139	142	148	156	167	187	215	222	213	198
(5) Motorcycle Races	21	20	20	20	22	24	26	30	33	34	35	31
(6) Lotteries	25	28	30	34	39	44	49	58	63	67	71	72
3. Food and Drink	1,193	1,235	1,290	1,336	1,401	1,463	1,564	1,610	1,775	1,895	1,960	1,968
(1) Eating out	946	982	1,018	1,056	1,104	1,153	1,229	1,268	1,412	1,495	1,550	1,568
(2) Bars, Cabarets, Clubs, etc.	247	253	272	280	297	310	335	342	363	400	410	400
4. Karaoke Box (Room)	—	—	—	—	—	3	9	13	29	38	46	55
Total	2,294	2,633	2,787	2,963	3,103	3,243	3,509	3,821	4,246	4,591	4,808	4,843

Figure 18.1 Turnover—games and amusements (Unit: 10 billion yen) (Source: Yoka Kaihatsu Sentâ 1994:72).

horse racing Chihô, which had once almost equalled JRA's turnover, gradually shrank to its present state largely because of poor management. Both Tokyo Racing Union and Iwate Prefecture Union, renowned for their imaginative services, are exceptional. Ôto-Rêsu is a small-scale organization and its turnover corresponds to its size.

The "post bubble" recession of the past six years has seriously affected all gamble races with the exception of JRA, and called for a radical revision of management and services. One response is the introduction of a satellite broadcast system combined with betting by telephone and computer. Kyôtei, Keirin, and JRA started it, yet the number of their users is still not many. In horse racing the cooperation between JRA and Chihô has improved by staging interorganizational races, sparking off fresh interest among fans, but the financial problem of the latter remains as before.

The effect of the recession is seen clearly in the change from 1988 to 1993 of the average spent per participant, as shown in Figure 18.2 (Yamada 1994:82). *Pachinko* is included for the sake of comparison, and we see that only *pachinko* scored an increase, that Ôto-Rêsu retained its betting level, and that the rest of races suffered a decrease in individual expenditure. Another interesting feature of the table is the high expenditure among *keirin* and *kyôtei*

	Participants (100,000)		Turnover (Billion Yen)		Amount per capita (10,000 Yen)	
	1988	1993	1988	1993	1988	1993
Horse Race JRA	56	124	2,207	3,745	39	30
HR Chihô	16	30	711	820	44	27
Keirin	15	20	1,439	1,787	96	89
Kyôtei	12	18	1,668	1,981	139	110
Ôto-Rêsu	6	7	258	310	43	44
Pachinko	285	292	11,528	17,500	40	60
Lottery	326	401	489	716	2	2

Figure 18.2 Participants and spending in gambling (1988–1993) (Source: Yamada 1994:82).

fans, more than twice than that of horse-race goers. This indicates their disposition toward heavy betting and, therefore, their more traditional attitudes toward "gambling."

This is the present state of gamble races in terms of market and participation. Economically, their share of about 15 percent of the entire leisure market is respectable enough, yet, despite the relatively high number of participants, the image and social status of gamble races does not match their economic status. None of them are listed among the twenty favorite leisure forms of the 3,272 people questioned for the 1993 white paper (Yoka kaihatsu sentâ 1994: 19), although among items of "joy and purpose of leisure" the item "to enjoy bet and chance" is ranked eighteenth.

In spite of this discrepancy, changing attitudes of ordinary Japanese toward gamble races in particular and gambling in general must be mentioned. The latest data available is an article of *Yomiuri shinbun* reporting the results of research conducted by the newspaper in March 1995 (Yomiuri Shinbun 1995:3). Of the answers to the question as to what might be improved about gamble races, 70 percent stated *status quo* and 6 percent expansion, while 13 percent stated minimalization and only 6 percent total abolishment. Three quarters of the sample are positive about gambling races. When these figures are compared with figures obtained in 1950—a poll of opinions regarding the continuation of *keirin* holdings in Tokyo, which resulted in a 50 percent rejection of them against 26 percent for continuation—it is clear that the general opinion has shifted, and still is shifting, toward a more permissive stance toward gambling, insofar as it remains within the range of entertainment. There is still some resistance among the older generation; about 30 percent of those above 60 years of age still consider gambling undesirable.

To a related question as to whether or not one approves of young women taking an interest in horse racing, as many do, the positive answer amounted to 67 percent, and even among the older generation only 17 percent found it undesirable. This change in permissiveness is parallel to the change in attitude toward betting in terms of the limit of total spending; more than half of the questioned persons considered it proper to spend less than 10,000 yen at one visit. The stereotypical image of the gambler and race goer used to be someone who spent a lot of money on betting at the risk of ruining his social life. The general tendency is shifting from risky gambling to entertainment with a mere spice of financial danger. What is actually happening among race goers, aside from these statistical figures, will be described later.

Gambling in Japanese History

Keirin, *kyôtei*, and *ôto-rêsu* were created after World War II on the model of horse racing, and they inherited its preestablished bad image. In order to understand the negative value imposed on these gamble races in the postwar period, we must investigate the position of both gambling and horse racing in the context of Japanese sociocultural history. Since the former is broader in its range than the latter, which has inevitably been involved in the sphere of the former, it may be more appropriate to start with gambling.

The oldest remaining record of gambling is found in *Nihon shoki*, according to which Tenmu Tennô invited high-ranking aristocrats, on September 18, 685, to play *hakugi*, a gambling game, and in the end he awarded ten of them clothes (Kida 1966:12). The type of game is not specified but is supposed to have been *sugoroku*, a dice game. The term *hakugi* is definitely Chinese, and games using dice were also of foreign origin. The very fact that the royal court held a gamble gathering, very likely as a new form of refined entertainment, implies that gambling itself was not deemed evil.

The irony was, however, that Jitô Tennô, who succeeded Tenmu, had to issue a decree prohibiting *sugoroku* gambles in 689, and this was followed by a stricter decree in 697 issued by Monmu Tennô, prohibiting gambling and punishing *asobite* (persons who engage in gambling) and the master and family of the *asobite* (Kida 1966:12). What emerges from these early records is a very ambiguous sociocultural position of gambling realized even in ancient times. The joy and excitement of a game are much intensified by combining it with betting. Yet various social harms are brought about by excessive indulgence in gambling. It was a big problem for the ruling class that those who served them tended to neglect their duties because of gambling. Hence a double standard had to be invoked, ruling who might indulge and who might not, according to class distinctions.

The vicious circle between the development of gamble fever among the common people and its incessant prohibition by rulers has continued from the Ancient Age up to the Modern Age. It was very remarkable for the cultural history of human beings that during the Heian era many complicated and subtle games were invented at and around the royal court, with the participation of ladies. These games seemed to have spread quickly among ordinary citizens, and gambling almost always accompanied them. It would be a very lengthy list, if we counted classic literature referring to games and gambling, notably *Kokin Chômonshû*. Hikaru Genji in *Genji Monogatari* (chapter Yadogiri) played *go* with Prince Kaoru, and Lady Ninomiya was the prize for the winner (Kida 1966:23). Here we discern the same double standard, game and gamble being highly commended among the aristocratic circle. In other words, among the upper classes gambling was regarded as a desirable form of leisure, comparable with the arts. Gambling among the lower classes was repeatedly suppressed with legal orders, but in vain (Masukawa 1980:15). For reference, vernacular terms related to gambling are listed below.

The policy of the Edo Bakufu toward gambling and gamblers was very prohibitive from the outset, due to their basic policy to consolidate the four classes. Kujikata Osadamegaki, the corpus of law published in 1742, specified penalties for gambling. It was regarded as a great crime, the source of all social evils. However, the more strict the law became, the more active underground gambling became. Partly as a compromise and partly as a convenient means to maintain law and order by making use of outlaws, the Edo government gave *bakuchiuchi* or professional gamblers an unofficial special status of law helper, with the condition that they were to be segregated from ordinary citizens (*katagi*, serious people). Here the word *asobinin* as opposed to *katagi* became firmly established and they became indicators of the two separate worlds, used as *katagi no sekai*. In other words, the Edo government turned a blind eye on the *bakuchiuchi*—they were semi-institutionalized. The origin of the present-day *yakuza* groups is generally attributed to this.

Parallel to the double standard applied socially to the practice of gambling, there seem to have emerged two types of betting culture. One was the upper-class mild betting to spice the games or matches. This type had a feminine touch on account of the participation of ladies of the Heian era and suits today's image of leisure. The other type was the lower class' heavy betting with the spirit of win or die. This was deeply connected with the Japanese aesthetics of machismo represented by the cherry blossom, emphasizing the beauty of a swift fall after a brief climax. This aesthetic notion was shared by both upper and lower strata of the Japanese population, but when associated with gambling it was definitely for outlaws and the lower class. It formed the core ideology of *yakuza* culture, expressed in the idiom of *otoko ni naru* (to become a man). This ethic of high-risk/high-return later dominated the gambling and racing scene, and brought to it the image of bad manners.

Horse Racing

It is not clear when the match-race type of horse racing originated in Japan, but it was surely connected with the royal family and Shintoism from the beginning. Tenji Tennô is recorded as having watched "horse running" (*souma*) on a holy day of May in 665, and the word *souma* appears frequently from the beginning of the eighth century in documents recording royal events (Wakano 1974: 20). It is more than likely that *souma* meant horse racing, since the terms *kurabeuma* and *kisoiuma*, both of which can be rendered as *keiba*, were also used. From the Heian era to the Edo era there was much literature describing or referring to horse racing; races that were held at a Shintô shrine, in the garden of an aristocrat, or even on the road according to circumstances, and racing at Kamo shrine in Kyoto took place since the Ancient Age. Betting on horse racing also appeared in the Heian era and continued into later periods, despite the inevitable prohibitions. This is a brief sketch of traditional horse racing in Japan.

Modern horse racing was introduced by British residents on a beach near Yokohama in 1861, and the Edo government was requested to establish it with a proper racing course, which request was granted, and so the Yokohama Race Club was founded in the following year. A new race course was built by the government and the first western type of horse race was held in the same year, 1862. Another new course designed by a British captain was built in Negishi of Yokohama in 1866. The Meiji government, which took over the Tokugawa regime, inherited and happily continued this system, presumably for both military and social purposes (Wakano 1974:33). The Ministry of Military Affairs held an independent race meeting at Kudan Shrine, Tokyo, in 1870, and the jockeys were all Japanese soldiers.

Meiji Tennô showed much interest in horse racing and he first visited the Negishi course accompanied by Saigô Takamori in 1893 and is said to have attended altogether fourteen times at different meetings (Wakano 1974:55). Saigô Jûdô, the younger brother of Takamori, became the first Japanese owner of race horses and helped the Yokohama Club, which had been exclusively managed by foreigners, to reorganize and form the Nihon Race Club with participation of Japanese in 1880. In various parts of Japan racing clubs were founded with new race courses, on the basis of traditional horse races held near Shinto shrines (Wakano 1974:59–59). The famous meeting at Shinobazunoike, Ueno, started in 1884 and is said to have attracted a large crowd of upper-class people and foreigners (Kida 1966:168).

There was nothing sinister at that time about Japanese horse racing. It was just like that of the West. Private betting on horses seems to have been practiced among foreigners, but the first official betting ticket was introduced by Nihon Racing Club in 1888, at one dollar per ticket. Theoretically it was the monopoly of the Club and therefore betting was, again only in theory, restricted to foreigners, but apparently some Japanese, especially businessmen dealing with foreign companies, started buying tickets illegally. Nihon Racing Club itself was aware of the fact that betting was illegal and claimed that the Japanese government had implicitly given it permission to sell betting tickets. A seed of radical change was sown when the newly founded Ikegami Club of Tokyo petitioned the government to permit the sale of betting tickets in 1904, upon which it was unofficially granted. The official justification of the government to permit horse racing was a military one, namely, as a means of improving the quality of horses in the army. In both the Sino-Japanese and the Russo-Japanese wars, the Japanese army had found its horses much inferior to the enemy's. For this purpose they helped racing clubs financially by permitting the sale of betting tickets. There was, however, an incompatible factor of criminal law, which categorically prohibited any kind of gambling. Here the government was faced with a dilemma.

The first day of the Ikegami meeting turned out to be a nightmare for the authorities, for many *bakuchiuchi* flocked to it without frock coats. It was their long-awaited fiesta, for they could gamble openly for the first time in their life. The price of one ticket was set at twenty yen, equivalent to the value of one dollar at the time, which was too expensive for a middle-class Japanese; it was about half of the monthly salary of a college graduate.

This betting fever was too conspicuous to be overlooked by the media, and newspapers began a fierce campaign against it. *Ôsaka asahi*, the predecessor of *Asahi shinbun*, went as far as to write that even an army general in uniform was *bakuchiuchi* and therefore criminal if he betted at all (Wakano 1974:101). A few years ago I asked an *Asahi* newspaper man to provide me with copies of *Ôsaka asahi* articles of that time. I received a thick package with a note by him. Indeed these articles tirelessly attacked the government practically every day about the "gamble scandal." This attitude of the media toward betting, regarding it as essentially evil for social life without questioning their own righteousness, continued until the early 1980s and deposited, as it would seem, a deep trauma in racing fans.

Eventually the Meiji Government had to give in, and an Act prohibiting the sale of betting tickets was issued in 1908. Fifteen years later the Statute Law of Horse Racing was enacted and the betting ticket was reintroduced. Although some aristocrats and *zaibatsu* tycoons like Yasuda Izaemon were still concerned with the racing world, most of the new customers were of dubious background, representing the counterculture of *bakuchiuchi* and/or *yakuza*, and race courses were regarded as *tekkaba*—a term referring to a traditional dice-gambling place filled with *bakuchiuchi*. It became unthinkable for an ordinary citizen to visit a race course, and if one did visit, he seriously risked his social status. Only some writers of popular novels (*taishûbungaku sakka*)—that is, not of pure novels (*junbungaku sakka*)—like Kikuchi Kan, Yoshikawa Eiji, and Yoshiya Nobuko, did not bother about the moral standard of the establishment; Kikuchi published the famous *Keiba dokuhon* (1936) and the latter two became owners of race horses.

Postwar Gambling Culture

The social values and atmosphere surrounding prewar horse racing were inherited by postwar gamble races, but there was one big difference between the two periods in terms of organization, and two other factors were new. Before the war any racing club was a private enterprise. All existing racing clubs were united into Nihon Keibakai with an amendment of the Horse Race Law in 1936, but the business still remained private. The enactment of the Anti Monopoly Law, recommended by the occupation administration, resulted in the dissolution of Nihon Keibakai. It was divided into Kokuei Keiba (run by the State) and Chihô Keiba (run by local governments) in 1948. This implied that horse racing and the other three newly created gamble races were put directly or indirectly under the responsibility of administrations. This organizational change brought into the racing world elements of the bureaucratic culture in its pejorative sense; arrogant, cold, inefficient, irresponsible, lack of services, and so on. The confrontation of these new elements with existing elements of the counterculture led to violent riots and hooliganism, worsening the image of gamble races cumulatively.

The first new factor introduced was the adoption of the straight-forecast bet based on the six-frame system in addition to bets on winner and placing. All the runners were divided into six frames, the number of which, not the number of an individual runner, became the object of betting. Hence, in the case of three runners in each frame, the frame number of the winner and that of the second-place runner were combined to provide the winning number. This means that the nine kinds of combination in the case of individual runners were reduced to only one combination, thus increasing the chance of winning, but at the same time much reducing the dividend.

Despite the restrictions of this frame system, both the expected and the actual amount of dividend was much higher than that of betting on win only, and contributed much to attracting gambling-oriented people.

The second new factor was the emergence of left-wing political parties (socialists and communists), both of which denounced gamble races as social evils and deterrents of progress. Professor Minobe Tatsuo was an economist who was elected Governor of Tokyo with much support from these parties and perhaps due to his frequent appearances on TV, coupled with his soft manner, which attracted many women's votes. He obligingly abolished *keirin* meetings at the Korakuen course situated in central Tokyo. As *Asahi shinbun* had demonstrated, it used to be very safe to attack gambling and its bad influences, simply because gamblers and racing fans had no means, nor theoretical justifications, to defend themselves against such unilateral attacks. In other words, "gamblers" were easy sacrificial objects, not for saving the Japanese from bad morality but for strengthening the social position of these sacrificers who could pretend to be killing socially evil dragons. This evil was expressed in the single word *shakôshin*—the spirit of obtaining a fortune with one shot. To prevent stimulating this spirit was the central theme for those who opposed gambling.

Changing Attitudes toward Gamble Races

Changes in the general Japanese attitude toward gamble races were largely due to what happened in the horse racing of JRA. Steady efforts of the organization from the late 1970s to attract ordinary citizens, especially of the female population, into the racing scenery gradually paid off. However, the real turning point was the sudden emergence of two heroes, Take Yutaka, a jockey, and Oguricap, a grey horse.[1] Both earned great popularity in 1988 not only for their superb performances but also for their attractive looks. Girls began to follow them from course to course just to watch one of them, or both if lucky enough. They never bothered about, or were ignorant of, the negative social values imposed upon gamble races, and simply obeyed their own spontaneous feelings. When race going became known as a new fashion, the tidal wave grew faster and faster, engulfing middle-aged women and young boys. The very successful sale of the stuffed Oguricap toy also contributed to the new trend. Then, Tokyo Racing Union, the largest Chihô racing organization, made a great impact by introducing night races (now named "Twinkle Races") at the Ôi racing course located at the waterfront near Haneda International Airport. The word *date spot* began to be talked about in connection with the night races, adding yet more popularity to horse racing. As indicated by *Yomiuri* research findings, permissive attitudes toward horse racing spread quickly in approximately five years. Newspapers started giving more and more space to horse races and even *Asahi shinbun*, which had been very unkind to race goers, began to cover horse racing. New authors on horse racing, especially certain lady writers, obtained popularity, and overseas tour companies started to offer visits to horse race courses. It has transformed into a socially acceptable form of leisure. This change is also affecting the image of the other gamble races in a positive way, despite the nationwide financial crises caused by the economic recession. One interesting aspect is the reaction of elements of the masculine counterculture, which had dominated the gamble races until the middle of the 1980s. They have now become very nostalgic of those days when horse races were simply a form of gambling.

As to criminal activities of *yakuza* groups, they become almost invisible to ordinary attendants. When they go to race courses, they no longer dress conspicuously in *yakuza* fashion, since their entrance is prohibited by law. Rumors of makeup races are very rare and riots fanned by *yakuza* groups on the spot, which used to be a cause of fear against gamble races, are much rarer now. Thus the mood of leisure at race courses is not disturbed by threatening behavior. This is of course only a matter of outlook. Illegal betting of the underworld seems prosperous as ever. The mere fact that racing newspapers are sold at many newspaper stands, even when there are no betting facilites within one hundred kilometers, tells what is going on underneath.

What matters from the point of view of leisure seekers is the sense of security at their activities, and security is almost guaranteed at race courses. This means that the social position of gamble races has moved from the very peripheral one in and before the 1960s to halfway towards the central one, led by the expanding popularity of horse racing. This increase in permissiveness towards gambling may be paralleled by the decrease in the moral objection against "earning without sweating in the forehead," which had been very strong among ordinary citizens. Successive revelations of the financial scandals of politicians, elite civil servants, and top-level executives in large companies may have contributed to this. It seems, however, to be due more to the spreading of the spirit of "enjoy yourself," as opposed to the workaholic mentality of the 1980s. In this sense, the establishment of gamble races as a form of leisure is both the cause and effect of these changes in the general moral values of the Japanese.

Terms

gambling/betting	gambler	to bet
hakugi, bakugi	*asobite*	
hakueki, bakueki	*bakuto*	
bakuchi	*bakuchiuchi*	
tobaku / toji		*tosu*
kakegoto		*kakeru*
tesukabi	*asobinin*	*utsu*
	noseru	
	nigiru	

Notes

1. I have dealt with this phenomenon elsewhere as "The Cult of Oguricap" in the forthcoming collection of essays on Japanese popular culture edited by Dr. Lola Martinez of SOAS.

References

Kida Junichirô. 1966. *Nihon no gyanburu*. Tokyo: Togensha.

Masukawa Kôichi. 1980. *Tobaku I*. Tokyo: Hôsei daigaku.

Nagashima Nobuhiro. 1988. *Keiba no jinruigaku*. Tokyo: Iwanami shinsho.

———. 1998. "The cult of the Oguricap" in L. Martinez (ed.), *Japanese popular culture* (in press).

Wakano Akira. 1974. *Nihon no keiba*. Tokyo: Kôbunsha.

Yamada Kosho. 1994. "Magarikado ni kita pachinko gyôkai," *Golf Management*, December, 80–83.

Yoka kaihatsu sentâ. 1990. *Leisure and recreational activities in Japan*. Tokyo.

———. 1994. *Leisure white paper*. Tokyo.

———. 1994. *Rejâ Hakusho 94*. Tokyo.

Yomiuri shinbun. 1995. "Gyanburu," April 17, morning ed.

Wolfram Manzenreiter

19

Time, Space, and Money

Cultural Dimensions of the "Pachinko" Game

Pachinko: For some people it is a mere pastime, for some it is hard work, for others an unpleasant nuisance, and for many others an enigma, but actually it is the most common form of gambling in Japan. This chapter sets out to explain the context in which *pachinko* has developed and maintained its appeal for "pleasure-seeking" Japan. I want to argue that particular notions of time and space are embedded in the context of the social and cultural practice of *pachinko*. In order to deal adequately with the cultural text of the *pachinko* phenomenon, we must first go back in time and space to the origins of the game. Some general remarks on the relationship between these fundamental categories of everyday experience and the various sources that determine their present representations are indispensable and shall be discussed at the end of the historical description. While trying to delineate the basic premises of the game's intranational success and the reasons for its international failure, I want to take a closer look at the meaning of *pachinko* leisure as a means of understanding contemporary Japan and her culture.

The analytical framework of cultural notions of space, time, and money in the present paper leaves aside questions of, for instance, legal history, political economy, and social structure. I have, however, treated the economic aspect of the *pachinko* game and industry elsewhere (Eils 1993; cf. Eils 1994). In this chapter, I treat money not in terms of market shares, productivity cycles, cash flow, or investment strategies, but rather in terms of the way its exchange value affects the commodification process of space and time in postwar Japan.

Pachinko and the history of leisure in postwar Japan are inseparably interconnected. In the mid-sixties media researcher Katô Hidetoshi praised *pachinko* as the most outstanding manifestation of popular culture during this period (Katô 1981:9). Twenty years later he reinforced his statement: *pachinko* was the unquestionable king of leisure ruling over a kingdom of thirty million subjects (Katô 1984:12–13). The fascination has not diminished since then. On the contrary, the *pachinko* industry has managed to double its annual turnover, estimated in 1992 at an impressive 17 trillion yen, or 5 percent of the GNP of the world's second largest economy (Foreign Press Center Japan 1993:53). This number is even a rather conservative estimate. As *pachinko* is a purely cash-manipulated business sector where even the turnover of goods used as prizes is barely controllable thanks to an elaborate circulation system, managerial authorities apparently find it difficult to resist the temptations of tax evasion. The National Tax Authority (Kokuzeichô) has recurrently listed the *pachinko* industry among the *zeidatsu uâsuto sangyô* ("most notorious tax-evading industries").[1] When the annual turnover approached 10 trillion yen in the middle of the 1980s, the rumor of *omote 10 chô, ura 10 chô, awasete 20 chô en* ("10 trillion for the tax office, 10 trillion for me, in sum 20 trillion yen") circulated throughout the business world (Mabe 1990:25). Although the figures must be handled with care, this oft-cited saying might indicate the true scope of the market.

In comparison to this impressive turnover the scope of the manufacturing industries that produce the game machines, peripheral equipment, hard- and software, hall interior, and the like, is quite moderate. The market size approaches 980 billion Yen. Half of the market is dominated by Heiwa, which was turned into a shareholding company in 1988. Fifty years ago a one-man enterprise, thus the prototype of the "Japanese dream," its success is based on innovative efforts in fields of product development (20 percent of the workforce are doing R&D), market approaches (game electronics, chains of *pachinko* parlors, and game centers), and practical-minded handling of the finance markets (Eils 1994).

Since the end of the high industrial growth period in the early 1970s, when the economic recession induced the dissipation of the work-focused value system and the massive invasion of large corporations of the young but promising leisure market, the scope of leisure types has gained considerable breadth. Despite the increase in complexity of contesting suppliers and leisure activities, *pachinko fans*—the players' connotative denomination coined by the operators of the *pachinko* business—loyally kept on coming. Virtually every year since the first white paper on leisure was published by the Leisure Development Center (Yoka kaihatsu sentâ), a semiofficial research institute founded by the MITI in 1973, the size of the player community has been estimated at a constant thirty million *pachinko aficionados*. Three million machines in sixteen thousand halls are ready to cater to the needs of their customers every day of the year from ten o'clock in the morning to ten o'clock in the evening.

And it all began with a children's game.

The "Pachinko" (Short) Story

Sources on the origin and early years of development in the prewar history of *pachinko* are fragmentary and inconsistent—those Japanese texts I have studied to date offer six different theories of evolution.[2] Yet it is semiofficially acknowledged that the earliest version of the game came to Japan from the mother country of pop culture, the United States, during the final years of the Taishô period, some time between 1921 and 1924. An Osaka-based retailer company had imported the predecessor of *pachinko*, so frequently and misleadingly referred to as "Japanese pinball," from Chicago, coincidentally the later capital of American pinball.[3] The *corinthian game*, in those times a children's toy, was a very simple construction consisting of a horizontal board with some scoring slots protected by nails, a steel ball, and a wooden dowel for shooting the ball onto the board.

The success story of the game began in the *roten* (open-air stalls) of Osaka's *sakariba* (amusement quarter) Sennichimae. From there it spread rapidly throughout the country. Stakes were low, as were prizes inconsiderable. A number of balls were allowed for a minor amount of *sen*. In the case of a sufficiently high score the lucky child could win candy or fruit. The prospect of winning

Figure 19.1 *Pachinko* originated as a children's game between the stalls and shops at amusement quarters, market fairs, and shrine festivals. Although it changed into a regular pastime for adults well before the 1950s, *pachinko* machines are even today an indispensable item at festivals and obviously still have appeal to youngsters.

some sweets was enticing for the children and at the beginning of the Shôwa period nearly every candy store and *depâto* had installed the *korinto gêmu*. At the same time, *tekiya* (itinerant merchants and artisans) brought the game to every local shrine or temple festival. When adult players discovered the fascination of the game that had already seduced their children, the exchange value of scoring balls had to be reconsidered. Regular prizes at that time consisted of consumable goods such as tobacco, vegetables, soap, and other everyday commodities. The practice of paying out cash can be traced back to these very early years (Katô 1981:10).

The adult customers provided a new opportunity for spreading the game into the *yatai*, street stalls of the *tekiya* that opened at night hours. To keep up with the ever-increasing demand the basic principle of construction had to be changed. The genuine idea of *pachinko* emerged when some clever constructors added a spring-

loaded handle and a glass cover to the main board and set it up ver-
tically. The transformation from the space-consuming horizontal
yokomono to the economic version of the *tatemono* (vertical machines) marked the diversion from the Western evolution that eventually produced the pinball machine. The new game deserved a new
name: *gachan-gachan* or *gachanko* in the Kansai area and *pachi-
pachi* in the Kanto area. Much like *pachinko*, these names are ono-
matopoetic and emulate the sound of the shooter hitting the ball.
Where and when the uniform name *pachinko* was introduced is not
precisely known, but it became common usage soon after the first
regular halls were opened in 1930.

The growth of the business was halted in the course of the late
1930s as the climate of a nation preparing for war prohibited the
use of raw materials for anything other than war needs. The machine production was interrupted, the factories retooled for war
needs. In 1938 all of the 380 *pachinko* halls were ordered to close
overnight. Only a few of them were granted compensations. Although others managed to stay in business illegally, legal *pachinko*
vanished until the end of the war.

The revitalization of *pachinko* occurred, immediately after the
war, between the barracks and stalls of the black markets. During
this time of general hardship, little amusement was available, and
this game provided the possibility to win some of the scarce daily
essentials such as sugar, rice, vegetables, and even cigarettes. The
production of machines was recommenced in the industrial area of
Nagoya and *pachinko* parlors opened across the country. When
daily life started to normalize at the end of the 1940s, it was escorted by the biggest ever *pachinko* boom.

Within five years, the number of *pachinko* parlors exploded from
4,818 in 1949 to 43,452 in 1953. New machine types emphasizing
thrill and the element of chance were chiefly responsible for this
rocket-like career. However, due to the increasing gambling character of the game the authorities felt prompted to halt this undesirable development. When the new over-successful models were out-
lawed in 1953, the *pachinko* business encountered a severe setback.
In 1957 the number of halls had dwindled to 8,792, which remains
the all-time low (Mitsui 1992:170–73). The slump was not as dramatic as the decline in parlor numbers would indicate. Most of the
enterprises that had entered the scene during the boom years had a

stock of only twenty or thirty machines. According to a report by the Tokyo Metropolitan Police the average stock in 1955 consisted of 61.2 machines (Kodama 1958:338). Hence the market recession primarily affected smaller enterprises. The same structural reorganization swept through the manufacturing industries. Of more than five hundred companies that were registered in 1952 only forty-seven survived the recession (Mabe 1990:158).

The following two decades (1960–1980) witnessed the rather quiet but steady and rapid consolidation of the business. Machine designs, hall policies, and management techniques changed considerably in compliance with the mood of the time—the high economic growth period. These processes, significantly referred to as campaigns of *kindaika* (modernization), *gôrika* (rationalization), and *imêji appu* (image cleaning), provided the solid foundation for doubling the turnover betweeen 1970 and 1975, the years in which the *pachinko* industries surpassed the one-trillion-yen borderline for the first time and attained the top position among leisure industries (Maeda 1991:24–25).

The new computer technology revolutionized the *pachinko* machine. Integral changes in the interior of the machine emphasized its gambling character. During the times of mechanical play an experienced and skillful player had had to spend several hours playing to have a chance of winning a few thousand balls. The electric spin-handle of the computerized machines could be mastered even by laymen and novices. If they were lucky enough, they could easily win five thousand to ten thousand balls in a matter of ten minutes. The new spirit of the game induced an incredible mega boom in the course of the 1980s. Whereas the entire leisure market doubled its size between 1982 and 1992, the *pachinko* market quadrupled and now held a share of 22.52 percent. When the Bubble economy collapsed, leading to Japan's most severe recession, and even the leisure market marked heavy losses, *pachinko* was able to account for another 7.4 percent (Foreign Press Center Japan 1993:61–63). As already mentioned, the number of active *pachinko* players has remained steady since the mid-seventies, and as the frequency of playing exhibits no remarkable changes either (between twenty and twenty-four times a year), the increase in turnover is explained only by the accelerating cash flow of the new machine types. Especially noteworthy is the introduction of *pachisuro* (the Japanized contraction of *pachinko* and the slot machine), which is in fact little else but a slot machine and has nothing in common with the nails and balls of traditional *pachinko*. The minimum fee for a stake is 20 yen/coin (compared to *pachinko*: 4 yen/ball), and with additional bets the stakes are rapidly multiplied. A single *pachisuro* machine had, between 1984 and 1988, an annual average cash flow of 8.75 million yen—three times more than a *pachinko* machine could make. In 1990 *pachisuro* contributed 40 percent of the turnover of *pachinko* industries despite its lesser number of machines, amounting only to 17 percent (Foreign Press Center Japan 1990:50).

Obviously, *pachinko* has been able to maintain its particular appeal for leisure-seeking Japan up to the present times, not withstanding the fact that the basic features of the game rely on a most simple concept—putting as many balls as possible into scoring slots. This career is a remarkable achievement considering that hardly any other business sector is changing as rapidly as the leisure industries, whose balance sheets are decided by the degree of ability to create, or at least to adapt to, the changing vogues and trendy lifestyle patterns of society.[4]

The "Pachinko-ron"

Certainly *pachinko* is no marginal phenomenon, nor is it the pursuit of a fringe group. It seems rather to emphasize the commercialized, industrialized, and bureaucratized character of play behavior in a mass society, as Japan is so commonly and so easily labeled. Yet the products of contemporary mass culture are characterized by their inherent ability to transcend national and even cultural borders.[5] Elements of Japanese popular culture that have been successfully exported to foreign markets include *manga*, animated movies, *karaoke*, popular music, but not *pachinko*. Despite recurrent attempts to popularize the game in countries of Southeast Asia, in Germany, and the United States, Japan remains the only country with a *pachinko* culture worthy of mention. As the meaning of leisure implies the freedom of choice, people outside of Japan have obviously chosen to get along without *pachinko*. People in Japan, however, must have their own reasons for sticking to the game. The ethnographer Ishige Naomichi explains the failure of export attempts with the legal restrictions on gambling and the gambling industries already established in the foreign countries.

But as virtually all attempts were abortive, he cannot but conclude that the game is somehow designed specifically for the Japanese mentality (Ishige 1989:183).

The rational perspective of this hypothesis is rather an exception in the field of *pachinko-ron*. Because of the territorial exclusiveness, *nihonjin-ron* analogies seem to come quite naturally. Katô Hidetoshi, for example, asserts that speculation, or "running a risk" (*atatte kudakeru*), are typical Japanese attitudes (1984:66–67). Or: *pachinko* serves as a master plan for the particular Japanese world view in which success depends less on effort but more on a mixture of competence and chance (1984:116–20). Furthermore, as *pachinko* can be played anywhere and at any time it is best suited to the needs of *himatsubushi* ("squashing time"), which refers to the Japano-characteristic "do-complex," meaning that an empty space of time that is not spent in activity is not supposed to be (1984: 131– 36). Katô's last argument refers to the particular "Japanese individuality" established in the process of cosmic integration of self and machine (1984:146–48). With the machine in mind, Tada Michitarô argues in *Asobi to nihonjin* in terms that might have been borrowed from critical theory and Walter Benjamin,[6] that in times of industrialization the relationship between man and machine determines the work process and extends to the private sphere. Strictly speaking, *pachinko* is no pastime but occupational education and preparation (Ishige 1989:183; Kôzuki 1978:34; Aoki 1978:34). The alienation from one's work in the bureaucratized society is made responsible also by Takeuchi Hiroshi. Due to the functional differentiation of the work process, workers are involved only in a limited part of the production process where satisfaction is mediated by income. After winning some thousand balls, however, the successful man can see, touch, and carry the fruits of his efforts (1979:304–05). Kubota Mitsusuke, chief editor of the journal of the *pachinko* industries, also praises the parlor as a place of "individuality in the group" (*shûdan no naka no kojinshugi no ba*). Noteworthy is Kubota's comparison of the flashing lights and electronic sounds to Caillois's categorization of play, especially to the element of ecstasy (*âlynx*), expressing the player's retrieval from perceiving the real (Ishige 1989:85).

Foreign voices contributing to the *pachinko-ron* argue in similar terms but with negative connotations. David Riesman, asked for the most eye-catching difference between Japan and America, recalled *pachinko*, and he must have had the same image in mind when he gave to this phenomenon the name of "the lonely crowd" (Riesman and Thompson Riesman 1967:127). The relationship of dependency between the player and the rhythm of play generated by the machine is another observation made by Riesman and Thompson Riesman (1967:116–117), Sepp Linhart (1990:89), Ian Buruma (1982:18), Donald Richie (1980: 19), and Roland Barthes (1981:43–45). For the latter, however, the lascivious feeling a winner must experience in the moment of pouring silver balls was more significant (Barthes 1981:46). The sexual allusion is even extended in the denotation of "Japanese masturbation" (Forbis 1981:168). Finally, when foreign voices attempt to decode "mystic Japan," the references to Zen Buddhism, meditation, and transcendency must occur, here made by Buruma (1982:18–19), Richie (1980:19), and Gérald Matzeler (1977:17).

To sum up and classify the main elements of the cultural discourse on *pachinko* in sociological jargon, we must keep four models or prototypes in mind. Most prominent are the convergence theory (the pattern of work determines the leisure behavior), the compensation theory (alienated work versus self-fulfilling leisure), the complementary theory (the individual in the group), and the particularity theory (genuinely Japanese qualities are matched by the genuinely Japanese game). Despite the diverging interpretations, most of the studies have at least one aspect in common: they are rather speculative and unsound in analysis and theory. In some cases they tend to overlook the fact that the premises they have used should cause similar repercussions in other societies, and, most obviously, they assume that the homogeneous community of *pachinko* players can be taken as representational of all Japanese. This makes one wonder—who are the thirty million fans, and when, how long, and how often do they play, how much do they spend on *pachinko*, and what makes them do so?

The Fan Community

According to the 1989 white paper on leisure, *pachinko* is predominantly a pursuit of Japanese males. Nearly every second Japanese male, but only every seventh female, played the game in 1989. Most outstanding is the proportional share of the young men aged twenty to thirty years. In this group 61.4 percent reported *pachinko* experience. Overproportional shares are further to be noticed among men aged between thirty and thirty-nine and those between forty and forty-nine. The interest in the game among the young (under twenty years) and among the aged (over sixty) is comparatively low. Similar patterns characterize the distribution of female players, with high participation shares among the twenty- to twenty-nine- and thirty- to thirty-nine year-old categories and extremely low rates for the young and the aged (Mabe 1990:54). A case study conducted by Ishige among *pachinko* players in a metropolitan parlor confirmed these results, although the differences in absolute numbers were rather large (Ishige 1989:173–75).

In another survey, Nikkôsô (Association of Manufacturing *Pachinko* Industries) questioned 5,000 active *pachinkâ* about their annual income. The share of those without any private income (25.8 percent) is eye-catching, though this group is likely to include professional housewives and students dependent on the income of another family member. 12.1 percent said that their income was less than 1 million yen, and a further 16.5 percent earned less than 3 million yen. An annual salary of 5 million yen, referred to as the average income of a white-collar employee with higher education and few years of occupational life, was surpassed by only 10 percent. Our first conclusion: *pachinko* is played by members of all age, sex, and income groups but it mostly attracts those young and middle-aged males with low incomes (Mabe 1990:62).

According to Ishige's case study, 45.5 percent of the players were salaried employees, 21.6 percent students, 12.8 percent self-employed, another 12.9 percent freelance workers, and 8.4 percent unoccupied. The stratification of occupational groups yielded significant differences for those who play four times or more a week: the salaried employees decreased to 22.5 percent while the freelance workers increased to 19.1 percent, the unemployed to 20.8 percent, and the students and self-employed remained without significant changes. Our second conclusion: regular players are apparently found among individuals who have a time schedule without restrictions (Ishige 1989:75).

Various surveys of Nikkôsô, Zenyûkyô (Association of *pachinko* Parlor Patrons), and the case study of Ishige come to the same con-

Figure 19.2   *Pachinko* is a social leveler—from 10 A.M. to 10 P.M. During the opening hours *pachinko* afficionados mingle in the illuminated parlors regardless of sex, age, income, and social status.

clusions concerning the structural relationship between average frequency of play, duration of play, and play expenditure. The higher the frequency of play, the longer the stay in the parlor and the higher the expenditure. With reference to these surveys we are now able to delineate more precisely the image of the thirty-million-member *pachinko* community. The average fan plays two times a week for 2.18 hours and spends 3,300 Yen. Twenty-five percent of all players are regulars who frequent the hall more than four days a week. More concretely, approximately eight million Japanese spend at least 4,000 yen nearly every day in three hours of playing *pachinko*!

With these results in mind one feels prompted to return to the question of the particular appeal of this game. Instead of recapitulating the assertions of more or less initiated observers, I will refer to two further surveys on play motivation. Informants of Ishige's sample were most attracted by the aspect of *himatsubushi* (45.8 percent), by diversion and recreation (33.9 percent), the prospect of winning (27.9 percent), and accessibility of the game (9.4 percent). However, such straightforward questioning seems to be rather problematic. Although another survey of a *pachinko* parlor yields similar conclusions, we have to take into account that the high share of people with "killing time" motivation on the one hand and the average play duration on the other can hardly correspond. Ishige comments that these responses are rather to be taken as tendencies: *himatsubushi*, which is given by every second player as his primary motive, must be understood as a typical case of *tatemae*. Two hours of play are unlikely to take place without the player's choice. The inner motive (*honne*) is more likely to refer to the gambling nature of the game, which Ishige believes is the main cause of *pachinko*'s popularity (Ishige 1989:188–89). Yet, in order to affirm his point of view, further research is needed.

Time to Play and Space for Play

The complex nature of the development over roughly seventy years deserves a second look in order to highlight some of the adaptive transformations that made of the Western original "the most Japanese of games" (Sedensky 1991:16). To apply a rather fashionable, yet, in this context, convincing term, the entire development of the former children's toy into the present-day *megatronic* pastime can be rendered as a perpetuating process of domestication. Among its many semiotic components, including those of civilization, taming, bringing under control, making familiar, the application of the term *domestication* here "suggests that Western goods, practices, and ideas are changed (Japanized) in their encounter with Japan" (Tobin 1992:4). Yet Japan itself has also changed. The simultaneity of the processes of change and providing guidelines of cultural orientation has resulted in two diverging patterns of transforming *pachinko*: on the one hand, the integration of the game into established patterns of entertainment, on the other, the consequent commercialization of the game in accordance with modern principles of rationality. More precisely, that what has happened in seventy years of *pachinko* history has been the passive and active adoption and adaptation of the game into the cultural text of Japan. Culture in this broadest of all meanings refers to the total of common world experiences that provide implicit and explicit models for structuring life for a given community. The knowledge of the cultural text—encoded in systems of symbols—is the basic prerequisite for understanding and behaving properly in any contextual situation. Due to the complexity and compactness of the links that shape and cohere the text, something that appears so absolutely strange to us is most familiar to those who have mastered the appropriate cultural knowledge. Discourses on phenomena such as orientalism or ethnocentrism are born out of the necessity to render the "Other's" text comprehensible, to proclaim the self-evident, the obvious. In intercultural studies there is nothing that goes without saying.

It does not go without saying that time and space and money belong to those points of reference that help people to organize and explain the world in which they live.[7] The arbitrariness of such concepts becomes most apparent in moments of intercultural experience, for example, in the discussion of the Japanese version of the modernization process or in the biased perception of order and disorder in the urban space (Müller 1984:542), or in the researcher's efforts to find an interculturally valid and applicable definition of free time, or leisure. The power of culture to shape the framework of everyday experience such as time and space deserves major attention, especially in the context of transcultural observations. The cultural text into which time, space, and money are interwoven, is recreated by the very act of living. But people also construct their notions, as all underlying concepts have been formed during historical constellations within particular cultural contexts and under certain social conditions. The contemporary rhythm of time and its reflective segmentization into distinctive and controllable entities makes sense only in the case of a denaturalized and secularized notion of time developed in line with certain specific technological, economic, and cultural changes. They commenced in the fourteenth century, spread with the invention and dissemination of the clock, and accelerated during the nineteenth-century industrial revolution (Giesen 1991:61–82). The conquest of time is parallel to the transformation of the space—as the workplace was separated from the household, or the world of men from the world of the family.

Space in this sense is defined by the arrangement of relations and the way these relate to surrounding spaces. However, the traditional Western perception is heavily influenced by the physical-mathematical concept of space as a three-dimensional container.

Based on the development of Newton's absolute theory and the historical background of the changing world view in Europe of the seventeenth and eighteenth centuries, space is regarded as an abstract entity without reference given to its content (Läpple 1991: 36–38). Finally, due to the logic of capitalism, money has gained a status of prominence in negotiating social relationships. By means of the monetary exchange value, both time and space attain the status of exchangable valuables that can be traded or speculated with, as they are limited and scarce resources on a trade market (Harvey 1991:150).

It is not too far-fetched to state that the power of this network was able to alter older concepts that had once signified the cosmology of premodern Japanese society. The development of Meiji Japan into a capitalistic economy and industrialized society stipulated the simultaneously occurring transplantation of Western thinking patterns that regarded and structured space and time in terms of their exchange value (Shimada 1994:70–165). Later transitions in the periods of high industrialization and postindustrialization only emphasized the degree of suitability these conceptions had for modern Japan.

In order to apply these theoretical considerations to the empirical world of *pachinko*, a deeper look at the way in which the commodification of time and space affected the development of *pachinko* is indispensable. Since the first transformation of the corinthian game, which was actually already naturalized as *korinto gêmu*, the manufacturing industries have been concerned with extending the commodification of time and space. The verticalization of the machines was a response to the simple recognition that the productivity of a machine is related to the space it requires. The same policy was acquired in the late 1950s, with the same success. Older halls required much more space for their stocks of machines because they were reloaded at the back. The transfer of the reloading hole to the front and, later on, to a fully automatic and computerized central system, doubled the rentability of space. As a by-product, wage costs were reduced. A *pachinko* hall of three hundred machines that had required a staff of thirty employees in 1960 could easily be run by fifteen staff members in 1980 (Takeuchi 1980:67).

As a second by-product, probably much more important, the rentability of time increased. The realization of this objective can be traced back to the ingenious inventions of Masamura Shôichi, the "godfather of *pachinko*." The mechanical handle of the *tanpatsu-shiki* ("one-shot-type") allowed sixty balls to be shot per minute, whereas Masamura's new *renpatsu-shiki* ("successive shots type") allowed up to 180, the number depending on one's skill. The introduction of the electric handle and the computerization of the interior also accelerated the shooting of balls onto the board. Actually it is the parlor's business to sell (or to rent) as many balls as possible, whereas it is a major concern of the Metropolitan Police Agency to keep the limit of prize balls and play balls under control. Because legal *pachinko* is supposed to be a game that requires more skill than luck, standards of licensing always had to consider that elements of speculation came second, or as the law (*Fûzoku eigyôtô torishimari hô*, paragraph 2.17) explicitly states, *shakôshin o sosoru ozore ga nai yûgi* ("a game that is unlikely to induce speculation").[8] Contemporary standards (1990) limit the amount of play balls to 100 per minute, and the maximum output to 2,400 or more, according to machine type (Sedensky 1991:86–87).

As I have stated elsewhere, the economic success depends on the creation and successful maintenance of supplier-induced demands by manufacturing industries. Catch phrases like *kindaika* (modernization), *gôrika* (rationalization), and *imêji appu* ("image polishing") headlined the campaigns following the logic of the High Growth Period. By constantly reinventing the game and its setting in correspondence with broader socioeconomic tendencies, the campaigns maintained the customers' high interest. Research and development of machine types—probably implied are the industries with the shortest innovation cycles[9]—are only one facet of the effort to prevent the *pachinko* world from any major recession. Guidance in matters of parlor management and administration, further education, and research in consumers' tastes, are all elements of the planning of coordination of the interests of all industries involved in the *pachinko* business (Eils 1994).

Yet *pachinko* implies not only business; for most people it denotes play. The exchange value of time and space is a common attribute of industrialized societies and does not explain the limitation of the game to Japan. By looking at the play aspect I hope to answer this last question. Considering the place of birth of *pachinko*—*sakariba, ennichi, matsuri*—it seems to be probable that as a

Figure 19.3   Have a nice day: play the balls and challenge "The Nagoya"!
Immediately after World War II Nagoya was the center of *pachinko* manufacturing, and still is in the eyes of most Japanese. Actually, the bulk of
machines is produced in Kiryû, Gunma prefecture. Each of the three big
manufacturers Heiwa, Sankyô, and Nishijin employs a large staff of designers and engineers who compete for creating ever more popular game
machine types.

form of play *pachinko* was adapted to more traditional, more natural perceptions of space and time.

Some people in Japan say that the traditional concepts of *ke*
and *hare* are indispensable for understanding modern kinds of
diversions (cf. Linhart 1984:208–10). Japanese ethnologists have
used the concepts of *ke* and *hare* to differentiate between the normal, the profane, days of work (*ke*), and the special, sacral days

(*hare*). The principle of this dichothomy followed the rhythm of nature which, typical for premodern and agrarian societies, determined the distribution of working time and free time in traditional Japan. As the fertility of the soil was regarded as a divine donor, days of rest were devoted to religious rites. With *kegare* the ethnographer Namihira Emiko introduced another concept, separating the impure, unlucky times from those of purity and luck. Times of *kegare* refer to situations of crisis in the life of the individual, such as menstruation, death, or illness, that also endangered the social organization of the village community and necessitated purification ceremonies for the sake of the community. But even before Western perceptions of time began to infiltrate Japanese society, these terms were said to have become meaningless. The extraordinary quality of the days of *hare* was absorbed by the urban amusement quarters where, without regarding *hare* or *ke* as time markers, pleasure was always at hand. However, the close connection between commercialized entertainment and the sphere of religion is signified by the presence of *yatai* and *roten* at every temple or shrine festival, as well as by the emergence of the urban *sakariba* in the neighborhood of the religious centers of pilgrimage in the Edo period (Tada 1984: 34; Graburn 1983). As both *hare* and *kegare* were seen as contrasts to *ke*, we might be able to identify a kind of "structural ambivalence" that allows attitudes toward the *sakariba* types of amusement to shift easily between affirmation and rejection.

The law that controls *pachinko* as well as other amusement enterprises prescribes the spatial borders within which *pachinko* is allowed. The legally defined allocation of *pachinko* halls, however, puts the pastime in line with more suspicious variants of entertainment, such as massage salons and love hotels, which are subject to precisely the same governing law. The negative image due to implied affiliations with morally questionable enterprises, prostitution, and the *yakuza* is one shadow the *pachinko* business probably will never get rid of, despite all efforts to create a respectable reputation. It seems that there is too much money in the game for organized crime to sever all ties. The biggest part of the price exchange system—the law forbids patrons to pay their clients in cash, thus lucky winners have to exchange their price balls for "special price goods" to be cashed in at the closest *kaiba*, often just a hole in the wall—is managed by *yakuza*-affiliated subcontractors. The estimated annual cash flow between parlors/customers, subcontractors, and wholesalers (*tonya*) is nine or ten trillion yen (for a detailed description of the exchange system, its agents and rituals, cf. Eils 1994, or the Japanese popular press on organized crime and *pachinko*: Hinago 1992).[10]

The integration of *pachinko* into *sakariba bunka* creates a tradition without a past. We can differentiate between five different types of *pachinko* parlors according to location, but only the two predominant models are of interest to us here: the *ekimae ritchi* (commuter terminal) and the *jûtakuji kinrin ritchi* (residential area) type. The former are the most typical and representative, sited in the proximity of commuter terminals, in amusement quarters and shopping arcades, while the latter are situated in the middle of residential areas. Even the other type, which is certainly not integrated into a greater amusement complex, links *pachinko* to its pseudo-past. Other possible sources of the *sakariba* were the open spaces between residential areas that were used as places of refuge in the eventuality of fire, but could also offer attractions to some people at certain times (Linhart 1986:200). These open spaces at the fringes of normality again offer attractions: *pachinko* parlors. The other three topologically determined types—*gakuseigai ritchi* (university), *bijinesu gai ritchi* (business quarter), and *kôgai ritchi* (suburban location)—seem to be variants of the "in-between character" of the open-space concept.

Characteristic features link the past with the present in the *sakariba*. First, a full-fledged *sakariba* has to be crowded, loud, and garish. Second, it is a space of male pleasure and male time. Third, it is a space for buying pleasure. And finally, it is a space on the exterior of time and space as it provides opportunities to transcend the social obligations and constraints of everyday life. All of these features can be found in contemporary *pachinko*, which is crowded, noisy, and sparkling. Also, *pachinko* is predominantly a male pursuit. It connects the very characteristic aspect of leisure in traditional Japan with that in modern Japan, namely that one must pay for entertainment. Finally, the fourth argument relates to the concept of *ilinx* (ecstasy), added by the French sociologist Roger Caillois to Johan Huizinga's classic model of play. The transcendence of the everyday social hierarchy in the ecstatic experience was a major aspect in the community festivals, the basic ingredient for the common reassurance of community bonds. We know that similar functions of renewing community bonds or transcending the everyday hierarchy have been extended to the *sakariba*, as the custom of *bureikô* indicates (cf. Linhart 1986:207; Allison 1994). Playing *pachinko* offers the postmodern version: the dynamics of the game machine and the signature of gambling eliminate the framework of time consciousness and open a space beyond the everyday world. The ecstatic experience of play reaches its climax in the moment of victory when man has triumphed over the symbol of modernity and, simultaneously, over the almightiness of predestination. The structural analogies between *pachinko* practice and traditional notions of time and space provide us with a reliable explanation for the intracultural success and for its intercultural failure. When the game first entered Japan it was smoothly integrated into historical spaces of amusement culture. After the defeat in World War II *pachinko* rapidly reestablished itself, without any serious competitors. Since then *pachinko* has established its firm position in the leisure market, and the custom of playing has become more and more part of the habitus of Japan's urbanized culture. All efforts to export the game had to face severe conditions of legal restrictions and missing chances, because any suitable space in the foreign cultural context—Las Vegas, game centers, and casinos indicate the existence of markets and demand—was already occupied by fierce competitors. An argument even more convincing than pure chance and market shares is the cultural illegibility of *pachinko*, which obviously cannot fascinate all the consumers of a steadily globalizing popular culture. You can transfer the game, actively, but you cannot transfer its historical background, even should it be a contrived one.

Notes

1. According to the *Asahi shinbun* (21. 8. 91), in 1991, for the seventh consecutive time, *pachinko* parlors occupied the first rank among tax-evading businesses. Some of the disappearing money is said to be used for financing political support, and, because of the large number of Korean parlor patrons, for presents to Kim Il-Sung, chief of state in North Korea at the time (Pohl 1990:7).

2. The "American theory," as opposed to evolutionary models of English, Korean, or Japanese origin, is most convincingly documented. The relationship to games of bagatelle and billard, however, relates to much older

and more distant predecessors in Russia of pre-Napoleonean times. For a more thorough-going analysis of the origins of the game and a detailed depiction of the *pachinko* history in Japan, cf. Eils 1993.

3. The development after the early 1920s exhibits two diverging patterns for Japan and the United States: whereas pinball and slot machines never fused in the Western setting, *pachinko* originally combined rudimentary elements both of game and gambling, of skill and chance. With the introduction of *pachisuro* in the early 1980s, however, a *pachinko* derivation emerged as a pure game of chance.

4. The rough competitiveness in this prospective market has produced a neverending chain of new machine types appearing in the *pachinko* parlors. Although most of them are barely variations on standard types—at the present time *hanemono, dejipachi, kenrimono, pachisuro* (for detailed explanation cf. Kiritani 1995)—quick-minded enterprises (*pachinko kyô-shitsu*), monthly periodicals, and a broad range of popular literature teach the puzzled customers to challenge the newest models.

5. Or, as Kogawa Tetsuo states, "nowadays the formation of mass culture means the transformation of popular culture" (Kogawa 1989:54).

6. Correspondent to the Marxist observation that in industrialized production systems it is the machine that controls both the working process and the worker, Benjamin noticed similar relationships of dependence among visitors to Hamburg's Lunapark who enjoyed the new machines at the amusement park (W. Benjamin, *Illuminationen*, cited from Warneken 1974:108–109).

7. Though the individual perception of activities-in-time might differ to a great degree, the underlying concept of time will usually not differ within a collectivity. The notion of time—by no means a neglected topic within the field of social or cultural studies—never loses the reference to the cosmology of the group even in times of deepest awareness of individuality or isolation (Nowotny 1993:9).

8. Not only *pachinko* manufacturers were always concerned with maximizing the productivity of machines regardless of legal restrictions, similar attitudes determined the development of the American slot machine. "The history of the slot machine is one of constant effort to devise ways to evade the law" (Anonymous 1950:62).

9. In best Schumpeterian tradition *pachinko* parlors frequently exchange and rearrange their machine stocks with innovative models, at least

once, more often twice a year, and sometimes every three months (Maeda 1991:28). Huge flower arrangements and billboards with signs of *shinki kaiten* or *shinsô kaiten* announce the occurence of another *pachinko* holiday. Being the only kind of advertisement this business seems to require at all, the output during these occasions is supposed to be very high.

10. The last desperate effort to get out of this vicious circle was the introduction of prepaid cards, to remove the cash from the game. However, forged or altered cards soon entered the market, causing the card-vending industries in 1995 a loss of 50 billion yen, and forcing them to introduce the fourth generation of card-reading hardware in less than seven years (*Mainichi Daily*, 24. 4. 1995).

──────────────── *References* ────────────────

Allison, Ann. 1994. *Nightwork: Sexuality, pleasure and corporate masculinity in a Tokyo hostess club.* Chicago: University of Chicago Press.

Anon. 1950. "Slot machines and pinball games," *The Annals of the American Academy of Political and Social Science* May 1995 (= vol. 269), 62–70.

Aoki Sadanobu. 1978. "Pachinko—sono hanei no mekanizumu (ka)," *Roajiiru* 4, 29–35.

Barthes, Roland. 1981. *Das Reich der Zeichen.* Frankfurt: Suhrkamp.

Buruma, Ian. 1982. *Buigzame emoties.* 's-Gravenhage: Uitgeverij BZZTÔH.

Eils, Wolfram. 1993. *Pachinko: Phänomen und Perspektiven: Kultursoziologische Anmerkungen zum Matador der japanischen Unterhaltungsindustrie.* Wien: Universität Wien (unpublished M.A. thesis).

———. 1994. "Die Ökonomie des Pachinko," *Nachrichten der Gesellschaft für Natur- und Völkerkunde Ostasiens / Hamburg* 152 (= Zeitschrift für Kultur und Geschichte Ost- und Südostasiens 1992, 152), 59–95.

Forbis, William H. 1981. *Japan today. People–places–power.* Tokyo: Tuttle.

Foreign Press Center Japan. 1990. *Leisure and recreational activities.* Tokyo: Foreign Press Center Japan (= "About Japan" Series 4).

———. 1993. *Leisure and recreational activities.* Tokyo: Foreign Press Center Japan (= "About Japan" Series 4).

Giesen, Bernhard. 1991. *Die Entdinglichung des Sozialen: Eine evolutionstheoretische Perspektive auf die Postmoderne.* Frankfurt: Suhrkamp.

Graburn, Nelson. 1983. *To pray, play and pay: The cultural structure of Japanese domestic tourism.* Aix-En-Provence: Centre des Hautes Etudes Touristiques (= Cahiers du Tourisme Série B No. 26).

Harvey, David. 1991. "Geld, Zeit, Raum und die Stadt," Martin Wentz (ed.), *Stadt-Räume.* Frankfurt & New York: Campus, 149–68.

Hinago Akira. 1992. *Pachinko sensô*. Tokyo: JICC.

Ishige Naomichi. 1989. "Pachinko—asobi no naka no shigoto," Moriya Takeshi (ed.), *Nihonjin no asobi 6: Gendai Nihon bunka ni okeru dentô to henyô*. Tokyo: Domesu shuppan, 173–96.

Katô Hidetoshi. 1981. "Pachinko bunka shikan," *Katô Hidetoshi zenshû* 5. Tokyo: Chûô kôronsha, 9–21.

———. 1984. *Pachinko to nihonjin*. Tokyo: Kôdansha.

Kiritani, Elizabeth. 1995. "Pachinko, Japan's national pastime," John A. Lent (ed.), *Asian popular culture*. Boulder, Colo.: Westview Press, 203–11.

Kodama Kôta. 1958. *Gendai: Zusetsu nihon bunkashi taikei. Dai 13 kan*. Tokyo: Shôgakukan.

Kogawa Tetsuo. 1989. "New trends in popular culture," Gavan MacCormack and Yoshio Sugimoto (eds.), *The Japanese trajectory: Modernization and beyond*. Cambridge: Cambridge University Press, 54–66.

Kôzuki Eisuke. 1978. "Pachinko no miryoku (ka)," *Roajiiru* 6, 29–37.

Läpple, Dieter. 1991. "Gesellschaftszentriertes Raumkonzept. Zur Überwindung von physikalisch-mathematischen Raumauffassungen in der Gesellschaftsanalyse," Martin Wentz (ed.), *Stadt-Räume*. Frankfurt & New York: Campus, 35–46.

Linhart, Sepp. 1984. "Some observations on the development of 'typical' Japanese attitudes towards working hours and leisure," Gordon Daniels (ed.), *Europe interprets Japan*. Tenterden: Paul Norbury Publications, 207–14.

———. 1986. "*Sakariba*: Zone of 'evaporation' between work and home?" Joy Hendry and Jonathan Webber (eds.), *Interpreting Japanese society: Anthropological approaches*. Oxford: JASO (= JASO Occasional Papers No. 5), 198–210.

———. 1990. "'Arbeite wie ein Präsident, vergnüge dich wie ein König': Bemerkungen zum japanischen Freizeitverhalten," Irene Hardach-Pinke (ed.), *Japan: Eine andere Moderne*. Tübingen: Konkursbuch Verlag, 81–95.

Mabe Yôichi. 1990. *Kyôi no pachinko bijinesu: Shirarezaru 13-chô en sangyô no uchimaku*. Tokyo: Sobokusha.

Maeda Susumu. 1991. *Pachinko ten no keiei no subete*. Tokyo: Keiei jôhô shuppansha.

Matzeler, Gérald. 1977. "Le pachinko," *Encyclopédie Permanente Japon* S72/2, 1–19.

Mitsui Yoshiaki. 1992. *Pachinko keiei kakumei—"Mitsui shiki" furanchaizu-shisutemu no susume*. Tokyo: IN tsûshinsha.

Müller, Rudolf W. 1984. "Das sozialwissenschaftliche Japan und der Okzident," *Leviathan* 12/4, 506–49.

Nowotny, Helga. 1993. *Eigenzeit: Entstehung und Strukturierung eines Zeitgefühls*. Frankfurt: Suhrkamp.

Pohl, Manfred. 1990. "Der '*Pachinko*-Fall' und japanische Vorurteile gegen koreanische Mitbürger," Manfred Pohl (ed.), *Japan 1989/90. Politik und Wirtschaft*. Hamburg: Institut für Asienkunde, 7–11.

Richie, Donald. 1980. *Some aspects of Japanese popular culture*. Tokyo: Shubun International.

Riesman, David, and Evelyn Thompson Riesman. 1967. *Conversations in Japan: Modernization, politics and culture*. Chicago: University of Chicago Press.

Sedensky, Eric. 1991. *Winning pachinko: The game of Japanese pinball*. Tokyo: Tuttle.

Shimada Shingo. 1994. *Grenzgänge—Fremdgänge. Japan und Europa im Kulturvergleich*. Frankfurt & New York: Campus Verlag.

Tada Michitarô. 1984. *Asobi to nihonjin*. Tokyo: Chikuma shobô.

———. 1989. "Osaka popular culture: A down-to-earth appraisal," Gavan MacCormack and Yoshio Sugimoto (eds.), *The Japanese trajectory: Modernization and beyond*. Cambridge: Cambridge University Press, 33–53.

Takeuchi Hiroshi. 1979. "Pachinko vs inbêdâ," *Sekai* 7, 302–09.

———. 1980. "The pachinko phenomenon," *Japan Echo* 7 (special issue), 63–70.

Tobin, Joseph J. 1992. "Introduction: Domesticating the West," Joseph J. Tobin (ed.), *Re-made in Japan: Everyday life and consumer taste in a changing society*. New Haven, Conn.: Yale University Press, 1–41.

Warneken, Bernd Jürgen. 1974. "Der Flipperautomat: Ein Versuch über Zerstreuungskultur," Jürgen Alberts et al. (eds.), *Segmente der Unterhaltungsindustrie*. Frankfurt: Suhrkamp, 66–129.

Notes on Contributors

Peter Ackermann is professor for Japanese Studies at the University of Erlangen-Nürnberg, Germany. During 1984–1989, he was lecturer for Japanese at the Universities of Freiburg and Zürich. His doctoral thesis was on Japanese musical traditions (University of Basel, 1982). In addition to methods and problems related to the approach of Japan through the medium of spoken and written Japanese, his research interests include intercultural communication and problems related to the historical development of values, value changes, and the encounter of differing values.

Eyal Ben-Ari is Associate Professor at the Department of Sociology and Anthropology at the Hebrew University of Jerusalem and took his PhD degree at the University of Cambridge. He receives the major part of his salary for being an expert on Japan and has carried out research on suburban communities and day-care centers in Japan and most recently on the Japanese expatriate community in Singapore. In addition, he has carried out research on (Jewish) saint worship in Israel and has done fieldwork in a battalion of Israeli military reserves.

Annegret Bergmann was educated at Sophia University in Tokyo and the University of Bonn. During 1990–1993 she studied at the Theatre Division of Waseda University. Presently, she is living in

Japan carrying out research for her doctoral thesis on "Theatre as private enterprise in Japan: Shochiku Kabuki as an example."

Katarzyna Joanna Cwiertka took M.A. degrees at Warsaw University (1990) and Tsukuba University (1994). Currently she is a visiting researcher at the Centre for Japanese & Korean Studies of Leiden University carrying out research on the evolution of Japanese food culture between 1900 and 1964 with focus on Western influence. Her publications include: "Kindai Nihon no shoku bunka ni okeru seiyô no jûyô," *Nihon chôri kagakkaishi* 28/1, (Feb. 1995), 76–81; "Wayô setchû ryôri no chôri bunka shiteki kôsatsu," S. Ôtsuka and A. Kawabata (eds.), *21 seiki no chôrigaku 1: Chôri bunkagaku.* Tokyo: Kenpakusha, 1996, 65–94.

Eckart Derschmidt studied at the University of Vienna (Japanese Studies, Korean Studies, Sociology) and took his M.A. in 1991 with a thesis on "Employment policies of Japanese labor unions after the first oil crisis, 1973–1978." He took part in a postgraduate program at Waseda University, Tokyo (1992–1994) and is currently working on a doctoral dissertation on "Jazz in Japan." His main fields of interest are sociology of music and popular culture. Derschmidt's publications include "Thrilling life performances: History of free jazz in Japan," *Resonance* 4/2, (Feb. 1996), 18–23.

Roland Domenig graduated from the University of Vienna, Institute for Japanese Studies in 1990. During 1991–1993 he was a research student at the Division of Sociology of Tokyo University. Currently Domenig is preparing his doctoral thesis about the Takarazuka Revue at the University of Vienna. His fields of interests include popular culture, film, and AIDS. He has published "AIDS in Japan," Eva Bachmayer, Wolfgang Herbert, and Sepp Linhart (eds.), *Japan von Aids bis Zen* (= Beiträge zur Japanologie 29), Wien: Institut für Japanologie, 1991, 506–25.

Susanne Formanek graduated from the University of Vienna with a M. A. thesis on birth control in premodern Japan and is presently a researcher at the Institute for the Cultural and Intellectual History of Asia at the Austrian Academy of Sciences. She has been engaged since then in the study of the social and cultural history of aging and the elderly in Japan. Other research interests include gender studies and the history of Japanese views of the Other World, with special emphasis on popular Buddhist beliefs as expressed in the context of pilgrimage and *etoki*. She is author of *Denn dem Alter kann keiner entfliehen: Altern und Alter im Japan der Nara- und Heian-Zeit* (1994), and coeditor of *Japanese biographies: Life histories, life cycles, life stages* (1992) and *Buch und Bild als gesellschaftliche Kommunikationsmittel in Japan einst und jetzt* (1995).

Sabine Frühstück earned her PhD in Japanese Studies at University of Vienna (1996) with a thesis in modern Japanese History and History and Social Study of Science. She is currently assistant professor at the Institute for Japanese Studies (University of Vienna, Austria). Her research interests include history and social study of science and sociology of modern Japan. Her publications include: *Die Politik der Sexualwissenschaft. Zur Produktion und Popularisierung sexologischen Wissens in Japan 1908–1941*. Vienna: Institute for Japanese Studies, 1997; "Sex zwischen Wissenschaft und Politik," *Nachrichten der Gesellschaft für Natur- und Völkerkunde Ostasiens* 155–56 (1994), 11–42; "Treating the body as commodity: 'Body projects' in contemporary Japan," John Clammer and Michael Ashkenazi (eds.), *Consumption and material culture in contemporary Japan*. London: Kegan Paul (in print).

Nelson Graburn is Professor of Anthropology at the University of California, Berkeley. Educated at Cambridge, McGill, and the University of Chicago, he started his researches on ethnicity and social change among the Canadian Inuit (Eskimo) in 1959. Through looking at their commercial folk arts, he developed broader interests in the topic, published as *Ethnic and tourist arts* (1976). This led to research on tourism itself. Since first visiting Japan in 1974, and again in 1978–79, 1987, 1988–90, 1991, 1993, and 1994, he has enjoyed conducting research on Japanese domestic tourism on numerous occasions.

Angelika Hamilton-Oehrl graduated from the University of Bonn, Germany, in 1994. She held a ERASMUS Scholarship at Rijksuniversiteitte Leiden, Netherlands. Her main area of study is socioeconomic relationships in the twentieth century. Currently, Hamilton-Oehrl is working at the Office of the High Representative in Sarajevo, Yugoslavia.

Inoue Shun is a graduate of Kyoto University. As a professor of sociology he was affiliated for many years to Osaka University until 1996, when he returned to his alma mater. A specialist for the sociology of culture, Inoue has been a pioneer in the field of the sociology of leisure and life course. He is one of the general editors of the new Iwanami series *Modern sociology (Gendai shakaigaku)* in 27 volumes, in which he edited the volume on *The sociology of work and play (Shigoto to asobi no shakaigaku)*.

William W. Kelly has been teaching at the Department of Anthropology of Yale University since 1980 and is currently professor and chair of the department. His current research projects include a book on the place of professional baseball in twentieth-century Japan and a book on the dynamics of a region in northern Japan. His publications include: *Deference and defiance in nineteenth-century Japan*. Princeton, N.J.: Princeton University Press, 1985; "Finding a place in metropolitan Japan," A. Gordon (ed.), *Postwar Japan as history*. Berkeley: University of California Press, 1993; "Tractors, television, and telephones: Reach out and touch someone in rural Japan," J. Tobin (ed.), *Re-made in Japan*. New Haven, Conn.: Yale University Press, 1992.

Sepp Linhart is professor of Japanese Studies at the University of Vienna. As a sociologist he has been mainly interested in the study of old people and of work and leisure in contemporary Japan, as well as in theoretical and methodological problems of Japanese Studies. He is presently editing a book on *Work and leisure in past and present Japan* together with Inoue Shôichi, and authoring another one on *The cultural history of the ken game*, both to appear in Japanese.

Wolfram Manzenreiter took his M.A. degree at the University of Vienna and is currently a researcher at the Institute for Japanese Studies of the University of Vienna. His research interests include leisure studies, sports sociology, and studies in popular culture. He is currently carrying out research for his PhD thesis on the sociology and history of mountaineering in Japan. His publications include: *Leisure in contemporary Japan: An annotated bibliography and list of books and articles.* Vienna, 1995.

Nagashima Nobuhiro earned his doctorate from Tokyo University and is currently professor of Social Anthropology at the Faculty of Social Sciences of Hitotsubashi University. His research interests in the field of Japanese Studies include ethnographical critique of Japanese Studies conducted by non-Japanese anthropologists, divination, and gambling in Japan. His publications include: "Regional differences in Japanese rural culture," *Senri Ethnological Studies* 14, 1984 (together with Hiroyasu Tomoeda); *Shi to yamai no minzokushi (An anthropology of death and illness: The concept of causality among the Iteso of Kenya).* Tokyo: Iwanami, 1987; and "A reversed world, or is it? The Japanese way of communications and their attitudes towards alien culture," Robin Horton and Ruth Finnegan (eds.), *Modes of thought.* Faber and Faber.

Emiko Ohnuki-Tierney is a Vilas Research Professor, Department of Anthropology, at the University of Wisconsin–Madison. Her books *Illness and culture in contemporary Japan* (1984), *Rice as self* (1993), and *The monkey as mirror* (1987) have become standard readings in the anthropology of Japan. Presently she is engaged in a larger research project on cherry blossom viewing and its history in Japan.

T. J. Pempel is Boening Professor at the Jackson School of International Studies, University of Washington. He has been on the faculty at Cornell University, the University of Colorado, and the University of Wisconsin, as well as being a visiting faculty member at Tokyo University and Kyoto University. Pempel's publications include: *Policy and politics in Japan: Creative conservatism.* Philadelphia: Temple University Press, 1982; *Uncommon democracies: The one-party dominant regimes.* Ithaca, N.Y.: Cornell University Press, 1989; and the forthcoming *Regime shift: The changing political economy of Japan.* Ithaca, N.Y.: Cornell University Press.

Jennifer Robertson earned her PhD in Anthropology at Cornell University (1985) and is currently Professor of Anthropology at the University of Michigan (Ann Arbor). She has published on a wide range of topics both historical and contemporary in scope, from Shingaku and farm manuals to gender attribution and theater. Among her recent publications are *Native and newcomer: Making and re-making a Japanese city.* University of California Press, 1991 (paperback 1994); and "Mon Japon: Theater as a technology of Japanese imperialism," *American Ethnologist*, 1995. Robertson is currently completing *Strategic ambivalence: Theater, sex, and gender in modern Japan,* and pursuing a book-length project on cultural strategies of Japanese colonialism, in addition to continuing research on internationalization and nostalgia. She has lived in Japan for about eighteen years.

Index

venereal diseases, 60, 65–68, 70, 74
victory, 114
video games, 7
virginity, 68, 75
visitors: 171–173, 176, 319; attractions for, 202
volleyball: 8, 121–122, 126–127; player, 131

white paper on leisure, 361, 367
women's magazines, 48–50
woodblock: printing, 222; prints, 4, 222–223, 232, 339
work: 2–3, 6, 8, 31, 38, 152, 158, 182, 195, 197, 225, 346, 366; ethic, 294; habits, 140; hard, 197, 199, 359; and home environment, 241; and leisure, 140; opportunities, 195; organization of, 247; pattern, 248; process, 366

workaholic, 200, 239, 357
worker, 294
workforce, 294
working: bees, 13, 247; day, 144; hours, 239–240, 246–247; overtime, 13; part-time, 197–198; time, 3–4, 13, 375; week, 14, 208
workplace, 2, 140, 146, 148–149, 152
World Cup, 134–135
World Jûdô Championships, 92

yachting, 38
yoka: 2, 5, 16, 28, 30, 38; *mondai,* 2
yokozuna, 128–131
Yomiuri Giants, 100, 105–107, 126
Yoshiwara, 59, 63, 72, 255
yûkaku, 4